THE RELEVANCE OF ECONOMIC THEORIES

INTERNATIONAL ECONOMIC ASSOCIATION PUBLICATIONS

Monopoly and Competition and their Regulation
The Economic Consequences of the Size of Nations
The Theory of Capital
Inflation
The Economics of Take-off into Sustained Growth
International Trade Theory in a Developing World
The Theory of Interest Rates
The Economics of Education
Problems in Economic Development
Price Formation in Various Economies
The Distribution of National Income
Risk and Uncertainty
Economic Problems of Agriculture in Industrial Societies
International Economic Relations
Backward Areas in Advanced Countries
Public Economics
Economic Development in South Asia
North American and Western European Economic Policies
Planning and Market Relations
The Gap Between Rich and Poor Nations
Latin America in the International Economy
Models of Economic Growth
Science and Technology in Economic Growth
Allocation under Uncertainty
Transport and the Urban Environment
The Economics of Health and Medical Care
The Management of Water Quality and the Environment
Agriculture Policy in Developing Countries
The Economic Development of Bangladesh
Economic Factors in Population Growth
Classics in the Theory of Public Finance
Methods of Long-term Planning and Forecasting
Economic Integration
The Economics of Public Services
The Organisation and Retrieval of Economic Knowledge
The Microeconomic Foundations of Macroeconomics
Economic Relations between East and West
Econometric Contributions to Public Policy
Appropriate Technologies for Third World Development
Economic Growth and Resources (5 Volumes)
Public and Private Enterprise
Unemployment in Western Countries Today
The Relevance of Economic Theories

The Relevance of Economic Theories

Proceedings of a Conference held by the International Economic Association in Collaboration with the Polish Economic Association at Warsaw, Poland

edited by
JOZEF PAJESTKA
and
C. H. FEINSTEIN

M

First published 1980 by
THE MACMILLAN PRESS LTD
London and Basingstoke
Companies and representatives throughout the world

Typeset by
STYLESET LIMITED
Salisbury · Wiltshire
and printed in Hong Kong

British Library Cataloguing in Publication Data

The relevance of economic theories
1. Economic development–Congresses
2. Economics–History–20th century–Congresses
I. Pajestka, Jozef
II. Feinstein, Charles Hilliard
III. International Economic Association
IV. Polskie Towarzystwo Ekonomiczne
330.9 HD82

ISBN 0–333–28733–9

4

Contents

PART FOUR THE NEW INTERNATIONAL ECONOMIC ORDER

PART FIVE ECONOMIC THEORY AND THE LIMITS TO NATURAL RESOURCES

PART SIX ECONOMIC DEVELOPMENT: THEORY AND POLICY

PART SEVEN NATIONAL ECONOMIC PLANNING

Acknowledgements

by the IEA

The Conference of the IEA recorded in this volume was held jointly and in collaboration with the Polish Economic Society. The latter bore all local expenses and made a generous contribution to travel costs. We are particularly indebted to its President, Professor Jozef Pajestka, for his perseverance in the realisation of the project and for his skilful guidance of the Programme Committee which designed the scientific content. We thank also his collaborators, Professor Aleksander Łukaszewicz and Dr Jan Kulig.

We should like, as usual, to express gratitude to the Ford Foundation and Unesco for their general support of the Association's activities and to the latter for a special contribution which facilitated the participation of economists from the less-developed countries.

Finally, our thanks are due to those who wrote papers and contributed to the discussion, to Dr Charles Feinstein who not only acted as Rapporteur and produced the record of the debate, but was also responsible for all the work of editing and preparing this English edition, and to Dr Bartlomiej Kaminski who acted as his Co-rapporteur.

List of Participants

Professor Henryk Cholaj, Polish Academy of Sciences, Warsaw, Poland
Dr Meghnad Desai, London School of Economics, UK
Professor Charles H. Feinstein, University of York, UK
Dr B. Fiedor, Economic Academy, Wroclaw, Poland
Dr Z. Fiejka, Institute of Planning, Warsaw, Poland
Professor Celso Furtado, University of Paris I, France
Professor Reginald H. Green, Institute of Development Studies, University of Sussex, UK
Professor Włodzimierz H. Hagemejer, Institute of Planning, Warsaw, Poland
Professor Wiktor Herer, Institute of Planning, Warsaw, Poland
Professor Amilcar Herrera, Latin American Faculty for Social Sciences, Mexico City
Professor M. Kabaj, Institute of Labour Studies, Warsaw, Poland
Dr Bartlomiej Kaminski, University of Warsaw, Poland
Mr Michael Kaser, St Antony's College, Oxford, UK
Professor Tigran Khachaturov, Academy of Sciences of the USSR, Moscow, USSR
Professor Jerzy Kleer, Co-operative Research Institute, Warsaw, Poland
Dr Rafal Krawczyk, University of Warsaw, Poland
Dr Jan Kulig, Institute of Planning, Warsaw, Poland
Mr Peter Lengyel, Editor, *International Social Science Journal UNESCO*, Paris, France
Professor Aleksander Łukaszewicz, University of Warsaw, Poland
Professor Edmond Malinvaud, INSEE, Paris, France
Professor Eugeni Mateev, Bulgarian Academy of Sciences, Sofia, Bulgaria
Professor Zofia Morecka, University of Warsaw, Poland
Professor Jan Mujzel, Institute of Planning, Warsaw, Poland
Dr Aleandro Nadal, El Colegio de Mexico, Mexico
Professor Jurg Niehans, University of Berne, Switzerland
Dr Jerzy Osiatynski, Institute of History of Science, Education and Technology of the Polish Academy of Sciences, Warsaw, Poland
Professor Marian Ostrowski, Institute of Planning, Warsaw, Poland

Dr Akinola A. Owosekun, Nigerian Institute of Social and Economic Research, University of Ibadan, Nigeria
Professor Józef Pajestka, Polish Economic Society, Warsaw, Poland
Dr Marian Paszynski, Research Institute for International Market and Prices, Warsaw, Poland
Professor Krzysztof Porwit, Institute of Planning, Warsaw, Poland
Professor Sir Austin Robinson, University of Cambridge, UK
Professor Justinian F. Rweyemamu, University of Dar Es Salaam, Tanzania
Dr Władyslaw Sadowski, Institute of Planning, Warsaw, Poland
Professor Zdzislaw Sadowski, Institute of Planning, Warsaw, Poland
Professor Kazimierz Secomski, Polish Academy of Sciences, Warsaw, Poland
Professor Dudley Seers, Institute of Development Studies, University of Sussex, UK
Dr Rier Simonyan, Institute of World Economy and International Relations, Academy of Sciences of the USSR, Moscow, USSR
Dr Paul Streeten, World Bank, Washington DC, USA
Professor Jan Szczepanski, Polish Academy of Sciences, Warsaw, Poland
Dr Shigeto Tsuru, Editorial Adviser, The Asahi Shimbun, Tokyo, Japan
Professor Victor L. Urquidi, El Colegio de Mexico, Mexico

Secretariat

Miss Mary Crook, International Economic Association, Paris, France
Professor Luc Fauvel, University of Paris I, France

Introduction

Jozef Pajestka
POLISH ECONOMIC SOCIETY, WARSAW

The subject matter taken up by the International Economic Association for its 1978 Warsaw Conference, The Relevance of Economic Theories for Contemporary Society, belongs to a rather sensitive area of debate among professional economists, though nobody would challenge its need or its urgency. With the rapid changes in socio-economic reality, and the appearance of new horizons for the future, social sciences have almost continually to rethink their relevance. This was the leading idea behind the Conference, and the Polish Economic Association was quite eager to be host to such an important and challenging intellectual venture.

It is far from my intention to give in these prefatory remarks any kind of general assessment of the merits and demerits of the meeting. After all, the book is before us, and any reader can judge for himself its results. Instead, I intend to present just a few personal impressions from the Warsaw meeting – as I formulated them immediately after it ended. Thus the afterthoughts become an introduction, which is not at all a rare practice.

It is right and desirable for any science to reflect upon its state and relevance. There appear, however, to be very special reasons for doing so for the social sciences, and for economics in particular. We are faced here not only by the necessity to develop paradigms, conceptual constructs and approaches which are more adequate to reality, which display more explanatory insight, and help in designing more rational activity patterns, but also by the fact that the subject matter of scientific reflection is more changeable over time than in any other field. When this is realised, there is a further issue which arises at the present juncture. It is maintained that the ongoing change in socio-economic reality is more profound in the present historical period than it has been previously. If this is indeed the case it provides an even stronger argument for critical analysis of the relevance of economic theories. But is it really so? Are the changes faster or deeper than before? This problem merits some attention.

There exists a feeling among certain social scientists that the rate of change in socio-economic processes has increased markedly in the recent historical period, and that it is going to increase further. This proposition is certainly difficult to prove. We have no yardstick for measuring this change (it would seem a great misunderstanding to measure it, for example, in terms of the growth rate of the Gross National Product), since it certainly is not the kind of change which we normally deal with in macroeconomics, measuring the quantitative features of the development process. In judging the proposition, the change envisaged has to be considered as one which involves transformation of the behavioural features of the system. Such transformations are not at all rare in human history. However, a judgement on whether such a change is more or less profound has to be, at least in part, of an intuitive character. I see no reason to discard such intuitive judgements, providing that there is behind them deep historical knowledge and wide humanistic orientation. One has to take it for granted, however, that opinions may differ widely when based on intuitive evaluations. And that is really what we are facing.

While some perceive the present and the near future as a continuation of the evolutionary process, just a further step in the development of human civilisation, others see a need for deep change in human behaviour, look for 'another development', and see it coming. This need for change is, in their view, a necessity called for by the changing environment of human activities, both natural and socio-economic. Changing conditions need a more profound adaptation of human behaviour than was the case during the long, past historical process. To face this challenge of life, much in the social sciences needs rethinking. Deep rethinking, re-evaluation and reorientation is therefore needed to assure the appropriate relevance of economic theories to the present and future conditions and needs of human development.

While the above problem was not explicitly discussed during the Warsaw Conference, I should like to venture the opinion that many of its participants would opt for the second of the two positions, that is for the one which acknowledges deep change in the human environment and, therefore, is inclined to rethink economic theories in relation to the requirements of present and future conditions. One would not have expected this position to be explicitly stated by all participants. Still, openness to new challenges was a general atmosphere of the debates. Therefore, in my view, certain important conclusions were developed which I shall try to formulate below.

Understandably, in view of these developments economic theories cannot be 'relevant' in any very strict sense of the term. What we should be seeking for, however, is an *increased* relevance in view of the nature of the changing realities, on the one hand, the need to assist in finding practical policy solutions, on the other. This seems to provide a measure for judging the merits, or the state, of economic science. While economic theorising tends to lag behind the needs of contemporary society – as can be demonstrated, for example, in the case of environmental problems, or the theoretical elaboration of the new international economic order – we should aim at minimising this lag.

The Warsaw meeting seems, to my mind, to have contributed quite a bit to meeting the above challenge. Whether it did so, and to what extent, can best be seen from the many valuable, sometimes quite innovative, papers and statements contained in the present volume. Before commenting upon some of its conclusions let me make one observation. A meeting of this kind undertaken by the International Economic Association, and particularly one which brings together scientists from various backgrounds: economic, social, ideological, intellectual, etc. – should be judged as a virtue in itself. Such meetings provide a powerful stimulus for mutual inspiration, they help in dispelling misjudgements and in creating better understanding of each other on the basis of personal debate and discussion that all of us need so much. Economists cannot easily apply experiments, which are so important in the development of physical sciences. Diversity of experience, diversity of views and theoretical approaches, can to some extent compensate for the lack of experimentation, and in this way contribute to scientific progress.

In the search for some guidelines for an enhanced 'relevance' of economic theorising to present-day society, the Preparatory Committee of the IEA selected several major topics as a basis for discussing and evaluating the state of economic science. The topics merit attention since they define the areas for which new thinking seems most pertinent. True enough, the selected topics are too large to allow for thorough and extensive discussion. This was not possible during the few days of the conference and, as a matter of fact, was not intended. The intention was to have a sort of 'brain-storming' discussion, showing the prospective vistas, throwing new light on the known problems, inspiring new thinking, confronting different views and theories. The reader is asked to look at the contributions presented here from this point of view.

The list of topics, of contributions to each of them, and of discussion around each, is contained in the pages ahead. In fact, the topics cover most of the crucial issues of political economy. Without attempting to comment on each of them, I would like to present a number of propositions which seem, in my view, to be the main contributions of the Conference. I fully realise that many participants would probably not agree with my propositions. In this case they will find in them an aid for formulating their own position; and this applies also to the readers.

As perhaps the most general conclusion, I should indicate the proposition that economic science needs a stronger orientation towards conscious shaping of the course of socio-economic development processes, seen in longer time-horizon. This relates to several dimensions, from a national scale, through the regional or subregional (international), to the global scale. This proposition is not tantamount to calling for a sort of universal planning. Still, economic theory and analysis should aspire to formulate well-founded judgements on what is purposeful and rational in development processes. Then it could have an impact both on public opinion and on policy-making. As a matter of fact, one can see this course of scientific development, and it seems to be on the increase.

Connected with the above is the proposition that economic science – in order to be better oriented to policy formulation – must depart from the position – which has been rather dominant in recent decades – that the aims of development processes lie outside the scope of socio-economic theorising. The Conference discussion stressed clearly and convincingly that *aims* must be included in scientific considerations as part and parcel of socio-economic theorising. This is particularly important at the present juncture in the historical development process. Recent international debates on various large topics: the predicament of mankind, the prospects and challenges of human civilisation, the new international economic order, socio-economic development feedbacks, etc, all touch increasingly on the problems of the aims and purposes of development. There seem to be good reasons for economic science to catch up with the problematique of those debates, if it is not to lag behind in important new trends of human thinking. Though for some schools of economic theorising this might seem a tremendous and even an awkward challenge, we are not without traditions in this line of thinking. There was a strong argument voiced during the Warsaw debates, calling for a turn from narrow theorising in economics to the good traditions of political economy. Personally, I would fully subscribe to this postulate.

These two issues are closely linked to a basic concept of economic theory, that of economic rationality. Should this concept embrace the aims and purposes, or only the ways and means, as hitherto largely considered? Is it justified to apply this concept on a global scale, and if so, what should that imply? Answers to those questions were far from uniform during the debates. Still, formulation of certain propositions in this respect merits attention. It is to be hoped that further discussion will bring more clarity to this problem.

While it proves rather difficult to accept the concept of global rationality in general, theoretical terms, it is much easier to agree on some of its specific aspects. Particularly when considering the natural environment and the resource base, thinking along the lines of what is rational not only on the national, but also on the global scale, is now widely accepted. In this context the Conference seems to have given wide support to an important proposition which merits emphasis: a major shift in theoretical approaches concerned with nature and natural resources is required, from the main focus on optimal allocation of resources to the focus on conservation and reproduction of the natural resource base. We are still rather far from having drawn all the theoretical conclusions from this proposition.

However, there is, perhaps, one problem area for which the debates showed the greatest gap between the state of economic theorising on one hand, and the needs of human development on the other. I have in mind the various aspects of development economics connected with international economics, which are discussed in political forums under the heading of the new international economic order. Formulating as a conclusion that in this area the 'irrelevance' is possibly greatest would not do justice to actual contributions made. Several authors have made important efforts to help eliminate this gap by showing certain lines of change in theoretical approaches to the problem. There was a proposition on the desirability of changing the perspective from 'international' to 'global' economics. I do not think it is necessary to indicate that this is not merely a terminological proposition, but one which implies a change of an important paradigm of theoretical thinking. Most interesting arguments were developed, supported by historical analysis, for considering the element of power and its working in the international setting. The role of control over new technology was particularly stressed in this context. Considerable attention was also given to the patterns of development strategy, particularly to the concept of 'self-reliance' and of the 'basic needs' strategy.

Consideration of these strategic issues seems to mark a most interesting departure in socio-economic thinking, closely linked to the lines indicated above. One can observe that it reflects policy orientation, takes a global view, and deals with the development aims of society. The last aspect stands out particularly in the problem of the 'basic needs' strategy. This issue has only very recently appeared as an important area of economic theorising; I have in mind here western-type economics. Without going into the details of the concept of 'basic needs', which was the subject of a most lively discussion during the Conference, I should like to make one particular observation. Disregarding the inspirations and the policy implications of this concept as a strategic premise, its introduction marks the acceptance of policy aims into economic analysis. This seems most remarkable whether one accepts 'basic needs' as a correct strategic concept or not, preferring to go deeper in consideration of the socially justified and economically conditioned development aims.

I fully realise that the above views on the IEA Conference are rather personal. They are marked by my own intellectual background. Coming from a socialist economy and from the socialist traditions of political economy I am particularly inclined to stress the conscious shaping of the development process, policy-oriented theoretical thinking, sensitivity to social aims, etc. Some other economists might consider the propositions to be very maximalistic. Still, it is my conviction that looking at the state of economic science and at its 'relevance' from this perspective may be significant and useful from many points of view.

PART ONE

General Review of the Relevance of Economic Theories

1 The Cultural Lag in Economics

Dudley Seers
INSTITUTE OF DEVELOPMENT STUDIES, UNIVERSITY OF SUSSEX, UK

I INTRODUCTORY

I was asked to provide a review of worldwide problems related to the evaluation of the relevance of economic theories. The topic[1] is a good one, because there is clearly growing doubt among students, lecturers and practitioners alike, in all parts of the world, about the relevance of received doctrines to social problems which are taking new and more severe forms, and increasing impatience with those who remain chained to obsolete models.

The concept of 'cultural lag' is a general one: it refers to the well-known tendency of attitudes and perceptions to lag behind changing reality, sometimes by years, sometimes by decades. In academia it takes the special form of reproducing throughout one's career the theories learned as a student, partly through inertia (e.g. the wish to avoid rewriting lectures and texts), partly because systems of appointment and promotion and criteria for publication enforce some degree of theoretical conservatism. Universities almost generate irrelevance. In the social sciences an additional cause is the pressure (even if only potential) from educational bureaucracies and governments, which usually have their own interest in current problems not being explored too deeply and may well find that theory inherited from the past suits their purposes very well. I shall examine the cultural lag in economics, concentrating on macroeconomics, suggesting that this may have grown recently with the accelerating pace of change, and argue that we now have a rare opportunity of reducing it.

1 Because of its scope, this paper is unavoidably rather superficial and unscholarly. Equally inevitably, it reflects my personal biases in the selection of what problems and what theories seem significant. This is perhaps more a 'sketch' than a 'review'. I am glad to acknowledge comments by Reginald Green and Percy Selwyn in particular.

II THE STATE OF THE ART TWO DECADES AGO

It may be useful to start by looking back at the state of theory in the 1950s, and asking how relevant this has proved to post-war problems. That may help us see the broad direction in which theoretical developments need to go.

In the 'developed' capitalist economies, Keynesian economics held sway, having spread rather gradually through the university world following (rather than during) the great slump of the 1930s.[1] A strong upward impulse was still provided in the 1950s by the tasks of making good wartime damage and meeting pent-up needs. But another big slump was considered inevitable about a decade after the end of the war. With the help of the proliferating systems of national accounts, economists were nervously taking the pulse of the world economy, and sharpening the counter-cyclical tools which had been implicit in the theories of Keynes and Kalecki.[2] The post-war slump would require sophisticated 'management' if a repetition of the 1930s were to be avoided. Otherwise, social and political problems might destroy the economic system.

Bitter memories of the 1930s also shaped perceptions of international policy needs. In the industrial countries, the main requirement was seen as one of avoiding the 'beggar my neighbour' policies which had, it was believed, propagated the depression in 1930–33. The establishment of the International Monetary Fund at Bretton Woods had set new 'rules of the game' designed to prevent competitive devaluation and inhibit recourse to exchange controls; under the aegis of GATT, tariffs and preferences were being 'bound' and reduced.

The older version of neo-classicism was in fact by no means dead, and as the years passed without a major slump it began to revive, especially in the United States and West Germany, and thus also the belief in the overriding need to limit the money supply, as it had been automatically limited by the rules of the gold standard.[3]

Thus in the advanced capitalist countries, economists were preoccupied with theory which had been developed in answer to much earlier needs. The

[1] It had encountered of course fierce resistance from the twentieth-century residue of nineteenth-century neo-classicism, a doctrine which drew its strength from the powerful surge forward of capitalism in the previous century. Its adherents (Pigou, for example) denied any inherent tendency to unemployment in the capitalist system.

[2] Thanks largely to the efforts of Joan Robinson, the Polish economist Kalecki is at last getting more credit for his simultaneous development of the basic theory of Maynard Keynes.

[3] In West Germany, the revival of neo-classicism was reinforced by memories both of the inflation of the 1920s and the state controls adopted by the Nazis in the 1930s.

main line of professional progress was to elaborate it in increasingly complex models.

It would of course be presumptuous of me, especially as a guest in Poland, to discuss how international or internal problems were then perceived in the socialist countries, or how relevant to them was Marxism, the other main neo-classical school. Nor can much be said on how they were viewed by the economics profession in the 'West', because they were considered a world apart – out of reach, in various senses, and only studied by a few specialists.

In the 1950s, there was also a small group at work on the problems of 'underdeveloped' countries. In retrospect, the economics profession had been blind in the colonial era to the scale of world poverty: there had been little study of economies other than those of Europe and North America, or of the world economy as a whole,[1] despite its increasing integration. (International trade theory after all covers only one aspect.) After the war, developments overseas (especially the independence of India) stimulated professional concern about conditions in poor countries for various reasons, partly humanitarian, partly political (based on a fear that decolonisation would be followed by revolution and the destruction of the world economic system). Associated with this was a new perception of the world as divided into three qualitatively different groups of countries – 'developed market economies', 'centrally-planned economies' and 'underdeveloped', later called 'developing' economies.

'Development economists' were in fact mostly nationals not of 'underdeveloped' but of the 'developed' countries (though there were notable exceptions such as Arthur Lewis, Prebisch and Mahalanobis), and they saw the central question as how the 'underdeveloped' countries could follow in the footsteps of the 'developed' and quickly achieve the same economic prosperity and independence, social welfare systems and parliamentary democracy, including institutional protection for human rights. 'Development' was essentially an economic problem. Economic growth was considered a suitable yardstick for it (indeed almost a synonym). In the end, growth would mean reduced inequality, unemployment and poverty (viz the Kuznets 'U-curve'). Such progress would be all the easier because the necessary technologies were already available – although medical technology had made the economic task more difficult by enabling the growth of population to accelerate.

The Harrod–Domar model, which had recently been elaborated (though primarily to make Keynesian economics dynamic, not for the sake of the 'underdeveloped' countries) provided a convenient framework for relating economic growth to investment. This led to a heavy emphasis on the need for

[1] Kalecki played a part in this too, by developing the United Nations World Economic Report in the early 1950s.

savings, and thus for aid and foreign investment, which would bring with them the latest technologies. Indeed, much work at that time consisted of building growth models which *inter alia* justified aid and guided the policies of donor agencies.

Although 'development economics' had its professional roots in 'developed' countries and was largely articulated by their economists, it helped – together with Keynesian and neo-classical economics – to shape the minds of the new generation of 'third world' economists and political leaders. These had mostly been students in one of the 'developed' countries (or in universities at home which had copied their syllabi). In a sense, their theoretical equipment was twice removed from reality – it reflected the doctrines developed for *other* countries in response to *earlier* events.

The chief theoretical schools of Europe and North America promoted their own recipes for accelerating growth as universally valid. At one extreme, the Chicago school (Simon Rottenberg, for example, teaching then in Santiago, soon to be followed by Harberger, or disciples such as Peter Bauer at work in West Africa) argued for opening the doors to foreign trade and investment, and avoiding planning and controls. IMF economists, from the same stable, saw inflation and payments problems – already widespread, especially in Latin America – as due to lack of monetary discipline. If this were put right, the basis would be established for a fast growth of output and employment.

Prebisch and Singer, however, developed a thesis with very different policy implications, based on an apparent chronic tendency for the terms of trade of primary producers to deteriorate,[1] which led to an emphasis on industrialisation and justified tariff protection. This thesis fitted another theme of that time, namely that to break out of historical stagnation, a simultaneous 'big push' was necessary, with the investment in each sector reinforcing and justifying investment in the others, which implied the need for 'planning'. It also helped explain the widening 'gap' between the incomes of 'developed' and 'underdeveloped' countries and reinforced the case for aid. This case was further strengthened by the argument of Rostow, that an injection of capital could make growth 'self-sustaining'.

On the Left were Marxists like Baran who also stressed industrialisation (referring to the Soviet model) but who, in contrast to Prebisch, believed that socialism was a necessary and very feasible condition for removing obstacles to growth. This approach has tended to lead to a classification of 'underdeveloped' countries by degree of socialism. It also suggested to some that fundamental and lasting worldwide growth would require and impel

[1] Actually, a stronger case lay in the lower income elasticities of demand for primary products: this is especially obvious now that subsequent research has thrown doubt on the empirical basis of the 'terms of trade' thesis.

worldwide revolution, encompassing also the imperial powers themselves.

Although there were profound differences among development economists, there were also common elements. It is not much of an exaggeration to say that a single frame of perception covered almost the whole ideological spectrum.

The belief in growth was of course convenient for all those who wanted to divert attention from the concentration of income (and economic power) in the hands of particular races or regions, but it was also theoretically acceptable to others with no such desire, including Marxists. There was almost universal emphasis, too, on capital accumulation as the source of growth. Product and factor market prices were (usually tacitly) assumed to be sufficiently competitive to validate market prices. The essential variables were believed to be quantifiable and the role of the economist was seen as a technical one of incorporating them in 'development plans' (actually *growth* plans). Such plans assumed the validity of the statistics available.[1] They also generally ignored the constraints on policy and the need for institutional change.

Another common characteristic of economists of those times (whether Marxists or members of the Chicago school) was a basic optimism. Inequalities within and between countries could and would in one way or another be reduced eventually, bringing an homogenised, modernised world within the reach of the next generation. Supply curves for oil and other industrial inputs were tacitly assumed to be flat, as they had been for decades. Nationalist aspirations and policies were ignored or deprecated as obstructive – in part a reaction against what was seen as a cause of the two great wars.

These similarities are not surprising since Marxist and other neo-classical doctrines all had their intellectual roots in the expanding European economy of the nineteenth century.[2]

[1] Actually, in mainly rural societies, i.e. in most of the world, measures of economic growth are largely hypothetical, because of the lack of regular statistics on economic activities in rural areas, especially construction, manufacturing and services. This does not stop economists using estimates of growth as if they were facts. (Such statistical difficulties are of course in a different category from those of interpreting aggregative indicators covering a great diversity of classes, races, etc.) See 'Urban Bias: Seers versus Lipton' (*IDS Discussion Paper* No. 116. 1977).

[2] See 'The congruence of Marxism and other neo-classical doctrines' by myself in *Towards a New Strategy of Development* (Pergamon, 1979).

III THE CAPACITY OF THEORY TO EXPLAIN RECENT DEVELOPMENTS

This whole set of doctrines is of course now in ruins.[1] In the first place, the 'developed' countries turned out not to have even nearly solved their social problems. The problems of submerged minorities (the blacks in the United States, southerners in Italy, etc.) became more visible and politically significant. The expectations aroused by modern technology for both consumption patterns and working conditions, and disseminated through the media, could not be universally realised. Far from economic growth being a panacea, it seems to have been associated with growing crime, drug addiction, alcoholism, etc. It creates a society difficult to administer (because of interconnections too complex for any input-output table) but easy to sabotage by strikes in key sectors, kidnapping of leaders, etc. It also involves serious environmental damage.

In brief, in the 1950s the economists of the industrial countries misperceived the problems as essentially cyclical – events have shown that they are essentially structural. In some countries, notably Britain, the basic problem was really adapting the socio-economic structure to a new and less privileged status, especially revitalising industry. When the major world depression did at last come, in the mid-1970s, the 'developed' countries started to experience inflation *plus* unemployment in a combination which had previously been considered characteristic of a number of 'developing' countries, especially in Latin America, and which was difficult to reconcile with Keynesian economics. Economic expansion now seems constricted by price inflation and related foreign exchange deficits. In any one country these can be moderated by productivity increases but then there is little net addition to employment. Moreover, the unemployed are not necessarily willing, nor are they compelled, to take unpleasant or boring jobs.

So the global 'management' techniques devised in response to the general demand deficiencies of the 1930s, and embodied in the sophisticated models

1 One might argue that neo-classical 'rules of the game' in international economics are not at all irrelevant for technologically strong countries, in this case especially the United States and West Germany (and now Japan), which need to break down nationalist barriers to their economic expansion. In these countries, too, the higher degree of factor mobility makes Chicago-type models at least less obviously inappropriate. This doctrine also remains useful for capitalists in any country who need arguments against state 'interference'.

of the 1950s and 1960s, turned out after all to be of limited relevance, as did – at least in the view of many – the monetarist policies which partially took their place. Government economists in Western Europe tend to see the solution outside – in the renewed expansion of Japan and the USA. But the stage has not after all been set for a steadily expanding world economy, despite the new institutions to stimulate the liberalisation of trade and payments. The uneven development of the main capitalist economies in the 1960s, with Japan and West Germany achieving particularly fast productivity increases, has undermined the post-war economic order. Following the Smithsonian conference, the monetary rules of the game were changed by the governments of the very countries which had earlier insisted on their strict implementation, and subsequently trade liberalisation was checked or reversed (e.g. by textile quotas). Indeed, the 'New Cambridge' school (Godley and Cripps), following earlier work by Frisch and Balogh, argue that protection (discriminating between sources of imports) will help to restore the expansion of the world economy, not hinder it.

Heavy and persistent unemployment in the advanced industrial countries has not proved as destructive as conservatives and liberals had feared and revolutionaries hoped. The capitalist system seems remarkably robust and able to survive many final crises. But the social costs of chronic unemployment are so heavy (and the political effects likely to become so traumatic) that we urgently require if not 'another Keynes' (or Kalecki), which may be impossible, at least big analytical innovations. Doctrines in the 'development' field have not fared any better. The Harrod–Domar model was undoubtedly a technical advance, but it was too simplistic to provide an adequate basis for explaining or predicting even growth. Already, at the end of the 1950s, the range in national incremental capital-output ratios implied, as did research on production functions, that there were other influences on growth – e.g. education. This was demonstrably a major requirement in Africa: it led to a new subject, manpower economics, and reinforced the political pressures for a big expansion in secondary and tertiary education which were already considerable, indeed in retrospect excessive.

Economic growth has, in fact, been fast by historical standards in most countries of the 'third world'; but we now see that no mechanisms, evolutionary or revolutionary, can be relied on to spread its benefits and ease social problems. Overt unemployment and associated emigration can increase even in (perhaps especially in) fast-growing economies such as Jamaica and Puerto Rico. The expected tendency to equality has not appeared even in countries where income levels have become much higher than they were in Britain a century ago, when the benefits of growth began to be widely dispersed. Concentration of economic power in the hands of capitalists, landowners, the bureaucracy and the labour aristocracy (the composition of the ruling coalition of classes varying from country to country) seems in general to have increased, not declined: so have associated urban-rural disparities, especially in social services.[1] Pakistan was merely the most dramatic case of a country disrupted by *inter alia* fast growth.

Such results were implicit in growth strategies that relied on capital-intensive import substitution, the benefits of which reached few sectors of the economy. Moreover, economic growth on this pattern has provided both the motivation and the resources for repression, which is also facilitated by imported technologies of surveillance, interrogation, police communications, crowd control, etc. In turn the erosion of parliamentary democracy has facilitated the concentration of economic power, including income.

It may be argued that it is not obligatory (perhaps not even desirable) for economists to venture into such 'non-economic' issues but if there are observable and recurrent socio-economic patterns, is it defensible for these to be ignored?

In the 1970s, it is true, interesting work was done on the compatibility of growth and equality,[2] in a relatively rapid response to growing awareness of the inadequacy of growth as such and there was an associated emergence of interest in 'basic needs'. But a big question mark hangs over this line of work, not about its economic rationale but about the realism of expecting those with economic and political power to yield it voluntarily.

Moreover, though foreign-financed industrialisation has left most countries less dependent on a narrow range of primary exports, they have become – the smaller ones especially – much more dependent on imports of technology, equipment, energy and intermediate products, as well as on foreign capital, which come increasingly via the transnational corporations, or TNCs. The TNCs fit badly into the neo-classical model. A large proportion of economic transactions, especially in international trade, are internal to the firm. Moreover the TNCs have so much expertise available (in advertising, legal and tax departments, as well as those containing scientists and engineers), that they can manipulate market forces to a considerable extent, and governments – including 'their own' – find them hard to monitor or tax, let alone control. To rely heavily on *their* capital and technology for economic growth, therefore, means in fact allowing them to influence its

[1] Though the distribution of even the most quantifiable element in economic power, income, cannot be measured in predominantly rural economies because of statistical weaknesses mentioned above. In countries with sizeable bureaucracies, allowance also has to be made for use of official cars, housing and educational privileges, government hospitality, access to foreign exchange at legal rates, etc. especially since these forms of income are non-taxable. In addition, of course, bureaucrats control the distribution of government services, recruitment to employment, allocation of contracts, etc. which can provide additional income as well as a degree of control over the lives of fellow citizens comparable to that of large property owners.

[2] E.g. in *Redistribution with Growth* (Ed. H. Chenery *et al.*, Oxford University Press, for IBRD and IDS, 1974).

pattern, including the origin and price of imports, the destination of exports, etc. Governments which have attempted to force the TNCs to conform to national interests (e.g. the decisions in Cuba in 1959, or later in Sri Lanka, to import Soviet oil) have had to face politico-economic retaliation. Attention was drawn to the political and military linkages (including aid) that restrict the liberty of governments, again especially of small countries, to choose their sources of capital, technology and industrial inputs. This was the background to the emergency of the *dependencia* school in Latin America, the first truly indigenous one outside Europe – though drawing to some extent on European theorists, especially Marx. Developing an earlier insight of Prebisch, Latin Americans (Cardoso, Furtado, Pinto[1]) saw the world as divided between a core of industrial countries and a periphery.

The obvious inappropriateness of many (not all) modern technologies to the requirements of the 'third world' raised the question why architects, engineers, doctors, etc. so often adopted them, and why this was tolerated by bureaucrats in government or public corporations. Why are syllabi in higher education, including economics, modelled on those of countries with quite different needs? And why are patterns of consumption that are capital-intensive, fuel-intensive and import-intensive, copied so widely?

These questions pointed to the importance of further factors that are 'non-economic' but inseparably connected to the 'economic'. Cultural dependence shapes the pattern of even material progress, both directly and via the mind of the policy-maker – who thus ceases to be an autonomous agent, as he has generally been considered in the past.[2] This provided the clue to why the historical models of the 'developed' countries (capitalist or socialist) could not be copied – as had been widely hoped in the 1950s. During embryonic stages in their evolution, these countries had not been

[1] A small school of 'plantation' theorists (Beckford, Best, Girvan, Thomas, etc.) in the Anglophone Caribbean, adopted a somewhat similar approach, but emerged independently – largely because of the linguistic inaccessibility of the dependence theorists. More Marxist variants of the dependence school were provided by Frank and Samir Amin.

[2] A doctoral thesis at Sussex by Chandra Randeni of the Bank of Sri Lanka, using official records to compare major projects aided by capitalist and socialist donors in the 1960s, shows that both groups were oblivious to the employment impact of their projects in a country with severe unemployment (which many projects aggravated) and the implications of this for choice of technology in either construction or operation. Both similarly made no allowance whatever for the effects on income distribution or on the country's economic dependence. In all projects, the only criterion used was how to maximise income, relative to purely financial costs. It is true that the Sri Lankan negotiators did not raise the real issues, so in a sense the responsibility is in part theirs, but then one must ask where they were educated and given a belief in the overriding importance of productive forces?

exposed to pervasive communication media disseminating attractive foreign life-styles, techniques and theories.

This line of thinking stimulated many economists to take an interest in China which was (at that time, anyway) following an autarkic and egalitarian policy, though with results hard as yet to evaluate, let alone assimilate into theory.

The successful action of OPEC governments at the end of 1973 in raising the price of oil more than threefold taught us further lessons. It exposed the danger of following economic models implying rapid industrialisation, unless energy resources were adequate, and reminded us of the finite limits to reserves of fossil fuels. While some governments of rich countries may be able to prolong growth by resorting to nuclear power, it would be financially out of the question for the poorer oil importers to solve their energy problems in this way. Despite the recent fall in fertility their population will double within the next thirty years. Techniques of harnessing solar, tidal, geothermal or wind power – even if economically feasible – take at best decades to develop and disseminate on a worldwide scale.

These dangers had already been stressed by ecologists, notably in 'Club of Rome' documents, but in an exaggerated and sensational way, so that few professional economists felt the need to take such warnings seriously. Yet there has apparently been a major qualitative change in the world economy. The dream of a completely 'modern' world, even in the next century, has started to evaporate. We are entering an era full of potential conflict.

Secure sources, especially of oil and uranium, are of paramount importance. In such a world, not at all benign, the level of living of a worker depends in large measure on the bargaining power of his or her government. Nationalism can no longer be ignored, nor can the nature of the state. 'Self-reliance' is naturally a common aspiration, as are the restructuring of the international order and the search for 'alternative' development strategies, eschewing capitalist or socialist economic models.

One cannot say that the cultural lag has disappeared. Developments in the middle of the 1970s have revealed the increasing professional irrelevance of the grouping of countries into three 'worlds'. At the end of the 1940s, when this classification was devised, advanced capitalist states typically had few public corporations and their regulating agencies were generally weak, whereas in socialist countries decision-making was heavily centralised. The latter were, moreover, importing little merchandise, technology or capital from the former. In the 1970s, the capitalist/socialist dichotomy has become less sharp or significant, trade and investment between them have increased (including a few joint ventures between TNCs and East European governments) and political tension has been relaxed.

In addition, the separation of 'developed' countries from 'underdeveloped' has become increasingly obsolete as several countries in the 'third world' have reached income levels above Portugal and other countries in Southern Europe, previously classified as 'developed'. The oil price rise, in particular, provided countries like Kuwait and Abu Dhabi with *per capita* incomes among the highest in the world. The 'third world' today covers too wide a variety of countries to have much conceptual significance.

The increasing differentiation has also undermined some core-periphery models – almost before European economists realised they existed. It is true that all 'peripheral' countries are still net importers of technology, capital equipment and arms,[1] but then the same could be said of the majority of countries up to now classifed as 'core'.[2]

In *all* countries, 'developed' as well as 'developing', capitalist or socialist, there is a lust for the products of modern technology, but technological progress facilitates the concentration of economic power (in geographical as well as social terms), destroys earlier (sometimes more humane) forms of production, causes unemployment (open or disguised),[3] requires the migration and retraining of labour, uses both capital and energy heavily, poses environmental problems, reinforces the centralisation of political and bureaucratic power, and spreads anomie.

Everywhere in the world, various analogous problems are being raised by what might be termed contradictions generated in technical advance, and no body of economic theory is well equipped to deal with them, certainly not those grounded in nineteenth-century Europe.

Towards more relevant theory

The general lesson of this review is that the adjustment of theory to reality is still delayed, often leading to dangerously inappropriate analyses and policies. One is reminded of the saying that generals tend to fight the *previous* war. If political leaders have used our prescriptions, e.g. by promoting growth, this has been because they have found these convenient rather than illuminating. However, some are now – as in the 1930s – desperate enough actually to feel in need of some professional guidance. We can, moreover, for the first time foresee some of the major characteristics of the world in the 1990s, which may help us avoid further theoretical lags. It

[1] In countries that count themselves as 'developing', there are also historic resentments against the former colonial powers – these too may be receding in practical effect as they are replaced by grievances against all countries, whether capitalist or socialist, which benefit from 'unequal exchange', to use the phrase of Emanuel, who pointed to the theoretical implications (especially for Marxism) of the enormous and still growing difference in wage levels between 'developed' and 'developing' countries.

[2] The subclass of 'socialist' economies within the 'periphery' has proved difficult to identify, as is shown by frequent reclassifications, e.g. of Egypt.

[3] In production units which are not responsive to market prices, especially public corporations, the problem appears as 'disguised' unemployment – i.e. excess labour and low productivity.

will, for example, be a world short of fossil fuels, and more heavily dependent on the technology of the TNCs. The imminent massive introduction of very cheap silicon chip microprocessors threatens to bring a new and more intense phase of international competition, unemployment and other social problems (while also holding out – as the latest technology always does – the promise of great benefits). Multilateralism is likely to be further weakened.

What are the implications for making economic theories more relevant, and university syllabi more appropriate, to today's problems – and if possible to those of the next two decades?

The first is the need to recognise that, while problems take different forms in different countries, there are theoretically significant common elements, arising out of the impact of similar, worldwide, technological changes. 'Development' is no longer just the problem of the tropics: the economists of advanced capitalist and socialist countries could learn much from their colleagues elsewhere – if they were prepared to. The growing irrelevance of the three-world classification suggests for some purposes, at least, that we need world models which, like that of Sunkel, do not deal only with national units, but are 'transnational systems' running across national boundaries, and with many non-economical dimensions.

Yet, and secondly, economics cannot be carried very far in generalities, ignoring the specific national context. Any usable national model incorporates the socio-economic characteristics of that nation – such as historically determined classes and ethnic groups, political institutions and social attitudes, structures of output and employment, etc. A student needs models based on the special nature of his or her country's economy. This implies making the discipline much less *a prioristic*.

Thirdly, of especial importance are the determinants of the national room to manoeuvre. These do indeed include economic factors, such as whether a country is industrialised, and whether its economy is planned. However, more basic – because they affect those factors too – are the following unalterable determinants, which have not so far been stressed, even by the dependence school,[1] though their importance has been demonstrated by recent events:

(i) size (both area and population);
(ii) location (proximity to more powerful countries, access to oceans, etc;
(iii) resource base (arable land, oil and minerals, etc).

[1] There may be some tendency to play down the importance of these geographical factors by those who wish to emphasise the overriding importance of social change. However, the serious effects on the Cuban economy of the recent fluctuations in world sugar prices, especially the re-emergence of unemployment, remind us that certain realities cannot be ignored.

These could lead to more useful typologies than the old 'three-world' classification; e.g. to models for petroleum economies, for more advanced industrial countries, and for small countries.

Fourthly, the agenda must clearly now also include a number of non-economic determinants of autonomy, and therefore of national development in all types of country, which *are* subject to policy, at least in the long term. These can only be very briefly noted here:

(i) technological (the size and quality of scientific manpower and institutions, civil and military and their capacity to select appropriate technologies, if necessary excluding or preventing the development of those that are inappropriate);
(ii) political (including an appreciation of the aims and resources of TNCs and of the governments of more powerful countries, and a willingness to exploit bargaining assets);
(iii) military (an arms industry, local military expertise, and thus a capacity to withstand great power pressures);
(iv) cultural (e.g. use of the main national language, proportions of films and TV programmes made nationally, and the effect of the system of education on national unity).[1]

Such determinants of development have up to now been hardly noticed by economists in any part of the world: even the theory and practice of planning take little account of them. They have no place in the main theories which were built for qualitatively different situations.

A final implication is to reinforce the rather hackneyed point that economics is not a separate subject (especially not 'development economics'). Analyses that use purely economic determinants, even of economic variables (such as growth), now run even greater dangers of serious distortion. This applies not only to 'macro' but also 'micro' analysis – e.g. project evaluation.[2] We can appreciate afresh the merits in the traditional subject, 'political economy', though naturally this now needs broadening to take account of the actual and theoretical trends of recent decades, and to give due weight to current political, military and especially cultural influences, which can no longer be grouped in a passive 'superstructure'. Unless teachers of economics refer to relevant 'non-economic' factors, they are really misleading their students.

[1] Cultural autonomy is perhaps of a different order of importance from the others, because a country without the pre-conditions for it can have little political basis for economic theories relevant to their own circumstances or for development strategies designed to increase autonomy in other fields.

[2] See the note on aid projects in Sri Lanka, p. 11 above.

It will not be easy to develop economics in ways more appropriate to this part of the twentieth century. For economists in all parts of the world, professional innovation is – as in past decades – painful and strenuous. Yet surely there are signs of the profession being humiliated as accepted models become obsolete and incapable of throwing much light on the problems that so badly need solution.

2 Some Global Issues

Jozef Pajestka

POLISH ECONOMIC SOCIETY, WARSAW

I A CRITICAL PERIOD FOR ECONOMIC THEORY?

At certain historical periods intellectual reflection on human reality seeks new orientations, looks for wider appraisal (or reappraisal) of the past and for new horizons, and turns towards more general, 'philosophical' questions. One may call such periods 'critical' in the sense that they mark a transition to a new state of comprehension of reality. Between such critical periods human thinking continues the existing patterns, adding to the sophistication of partial argumentation, but still keeping in line with the basic questions and established paradigms. Economic theorising could be expected to follow this pattern in its development since it is part and parcel of general human reflection on socio-economic reality.

It is argued by some that we are coming to such a critical period in the development of socio-economic sciences. To support this proposition one can indicate existing feelings of the necessity for a reappraisal of human past and predicament, for opening new horizons, and formulating new questions. And indeed dissatisfaction with the state of economic theories, visible in certain circles, may be considered a sign indicating a critical period.

Whether we are really in a critical period of the historical process which demands and evokes new comprehension of reality is still, in my opinion, an open question. It first derives from an evaluation of truly new material and socio-economic phenomena and processes engendering these critical stands. Such judgements are usually more justified *ex post*, when it can be seen clearly that new comprehension has indeed been shaped, changing the patterns of thinking and seriously influencing both explanatory and predictive values of theory. We will certainly hear different views on that during this conference.

For an introductory comment, let me observe that feelings about a possible critical state of economic theory tend to appear among western economists, while Marxian economists in the socialist countries tend rather to rely on continuity, though remaining open to new questions and horizons. Where, however, I would expect a relatively wide consensus on the necessity of rethinking the state of economic theory, there is the emerging question of major world issues.

II NEW AREAS FOR ECONOMIC THEORY

There appear to be at least four major areas which mark new openings of recent socio-economic thinking:

(i) the global problematique (world models, the international economic order, etc.);
(ii) the long-term future (futurology, long-term forecasting and programming, etc.);
(iii) society's development objectives and the socio-economic feedback from the development processes;
(iv) interdependencies between mankind's patterns of civilisation and the ecosphere.

Good grounds seem to exist for asserting that economic theorists have lagged behind in developing thinking in these areas, and this is a problem to ponder about. By that I do not mean that individual economists have not contributed to the advancement of thinking in those fields. But, to the extent that they actually have, it has been more by virtue of abandoning the strict pattern of economic theorising than by adhering to it.

Once again, as so many times before in history, new openings in social thinking have been inspired by real life and not by deductive theorising. It is probably inevitable that theories lag behind the newly emerging tendencies and the arising challenges of reality. Still, the length of this time-lag is not irrelevant and strongly influences the relevance of theories. I am tempted to observe that excessive lagging behind of economic theories is due *inter alia* to the complacency of many theoreticians who resort to sophisticated mathematical theorising, finding in it both intellectual satisfaction and professional approbation. There seems to be a poor balance in the evaluation of scientific achievements between elegant, deductive theorising on one hand and innovative thinking on the other. We clearly need both and should praise both.

When science aims at grasping the real issues, the problem of appropriate theoretical equipment is of utmost importance. Economists here face a dilemma. Usually they are equipped with a set of theoretical and methodological devices with the help of which economic problems are approached. But real issues (like the ones mentioned above) are never purely economic. They are also social, political, informational, etc. This problem is well known. Many believe that it can be solved by a multidisciplinary approach, and strongly advocate this. Usually, however, individuals do not have multidisciplinary theoretical equipment at their intellectual disposal. Science has tended to develop by way of specialisation, and universally minded individuals are rather rare. Team work can be very valuable for some specific research, but it rarely produces synthetic comprehension of general issues. There is no simple way of solving this dilemma. Let me make two observations in this respect.

One can visualise two approaches in tackling new problems. The first consists in relying heavily on the existing set of intellectual instruments (theoretical and methodological). The second starts without preconceived instruments and relies rather on achieving an intuitive grasp of the problem considered, and on selecting appropriate intellectual devices for dealing with the problem. One might label the two approaches respectively as 'theory-abiding' and 'problem-solving' thinking. I suggest that the theory-abiding thinking is often unsuitable for tackling and solving new socio-economic problems. Turning to problem-solving thinking may prove very productive. It demands, however, a critical attitude towards the existing conceptual equipment and a willingness to draw on the theoretical and methodological experience of various schools and disciplines. This does not imply abandoning or neglecting the existing theories but does mean a more practical understanding of theoretical concepts.

It may be worth noting that when social thinking faces new challenges, a number of scientists (including, in particular, economists) tend to abandon strict theoretical considerations and turn to social philosophy, to intuitive judgements and to various types of relatively loose argumentation. Senior economists particularly demonstrate this tendency. This is the situation at the present time, and it supports the arguments presented above. Such attitudes should be appreciated and fully understood. They may be creative and may develop our knowledge no less than strict deductive theorising.

III THE WORLD PROBLEMATIQUE

The world problematique has become in recent time a most crucial issue in social thinking. It should be noticed, however, that its main thrust has come more from political tendencies than from theory. And, a remarkable fact, some very influential writings (the first two reports to the Club of Rome) were inspired by thinking not closely associated with the main stream of economic theory.

Looking at the world problematique as it has recently developed, and confronting it with the traditional patterns of economic thinking, the following points seem to merit attention:

(i) there has been a shift in perspective – from international economics to a global problematique;
(ii) the global issues are considered in a long-term perspective;
(iii) there has been a strong tendency towards normative and policy-oriented thinking;
(iv) the economic problems appear in close connection with socio-moral problems, particularly those of justice and equity.

I do not think that extensive argument is needed to show that the above points pose serious challenges for economic theory. Economists in the socialist countries are generally accustomed to consider the development processes in a prospective, normative and policy-oriented perspective. Yet the global problematique seems to call for a certain reorientation in theoretical considerations.

IV SHAPING THE FUTURE

The conscious shaping of socio-economic processes is one of the leading ideas of contemporary thinking. It originated as a basic premise of socialist ideology, but has slowly grown to become a widely acknowledged paradigm of socio-economic thinking.

This paradigm has (or should have) a deep impact on economic theory. Above all it leads to a new interpretation of the functions of economic theory: that it should serve not only in its explanatory and predictive capacity but also for policy design. This is how the functions of economic theory are understood in the socialist countries, and it serves as a basis for evaluating the relevance of theoretical considerations and of economic research.

In performing the above function, theory encounters certain difficult problems. Let me indicate some of them.

Conscious shaping of the development processes has to deal both with the aims of socio-economic activities and with the long-run development process and the ways and means of performing the various activities. It should be noticed that theory is not equally well equipped for dealing with these two sets of issues.

For a long time the problem of the aims of development has been left rather on the margin of theoretical interest. When it was necessary to deal with it for the sake of the completeness of certain theoretical schemes, e.g. in programming theories, the aims were treated as unexplained, exogeneous variables (often taken as political decisions) or as maximised variables of aggregated final effects of activities. This way of dealing with the socio-economic aims of development – or, still more, leaving the subject altogether outside the scope of theoretical considerations – seems to have been mainly a result of the fact that scientific analysis is not well equipped to deal with it. There were several reasons for this.

(1) The socio-economic sciences have been largely concerned with past and current issues, and have paid relatively little attention to the future. It is a new trend that there now appears to be a shift of interest towards concern with the future, and, it is particularly in this connection that the problem of the aims of development stands out predominantly.

(2) There is a specialisation in socio-economic sciences which, as already indicated, is not particularly suitable for dealing with such a complex problem as the aims of development. This is a problem which requires

a synthetic approach, and no one narrow, specialised science is able to deal with it.

(3) It should be noticed that it was something of a tradition among economists to shy away from the question of the socio-economic aims of development. There was a strong feeling of scepticism about the possibility of dealing with this in a strict, scientific manner. It is notable that this problem appears at most only very marginally in the writings of outstanding economists.

However, although the reluctance of economists to tackle the subject may be understood, the subject itself cannot be escaped. The policy-makers have to give answers to it, and are certainly right to demand some aid from scientific analysis.

Since we already have a wide historical experience in conscious shaping of the processes of development, this should become a subject of analysis, allowing us to discern the aims of actual development policies, and revealing certain regularities and tendencies in this field. While, however, this line of analysis seems promising, I would not expect much from any kind of deductive theory of aims. Theoretical deliberations on multi-aims systems, or on hierarchical structures of aims, etc., can certainly be helpful, but too much should not be expected from them for the guidance of development processes.

The most promising path to follow seems to be the diagnosis of the justified aims of society in changing the pattern of development. Socio-economic theory can contribute much in this way, using both analysis of the past and consideration of the future. Development of the latter is of special significance since it is particularly in consideration of the future that the problem of aims becomes most important, and without tackling it those considerations may be devoid of any meaning. Reflection on the future, particularly for the longer run, reveals the mutual relationship between the aims and the changing environment (social, economic and physical). And it is on this basis that some of the arguments for evaluation of the aims tend to arise.

A question may arise whether we can rationally formulate judgements on the aims of future development. This is a question with wider implications, and it concerns the whole value of future projections and programming. It is my view, however, that when we formulate the aims of the long-run development process we are not setting the aims for future generations. Even if we wanted to do that, there would seem to be no reason at all why our aims should be accepted in the future. Our vision and our judgement concerning the distant future are bound to be rather defective, and in time many of them will look very limited, naive, or even faulty. Future generations will certainly set their own aims, and these may be quite different from ours. But it must be noted that purposeful shaping of the development process is a continuous exercise. The future has roots in the present, and our present actions shape the future whether we are conscious of this or not. Long-term programming or planning thus has its main value as a method of helping to achieve greater rationality of contemporary activities, allowing also for the point of view of the future. The assumed or explicitly formulated aims of development can be understood as a kind of contemporary ideology which takes into account future needs and conditions in so far as they are currently understood. We are not able to foresee and evaluate everything, but what we can do is certainly better than to assume complete blindness with regard to future needs. It is this blindness which is assumed by the proposition that we cannot reasonably evaluate the aims of future generations, and so should not attempt to formulate long-term goals.

The problem of the aims of the development process presents a great challenge to socio-economic theory. In the socialist countries it is discussed under various headings, e.g. 'the patterns of life', 'the socialistic life styles', 'the features of the mature socialist society', etc.

As already indicated, the problem of the aims of development arises within the context of the paradigm of conscious shaping of the development processes, and then appears principally within the scope of the national economies. But there seem now to be good reasons for considering these aims within a global context; tendencies to do that are clearly discernible, and create new openings in social thinking.

V GLOBAL RATIONALITY

The global and policy-oriented approach to the world development process requires the formulation of a global rationality paradigm. Let me submit within this context the following considerations.

The conscious shaping of the process of large socio-economic systems assumes that they form some sort of unity. This makes sense only when firmly based on reality. The systems demonstrate this unity when there are grounds for considering their elements as component parts, encompassed by a community of purpose and rationality.

Let us describe the characteristics of the socio-economic systems which determine their susceptibility to conscious shaping by the following symbolic formula:

$$U(A) \rightarrow R(M)$$

The formula denotes that this susceptibility requires a certain unity of aims – U(A) which implies the rationality of policy measures – R(M).

When considering the various systems a great diversity in the element of U(A) should be perceived. My proposition is that (a) this diversity is very important and should necessarily be observed, and (b) the rationality should correspond to the ascertained unity of aims. For social systems without a unity of aims the rationality is meaningless, and the two are very strongly connected.

The unity of aims and the corresponding rationality can be defined for economic organisations (firms) and for the national economies. One might assert that the existence of the unity of aims is a basic assumption of economic behaviour of economic systems (like that of economic organisations or that of the national economies), whether explicitly formulated or not. The discussed 'unity' may differ substantially, and this is particularly relevant with respect to national economies. We can note here certain historical trends showing a tendency towards an increase in unity as well as differentiation due to the basic features of the socio-economic systems (capitalist or socialist). Though discussing the economic behaviour of national economies in the light of the defined unity of aims is important, we leave this problem aside here, concentrating rather on the global issues.

It seems justified to suggest that it is also possible to define a certain unity of aims in global terms and, therefore, that there are grounds for considering a global rationality corresponding to it.

It seems appropriate at this juncture to observe that one can visualise two approaches to the comprehension of global rationality. The first relies on an abstract concept of rationality, resembling the one applied to economic organisations or to national economies. Following this concept one could visualise for example an optimisation model built up to determine the optimal, international division of labour within the framework of the world economy. The second considers 'rationality' in close connection with the defined unity of aims of all mankind. It is the second concept which seems right and defensible. Moreover, it is only on the basis of a firmly ascertained unity of aims that the rationality of any measures can be considered and devised.

If we attempt to define the common aims of the world community at present and for the foreseeable future, the following can be firmly defended:

(1) The preservation of world peace, and in particular prevention of a possible outbreak of a thermonuclear war that would pose a threat to all human civilisation and to the very existence of mankind.
(2) The elimination of the flagrant worldwide socio-economic disparities whose continuation – and, even more so, intensification – threaten world peace and harmony.
(3) The observance of an equilibrium between mankind and the ecosphere which, if undermined, could check progress and possibly cause a regression of the human race.
(4) The attainment of greater order and justice in international economic relations, which would in the long run promote progress in the interests of all nations.

Basing the concept of global rationality on this kind of definition of the unity of aims might seem a minimalistic approach. But, let me emphasise, such theoretical concepts should be based on firm grounds, on facts and tendencies appearing in real life. Considering the world development patterns in the light of some abstract, universal rationality might look nice and attractive, but this is not a virtue which makes it the correct concept for explanatory and predictive purposes. It should also be noted that implementation of the global rationality corresponding to the defined unity of aims is still so far away from reality that it should by no means be described as 'minimalistic'. One can forecast that in the future the scope of the global unity of aims will expand. This tendency, which should be analysed and anticipated, does not change the correctness of starting from the observance of the real unity of aims appearing in the historical period considered.

VI THE INSTITUTIONAL FRAMEWORK FOR A GLOBAL UNITY OF AIMS

The concept of global rationality can serve as a point of departure for further considerations. Three groups of questions seem relevant in this context:

What is the nature, and the working 'mechanism' of the unity of aims?
What patterns of global rationality follow from the defined unity?
What are the policy measures corresponding to the global rationality?

A few problems belonging to the first group will be briefly discussed.

A community of aims developing in the historical process appears primarily in human comprehension as a pattern of understanding reality, its requirements for human behaviour; this comprehension develops from narrow intellectual and political circles but has a tendency to spread. As long, however, as a certain unity of aims is no more than a mere exercise of intellectual argumentation, it can hardly become an operating factor and serve for conscious shaping of the development processes, even if the arguments seem very strong.

Historical experience shows that for the unity of aims of a socio-economic system to become effective, it has to be 'institutionalised'. We do know something about the institutional set-up of economic organisations and of the national economies. One can also perceive institutional developments corresponding to the global unity of aims and global rationality; this takes place particularly in the development of the United Nations framework. But, in my view, this has hardly started to become a subject of theoretical analysis. Economic thinking seems to be particularly poor in analysing socio-economic institutions and, therefore, poor for predicting a new institutional set-up. This is probably why this important line of institutional development connected with global rationality goes on almost unnoticed in economic theorising.

Whatever the institutional set up of the global unity of aims, its working has to be seen in the light of the existence and functioning of the important institutions acting on the international scene. There are, in particular, the national states and the transnational corporations (TNCs). My contention is that the interplay between these three types of institutions (global, national, TNC) is of great importance for the global system, and deserves much more attention than is usually given to it.

Assume that the world community is organised in a pattern relying heavily on the existence of the national states. Then we have to do with the relatively strongly integrated unity of aims and the corresponding national rationality, supported by a strong institutional set-up defined as a national state. If the national states are a dominating element of the world institutional system, then the working of the global unity of aims and rationality acquires a specific pattern. For implementation they have to be 'internalised'. By that I understand a way of accommodating the rationality and wider aims than those belonging to the narrower scope of national interests into the national economy set-up. This accommodation can eliminate, at least partly, an outright contradiction of national and global interests.

However, consideration of the forms and patterns of this 'internalisation', can be inhibited by treating the national state as an obsolete institution which should preferably perish. This line of thinking is fostered by some western economists; its final conclusion leads towards the establishment of 'world government'. Institutionalisation of global rationality in the form of a kind of 'world government' does not correspond, in my view, to the scope and character of the global unity of aims as it appears at present; it is obviously premature. One should also not forget that the national state constitutes the main institutional form in which the poor nations are organised; and this is the only institution which can protect their interests in relation to the transnational companies.

The above considerations justify the necessity of studying the world institutional system. Let me indicate that within the CMEA the socialist countries have developed ways to accommodate this broader rationality while keeping national states as the dominant institution. Many interesting observations of a general character can be drawn from this experience.

VII JUSTICE, EQUITY AND THE NEW INTERNATIONAL ECONOMIC ORDER

Recently a tendency towards the implementation of a global rationality has appeared most strongly in the attempt to establish a new international economic order (NIEO). This is a historical lesson which must not go unnoticed in economic thinking.

The genesis of NIEO can be found in particular circumstances appearing in the first half of the 1970s (connected with the 'energy crisis'). My contention is, however, that not disregarding the particular circumstances, the basic propelling force for NIEO should be seen in the socio-political drive towards greater equity among nations. A striving towards greater justice and equity can be seen both on the internal scene (for many nations) and on a world scale. This statement is, in my view, strongly substantiated by recent developments, though they need further observation assessing the strength and the patterns of the driving forces.

The above proposition gives grounds for formulating certain observations and conclusions:

(1) The drive towards equity is a function of time and will in future grow and intensify. Two factors seem to make for this:
   (a) the economic tendencies creating growing discrepancies and thereby stimulating socio-political reaction against them;
   (b) education and the mass media awakening wide social strata to new needs and aspirations.

(2) A NIEO should then be conceived as a process and not a single reform of world patterns. Factors lying behind this process are growing in intensity, and so will the process itself. There is before the world community a whole era of shaping a new order which has hardly started. If the initial action does not achieve full-fledged results, one should not be disappointed.

(3) The forces behind NIEO are of a socio-political nature, and the mechanism for shaping NIEO and running it has to be politico-economic. The feedbacks between political factors on the one hand and economic patterns on the other, acquire a particular role here; disregarding this aspect of the problem would lead to conceptual errors.

The striving towards NIEO, being of a socio-political nature, is associated with an intellectual movement elaborating new concepts of development, both internal and international. This has already proved theoretically creative and stimulating. But it needs steady conceptual and theoretical support; no great movements in history have succeeded without such support.

New thinking accompanying the drive towards NIEO concentrates particularly on developing strategic concepts, and seems to have a tendency to move from strategic diagnosis to strategy design. While, for example, the concept of 'capitalist metropolis–periphery relationship' has had mainly an explanatory value (though it is not devoid of certain policy implications), newly developed concepts such as 'collective self-reliance', 'basic needs', 'the international management of resources' clearly take the form of a strategic design.

Probably as a result of the fact that it develops these strategic concepts, the new thinking demonstrates one common feature: it belongs to political economy rather than to economics *sensu stricto*, and it is strongly policy-oriented. This is not only a mere statement of facts. There are reasons for considering it a most desirable line of change in economic thinking. Whenever real world issues are analysed, economics narrowly conceived has not much to offer. However, while economics has developed a rather strict logical system, political economy is sometimes much more loose in its argumentation. In certain applications it demonstrates a tendency to create concepts which are not well defined and are subject to various interpretations. It would seem desirable, therefore, that some of the concepts currently in circulation, including those mentioned above, should be very thoroughly scrutinised.

Discussion of the Papers by Professors Seers and Pajestka

(Chairman Professor S. Tsuru)

Professor Pajestka and Academician J. Sczepanski welcomed the participants and formally opened the conference. Professor Tsuru explained that at the first session the two authors would each introduce their papers and there would also be a brief statement by Professor Furtado. Subsequent sessions would be opened by discussants.

Professor Seers (UK) raised three issues as an introduction and extension of his paper. First, he asked whether it was still relevant to use the standard division of the world into three. It might have some political rationale, especially for the 'third' world, but economically there was a large degree of differentiation within, and of overlapping between, the three 'worlds'. In his view the framework was no longer useful professionally and it was better to see the world as a continuum which could be classified in *various* ways. While not denying the existing differences he thought there were certain similarities which were worth stressing: all countries have problems with bureaucracies and the process of policy-making; all have to face the effects of imported patterns of consumption and of imported technologies; and all have to deal with transnational corporations (TNCs). There would be varying constraints of size, location, national economic and political conditions, etc., but no governments were now fully autonomous agents in dealing with TNCs or setting their development strategies. All countries were strongly affected by external cultural influences via films, television, educational exchanges, etc. Arising from this there was a real danger that their analysis and policy-making would be harmed by theories derived from the wrong time and the wrong place.

Professor Seers' second point followed from this and concerned the relevance and usefulness of the education currently provided for economists. He considered that many had first to unlearn what they had been taught and that this was especially true of newly-qualified PhDs. Economics tended to start from a set of abstract concepts and derived propositions from this which were logically sound but bore little relation to reality.

One of the main problems was that academic excellence was measured in terms of skill in mathematical manipulation, elegance and novelty rather than ability to illuminate important and relevant questions. The underlying assumptions of economic theory – including rationality, primacy of economic motives, universality of competition, and the homogeneity and perfection of markets – were all of very doubtful relevance.

The doctrines normally taught also took for granted the importance of growth. This was taken to be synonymous with development and accumulation was seen as its source, requiring savings (sacrifice) and/or imported capital and associated technology. The actual experience of most countries where fast growth had occurred – judging from admittedly very inadequate data – was that it had been accompanied by increased unemployment and poverty, and a widening inequality in the distribution of income.

The great lesson to be learned from this was the fallacy of a policy of 'growth first, distribution later'. The type of growth adopted would itself determine the pattern of redistribution; for example, by creating a group with a vested interest in the continuation of particular policies. This group might cut across conventional social classes and include sections of the organised urban working class.

The framework of perception which gave rise to these errors regarding growth was common to both capitalist and socialist economists in the developed countries – they had common roots in the theories of Adam Smith and Ricardo and in the experience of growth in Europe in the nineteenth century. A more relevant framework would include the following:

(a) a world economy involving flows of technology, capital and labour and allowing for the role of the TNCs;
(b) the specific relationship of any individual country to the world economy;
(c) the specific features of each individual country, and especially size and resource base.

Professor Pajestka (Poland) then summarised his paper. He emphasised four areas where a new approach was needed: the problems of the world economy, forecasting and shaping the future, the formulation of objectives for the world economy, and the interdependence of human activity and the ecosphere.

Traditional theory had not, in his view, been very productive in these areas and lagged too far behind the problems set by the real world. He identified two main reasons for this. Firstly, the complacency of abstract mathematical theorists; this type of economic theory gave personal satisfaction and gained professional approbation, including Nobel Prizes, but it was quite often of little relevance. Secondly, the fact that real world issues were never purely economic; they were also political, social and institutional and therefore required a much wider approach than economics alone could offer.

Realisation of this led to suggestions for a multidisciplinary approach, but few individuals are able to operate with the concepts and tools of several disciplines, and teams of scientists are of very limited value for development of theory.

Turning to the problems of the world economy, Professor Pajestka listed four recent tendencies which he thought deserved attention: the movement away from traditional 'international economics' towards examination of the economic problems of the world as a whole, the consideration of these problems in a long-term framework, the emphasis on normative and policy-oriented thinking, and the concern with issues of justice and equity. A major element of contemporary thought was thus the conscious shaping of global socio-economic processes and this would have important implications for economic theory.

Earlier generations of economists, including Lange and Kalecki, had accepted the aims of economic growth as given, but this was no longer satisfactory. Economists must now be as concerned with ends as with means; rational aims were as necessary as rational methods for the attainment of these aims.

This raised the question of global rationality. Rationality is not a purely economic concept, and one cannot discuss an issue such as the optimum allocation of resources for a given set of countries without consideration of all the circumstances – economic and political – of these countries. Only if there is a real unity of aims among a group of countries can there be a rational set of measures.

Professor Furtado (Brazil) said that the main theme of the conference had to be seen from an epistemological point of view, rather than as the failure or irrelevance of economic theory. The social sciences, in particular economics, might have to undergo some fundamental change. The evolution of economic thinking reflected the evolution of historical processes. A key aspect of this evolution had been the periods of concentration on accumulation during the last two centuries. The first period was dominated by Great Britain and led to the expansion of world trade in the mid-nineteenth century. In the second period, from about 1870 to 1950, new economies developed, generally on the basis of protective tariffs, and this development was accompanied by tension, wars and socialist revolutions. By the end of this second period the process of accumulation and development had been diffused throughout the industrial core. In the third period, beginning *c*.1950, there had been a new phase of diffusion in the periphery.

The subject matter of economics had evolved in relation to these three periods. In period one the engine of growth was the Schumpeterian entrepreneur and the enterprise, and this gave rise to the microeconomic approach. In period two a major feature was the co-ordination of decision-making at the national level, and the greatly enhanced role of the state gave rise, after a long time-lag, to the development of Keynesian macroeconomics. In period three the major new element was the transnational corporation and the problem for economic theory was to incorporate in its basic framework both this factor, and the position in the world economy of the third world countries on the periphery.

In Professor Furtado's view Professor Pajestka's approach was similar to his own, but he could not quite agree with him on the question of global rationality, and he doubted whether it was possible to formulate a satisfactory concept of rationality at the global level which would correspond to the earlier concepts of micro- and macro-rationality.

Finally, he wanted to stress the need for economic theory to adopt a much broader approach. It should not be seen as a narrow formalising science but should incorporate aspects such as the origins and legitimacy of power. Without this the present crisis of economics could not be overcome.

Academician Khachaturov (USSR) said that he wished to comment on one point. Professor Pajestka had suggested that the world community might have four common aims (see p.23). In his view these aims were too general and were political rather than economic objectives. Given the existing divisions in the world it was a very important task for economic science to formulate specific economic aims for each of the separate groups of countries.

Dr Desai (India) suggested that speakers were too readily taking for granted the demise of economic theory. There was more to it than mathematical economics, and it was not true to say that economics had failed to discuss urgent problems or to provide solutions. However he would accept that in some cases the solutions proposed have led to further problems. He said that Professor Seers had pointed out that while growth had taken place over the last thirty years, poverty and unemployment had also grown. But here we could recall England's growth experience, say between 1790 and 1830. This was a period of rapid economic growth as well as of misery. Malthus was generalising from the society around him, not building an abstract theory *a priori*. Growth became benevolent only in the late nineteenth century.

Today we lived in a much more democratic age and the poor were not willing to suffer patiently as they did in the late eighteenth and early nineteenth centuries.

Dr Desai's third point was that global rationality as proposed by Professor Pajestka required a global harmony of economic interests, whereas the actual situation was one of conflict.

Academician Mateev (Bulgaria) thought that the great pessimism about the relevance of economic theory expressed by Professor Seers was exaggerated, and was not applicable to all schools of economics. For example, the emergence of the giant corporations had not come as a surprise to all economists: precisely this feature had been stressed by some theorists in their discussions of capitalist economies many years earlier. Similarly, the breakdown of the Bretton Woods system, to which Seers referred, had been anticipated by those theorists who had stressed the importance of the unevenness of development at the foundation of the system.

Dr Owosekun (Nigeria) referred to Professor Pajestka's comment on economic aims. He said that in the third world, aims were too vaguely defined. Since economic development was multidimensional, involving improvements in a number of indices, it was important to define economic objectives to incorporate other indicators besides per capita GDP. These other indicators should include access to safe water, health services, communications, etc.

Dr Owosekun also thought that there were good reasons for preserving the much-used three-part classification of countries despite the criticisms of this by Professor Seers. He thought this helped the developing countries to appreciate the gap between them and the developed countries and to be fully aware of the enormity of the problems of development, and the distinct cultural and other differences between them and the developed nations. This awareness should help the developing countries to formulate policies for economic growth, education, health, etc., which would avoid mistakes made by the developed countries.

Professor Urquidi (Mexico) said that he thought that there was a serious gap between theoretical knowledge and actual problems and gave four examples to illustrate what he saw as the inadequacy for the developing countries of the orthodox market-allocation economic theory of the developed countries. It could not deal with the role of the small peasant producer who failed to react to market forces in the manner predicted. Its theory of industry was based on the operations of the entrepreneur who combined the various factors of production in a free market economy, and was of no help to developing countries where entrepreneurs were few in number, lacked the necessary information about the availability of resources, and were subject to unequal competition from the transnational corporations. His third example was the failure of orthodox neo-classical theory to allow for the high rates of population increase experienced by the developing countries; this tended to produce a large labour surplus which could not be absorbed even at high rates of growth. This was in turn linked to the fourth question – the choice of the appropriate technology and the process of technological innovation. He recognised that on these and many other issues it was easy to criticise, but so far they had not been able to build a new body of economic or socio-economic theory which would be more relevant to the structural problems of the developing societies. Could this be done?

Professor Ostrowski (Poland) said that the fundamental question to be considered was the role played by economic theory. In his view it should provide some organising principle for action. There was the concept of the individual entrepreneur acting on the basis of microrationality and of the national state acting on the basis of macrorationality, as mentioned by Professor Furtado. Was there a corresponding agent at the global level? There was interdependence of nations at this level but no world government, and since there was no agent it was a mistake to look for global rationality. It was thus not possible at this stage to introduce the concept of global rationality as an organising principle, though it could remain as a noble ideal for the future.

Professor Rweyemamu (Tanzania) referred to further deficiencies of economic theory as observed by an economist from a developing country. Orthodox theory started from an existing structure for which small changes were required. Furthermore, economic theories of international trade were based on an assumption of equality of actors whereas nations were in fact very unequal, and the effect of this on their economic relations should be allowed for if the theories were to be relevant and helpful.

Dr Simonyan (USSR) said that Professor Seers had considered economic growth *per se* without adequately taking into account the socio-economic system as a whole. For example, the problems of oppressed minorities or of the increase in crime were not the consequence of growth as such, but of the absence of the appropriate social changes which should accompany economic growth. He also thought that Seers was generally too pessimistic and too negative. He had said what the developing countries should not do, but not what they should do.

In reply to the discussion, *Professor Seers* said that the issue of what the developing countries should do was a matter for them, not for him. He could only point to some of the lessons to be learnt from past experience of economic growth, e.g. the tension it could generate. Dr Desai had mentioned the example of England in the late eighteenth and early nineteenth centuries, but he did not think that one could expect England's experience to be repeated in the present day. At that time there was no foreign country with higher standards than England's to raise the consumption levels of the minority and to set patterns that were harmful to development. In countries in Latin America which had apparently achieved a certain degree of industrialisation – comparable to the level of England in the second half of the nineteenth century – no redistribution had taken place because the consumption standards of the minority were set by more advanced countries, and could only be maintained by the denial of economic and political rights to the majority of the population.

He agreed with Professor Pajestka's emphasis on lags in the development of relevant economic theory. It was largely explained by what he called 'academic inertia': the academic world rewarded those who could absorb and reproduce the current doctrines. It also created an environment in which economists were cut off from economic reality and discouraged from dealing with it.

Academician Mateev had said that the development of the transnational corporation had been envisaged by some earlier economists. This was so, but the TNCs had become qualitatively different from what had been foreseen: they had moved into new spheres of activity including manufacturing, banking and communications; they no longer operated only within the old colonial empires but were worldwide; and there was no longer the same degree of identification with the government of their country of origin. This was a problem not just for the third world but also for the developed countries: for example, the UK's North Sea oil resources were being developed primarily by US companies. The relationship between these companies and the governments with which they dealt was a major issue.

Professor Pajestka said in his reply that he did not think it was possible to abandon the concept of global rationality. He accepted that there were conflicts of interest, but still thought that there were aims which were in the interests of the world as a whole, and that the attainment of these aims implied some concept of global rationality.

PART TWO

Economic Rationality

3 Theoretical Concepts of Economic Rationality

Zdzisław Sadowski
INSTITUTE OF PLANNING, WARSAW

I INTRODUCTORY

Economists are so attached to the idea of economics as a body of knowledge concerning the best possible use of available resources that the concept of rationality seems a sacrosanct cornerstone on which the whole structure rests. But, on close scrutiny, this concept – and its meaning for economics – becomes much less clear. What makes things difficult is probably the fact that the understanding of the role of rationality in economic activity has been undergoing continuous evolution. Two hundred years ago it was possible to assume that man by his very nature acted rationally in his economic life. This assumption eventually became obsolete. Today, it may at best be claimed that, amidst various obstacles and difficulties, man only endeavours (or, perhaps, should endeavour) to act rationally. There is a vast difference between these two assumptions. The first gave birth to an interpretative body of theory, claiming to explain what is. The second may give rise only to theories describing what should be, given additional assumptions on what is desirable.

In what follows a closer look will be taken at some implications of both approaches, and an attempt will be made to draw a few conclusions concerning the present needs and possibilities of economics.

II THE HISTORICAL ROOTS

The idea that man acts rationally was launched two hundred years ago by Adam Smith. The individual human being in his economic activities, i.e. activities concerning his material wellbeing, was approximated by an abstract notion of 'economic man'. Faced with information coming to him from the market, he was able to behave in a rational way, i.e. so as to maximise his benefits given the resources, or – alternatively – minimise his costs of attaining a given level of achievement. The working of the whole socio-economic system was interpreted in terms of this assumption: rational behaviour of individuals pursuing their selfish goals became – in the eyes of

Adam Smith and his followers – a blessing for society. Owing to it, a self-regulatory market mechanism was set in motion, taking care of an allegedly optimum allocation of means of production and an optimum distribution of output.

We all know how vast possibilities for intellectual development were opened by this line of thinking. A whole theoretical discipline supposed to explain the working of the economic system based on the market mechanism was established and acquired high academic status. It was subsequently developed and refined over many decades. It is important to note that this discipline called economic theory was purely deductive: it was based on the *assumption* of rational behaviour of man in his economic activity.

When the validity of this assumption was eventually disproved, the discipline did not lose any real meaning: its main structure was absorbed into a broader philosophical discipline of praxiology – the theory of how to make optimum decisions given the aims. But before that happened, economics had a long way to go and a multitude of problems to face.

The first of these was that of defining the criteria of rationality in economic behaviour. Even the basic concept was not easy to formulate.

Among the founding fathers of political economy, Quesnay was probably the first to try to define the ideal objective of economic activity by saying that it should seek the greatest possible augmentation of benefits while at the same time seeking the greatest possible reduction of expenses. The error of this formulation has been repeated ever since by new students of economics, not yet familiar with the notion of a clearly defined goal function: they learn only after a while that one can only either maximise one thing or minimise another. There are, therefore, two forms which can be taken by the principle of economic rationality: it is either the maximisation of effects, given the outlays, or the minimisation of outlays, given the desired level of effects.[1]

This interpretation underlines the fact that the concept of economic rationality is necessarily linked to the idea of pursuing a clearly defined objective. Depending on the choice of the objective, the goal function may take the form of either maximisation or minimisation. Which of the two it happens to be in an actual situation, does not seem to have conceptual importance, though it may be relevant for practical solutions. What is more important, is the fact that economic rationality can have no real meaning before the benefits and outlays are clearly defined.

It is a commonplace for present-day economics that neither effects nor outlays can be defined in a clearcut way for any possible decision-maker. The best we can do is to use some kind of approximate ways of presenting (and quantifying) them. This is a serious problem which will need more discussion

[1] This formulation was made by O. Lange in his *Political Economy*, vol. I. In this shape, the principle of rationality was adopted by praxiology, cf. T. Kotarbiński, *Traktat o dobrej robocie*.

later. It did not seem as serious to the founding fathers of economic theory.

The reason for that can probably be found in the fact that the birth of the 'science of economics' was linked to the development of money-making activities as the standard type of activity concerned with the satisfaction of human needs. Money income, representing the universal tool for satisfying all possible needs, became *the* universal objective, and hence *the* magnitude to be maximised, the single objective of economic activity, and a measure of the level of satisfaction. This fact gave some ground to the theory, put forward by Max Weber and reiterated by Oskar Lange, that the very emergence of rationality in economic activity should be linked to the separation of money-earning activities from those which had a traditional, habitual nature and were dominant in pre-capitalist societies.

The need for a distinction between the two types of activity was clear already to Aristotle, who distinguished what he called *chrematistics*, from the traditional ways of household administration called *oikonomia*. There is some irony in the fact that it was eventually the latter term which was applied to the activities which had originally been described by the former one. What is important is to try to understand why it happened that way. A good reason seems to be that traditional *oikonomia* was difficult to deal with in terms of rationality in the sense described above. It was concerned with pursuing a large number of habitual goals of the household which was best done by adopting standards of behaviour established by routine or habit, in other words inherited from previous generations. No maximisation or minimisation of any tangible magnitude could have been applicable in these circumstances, as no such magnitude was visualised. Such magnitude, by contrast, was readily visualised in money-making *chrematistics*. Owing to this, activities concerned with making money income readily became the field for applying the principle of economic rationality.

This, however, does not seem to imply that economic activity based on routine determined by habitual or traditional rules of behaviour deserves to be labelled as non-rational as is done in the Weber–Lange approach. One is inclined to think that even in an economy governed by traditional behaviour a kind of rationality underlies the pursuit of routine behavioural patterns: it could also have been based on the idea of making the best use of resources. To the prevailing type of conventional wisdom, any departure from the habitual patterns meant departure from optimum allocation.[1] What was different, was the understanding of how the optimum was determined and the measures used for this purpose. One can describe the strict adherence to traditional rules of behaviour as a risk-minimisation programme for resource allocation in the pursuit of goals which were also determined by tradition.

The distinction between a tradition-governed economy and one of

[1] Cf. the criticisms of Lange's approach by Lipiński and Kula in O. Lange, *Dzieła*, t.3, p. 926 ff.

money-makers is, therefore, important not because it pinpoints the historical divide between non-rational and rational economic behaviour, which it does not, but because it shows the relativity of the concept of rational economic behaviour in relation to the type of decision-maker and his environment. The 'rationality of money-makers' loses ground for claiming that it is the only possible rationality.

The fact remains, however, that the science of economics did not adopt this line of approach and, instead, attributed an absolute value to the 'rationality of money-makers'. This reflected a confusion between rationality related to the existing level of knowledge about how to secure efficient use of resources, and absolute rationality in the sense of securing maximum efficiency of allocation. It is very clear to us nowadays that rationality of human action is unavoidably limited by the level of knowledge, and the same must be true of economic rationality. Thus, the relative nature of the concept of rationality has a second aspect. But economics in its earlier days did not seem to be aware of this fact, and confused the relative rationality limited by the knowledge of decision-makers with absolute optimum-allocation (or perfect-knowledge) rationality.

What economists then did was to adopt a fundamental principle of rational economic behaviour, attributing to it a universal value in explaining the actual behaviour of decision-makers in a market (and money-oriented) economy. On this basis they erected a structure of deductive theory which (until Say's law was rejected) claimed to explain how the system actually works to secure optimum allocation of resources.

In the development of economic thinking the idea of the 'economic man' was soon disproved as an oversimplification. Rationality in terms of maximisation of a well-defined money magnitude was found applicable, not to a human being in his individual behaviour patterns, but rather to an organisational unit called a capitalist firm, or, alternatively, to its personification – the individual or collective capitalist entrepreneur. (In this respect the profit motive was long considered an adequate approximation of the goal of economic decision-making. Even this, however, eventually came under scrutiny as a result of some doubts concerning its adequacy.) Economic behaviour was thus divided into two parts: behaviour of producers and of consumers. In a sense, the previous concept of 'economic man' survived, but only with regard to the former.

III THE CHALLENGE TO THE CONCEPT OF ECONOMIC RATIONALITY

It seems worth while to consider some implications of this development for the concept of optimum allocation of resources in a society based on the competitive market system. This concept needed the idea of consumers' rationality as the ultimate explanation of the efficiency of the whole system. Producers' rationality was not enough to explain how a system was run efficiently, as producers had to be guided by the final demand of consumers. Hence the notion of consumers' sovereignty was indispensable for the logical consistency of the theory of resource allocation.

In view of the difficulty of simplifying human motives to money-making, the need to defend the idea of a rational consumer gave rise to the line of thought which tried to interpret the economic behaviour of consumers in terms of the maximisation of utility or satisfaction. If this could have been made into a workable proposition, nothing would have been lost from the basic approach to rationality; it was only a question of identifying the right kind of goal function best suited to every type of decision-maker. The trouble was that utility proved to be immeasurable, both in a cardinal and even in an ordinal sense (though it should be noted that the issue is still under debate).

This undermines the whole structure. What, indeed, can be assumed about consumer's behaviour? Is he acting at all rationally? If he is, how is his goal function formulated? If he is not, what becomes of the optimum allocation of resources?

The most recent development in the treatment of these questions is Harvey Leibenstein's idea of selective rationality, which seems to represent an elegant endeavour to fight a losing battle in defence of consumer's rationality.[1] He takes for his paradigm the proposition that the consumer acts rationally only from time to time, selectively, and builds it into a theoretical system. This approach deserves more attention than it is possible to give it in this paper. But why should we not take one revolutionary step further and say what seems quite reasonable on the grounds of everyday evidence: that the economic behaviour of consumers in any developed economic system is erratic?

This proposition is in full contrast to the above mentioned Weber–Lange approach, as it would imply that there is more rationality (admittedly at a lower level of knowledge) in the routine behaviour of a traditional household than – at a much higher level of information – in the economic behaviour of a modern man. He is exposed from early childhood to senility to a continuous shower of totally inconsistent information on what is best for him and his family, where he should go, what he should see, what he should buy and how he should spend his income and time. What rationality of economic choice is possible in these circumstances?

However, trying to avoid an excessively emotional approach, let us suppose that there exists a consumer who has a strictly determined criterion for the maximisation of his satisfaction, i.e. a preference function, and wants to apply it with consistency. It seems that, even if one day utility were to be proved measurable (which is hard to believe), there would still be one factor which would condemn his efforts to failure: the influence of the time factor. There is no way for any decision-maker to apply consistently to all his

1 H. Leibenstein, *Beyond Economic Man*, (1976).

decisions a single time-horizon. This problem was never perceived adequately by the early classicists, who – following Adam Smith – tended to adopt a year-to-year approach. It was perceived by Alfred Marshall with regard to the equilibrium of a firm; but it does not seem to have been solved. It still persists in the shape of a conflict between time horizons of differing lengths: the rationality of economic decision is relative also in relation to the time horizon adopted. There is no theoretical or practical foundation for using one single time-horizon for all decisions, but a change of horizon renders alternative lines of action incomparable, as they differ qualitatively, and not only quantitatively. This is too well known to deserve elaboration. But, for some reason, it was long neglected by economic theory.

If the consumer is bound to act erratically, he may still preserve his sovereignty, but the claim that a system based on such sovereignty leads to optimum allocation of resources can hardly be defended.

IV RATIONALITY OF THE SYSTEM

The question of evaluating how an economic system works was simple as long as consumers' rationality was the paradigm. The theory maintained that a system composed of rationally acting elements was necessarily rational also as a whole. This proposition is subject to doubt from more than one side. Even if the elements of a system act rationally, the whole system can still have certain specific features which make it deviate from overall rationality. However, this criticism seems less important than the more basic doubt with regard to the idea that the elements of the system act rationally. As was shown above, at least some of these elements – the consumers – can hardly be assumed to be rational. Without that, the more tenable assumption of the rationality of producers does not suffice to ensure the overall rationality of the system.

Thus, at a certain stage of socio-economic development the question emerges of rationality viewed from a higher level than that of an individual consumer or individual entrepreneur. This question first emerged implicitly through the doubts about the beneficial nature of free market capitalist systems for society as a whole (whatever its meaning). Hence, it appeared in the shape of the proposition that economically rational behaviour of individual decision-makers does not necessarily produce results which can be considered rational from a broader point of view, or even that it must produce results which have to be considered non-rational from the viewpoint of the whole society.

The argument took two different lines. One was that a free market society fails to produce an equitable distribution of the product of its activity – which is a proof of waste, and waste is the antonym for economic rationality; the other was that such a society is bound to create monopolistic deformations which lead to irrational allocation of resources.

The introduction of the problem of rationality at the level of society as a whole may perhaps be attributed to the Marxian theory of historical materialism, with its concept of the law of concurrence between productive forces and productive relations. The revolutionary adjustments of productive relations to the level of productive forces may be considered a form in which higher level, overall rationality is infused from time to time into the socio-economic development process. The most relevant example of such adjustment in the Marxian approach is the revolutionary transformation of the capitalist into the socialist system which becomes due when capitalism ceases to be able to perform the historical task of promoting growth to the common benefit of the people.

Once this idea was formulated, it opened new ground for asking further questions, also from different standpoints. Thus, the question was raised whether something could be done to make capitalism more rational at the overall level and thus save it as a social system. This was the Keynesian line. The fundamentally controversial nature of these approaches is both obvious and well known. What is common to them is that both of them make use – even if to some extent only implicitly – of the idea of overall rationality.

But obviously this adds a new dimension to thinking about economic rationality. It implies a different understanding of rationality than that based on the notion of individual advantage. What appears here as the basic idea is the notion of common good and common advantage.

V RATIONALITY IN A SOCIALIST ECONOMY

The need to articulate a definition of how exactly this common good is to be understood becomes particularly strong in the socialist socio-economic system. It would not make much sense to try to derive this definition from individual rationalities in view of the basic doubt about the latter, unless the doubtful assumption is made that socialism creates conditions which secure rationality of individual consumer's choices.

This can hardly be expected; the most important reason is that a socialist society is characterised by universality (as opposed to individualism) in its approach to social goals: in principle the advantage to individuals is considered a by-product of the advantage to society, not the other way round. Hence, in a socialist society, the idea of deriving the notion of common advantage from that of individual advantages loses its sense. Common advantage, and hence the measure of economic rationality from a social standpoint, has to be defined autonomously.[1]

If we assume that a satisfactory definition is available it may be further assumed that, in centrally controlled socialist economies, conditions do exist for conscious application of a higher level rationality principle by the

[1] The problem of social rationality was extensively discussed by J. Pajestka in 'Conscious Shaping of Socio-Economic Processes in a Socialist Economy', *Oeconomica Polona* No. 1 (1977).

controlling authority. Within the Marxian approach these two assumptions indeed led to theoretical and methodological developments, mainly attributable to Oskar Lange, which led to the elaboration of the theory of plan optimisation under socialism.

The asumption of full rationality of the central decision-making authority (which can be traced back to Enrico Barone) is very useful for theory building, just as was that of consumer's rationality in the case of the capitalist system. It is also very useful for practical purposes as a statement of intention: the authority should indeed try to act rationally. However, it would not be realistic to maintain that it does. Why? One reason is that it is too difficult in view of the limited information available. The other difficulty may be that the working of the socio-economic mechanism creates by itself obstacles to rational action.

It seemed easier for theory (perhaps because more in line with tradition) to reason in such a way as to get rid of the first of the two difficulties. This was done by making assumptions which helped reduce the working of a planned economy to the solution of the problem of plan optimisation.

Let us consider what conditions would have to be satisfied to justify this kind of approach. It seems that they can be reduced to four:

(i) a clearly defined criterion or goal function must be available in terms of a scalar magnitude;
(ii) this criterion must be consistently applied to all decisions;
(iii) the decision-maker must be capable of collecting and quickly processing a wide body of information on the existing alternatives for action;
(iv) he must be also capable of comparing the costs and benefits of various alternatives.

In the theory of plan optimisation it is assumed (often implicitly) that these requirements can be met to a certain extent in a socialist economy. How realistic is this assumption? There are very clear difficulties in meeting them.

The problem of criterion is well known and widely discussed. In the earlier stages of economic development of a socialist society it is possible to use the criterion of maximisation of the national income or its part – the consumption fund. But in the course of development this gradually becomes less and less satisfactory. The reasons for this are that the basic material goals of development lose their share in the notion of overall social satisfaction in favour of less tangible elements, some of which can hardly be evaluated in terms of money units. The inclusion of these social objectives again brings a new dimension into the concept of rationality, a dimension which is very difficult to deal with. All recent endeavours to work out new measures of economic welfare show the deficiencies of such proposals, whether they are based on monetary evaluations or other methods of weighing various welfare components.[1] Technical difficulties of evaluation are, however, only a part of the story. Perhaps more important is how to decompose the global measure, whatever it may be, into a set of specific objectives.

The decomposition of objectives is possible through a decision of the central authority, but, in one way or another, it needs social verification, *ex ante* or *ex post*. The best socio-political or economic machinery for such verification cannot be expected to produce one result: to secure full consistency in applying the given criterion.[2] The application of the criterion will have to depend on changing situations, at least with regard to the time horizon. It may be worth noting that, as a rule, the tendency for the central decision-maker should be to use a longer time-horizon (than individual decision-makers), which he often cannot do under the pressure of current events.

Added to all this is the always limited – and fluctuating – information on existing alternatives which is unavoidably hampered in any society by the existence of various sectorial interests. This can hardly be overcome, since it is a vital and characteristic feature of any existing social process.

Out of the four conditions listed above the easiest to meet, though technically not at all simple, is the last: that of the availability of methods for comparison of alternatives. When taken alone, however, it loses much of its significance for overall rationality.

The outcome of all this seems to be that there is not much point in using the term 'rationality' simply to denote the fact of using certain techniques of computation, given a goal function. The question must necessarily be asked, how was the goal function arrived at, or how is it to be determined. The traditional standpoint of many economists, described as: 'tell me your goal function and I will tell you how to act rationally', can no longer be accepted, in either the East or the West. The determination of the goal function, or the set of objectives, is itself a basic part of the game of rationality.

Therefore, we avoid the conclusion that, as long as we consider rationality in the traditional sense of maximisation of a well-defined magnitude, we must doubt the possibility of fully rational decision-making at the national economy level. This results from socio-political limitations.

[1] An interesting attempt to formulate theoretical foundations for a social welfare function is made in A. Aganbegian, K. Bagrinowski and A. Granberg, *Sistema Modeley Narodnolhoziajstwennogo Planirovanija* (Moscow, 1973), particularly Chapter III.

[2] Cf. J. Kornai, *Anti-Equilibrium*. Also, in the treatment of this subject I lean to some extent on the argument developed earlier in co-operation with M. Ostrowski in our forthcoming book, *The Development Challenges* (in Polish only).

However, similarly to what was said above in the context of the traditional economy, we would perhaps be well advised to think of redefining rationality – and the tasks for economics – rather than trying to fit new problems into old frames.

There is one further problem which has recently emerged and needs mentioning: why should high-level rationality be confined to the dimensions of a national economy if more and more of the problems facing mankind are of a global nature? Why not elaborate a concept of worldwide rationality? This has been done by various authors in different ways. But there is one serious limitation to its applicability: it must remain impracticable until decisions at the level of individual countries are made more rational in some new sense of the word.

What can be done at the country level is to adopt the view that economics only articulates a dream about rationality which does not exist in the real world. It is a postulate, at best an inspiration. Further developments based on the assumption of rationality may be useful for a remote future, but have very limited explanatory value for what happens in current reality. There seems to be a growing need for new economics, concerned with the description and analysis of real socio-economic processes rather than with any deductive constructions.

4 The Problem of Global Rationality

Aleksander Łukaszewicz
UNIVERSITY OF WARSAW

Redefining the concept of economic rationality is as desirable as it is difficult. What I am going to attempt is simply to propose some lines of reasoning. The emphasis throughout will be on the growing role of macro rationality; this includes the fact that, parallel to the strengthening of its foundations, another line of thought and activity is emerging – the problem of global rationality.

I THE CONTEMPORARY BACKGROUND

The behaviour of individuals and social groups has always been determined, both directly and indirectly, by the environment, particularly the socio-economic environment. The concept of rational behaviour must, accordingly, be looked at against the background of some kind of synthetic panorama of the contemporary world. The question is whether it is at all possible to create such a panorama which would be based on generally acceptable views of what are the crucial phenomena.

If we adopt the assumption (often taken as implicit) that socio-economic development is a process ruled by objective laws, we are led to the conclusion that there are certain basic characteristics of the real world which deserve to be treated as crucial. These have not emerged by accident or from the totally unconstrained choices of individuals or social groups, but from the interplay of activities of people pursuing certain goals. This does not imply that the result can ever be fully deliberate; in many cases it is merely the outcome of numerous incoherent activities. But even incoherent activities are by no means ruled by blind chance. On the other hand, even with activities which are coherent, the final outcome is not necessarily consistent with the designed pattern, ultimately because of the limited knowledge of those responsible for the design.

The idea of identifying the crucial phenomena in the real world which are subject to continuous change may be suspected of a static bias. Let us therefore assume that we are dealing with a certain time interval in which the most important features of the world panorama remain basically unchanged.

In the picture of the contemporary world the following features deserve to be considered as crucial:

(1) The tendencies in the world economy towards integration of smaller into larger entities. Various regional integration schemes, including the EEC and the CMEA, represent one line of the secular process of integration in the world economy. The other line, which has emerged from the historical process of private capital concentration, is the development of multinational corporations which have already become an autonomous factor contributing to the shaping of the present-day world economy.
(2) The basic components of the world economy are still nation states. To a historically unprecedented degree, governments of these states have undertaken responsibility for economic, social and political developments. There is a wide range of forms in which this responsibility manifests itself, from centrally planned socialist economies to various types of government intervention and planning in the capitalist market economies.
(3) Industrial development and the resulting urbanisation, the concomitant development of techno-economic infrastructure, demographic expansion, large-scale internal and external migration, all these led to profound changes in the socio-economic structure of societies. 'Mass consumption' together with the unprecedented congestion of industrial activities and human settlements, and the largely uncontrolled exploitation of the natural environment, created a situation in which shrinking natural resources endowment and diminished ecological absorptive capacity acquired the status of barriers endangering the further development of mankind, and perhaps even the very survival of civilisation.
(4) At the same time, the unevenness in the levels of socio-economic advancement between national economies and world regions became more conspicuous than ever, and the disparities are still tending to deepen rather than to diminish. The very timely cry for the 'New International Economic Order', strengthened by various assessments of prospects for the world economy (whose cognitive, advisory and warning qualities should not be underestimated) made social sciences face a challenge so enormous that to label it simply as 'new' would dwarf its real dimensions.
(5) As a result of these phenomena, the need for effective control over the development of national economies became widely evident for the first time in history. None of the historical examples of economic development governed by a central strategy seems qualitatively comparable with the contemporary situation. In these conditions the common understanding of 'economic' decisions seems to acquire increasingly macro undertones.

(6) Since the revolutionary emergence of the socialist system, the socio-economic system based on private ownership of the means of production has lost its historical exclusiveness. The coexistence and parallel development of the two systems, along with political contradictions and tensions, continues to produce not only rivalry in the economic, social, cultural and moral spheres but also mutual influence and unavoidable interaction. The coexistence of two socio-economic systems which are contradictory by their very nature, cannot but have a strong impact on the approaches to the understanding of social objectives, to general socio-economic and moral praxiology, to motivation of human activities under various institutional conditions. In these circumstances individuals, social groups and whole societies are facing new conditions of choice and decision, new challenges in their striving for survival as well as new opportunities in their search for advancement and progress.

II THE DOMINANCE OF MACRO RATIONALITY

All the above factors, taken together, including the competitive coexistence of two systems, determine the dominant scale of economic problems, choices and solutions. National and – all the more so – international development strategies may be implemented only by national states and their groupings. The dominant problems are macro problems, the relevant instruments are predominantly macro instruments, and decisions preceding strategical actions are macro decisions made with a view to achieving macro results. In brief, the macro approach reigns supreme in contemporary socio-economic strategy and policies. Consequently, the motivational set-ups also evolve in the aggregative direction; the individual's choices and decisions depend to a growing degree upon the behaviour of the aggregate he belongs to – be it the social group or class, professional group or the nation as a whole.

Thus in redefining economic rationality for present-day purposes, it is necessary to focus attention on macro dimensions, hence on macro rationality. It would seem false, however, to forget about the micro and mezo dimensions. They have not faded away; they have only to be fitted into the whole picture in a new way.

The dominance of the macro approach changed the general framework for the functioning of the entities of which the national economy is composed. Similarly, the emergence of a global approach is changing the general framework for the functioning of national economies which are integral parts of the world economy. This framework of macro or global structures is itself subject to changes which, in principle, should lead towards more rational shapes and forms. Be it as it may, the micro and mezo entities within the national economy are more or less strictly determined in their striving for rational behaviour by the macro environment and – to a slowly but constantly growing degree – by the global environment. Under these circumstances it now seems to be unacceptable to look at the concept of economic rationality taking as the point of departure the firm, and treating all the rest as 'externalities'. Rather the opposite is true: the macro scale, the macro environment, constitutes the framework for the firm, and hence should be the point of departure for the analysis of micro rationality. Constraints on micro choice should not be confused with externalities.

III DIMENSIONS – SCALE AND TIME

The main dimensions of any socio-economic activity are its scale, its time-span, and the location in which the activity is organised.

The need for a macro approach in terms of dimensions applies first of all to the scale of activity. The macro scale is today overwhelmingly present and emphatically colours the rules of behaviour of individuals and other basic economic units.

Traditionally the concept of rationality has been analysed and discussed mostly in static terms. The concept reveals some of its weaknesses when confronted with the dimension of time. Built into the framework of static analysis was the tacit assumption that choice which is rational in a given moment is thereby rational throughout time. This assumption requires scrutiny.

The time factor has always been taken into account in economic decisions as the main cause of risk and uncertainty, the twin brothers of any undertaking. Its role must have increased with industrial development which has brought about more and more structural diversification; due to technological requirements methods of production continually grow longer and more roundabout.

True, earlier societies also engaged in huge undertakings such as European medieval cathedrals which needed a substantial time for their implementation. But there is a qualitative difference in this respect between historical epochs. While in pre-capitalist societies large-scale undertakings, whatever their motivation, were focused predominantly on the physical product, the large-scale undertakings of industrial societies (both capitalist and socialist) are focused on the *surplus*, as these societies are development-oriented.[1]

[1] One should not overlook the difference between the capitalist surplus which is both motivated and appropriated privately and the socialist surplus which is both motivated and appropriated collectively. Collective appropriation in modern capitalism which is making headway with the increasing significance of welfare policies and R and D promotion policies is a form of indirect redistribution of the surplus for the sake of strengthening the safety conditions for maintaining direct private appropriation of the surplus. The socialist collective appropriation of surplus has always been direct, while indirect ways and instruments of its redistribution are applied only for allocative purposes.

These surplus-oriented large-scale undertakings were made both possible and necessary by the available technology and organisation. Because of the surplus orientation these undertakings require long and painstaking pre-investment studies, advanced organisational and financial facilities, phasing of outlays. Along with the scale, gestation periods increased. Risk and uncertainty acquire such proportions that a single economic unit (be it a capitalist or a socialist firm) cannot bear it by itself, therefore ultimately seeking some form of partnership with the state (credits, subsidies, licences, guarantees or political safeguards).

In the conditions created by the expanding time dimension, the rudimentary cost-benefit approach to such projects, based on the general praxiological principle of economic rationality, cannot but lose ground, at least partly. Although, relevant for a single economic unit, it can hardly be applied by the state, whose activity cannot be governed solely by the criteria of economic rationality.

This shows the point at issue. In a case-by-case approach (which may include parts of a project whenever it is divisible) economic micro criteria of choice can be readily used. But there is no additive consistency of the whole composed of such individual cases; the consecutive stages of aggregation bring about both new constraints and changes in the substance of the goal function. This is true even with regard to a large and complex investment project composed of complementary elements. It is all the more true with regard to a large corporation, a region or a national economy.

This problem manifests itself conspicuously in development planning. In socialism, the hierarchically constructed goal function (or rather the set of mutually dependent partial goal functions) has much more to it than simply maximisation of some magnitude under given outlays. But even indicative planning in a capitalist market economy necessarily has more complex goals to pursue than just aggregation of a number of individual profit-motivated undertakings (private or public). The contemporary capitalist state cannot depend on private rationality for its goals. *Mutatis mutandis*, the contemporary socialist state cannot merely depend on group rationality whether it be of a commune, a co-operative or the staff of a state enterprise).

In other words, in the conditions of contemporary capitalism the state (with its specific preferences) steps in to take active control over the development process, as market forces fail to reach the goals which are considered necessary. This means that micro rationality as a universal basis for economic decision-making is replaced, or at least complemented, by other criteria related to macro rationality. To what extent and how this is done, needs to be established; we will return to this problem later.

What happens in a socialist economy where the substitution of macro for micro rationality has been formally achieved? One interesting observable phenomenon is that central control is found in some respects to be inefficient at the level of the units subject to control; in such cases some degree of autonomy is given to these units, within the general framework of central planning. This is accompanied by the employment of a combination of directives and economic parameters (economic and financial instruments) which are supposed to create favourable conditions for economic choice, initiative, innovation, etc. This kind of action may also be described as introducing a degree of substitution of micro rationality for macro rationality. It is done with a view to reconciling and eventually harmonising both. This requires relevant adaptation of the planning and management procedures, as well as adaptation of the rules of the game for economic units. But it reveals a recognition of the fact that what is needed for efficient functioning of the economy is a combination of both rationalities.

IV TOWARDS HARMONISATION OF MICRO AND MACRO RATIONALITY

The problem of reconciling and harmonising micro and macro rationality creates formidable difficulties both for making theoretical generalisations and for finding practical solutions. These difficulties invite arbitrariness on the part of decision-makers who may feel this to be justified in the absence of analysis and expertise, or who may be sufficiently powerful to forego such expertise and experience as are available. But arbitrariness may easily spell irrational behaviour.

It is easy to stipulate that harmonisation of macro and micro rationality is desirable, but it is still not clear how this is to be achieved. It may be useful to ask a few supplementary questions concerning the very concept of harmonisation:

(i) is it an act or a process of an asymptotic nature?
(ii) if it is a process, is it continuous or discontinuous (going by stages)?
(iii) what should be the balance between spontaneity and conscious shaping (or imposition) in this process?
(iv) to what extent is imposition (using coercive methods) reconcilable with rational economic choice?

These questions seem to be highly relevant both to economic theory and to the practical shaping of strategies and policies in present-day societies.

Some answers may be ventured. First, harmonisation of macro and micro rationality is probably best viewed as a process of iterations, spontaneous or regulated, which should eventually lead to mutual adaptation of the participating agents. The nature of the process may thus take the shape of certain curves where the relation of both types of rationality is asymptotic within a relevant time-span. Secondly, due to various factors, including the character of technology, as well as the economic and organisational autonomy of economic units, this iteration is discontinuous, it goes from stage to stage. Thirdly, some elements of regulatory intervention are often involved, which means that a certain amount of coercion is injected into the economic process.

Coercive methods (such as legal norms, directives etc.) are inseparable from the existence of a polity. The extent to which these methods are used, and their impact on the rate and direction of economic development, differ substantially in time and space, particularly between different socio-economic systems.

In present conditions economic choice is inseparable from some imposed variables, at least for major undertakings and decisions. The degree of their concordance depends largely on the understanding of economic rationality on the part of those who generate the imposed variables. The rationality requirement for the decision-making centre is that it should be aware of the consequences of the resulting allocation of resources. But this requirement can be met only partly, by formulation of certain rules, for example with respect to the question of balanced or unbalanced growth. Equilibrium is not necessarily a virtue, nor disequilibrium necessarily a vice. Disequilibrium may of course result from exogenous forces such as natural disasters. There may also be strategically designed disequilibria which involve risk, but which may be necessary for the stage-by-stage iteration required to harmonise micro and macro rationality. This situation is well known to long-term development planners; whether or not it leads to success depends on the effectiveness of the compensatory measures built into the plans.

The decision-making centre, whether corporate or public, is only partly able to rely on price relatives in its allocative decisions, irrespective of the fact that they may be differently motivated. For a corporate body, social rationality tends to be only a metaphysical category, totally unsusceptible to accounting. Hence, for public bodies there is no other way but to impose such rules of the game as would ensure the general observance of whatever is meant by social rationality. Thus, once the categories of social interest and social (macro) rationality are accepted, the need for coercive methods follows. But, obviously, coercion void of responsibility rooted in knowledge and goodwill must be a blind and socially harmful force. On the other hand, coercive methods, unavoidable as they are, do not *per se* guarantee that the desirable level of economic rationality will be achieved. Their application whenever deemed socially necessary, is auxiliary to the attempt to achieve macro rationality.

Another aspect of our problem is how the harmonisation between micro and macro rationality may appear with regard to the factor of time taken as an economic good. The principle of rationality requires time to be used economically. This leads to the need for a discount rate. But the social and individual discount rates are not synonymous. In development-oriented societies the role of the social rate of discount increases together with the role of macro choices.

In a structurally diversified economy, the central decision-maker may have a greater propensity to embark on development ventures (such as ambitious welfare schemes, exploitation of relatively poor quality or unfavourably located natural resources, exploration of outer-space, preferential treatment of selected R and D fields, etc.) to which the ordinary cost-benefit approach is not applicable.

The factor of actual historical time seems to be both very important and relevant to revised thinking on economic rationality. Even at the micro level decision-making has to resort to ever longer time-horizons, and this tendency increases the more the macro framework explicitly influences the micro decisions. For a macro approach, however, recourse to distant time-horizons tends to become increasingly common as a principle of strategy. The impact of global problems is one of the factors which contributes most strongly to this process.

Against this background one other observation is important. The macro-level decision-making centre, while aware of its responsibility for the future shape of the economy and society, is nevertheless very susceptible to the pressures of current needs and requirements. As a result, the harmonisation of micro and macro economic rationality is necessarily concomitant to the harmonisation of rationalities viewed from shorter and longer time-horizons. Needless to say, the complexity of our problems therefore appears to increase, but we do not face this situation with an empty box of tools. The contemporary theory of graphs, very modestly applied in economic analysis so far, may supply the relevant tools of analysis and operational solutions for these very problems.

V THE LOCATION OF ECONOMIC ACTIVITY

Along with the scale and time dimensions, the contemporary state of knowledge in social sciences makes it necessary to take into account the space dimension. The crux of the matter here is the determination of rules for the location of economic activities and their spatial interactions.

In this area the spontaneous working of market forces, that is non-coherent behaviour based at best on principles of individual rationality, inflicted deep and long-lasting harm on the community. The territory on which socio-economic activities are located has been for too long taken simply as a subject to be conquered. For too long individual costs and benefits of this conquest have been the sole object of accounting, while social costs and benefits have been neglected. True, some rules and regulations have been introduced at times by state or communal authorities, but these have usually been too weak and too inconsistent to avoid such disasters as we are now facing. Moreover, the concentration of economic activities in some areas, determined by market forces, created external economies exerting a self-enhancing effect on further concentration, eventually leading to overconcentration, and to overcongestion and unmanageability of huge metropolitan and industrial centres. All this is too well known to require elaboration here.

The links and feedbacks between socio-economic space and the scale and time dimensions are evident. Flows accumulating into stocks determine the spatial structure and infrastructure which is inert by nature. Its inertia, however, should not be visualised as a purely adverse phenomenon from the social point of view, even when full heed is paid to its negative petrifying effects. The spatial concentration of material social wealth creates both economies of scale and external economies, induces creative competition yielding technological progress, and lays the ground for an unprecedented flourishing of arts and sciences. While all these blessings must be appreciated, the questions persistently recur: what are the rational limits to this concentration? What is the level of endurance of spatial environment to human actions? What rational criteria should be applied to decisions concerning location in order to secure and sustain harmony between human actions and their natural environment?

It is not for me to answer these questions. Within the scope of our main interest, however, some suggestions may be relevant.

Spatial strategies and policies may be roughly divided into promotive and corrective. The former are applicable mainly to the less developed economies (or, in the case of the more developed ones, only if, due to polarised development, some backward regions have been left behind). The latter are applicable mainly to the more developed economies. In both cases the formulation of strategy and policies as well as supervision over their implementation are usually the responsibility of public authorities. Thus macro rationality comes to the fore.

Indeed, irrespective of particular institutional conditions, successful coping with environmental problems goes nowadays far beyond the abilities, skills, and financial, technological and organisational potential of any single economic unit, even if it is a very large capitalist corporation or a socialist industrial association and/or combines of enterprises. In many cases it already surpasses even the powers of single national states. What is the basis for macro rationality in this respect? One might say that where sheer survival is at stake, there is no room for pedestrian accounting. But the problem in question can hardly be compared with a situation of natural disaster where rescue squads are put into action without any regard to toil and expense. Environmental problems have become permanent and they need to be dealt with on a continuous basis. This seems to require an approach based on extra long time-horizons. But here the imaginable magnitudes involved appear to be exceptionally difficult to quantify because of the limitations set by the existing state of knowledge.

What happens in real life is that under the impact of the critical situations with regard to the state of natural environment, the relevant national organisations involved to some extent in international co-operation have to take regulatory and controlling action by imposing specific constraints on individual and group decisions. In this way such dispersed decisions are harnessed and subordinated to higher level objectives and preferences. This process can probably be expected to continue, broadening the scope and increasing the strength of constraints on individual and group decisions, but at the same time providing a new perspective for economic macro rationality and eventually global rationality at an international level.

VI SOME CONCLUDING REMARKS

Whatever conclusions may be drawn from past contributions and debates, the present-day generation has a crucial question on its hands: since the old criteria of rationality have been made obsolete by developments which have so profoundly altered the contemporary world what then is rational? Can the market prices of either capitalist or socialist markets reflect conditions for rational choice? Whose rationality do they reflect if they are more subject to manipulation and setting than to spontaneous determination? What really are the new rules of the game which by their emergence undermined the foundations of comfortable theorising about the economy and society?

These and many similar questions are too persistent and too vital for economics as a social science to be pushed aside. They not only touch the pivotal problems of this theory, they are the pivotal problems.

The point of departure for fruitful discussion seems to be the proposition that any economic choice may be rational provided that the constraints are identified and the goal function properly determined. The number and nature of constraints depends on the level at which the choice is made (e.g. micro or macro). The proper determination of the goal function depends on the revealed preferences corresponding to the level of choice. The difficulty of identifying these preferences is obvious and includes the need to keep up with their changes.

The next difficulty is that constraints cannot be taken for granted. Some of the constraints are objective (exogeneous or autonomous) within a given period, and these need only to be identified. But the other group of constraints result from our own decision expressed in the plans for our activity. These constraints are endogenous (or induced) to the process of rational choice, as they are themselves subject to choice.

On the basis of this reasoning one has to conclude that in most cases two stages have to be passed on the way to rational choice: first, identification-cum-choice of constraints; and second, optimisation procedure as a choice among admissible alternatives.

At this juncture the possibility must be taken into account that our weighing of admissible alternatives can lead to the change of constraints in a feedback manner. This possibility results from the power which can be exerted over the feeding and steering mechanisms specific to the unit on behalf of which the choice is being made. This power may have various forms: implementation and execution of legal norms, normative rules and conventions, administrative directives, economic instruments and – last but not least – persuasion (ideology, propaganda, advertising, etc.). Depending on the level, the importance of each form as well as the time sequence of its application, may be different.

The interaction between hierarchically located socio-economic units and the forms of power unleashed against concrete constraints is strongly influenced by the nature of the socio-economic system – capitalist market economy or socialist planned economy. This interaction, moreover, depends to a considerable extent on the level of socio-economic development: the greater the economic potential and the more structurally diversified the economy, the greater will be the number of admissible alternatives, and the freedom of choice among endogenous constraints (for a given moment, and all the more so for a period of time within a given time-horizon).

Taking for granted the profound motivational differences between the agents of socio-economic processes under capitalist and socialist conditions, one is bound to find equally profound differences in the identification of social preferences, in the procedures of choice among admissible development alternatives and in the manipulation with constraints. Generally speaking, in a socialist economy all this is done more directly than elsewhere, its mechanisms are more transparent. This, however, does not guarantee satisfactory results nor automatic harmonisation of micro and macro rationalities.

With the exception of last-ditch proponents of perfect competition as a make-believe reality, there seems to be much agreement between contemporary economists on the proposition that macro rationality is not an additively consistent category and therefore cannot be constructed in an additive way. The real problem, however – repeatedly present in our discussion – is the relation between micro rationality and macro rationality and how to make them coherent. It does not seem to us that there exists a single and unambiguous answer to this question. At the same time we are convinced that some answers can be sought in the area of choice among endogenous constraints. It may well be that among these constraints price setting and price manipulation rank very high in relevance irrespective of the socio-economic system.

Discussion of the Papers by Professors Sadowski and Łukasjewicz

(Chairman: Professor K. Porwit)

Mr Kaser (UK) opened the discussion by noting that the common theme of the two papers was the antithesis of micro- and macroeconomic rationality regardless of the nature of the economy. Both distinguished the three tiers: individual (household or enterprise), national and global, and both attached crucial significance to the limitations of information flows about objectives within each tier and between the three tiers.

Professor Sadowski took a path from Adam Smith's certainties to his own agnosticism, though he set no signposts clearly to distinguish mercantilisation (i.e. Smith's perception of the process, whereby the market determines the optimum flows of production and distribution) from monetisation (i.e. the acceptance of a money numeraire for the majority of economic activities). Sadowski criticised the Smithian equilibrium position based on the assumed rationality of the agent, but he did not appear to criticise the conceptualisation of Smith's procedure, i.e. of the mechanism.

Surely it was only a necessary condition for economic activities to become mercantilised that they had to be monetised. The point was well set out in Sir John Hicks' *Theory of Economic History*. Mr Kaser said that he thought Hicks' distinction between customary and command economies was preferable to the separation of the traditional and monetised economies. It had the advantage that the command economy covered a range of economies: the early theocratic state, or Ghengis Khan's taxation under the Tartar Yoke, or a modern demonetised bureaucratic state.

The issue of a command economy arose as much for the Department of Health and Social Security in Great Britain as for an industrial ministry in the USSR. The papers stressed the constraints on information, and Mr Kaser also found particularly relevant the mention by Professor Łukaszewicz of the transparency of objectives. He focused on the perception of direct or indirect objectives by households, firms and governments, and put special emphasis on the growing indirectness of the ends towards which the means are mobilised.

Mr Kaser said that Professor Łukaszewicz also analysed the complex interaction between information and decision-making, rejecting the arbitrary choice of macro goals as leading all too easily to coercion. The difficulty for a centrally planned economy, as for any government department that operated on other than a fee-for-service basis, was to verify the preferences of those on the periphery, whether households or enterprises. A consequence of ignoring such preferences was counter-productive coercion and its avoidance one of the main reasons for the moves towards decentralisation of some of the socialist economies.

Both authors rejected the assumption that the rules for microeconomic rationality assured some consistency of criteria over time, which, Professor

Łukaszewicz added, was rendered more intractable by the indirectness of production. But it was one thing for the latter to say that the micro rationality of the components cannot be added together to constitute a national goal and another to assert that neither contemporary capitalist nor socialist governments could formulate a social-welfare function on the assumption that lower-level decisions were rational.[1] This was tantamount to throwing the baby out with the bath water, and Professor Łukaszewicz was insisting that economics continue to rely on the concept of rationality at all levels.

Dr Desai (India) thought that the distinction between systems rationality and component rationality might be more helpful than the micro-macro-global classification. Adam Smith could be said to have pioneered the notion that if the components acted smoothly (rationally), the system would take care of itself. Marx concentrated on the rationality of the system itself. He tried to formulate the laws of the dynamics of a system – of a mode of production. He showed that components may be rational but the system may be irrational, thus contradicting Adam Smith. He thought the authors might be helped by taking Marx's notion of reproduction rather than that of allocation as a starting point. The notion of reproduction was dynamic. Traditional systems underwent simple reproduction and this required little conscious decision, but in modern economics reproduction took place on an extended scale, and this added uncertainty and made conscious decision-making essential.

In his view there were some hasty judgements in the papers regarding economic theory. They took for granted the failure of economic theory. Take for instance their statement that consumer behaviour was erratic (p. 42): it was not enough to say that, we had to provide a systematic explanation of such behaviour. People often said that they preferred disequilibrium to equilibrium characterisation, but this made the task of economic explanation more, not less, difficult. Economists preferred equilibrium concepts because it made the task of explaining economic phenomena easier. But whether economic phenomena were equilibrium/disequilibrium or stochastic/deterministic, it was our duty to explain them.

He was also unable to agree with Professor Sadowski's view that since different commodities had different horizons in the consumers' decision-making function, this caused insurmountable problems for economic theory (pp. 41–2). Different horizons caused no technical problem in maximisation behaviour though there might be a practical problem.

Dr Desai's final point related to Professor Łukaszewicz's statement (p. 53) that the social rate of discount was a complicated function of several variables rather than a simple quantity. This might be so, but once again we could not

[1] The relevant arguments and references to much of the previous literature are in A. K. Sen, 'On Weights and Measures: Informational Constraints in Social Welfare Analysis', *Econometrica* (October 1977).

escape the responsibility of explaining what it is. People would make decisions which would have an implicit social rate of discount. It was up to economists to explain what was the rate of discount being actually used and what it should be.

Dr Nadal (Mexico) asked what was meant by rationality. Was it a characteristic attributed by economists to economic agents, or was it an observed feature of given socio-economic systems? He thought that Professor Sadowski's statements about the impossibility of rational behaviour, on the part of the consumer (p. 41) ignored the possibility that such behaviour, including waste, might under certain conditions actually be rational for the system as a whole.

Academician Khachaturov (USSR) said that rationality must not be confused with equilibrium. In many cases disequilibrium was necessary in order to achieve structural change. It was also important to appreciate that what was rational for the consumer might not be rational for the salesman, and what was rational for the salesman might not be rational for the industry or for society. He thought that it was better to speak of interests rather than of rationality. Under capitalism the main interests were those of private entrepreneurs whereas under socialism the main interest was that of the whole society. It was necessary to arrange the combination of different interests within the system.

Dr Fiedor (Poland) said that in his view it was necessary to consider not only the explanatory power of the concept of economic rationality but also the ability of particular economic units to express and achieve specific goals. The notion of rationality necessarily involved the specification of ends and means and if economics was to be more than a statement of the deductive logic of pure choice it must include an analysis of the actual technical, economic, social and institutional conditions of production, distribution and consumption. Until recently the prevailing view of neo-classical economics was that there was only one notion of economic rationality and, therefore, only one notion of social welfare, based on the principles of Pareto optimality. Now it was realised by some western economists (for example Koopmans) that concepts of economic rationality and social welfare must be related to concrete social and economic systems. This change had come about as a consequence of the confrontation of the orthodox assertion of the *ex definitione* inefficiency of socialism by the actual economic successes of the socialist countries.

With respect to the notion of consumers' sovereignty and its associated micro rationality Dr Fiedor thought that under modern conditions, including mass output of diversified consumer goods and services, the pressures of advertising and the international demonstration effect, the concept of individual rationality was no more than a pleasant fiction. In practice the problem of consumers' rationality could be solved only on a macro scale and with an interdisciplinary approach. In his view a number of countries would, in the foreseeable future, achieve a degree of opulence in which entirely new criteria for macro rationality would be needed. These would not be based on the scarcity of resources but on the formulation of socially desirable rules of behaviour under conditions of affluence.

Professor Rweyemamu (Tanzania) said that Professor Łukaszewicz's paper referred to market prices reflecting conditions for rational choice (pp. 52–3) This seemed to imply that there had been a system of rational prices which had been lost and needed to be replaced. He disagreed with this. In his view neither Adam Smith's invisible hand, nor Walras' tatonnement process, nor Hicks' elasticity of expectations could provide a rational basis for price determination. Sraffa's framework of relations between basic and non-basic goods could provide a useful starting point for price determination.

Mr Lengyel (UNESCO) said that he would like to supplement the terms micro and macro rationality by 'megalo rationality'. There had been a process of pushing externalities further out, from firm to nation and from one nation to another (perhaps weaker) nation. Once we reached the global level it was no longer possible to do this and economic theory would have to adapt to this new situation by developing an appropriate megalo approach.

Dr Streeten (UK) observed that there had been two strands in the discussion: (a) an increasing degree of national integration had led to international disintegration; and (b) international integration (by transnational corporations and cultural élites) had led to national disintegration. With regard to the former tendency governments had adopted a wider range of objectives and no longer saw themselves simply as 'night watchmen'. These objectives included economic growth, full employment, reduced inflation, more equitable distribution of income, care of the environment and regional policy. At the same time they had abandoned certain constraints on policy, such as the gold standard, a balanced budget and fixed exchange rates. By behaving nationally more rationally, national governments had made the international economy less rational and had increased the difficulties of international management.

The second tendency had involved an international alignment of, for example, the consumption patterns of the upper classes and of technology, but left the poor untouched and this promoted national disintegration. The international dissemination of culture, dress, *mores*, sexual habits, even crimes, etc. had left institutions behind, and the reality of interdependence was ahead of institutional adaptation.

What was required was joint action in areas where it was possible to avoid 'negative sum' outcomes. Examples would include disarmament, preservation of the world environment and the avoidance of 'beggar-my-neighbour' policies of protection or deflation as a means of escaping the problems of global stagflation. In these and many other areas some degree of global co-ordination and co-operation was necessary.

Professor Dudley Seers (UK) questioned whether there was such a sharp distinction in practice between individual and social decisions as implied in the paper by Professor Sadowski. Politicians and officials always had their own career interests. No doubt they considered these identical with the national interest, as they interpreted it, and believed this required them to retain power against competitors (whether other individuals, factions or parties). Yet public relations needs might produce biases in policy and project choice, for example a tendency to prefer very large projects, or projects near the capital city, or projects embodying the latest technology, or projects which were photogenic. The room for subjective judgement, for example on discount rates and shadow prices, facilitated this sort of bias. More important, it was very difficult for decision-makers to abandon a project if the cost/benefit balance changed once it had been started – or even announced – because of the possible damage to their careers (Concorde is the *casus classicus*). Such individual interests might produce substantial biases in social decisions.

Professor Green (UK) suggested that in the course of the discussion, and, to a degree, in the papers, rationality had been used to refer to five quite different concepts, and these needed to be distinguished.

(1) Internal consistency, as in the Walrasian general equilibrium system but also in certain attempts to construct an applied theory of efficient managed markets.

(2) Consistency of an actor's decisions with each other and with his own objective function. This posed a series of information requirement issues. These were especially acute when feedback was significant, i.e. the actor's present decisions affected the future structure of choices open to him in a way which was substantial but often hard to forecast.

(3) Consistency with the general interest. Smith saw micro rationality by competitive actors aggregating to social rationality. Keynes adumbrated the macro hypothesis of general interest and from it built a case for macro policy to induce micro rationality conducive to the general welfare.

(4) Particular individuals' class or interest group rationalities. Here the questions were not whether actors acted in accordance with what they perceived to be their interests nor, any longer, whether such actions led to conflicts of interest. They now turned on whether data allowed rational decisions – and if so by which actors under which conditions – and on whether the perceptions of interest were stable and orderly enough to allow construction of usable objective functions.

(5) Action in accord with stated normative principles, e.g. the suggested global or megalo rationality. To be operational this type of rationality would appear to require to be consistent with macro (systems) and micro (component) rationality through alteration of perceived possible and desirable actions whether by education (altering functions), provision of more information (altering perceptions) or creating new structures (altering the possible).

Given the general agreement that more than one rationality could exist (and usually did) – whether on component/system or class or national/global axes – and that these rationalities could be contradictory, major theoretical and practical questions of power, co-ordination and synthesis arose. Dr Green asked how divergent rationalities could be controlled, interpenetrated, co-ordinated or otherwise influenced to act in a more harmonious and less mutually damaging manner.

Professor Malinvaud (France) said that he liked the two main messages of the papers, but he did not think that full justice had been done to the theoretical work of the past thirty years on how to define and implement economic rationality.

He agreed with the authors that one should not rely on a dogmatic doctrine to provide the appropriate criteria of rationality, either the ultimate criteria of rationality of our economic activity or the proximate criteria that were necessary to help in current decision-taking about productive operations. By now this point should be widely accepted.

Similarly he agreed with Professor Łukaszewicz that the problems raised by economic rationality were now less often than before micro problems and more often macro problems, which were indeed much more difficult to solve in a society in which information was imperfect and costly to transmit. But it should also be recognised that a lot of significant theoretical work had been done recently. This work was stimulated by concrete problems: the height of the dykes in Holland after the big flood (with obvious uncertainty components); the macro decision concerning the closing of coalmines in France; the rate of discount to be used for investment project appraisal in the public sector of an incompletely controlled economy; the management of exhaustible resources, and so on.

It was true to say that, confronted with the complexities of space, time and uncertainty, confronted also with the macro dimension of many programmes, the economic theory of resource allocation had become quite difficult to follow. We were no longer in a period when the conclusions of this could be summarised by such a sentence as 'Do what any plain businessman would do'. But the fact that the literature was difficult did not make it negligible. The literature was a guide to those who had to consider, analyse and decide about concrete programmes.

Professor Sadowski, replying to the discussion, said that he agreed to a considerable extent with Professor Malinvaud's comments. He had not attempted an exhaustive treatment of the subject but had asked whether the concept of rationality had anything to do with the relevance of economic theory, and what use was made of the concept. He found that the concept was almost always linked to the notion of some kind of goal function expressed in terms of maxima or minima, and concluded that this approach was not relevant when confronted with problems of choice at the macro (or systems) level. The reason for this was basically that because of the variety of goals to be pursued there was no maximand or minimand.

Another way of looking at the problem was the 'rationality of aims' approach, but this led to ideas which involved exactly the same kind of maxima or minima which he was trying to avoid. However, he would plead 'not guilty' to the charge of agnosticism. That would suggest that the problems could not be solved, and he did not take that view.

Professor Łukaszewicz, in his reply, said that the main purpose of his paper had been to draw attention to the conditions which had led to a decisive shift from micro to macro rationality. This shift had been explained in terms of the historical process which had taken place, and it was a reflection of the change in the interaction between the productive relations and the social productive forces. Some of the participants in the discussion, including Academician Khachaturov, had not sufficiently appreciated this aspect of his paper. In his view the identification of rationality criteria, i.e. of criteria for the efficient organisation of the social process of reproduction, was the most important task facing economic theory, and these criteria could not be identical for all economic systems.

He also wished to stress that he did not regard rationality as synonymous with equilibrium, and global equilibrium did not assume *per se* partial equilibrium, or vice versa. In general, balanced growth created more favourable conditions for rational choice than unbalanced growth. For precisely this reason, the centrally planned economies paid so much attention to the attainment of balanced growth. The supply of information, in the proper time and place, was a crucial condition for the efficient planning of the economy. He felt that Mr Kaser's interpretation of his discussion of this problem had not been entirely correct.

Finally, he feared that the fragmentation of the problem of rationality could lead to the apparent disappearance of the problem. He considered that economic processes observed certain rules, and that generalisations were justified and necessary. This was true of the concept of rationality, which had always been present in economic theory but which was subject to historical changes in the same way as any other category of economic theory.

PART THREE

Efficiency, Equality and Socio-Economic Progress

5 Economic Efficiency and Income Differentials

Wiktor Herer and Władysław Sadowski
INSTITUTE OF PLANNING, WARSAW

I THE PROBLEM OF CONTEMPORARY ECONOMICS

In recent years the relevance and achievements of economic theory have been severely criticised. Some aspects of this criticism certainly deserve great attention. It is said with some justification that economists waste energy on solving technical issues of little or no social importance and that it is the perfection of the increasingly sophisticated and refined tools of mathematical analysis, which takes a growing proportion of their time and energy. It is also true that economics turned its back on the major economic problems and contemporary social conflicts, escaping into the safety of an imaginary world of perfect competition, perfect central planning, etc. Economics does not take up the problems which are relevant and socially painful, but prefers those which promise technically interesting and formally elegant solutions.

It should be noted, however, that the criticisms of economic theory are not always correct, and the proposed remedies are sometimes no better than the illness. In its extreme forms this criticism explicitly or implicitly denies all the achievements of quantitative economic analysis; it directly attacks model-building and deductive methods of economic research, though it is to these methods that economic theory owes its existence. The investigation of material causes and effects of economic activity is denied its central place in economic research (for instance, for some economists the very concept of national income became a *bête noire*). Under such catchwords as 'a turn towards man', 'multiplicity of his needs and aims', 'quality of life', 'social equity', etc., some critics would like to turn economic theory into a collection of more or less commonplace stories, perhaps beautiful (when written with intelligence and literary talents) but rather banal.

Once economics is limited only to correcting our ideas on the *aims* of economic development, even if the proposed corrections are sensible, it will not live up to the new social needs. It is the *means*, where the crucial interdependencies must be looked for, and the study of these interdependencies must always be the *fundamental* task of economic theory. We shall fulfil this task the better the more we can apply all that is sensible in the available stock of economic knowledge to solving the new problems of our times.

In our opinion, the weaknesses of economic theory, which come to surface especially during periods of crises such as the present, are rooted not so much in the inadequacies of positive economic knowledge, but in our inability to apply this theory to *socially useful* purposes. Scientific research is too often inspired not by real life but by the intrinsic needs of the 'logic' of the model-building process, while the models themselves though formally beautiful lack any authentic inspiration, or are malabstracted from reality. The positive economic knowledge available today would quickly bring significant results if it were broadly applied to solving authentic social problems. It is precisely in the *authenticity of inspirations* that the crux of the matter lies.

Thus we see an urgent need to make use of the existing theories for solving many new 'qualitative' problems of economic development. These problems include the relation of society towards the environment, 'quality of life', 'social equity', etc., and hence the implied necessity to transform economics into a more general theory of 'social reproduction' which would embrace these problems.

In what follows we shall devote our attention to some aspects of the problems of social equity in relation to the distribution of income. We shall not consider systematically all the general implications of this problem; but will simply attempt to present a theoretical approach to one of the more significant aspects of the matter: the *costs* involved in an equitable distribution of national income.

II ECONOMIC EFFICIENCY AND THE PRINCIPLES OF INCOME DIFFERENTIATION

In economic discussions it is often emphasised that certain principles of social equity must be implemented. However, most of what is said about social equity is stated as a matter of faith and an autonomous function of social development; increasing social equity is, unfortunately, never seen as a target, the achievement of which may involve costs and may compete with increasing economic efficiency.

It appears, however, that in a centrally planned socialist economy a contradiction may arise between an increase in equity and in efficiency. One of the areas in which this contradiction may arise is an equitable distribution of consumption, 'equitable distribution' being usually understood as limiting excessive wage differentials. To see the problem in a broader perspective let us note that although a more equitable distribution may involve costs, this does not imply either that increasing wage differentials never involves costs, or that there is always a positive correlation between increasing wage differentials and economic efficiency.

Since we make use here of the concept of economic efficiency, this must be measurable; it is convenient to present it as a ratio of effects to outlays. By economic effect we mean the increment of consumption fund achieved during a certain period which is obtained by means of additional labour and capital outlays incurred during the same period. The maximisation of the incremental consumption fund may be considered the objective function of the central planner. The central planner should assess various degrees of realisation of this target against various degrees of realisation of other social targets, for instance, against various degrees of limiting wage differentials (and thus of achieving greater social equity). Decisions taken with respect to these latter postulates are ultimately always political choices. Still, in taking those decisions the planning authorities should have a clear and possibly well-quantified view on the cost of satisfying the respective social targets, the cost being expressed in terms of a lower degree of realisation of the target for incremental consumption.

It is convenient to introduce here some additional constraints which limit realisation of the consumption target. First of all we assume that outlays on development of the so-called 'non-productive sphere' (i.e. on education, culture, health care, and natural environment protection) are given. This implies that we rule out a choice between higher economic efficiency on the one hand, and better satisfaction of, say, health care or environment protection needs on the other. The concepts of effects and costs applied here are restricted to those in the productive sphere only; also the possible choices of economic efficiency refer only to this sphere.

Let us further assume that the economy considered maintains full employment of the available labour force. Thus we also rule out a choice between higher unemployment and higher efficiency of the employed labour force. (Full employment considered as a social target may involve costs, because under certain conditions it must be paid for in terms of lower output per every person employed, and lower wages for the employed.)

In our analysis we are interested in incremental magnitudes; hence, to measure economic efficiency we shall use the following formula:

$$E = \frac{C}{L + Mq}, \qquad (1)$$

where:

C = that part of the increment in national income (expressed at constant prices) which in the period considered is destined for individual consumption;

L = the incremental outlay on labour (expressed at constant wage rates) employed in the productive sphere;

M = the increment in fixed capital stock created by investments in the productive sphere in the period considered;
q = the rate of interest on capital.[1]

All three variables in (1) refer to a certain time period; thus they are all streams. True, one may have legitimate doubts whether the summation of M, which is expressed at constant prices, and L, which is expressed at constant wage rates, is logically sound. However, for the limited purposes of our analysis equation (1) may be considered satisfactory.

We may now consider interdependencies between changes in efficiency, measured in accordance with equation (1) and changes in wage differentials in a centrally planned economy.

The choices contained within the range of socially acceptable wage differentiation may be looked at from two points of view. Solutions close to the bottom end of this range secure a more equitable distribution of national income. Those close to the top end of this range will more effectively stimulate productivity in all industries.

In the national economy, there are always some macroeconomic interdependencies of a technical character. They constitute a sort of feasibility test which every principle of income distribution must pass. Ultimately it is also this test which determines the impact of each of those principles on the actual income distribution and economic efficiency. Therefore, in order fully to appreciate their macroeconomic implications it is necessary to understand the character of those interdependencies. For instance, it may well emerge that the differences between the advocates of greater equity and of increasing wage differentials are illusory, and that what both parties have in common is lack of knowledge of the macroeconomic consequences of their programmes. In given economic conditions these consequences may well be very much alike, regardless of whether in economic planning and policy-making we choose to follow the first school or the second.

Our basic hypothesis is this: the degree of wage differentiation influences the composition of effective demand. This affects the raw materials intensity and the import intensity of the incremental consumption fund. Thus, bottlenecks may appear which to a greater or lesser extent limit the rate of growth of the consumption fund for society as a whole. This may contradict the intentions of the policy of redistribution of the consumption fund, either when this aims at the reduction of wage differentials in the name of social equity, or when it aims at increased differentials in order to stimulate

[1] For simplicity we abstract here from a complex problem of costs of use of land and other natural resources. The concept of the rate of interest is equivalent to the so-called 'efficiency norm' which is applied in the calculus of economic efficiency of investment projects, and equation (1) is a simplified version of the so-called 'efficiency formula' used in the planning accountancy.

productivity. The possibility of such a result must at any rate be taken into account.

In this way the centre of gravity of our argument shifts towards analysis of the macroeconomic interdependencies of a technical character which set limits to the growth of the consumption fund. We must first deal with these interdependencies; then we shall revert to the problem of wage differentiation.

III RAW MATERIAL AND IMPORT BOTTLENECKS

The economy may be divided into a sector producing agricultural and mineral raw materials and another producing all manufactured and other goods and services. Increased output of the former encounters increased resistance of nature, and so is subject to diminishing returns, i.e. to a declining efficiency (in the sense of equation (1) above) of marginal units of inputs. In the latter sector it may be assumed that over a certain range of output changes there will be increasing returns, because greater outlays lead to larger plants and economies of scale. Beyond a certain point, however, this sector will have constant returns to scale.

Increased output also involves a rise in imports and these must be paid for by increased exports (assuming no foreign credits). However, attempts to increase exports often require a shift to goods with high domestic outlays per unit of the foreign exchange earned. Further, for Poland it generally necessitates increased foreign sales of capital-intensive primary products, and a shift to markets where the same goods fetch lower prices. The intensity of these unfavourable developments depends largely on the share of exports to developed capitalist countries (i.e. to these markets where the expansion of our exports meets the greatest difficulties) in total exports.

On the other hand, a higher rate of growth of output and inputs must inevitably be followed by a correspondingly higher share of imports from these same markets. (Demand for sophisticated machinery and equipment grows more rapidly than total imports.) This, in turn, makes it obligatory to increase the share of exports into these difficult markets.

However, due to the specific influence of external markets the outlays on export promotion are accompanied by falling foreign exchange proceeds; in fact it is the same phenomenon which we have already encountered in the raw materials and agricultural sector. Thus diminishing returns embrace not only mining and agriculture but also the export industries.

We shall now take into account diminishing returns in the way the central planner would approach them. In constructing the plan for a certain medium-term period (say, for five years) he should confront different variants of physical composition of national income and consumption, taking into account the impact which implementation of each of these variants would exert upon economic efficiency.

We shall assume here that in the period covered by a medium-term plan the total investment outlays, as well as the total increase in employment (which is determined by demographic factors and by policy programmes on education and job training, etc.), are both given. A part of total outlays on investment and new employment must go to industries producing capital goods. The remaining part of these outlays, which we denote by N*, is earmarked for producing the increment in consumer goods and services.

The total increment in the value of consumption goods produced during the planned period may be seen as resulting from two different sources:

(i) from technical progress and a better utilisation of capital and labour employed in industries producing consumer goods;
(ii) from additional outlays on capital and labour which enlarge the productive capacity of these industries (we abstract here from the corresponding outlays on research and development).

During the planned period, that increase in output which results from technical progress, better education, learning by doing, etc., may be considered as determined by outlays incurred in earlier periods because the 'gestation periods' in science, technology and education are rather long. While fully appreciating the contribution of these factors to the growth rate of output we may therefore abstract from them in our further analysis. There remains, however, that part of the increase in consumer goods output which depends on the outlays, N*, incurred during the planned period in the consumer goods sector; we shall now concentrate on this increment only (we shall denote it by C*). What determines its value under the assumed conditions?

In so far as C* depends on the volume of outlays, N*, we have no freedom of choice; in accordance with our assumptions N* is given. We may assume that decisions concerning the choice of techniques of production, the modernisation of existing equipment, etc., have also already been taken. Thus all possibilities of obtaining additional output from these sources have already been exhausted. However, there still remains the choice of the *composition* of the incremental consumption fund, and, consequently, of the composition of incremental inputs of machinery and equipment, raw materials and labour. It is precisely this composition of the incremental consumption fund which – by influencing the economic efficiency of outlays – may significantly affect the incremental volume of output which we want to investigate.

Now, in line with our earlier argument, the total increment in the value of consumption fund, C*, may be divided into two parts, according to the sources of its origin:

$$C^* = C_s + C_p, \qquad (2)$$

where:

C_s = the value of home-produced additional mineral and agricultural raw materials which were directly and indirectly used as inputs in manufacturing of final consumer goods (the value of these inputs being calculated from input-output tables); it includes the value of incremental imports of final consumer goods, raw materials and semi-products used for manufacturing final consumer goods;

C_p = the incremental value added generated in the last and earlier stages of processing domestic and foreign mineral raw materials and agricultural products into final consumer goods.

We may postulate that for reasons similar to those discussed above (p. 71) for total output, C_s is subject to diminishing returns, while C_p experiences first increasing and then constant returns to scale. The actual value of C^* will depend on the balance between C_s and C_p: the greater the raw material and import intensities of the incremental output of consumer goods the stronger will be the tendency for diminishing returns to appear.

The bottlenecks in the growth of consumption thus manifest themselves in diminishing returns which reduce the economic efficiency of outlays. From the above considerations it follows that the factors limiting growth are stronger, the more difficult the natural and technical conditions prevailing in the raw materials industries and the worse the terms of trade on the world market. Once these conditions are given the factors limiting growth rates are determined by the composition of consumer goods output alone.

The above description of the factors limiting growth rates corresponds to the actual conditions of many countries, and of Poland in particular. The position of this country is determined, among others, by the following conditions:

(1) Low-fertility soils and on the whole rather unfavourable climate conditions for agricultural production (much less favourable than in the countries west, south and south-east of Poland).

(2) Poor geological accessibility of raw materials deposits; high operational costs of their extraction (e.g. new coalmining fields near Lublin involve, *inter alia*, great outlays on the infrastructure).

(3) Demand for imports from capitalist countries steeply increasing with investment outlays.

(4) Demand for technology and equipment imported from developed capitalist countries grows much more rapidly than total outlays and total imports. This demand is reinforced by the need to modernise existing productive capacities quickly in view of the now rapidly falling supply of labour (due to demographical changes).

(5) Difficulties in exporting manufactured goods to the developed capitalist countries make it necessary to increase the extraction and export of raw materials.

In the conditions specified above, attempts to increase the consumption fund should not consist of a direct attack on the bottlenecks at the expense of huge outlays. If outlays are already at a high level expanding them still further may simply reduce their efficiency and cause increased strains in the whole economy. The solution should consist rather in searching for every possibility of avoiding the bottlenecks. In the actual conditions of the Polish economy this implies first of all searching for ways and means of reducing the raw materials intensity and import intensity of the incremental consumption fund. To a certain extent this can be achieved by an appropriate choice of the composition of the incremental consumption fund. However, such a choice may prove impossible because it may appear to conflict with the realisation of other social targets.

IV CHANGES IN INCOMES DIFFERENTIATION AND BOTTLENECKS OF GROWTH

We shall now consider, in the light of the above relationships, the impact of wage differentials on raw materials and import intensities; in other words, we shall discuss the sensitivity of economic development with respect to the bottlenecks which result from the natural and technological conditions of raw materials extraction and from the terms of trade achieved on world markets. In what follows we shall assume constant retail prices for consumer goods and services (especially for foodstuffs) during the planned period. This assumption is a close approximation to the actual conditions in socialist countries, and those in Poland in particular.

The raw materials intensity and import intensity of the incremental consumption fund depend mainly on the physical composition of effective demand for consumer goods. It will be noted that various income groups differ significantly in the composition of the consumer goods they demand, and also with respect to their income elasticity of demand for individual goods and services. Thus, changes in income differentials will result in definite changes in the physical composition of incremental demand, and therefore also in the composition of supply of consumer goods and services. We have already noticed that the conditions of manufacturing various goods differ sharply from the point of view of the economic efficiency of outlays. Hence, at constant retail prices and at given total outlays during the planned period, changes in income differentials will influence the economic efficiency of outlays and the rate of growth of total consumption. We must now determine the relationship between economic efficiency and the degree of income differentiation, so that we may know how changes in the latter will influence the incremental consumption fund.

The available statistical information indicates that two different tendencies exist, characterised by the following features.

The first tendency

The consumption of the lower income brackets is characterised by:

(i) A relatively high share of agricultural products in total consumption as a result of relatively high shares of foodstuffs, and raw materials in the value of the food consumed (low degree of processing of the basic foodstuffs). This is combined with a relatively high income elasticity of demand for food, and consequently for agricultural products, characteristic of these low incomes;
(ii) A relatively high share of the low-processed industrial goods; these, in turn, require relatively big inputs of raw materials and semi-products; the share of value added generated in the manufacturing of these goods is low; the high share of such products in the total consumption of low-income groups is again combined with a relatively high income elasticity of demand for these goods.

From these features it follows that every attempt to increase equity in income distribution involves significant social costs. It reduces the efficiency of outlays and thus sets limits to the growth rate of total consumption. As we see, there appears to be a contradiction between increasing social equity and increasing economic efficiency.

In our opinion it is precisely this first tendency, resulting from the levelling of income differentials, which clearly dominated in Poland in the years 1945–70. The decline in income differentials which was achieved in that period was quite remarkable – especially when compared with income differentials in inter-war Poland – and resulted in a steeply increasing demand for agricultural products,[1] and for the low-processed but highly material-intensive manufactures. Thus we may say that the levelling of incomes in this period caused a rise in unit costs of production and diminished the efficiency of outlays in terms of the incremental consumption fund. It must be noted, however, that this tendency was seriously mitigated by the possibilities for the better utilisation of agricultural labour. By the 1970s these possibilities had been exhausted. Marginal increments in agricultural output became very expensive both in terms of unit costs (the reciprocal of equation (1) above),

[1] This was the most important factor. In the inter-war period, with very high income differentials and an average consumption of meat equal to *c*. 19 kgs per head, there was 'overproduction' of agricultural goods. Today, with the consumption of meat equal to 70 kgs per head, and consumption of milk one of the highest in Europe the shortages in meat supply cause serious disturbances. Such a great increase in the consumption of animal products results, *inter alia*, from the levelling of income differentials. This, in turn, results from elimination of unemployment and also from significant levelling of wage rates.

and in terms of direct and indirect capital intensity. These factors may at present reinforce the contradiction between attempts to reduce income differentials and attempts to increase economic efficiency. This contradiction is even more important when the cheap resources of mineral raw materials (i.e. those deposits which require relatively lower investment input per unit of output) become exhausted, and also when the world 'energy crisis' makes it necessary to resort to expensive home deposits of coal.

The second tendency

The tendency for unit costs to rise may also result from the pattern of consumption specific to the high-income groups. First of all, expenditures from these incomes are characterised by a high demand elasticity for cars and oil,[1] a high elasticity of demand for final consumer goods and services imported from developed capitalist countries (e.g. foreign tourism), and for highly processed industrial goods, the manufacture of which often requires foreign materials, equipment and technology. The composition of demand characteristic of these income groups may mean that because import intensity rises with the level of income the effect of increasing income differentials will be a falling tendency in the efficiency of outlays.

From the above considerations it follows that the impact of income differentiation on economic efficiency is not unequivocal: a more equitable distribution of the consumed part of national income adversely affects economic efficiency (the first tendency); on the other hand, the increase in income differentials causes similar results (the second tendency).

One may ask which of these two tendencies exerts a greater impact on economic efficiency in the present conditions of development in Poland? It seems legitimate to claim that it is still the first tendency which dominates, but the second tendency may gain in strength at the present stage in the development of the Polish economy. As in all countries entering the medium development level, the assortment of home-produced, highly processed industrial goods (the manufacturing of which is based on home technologies and home-produced materials) will prove insufficient for many sections of the population.[2]

[1] In the Polish conditions running of cars is highly import-intensive and also requires significant outlays on infrastructure which are again highly import- and energy-intensive.

[2] The adverse influence of the above tendency may be mitigated by means of high prices for cars, imported industrial goods, and goods produced at home but requiring substantial inputs of foreign equipment and materials. Such measures, which in fact boil down to imposing taxes on selected goods, result in a much higher differentiation of money wages than the respective differentiation of real social outlays incurred in production of goods consumed by various income groups. Such measures are commonly used in this country (e.g. low food prices and high prices for cars); incidentally, this makes it difficult to compare income differentiation in this country with that in capitalist countries.

So far we have discussed in some detail the impact which various patterns of demand for consumer goods – due to various degrees of income differentiation – exert on the economic efficiency of outlays earmarked for increasing the total consumption fund. In conclusion let us note that the elasticity of efficiency of outlays for increasing total consumption with respect to changes in income differentiation depends on the absolute level of consumption which is, of course, correlated with the level of overall development achieved by the country in question.

At a *low* stage of development the adverse impact of equitable distribution on the efficiency of outlays is to a great extent offset by relatively more favourable conditions of raw materials extraction and especially of agricultural production (owing to the abundance of labour in agriculture). On the other hand, at a relatively low absolute level of income (even with regard to higher income groups) a greater income differentiation does not yet exert significant pressure on imports as compared with the situation in more developed countries.

At a *high* stage of development the consequences of more equitable distribution of income are partially offset by a relatively low income elasticity of demand for agricultural products and low-processed industrial goods, because the absolute level of consumption of these goods is fairly high (even for low-income groups). On the other hand, greater income differentiation does not necessarily involve any significant difficulties in balancing the increased import requirements, because a well-developed economy has abundant possibilities for expanding exports of highly processed manufactures.

Thus it may be concluded that the elasticity of efficiency of development with respect to income differentiation is highest *in a country at an intermediate stage of development*, where – for a time – certain characteristics of both low and high stages of development are combined in an obviously unfavourable way. In such a country, there continues to be a relatively high elasticity of demand for agricultural products and low-processed manufactures. At the same time the conditions for agricultural production and mineral raw materials extraction at home become as difficult as those which, *ceteris paribus*, appear in highly developed countries. The pattern of demand generated by higher income groups is very close to that of higher income groups in well-developed countries. The capacity to export, however, can hardly move beyond the limits set by the low stage of economic development.

The above circumstances can be of significant importance. At an intermediate stage of development the level of satisfaction of the basic consumer needs of the whole society will be relatively high. This may lead to the conclusion that it is time to start a new phase in economic policy, relying on acceleration of economic growth by means of a distinctly better remuneration (in relative terms) of jobs performed by skilled workers, managers, and all who offer good prospects for increased productivity. According to our earlier argument, in a country where the bottleneck of growth is not the dynamics of productivity in manufacturing industries but rather the supply of raw and imported materials, the actual macroeconomic results of such a policy ultimately depend to a great extent on what the newly earned money is spent on. Therefore, when the need to pursue such a policy arises it must be remembered that it involves the risk that the growing stream of money incomes may boost consumption needs, and that these will then get painfully hurt by the declining efficiency of outlays due to the bottlenecks to growth.

6 Social Equality as a Criterion and Condition of Socio-economic Progress

Zofia Morecka[1]
UNIVERSITY OF WARSAW

I INTERPRETATION OF THE TERM SOCIO-ECONOMIC PROGRESS

The notion of socio-economic progress is of great importance and interest to both governments and social scientists. However, the term is interpreted very differently, while evaluations of socio-economic changes are frequently based on divergent criteria and highly unsatisfactory measures.

The term 'socio-economic progress' contains a valuating element, i.e. 'progress', and two elements defining the fields or rather aspects with which this progress is concerned. 'Progress' as a favourable change, a change for the better, is subject to evaluation from the point of view of a definite system of values conditioned by numerous ideological, socio-political, cultural and economic factors. This is the source of the possibility of highly divergent evaluations of the same events and processes. The possibility seems considerably greater in the analysis of social progress than of economic progress, partly because economic changes concern the world of material things to a much greater extent than social changes. In the field of interdependence between the distribution of national income, models of consumption and socio-economic progress with which this session of our conference is concerned, the generally accepted symptoms of economic progress are: growth of the national income and increasing possibility of accumulation, modernisation of the economic structure, more rational utilisation of resources, increasing effectiveness of production factors, and improvement of the structure of the social product.

The interpretation of social progress, depending on the accepted systems of values and conditioned in turn by the socio-economic system and its ideology, converges only in the most general formulations: improvement of living conditions and perfecting of social relations. They will be concretised and worked out in detail on the basis of the accepted system of values, especially elements concerning man himself, the ideal of his personality and

[1] The help of M. Bednarski and S. Golinowska in the preparation of this paper is gratefully acknowledged.

the type of social order. This will be the basis of a differentiation of views on the basic elements or criteria of social progress, on the content of prosperity which is to be propagated, on the subjective and objective range of social equality and justice, on the desirable influence of the society (its concrete groups) on the shape of community life, and finally on the content and character of social coexistence on the micro and macro scale.

The heterogeneity of the term 'socio-economic progress' is a reflection of the heterogeneity of actual economic and social processes, conditioning each other and showing a comparative independence in both their spontaneous and their regulated course. The thesis of the mutual conditioning of economic and social processes is today widely accepted. Economic and social aspects of the functioning of economy and society constitute an inseparable whole. They are marked, however – as has already been pointed out – by a comparative independence causing the appearance of contradictions between them, which become graver under certain conditions. This independence, the contradictions revealed and the evaluation of the self-operating social effects of economic progress as unsatisfactory constitute the main premise of the formulation of social policy and its rapid development in the contemporary world. However, social policy does not guarantee the integration of economic and social progress as a uniform socio-economic progress. On the other hand, such an integration seems ever more desirable at the present time, with a rapidly growing population, limited resources, increasing needs and aspirations and a rising standard of education. With integrated socio-economic progress the highest priority is given to social goals and processes, because in the final account they have stimulated human activity since the dawn of history. The striving to meet the ever growing and ever more variegated needs, the striving for one's own all-round development and happiness, constitute after all the natural aim of economy, even though it is veiled by the specific aims of alternative socio-economic formations or the immediate tasks of a given stage, which are full of contradictions and antagonism. Restoration of the proper priority to this natural aim is a highly complicated process, requiring far-reaching economic and social transformations. For it means the necessity of the application of twofold criteria in the evaluation of the situation and in the making of decisions in every field of social life: general social criteria and criteria specific for a given field, for example economic ones in the economic field. Thus economic decisions would be made with due consideration of both their social effects and their feedback as regards the course of economic processes. Such criteria should be used on the macro- and microeconomic scale. The calculus of economic effectiveness would be transformed into a calculus of socio-economic effectiveness, in accordance with the standpoint that the final effectiveness of every effort of society as a whole and of its every part is expressed in social progress. Economic progress would be treated as a stage and condition indispensable for the current and future achievement of social progress. It appears that socio-economic progress treated in such an integrated manner can be achieved only under specific conditions of the social system – economic development must be submitted to the social control exercised by the widest masses of society. A socialist society is in our opinion closest to these conditions: the economy is based on social ownership of the means of production and a planned central steering of all fields of social activity.

The specific factors of integrated socio-economic progress, as well as the market symptoms of its achievement are income distribution and the transformation of consumption models. Their analysis permits us to answer questions about what and whose needs are really met by economic development, the extent to which there are disproportions between the living conditions of the various social groups, the degree of equality and justice in the basic economic components of the quality of life, and so on.

We should like to devote our further arguments to problems of egalitarianism in the field of income distribution, concentrating, however, not on a statistical picture of achievements and tendencies, but on the mechanisms and conditions of the application of principles of social equality and justice. The influence of the socio-economic system on these mechanisms and principles is the reason why the arguments are confined to the conditions of a socialist economy.

Essential differences in the interpretation of the concept 'social equality' make it necessary briefly to present our standpoint on this subject.

II AN ATTEMPT TO INTERPRET THE CONCEPT OF 'SOCIAL EQUALITY'

By social equality we understand the absence of glaring, objectively unjustified and socially unaccepted, differences. It is an ideal system to be reached. We call development in this direction egalitarianisation or equalisation of society. This means that the equalisation of society consists in:

(i) a reduction of social differences so that they are no longer glaring (particularly in cases of poverty or insufficiency);
(ii) elimination of differences which do not have an objective social justification (derived from work done, its effectiveness or its importance for economic development);
(iii) elimination of differences unacceptable to society (because of their size, causes, etc.).

The introduction of equality depends on the prior creation of proper material and social conditions, first of all in the form of proper legislation. From this point of view we distinguish a formal equality, that is equal rights of all classes, strata, social groups and individuals; and real equality, characterising the extent to which these rights are used. This depends both on the 'right-holders' and the objective, material, organisational and other possibilities of their use. Most frequently formal equality precedes and conditions real equality. This, however, is not an indispensable correlation.

Real equality (or inequality) need not have its counterpart in formal legislation. We can distinguish three main forms: equality of measures, of opportunities and of situations.

'Equality of measures' means identical treatment of all social subjects, or conduct caused by a specific case and not a specific person, and the application of identical norms and evaluations in particular fields of economic and social life. Typical examples of this form of equality are the equality of citizens before the law or remuneration for work according to its quantity and quality. The principle of 'equal measure' under conditions of differentiated social characteristics of individuals or groups exerts an obvious influence differentiating their current and future situation. Despite, therefore, its considerable similarity to the norms of social justice, it does not solve the problem of the elimination of excessive differences in the economic and social structure.

'Equality of opportunities' is undoubtedly a higher form of social equality. It is also more effective from the point of view of socio-economic progress. It means that all social classes, groups and individuals have equal access to ways to development, to occupying social positions and the various advantages connected with them. The absence of limitations to this accessibility resulting from the social positions held at or before the moment of 'starting' is another of its characteristics. Equality of opportunities does not mean that everybody has an identical prospect of achievement. It means an identical prospect for individuals of the same value from the point of view of the possibility of meeting certain definite requirements. If under such conditions the mechanisms of selection are based on an objective evaluation of usefulness for concrete social roles and functions, the individual has the chance of fully mobilising his possibilities and society will enjoy the optimum exploitation of talents. Both effects are directly connected with socio-economic progress, and at the same time they initiate mechanisms motivating further progress.

The next form is 'equality of situations', defined sometimes as equality of participation. This is the most controversial form of equality in the system of values, the most utopian from the point of view of the possibility of its introduction and the most complicated as an object of analysis of an actual state of affairs. The demand that excessive social differences should be eliminated contains, however, an element of the reduction of 'differences in situations', particularly in some especially important fields or with regard to different social groups. The problems of egalitarianisation now being discussed and solved in practice include first of all in our society the question of reducing differences in the living and environmental conditions of the younger generation, conditioning the equality of their opportunities in life. The three basic forms of equality are strongly correlated and condition one another. Equality of measures can cause inequality of situations. A real inequality of opportunities (impossibility of using an opportunity) results from inequality of situations. Even given equality of opportunities, their full exploitation brings about an inequality of situations. The introduction of one form of equality might, therefore, either be conducive to the introduction of another form or it might threaten it. Processes of a cumulation of effects or of their mutual reduction might appear. Hence the particular importance of a comprehensive approach to the problem of equality.

One cannot speak, therefore, of equality 'in general'. For what matters can be an actual state of affairs (trend) or norm, a materialised objective reality or an element of socio-economic policy, a formal or real equality in the field of duties or rights, an equality of measures, of opportunities or of situations. A precise and comprehensive analysis of real processes and tendencies, as well as their evaluation, and the formulation of tasks or ethical norms, is a necessary condition if misunderstandings, illusions and disappointments are to be avoided.

III INCOMES IN A SOCIALIST SOCIETY, AND THE PROBLEM OF EQUALISATION AND SOCIO-ECONOMIC PROGRESS

Socialist society becomes more egalitarian than other societies almost from the beginning of its creation, thanks to the liquidation of high incomes connected with private ownership of the means of production, ever wider application of the principle of distribution according to the quantity and quality of work, and the expansion of social consumption funds. All these premises promote the immediate limitation of differences, and favour processes of egalitarianisation. However, they do not determine them in an unambiguous manner; that is, they do not guarantee their implementation. The problem is that both distribution according to work and the so-called 'desiderative distribution' of social consumption funds can lead either to greater social equality or to growing differentiation, depending on the detailed principles and mechanisms of distribution and the conditions under which it is made, or even depending on the behaviour of the subjects profiting by it.

The results of division according to the quantity and quality of work depend, as is known, on indices of work and changes in its quantity and quality. These characteristics of work are shaped partly by the requirements of production and partly by employees themselves. Without even descending, therefore, to the level of the individual, but speaking of qualified professional groups, we find multidirectional changes in their positions in relation to each other under the influence of technical and organisational progress going on at a varying rate, and in a variety of concrete forms in the separate fields of professional activity. In specific fields of application the process tends to equalise the characteristics of work and the conditions of its performance, while on the scale of the entire economy it increases differentiation in the qualifications, harmfulness, responsibility, etc., of jobs affected by this progress. Even in modernised fields, the concentration of the basic mass of employees is accompanied as regards characteristics of work by the appearance – at the extremes – of groups considerably different from the norm for the given period and type of progress.

This means that the most highly materialised and measurable factors – changes in work itself – bring about simultaneous concentrating and differentiating processes. With the assumption that an equal measure must be used for the remuneration for work this must lead on the one hand to equalisation and on the other to differentiation of the remuneration of groups of employees. Propagation of progress liquidates certain differences, while the maintenance of distinct privileges in certain fields over a long period of time perpetuates those differences. They will be transformed into more enduring social differences unless there are conditions of high social and spatial mobility.

When it comes to the shaping of incomes from work, or more narrowly of wages alone, an essential role is also played by non-technological characteristics of work: the labour market situation called in the literature 'scarcity of work', and the so-called social weight of work resulting from developmental preferences established by the central economic organs.

We have to deal here, therefore, with an extremely important phenomenon: the application of the principle of equal measure under conditions of considerable changeability of the elements of that measure. This causes methodological complications: difficulties of measuring and comparing various characteristics of work are accompanied by the necessity of taking due account of their uneven changes in time.

The term 'equal measure' becomes an approximate, directional signpost. Moreover, it becomes subject to an additional modification at the moment of translation of all work into the language of money, that is into the rates of wages paid for each job. For an essential role is played in the establishment of these rates not only by work evaluation but also by the levels and relations of wages shaped so far, the possibilities of the wages fund at our disposal, and the immediate aims of economic and social policy.

As a result, the wages reflecting the basic indices of work deviate from the principle of 'equal measure' in the strict sense of the term, because they contain numerous additional elements which it is sometimes difficult to measure and which are exposed to the influence of subjectivism. Depending on the mechanism for their establishment and on the attitudes determining the wage policy, they can be a tool for either the observance or the infringement of the principle of equal measure. At the same time, the field for manoeuvre found here may favour the implementation of the principle of the equality of situations, i.e. by preventing marked differences in rates of wages, even those 'technologically' and 'economically' justified, which lead to a differentiation of income considered to be excessive in relation to the general living conditions in a given period.

Another difficult point in the observance of the principle of equal measure in wages policy is the measurement of labour outlays and its effects, as well as the use of different systems of remuneration for work. Neither working time nor working norms are reliable indices of the quantity of work. What particularly escapes the records is the waste of working time in the time systems of remuneration, while reservations are also aroused by the uneven intensity of working norms in piecework and bonus-carrying systems. Both shortcomings cause serious infringement of the principle of equal measure and are the source of disproportions in earnings, dangerous not only from a social but also a productional point of view (excessive mobility of personnel, weakening of incentives for work and of discipline, etc.).

As can be seen from these arguments, the problem of the observance of the principles of social equality is very complex even in such a simple form as the equality of measure and in such a strongly objective field as the quantity and quality of work performed. This complexity is the reason why the tendencies for increasing equalisation of the quality and conditions of work dominating for a long time in the planned socialist economy are not automatically reflected in the structure of incomes from work. Statistical studies of income distribution and the structure of wages in Poland show an astonishing stability. Although the level of wages has been increased several fold, the sectoral proportions of average wages remain almost unchanged, though with increasing disproportions within the various branches. A further distinguishing characteristic is the concentration of wages paid in a comparatively small part of the total range: the overall range exceeds 1:12, but 80 per cent of wages are contained in an interval of 1:3, and 60 per cent in an interval of 1:2.

It is possible, therefore, to state a very specific effect of changing remuneration for work done on the process of the egalitarianisation of Polish society: there are essential processes of equalisation of the wages of the majority of employees, and the simultaneous maintenance (in some periods an increase) of the difference of extreme wages despite a systematic and considerable raising of the minimum wage.

The differentiation of wages, and particularly of their range, is the object of specially keen observation by wide masses of employees. It is subject to a sharp critical evaluation, often sharper than would be justified by the objective role played by wages in the final shape of the prosperity and conditions of life and development of employees' families (the livelihood of over 62 per cent of the population is based on wages, which represent 80 per cent of the incomes of employees' families, while about 20 per cent are derived from incomes from social consumption funds). It has been found in an irrefutable manner from numerous studies that the main influence on the level of prosperity is exerted by the demographic characteristics of households (size, structure according to age, phase of the development of the family, the degree of professional activeness).

While rejecting the utopian slogan of equality of the living situations of classes, social groups and individual households, we consider it indispensable under socialism to prevent their differentiation to a degree which would permit areas of poverty, limit in an essential measure the possibilities of individual development and eliminate real equality of opportunities. This requires a widely expanded system of social benefits (in cash and in kind) functioning as the so-called *social consumption fund*. However, this fund has a number of specific functions to perform and cannot be used solely as a means of promoting equalisation.

The main function of social security is to prevent the deterioration of the 'normal' situation of persons protected by it in such cases as old age or families with an exceptionally large number of children. The task of social care is to guarantee an indispensable income for persons who are chronically in a difficult situation which they are in no position to improve. The main function of basic benefits in kind is to stimulate and satisfy some of the needs of the population particularly important for society (health service, education, recreation and physical culture, etc.).

Without going into details, it may be generally stated that the social consumption funds in their role of providing social security and social welfare do not play a major part in the elimination of differences in the prosperity of families. Most of the funds are distributed in proportion to wages and incomes from work (family allowances, which increase with the number of children, are at present only a small part of overall incomes).

Of a different character are the basic benefits in kind – education, protection of health, physical culture and social welfare. These are free and available to everybody, not conditioned by membership of a class, stratum or social group, nor connected with the amount of income or the degree of individual prosperity; they operate by their very nature in an egalitarian manner – and create equal opportunities for satisfying certain definite needs. It is true that it is not easy to observe these principles in practice. Their observance is still made difficult by economic and material barriers, even though they have been considerably weakened: the former connected with the additional costs of consumption of services, the latter with the distribution of infrastructure, which still continues to be much better in cities. The creation of equal opportunities also does not guarantee a reduction of the differences in the consumption of goods or services because of the unequal degree of the development of needs of a higher order, which are determined to a considerable extent by the level of prosperity and education.

A separate group of benefits from the social consumption fund is made up of services in the field of recreation, child care and up-bringing. Although treating the problem generally they are based – like social insurance – on priorities for employees in the socialised sector, the activity of the local organs of people's authorities in some of these fields is concerned with all inhabitants of a given region. Within the framework of the social consumption funds they have the strongest levelling effect, because payment for them increases proportionally to the family income.

Benefits provided by industrial plants include housing, workers' hotels, vocational schools, school hostels and scholarships, health protection, cultural, tourist and sports centres, canteens, buffets, etc. These benefits are partly paid for by the users and are financed from the enterprise turnover fund, the works' fund and a state subsidy. Both unequal investment possibilities in previous years and also differences in the subsidies received from the central budget have caused increasing differences in this component of the social benefits. This is why the principles of the creation of these funds aimed at limiting the differences appearing here were reformed in 1973 and again in 1978.

The variety of the social consumption funds and their functions, together with the multidirectional tendencies of wages and incomes from work, and also the demographic changes, are the reasons why general equalising tendencies – particularly in respect to equality of measure and of opportunities – may be accompanied by periodical and sectional deviations from them. It would seem, therefore, that what is indispensable is an active and quickly reacting policy in this field. As we have said already, however, the policy of wages (and incomes from work) must be subordinated to the needs of employment and efficiency.

We may draw from this the general conclusion confirming the opening thesis of the paper concerning the inseparability of social progress and economic progress, and the indispensability of their integration in order to create proper economic conditions for the observance of the principles of social equality and justice under a socialist system.

7 Accumulation, Efficiency, Equity and Basic Human Needs

Reginald Herbold Green
INSTITUTE OF DEVELOPMENT STUDIES, UNIVERSITY OF SUSSEX

I HISTORICAL ANTECEDENTS: INTELLECTUAL AND OPERATIONAL

Basic Human Needs (BHN) as a concept was not invented in a vacuum by the technical paper preparers and consultants for the ILO's World Employment Conference,[1] even though it was the first occasion on which that concept was discussed under that title in a major forum. Like any other concept it represents both existing elements, reordered in a new pattern, and also newer ones. The strands influencing the emergence of the concept in 1975 included:[2]

(1) The Indian (e.g. K. N. Raj, B. Minhas) basic and minimum needs work of the 1960s, including the studies of differences in their attainment not directly correlated to average productive forces and the attempts to design state action packages to enable communities to meet these need as a central aspect in development strategy as embodied in the draft (albeit much less in the final) version of the Fifth Plan, plus related South Asian studies (e.g. those of K. Griffin).

(2) The attempt to articulate a socialist economic and pricing calculus more relevant to a socialist society's aims (associated with Kalecki and I. Sachs).

(3) The 'mass needs' debate, particularly in its Mahgrebian-Egyptian aspects centred on examining the limits of socio-economic recon-

[1] The conference was the first broad forum to centre on discussion of the concept and its preparation – especially the writing of *Employment, Growth and Basic Needs*, ILO, 1976 – brought a number of strands together. However, this is not to suggest that a slogan was invented by ILO with no prior conceptual base or that a model was fabricated out of thin air.

[2] Concept dating is always difficult – when do precursors and early formulations begin? Here *What Now*? (1975 Dag Hammarskjold Report) and *Employment, Growth and Basic Needs* are treated as the first full formulations, but claims could be made for some works within the strands cited here as influences and antecedents.

struction under Nasser and those imposed by the initial heavy-industry-centred Algerian strategy.

(4) The Latin American thinking flowing from perceptions of the limitations and failures as well as the insights of the basic ECLA 'gapmanship' model (e.g. E. Cardoso), and the disaggregation of the dependence models to study the detailed impact on exploited and excluded groups as a foundation for studying dynamics, (e.g. R. Stavenhagen, C. Furtado).

(5) The interaction or contradiction of the New International Economic Order dialogue and that on Self-Reliance. Especially relevant was the perceived inadequacy of changes at international level without parallel or prior national strategic changes since otherwise, while interterritorial gain divisions might be altered, the exploited and oppressed in the periphery would be unlikely to benefit.

(6) The reaction against arguments based on *Limits to Growth* that world resource constraints required continued inequality (or even the aseptic genocide advocated by the 'triage' theorists), and in particular the work of the Bariloche Foundation in creating a Latin American model to demonstrate the feasibility of meeting basic material needs in a brief time period if that were to receive top priority.

(7) The attempt by the United Nations Environmental Programme (and particularly by Maurice Strong) to develop an 'inner limit' of minimum human needs as a co-constraint with the ecological 'outer limit' in the development of environmental policy.[1]

(8) The World Bank's (and particularly Robert McNamara's) growing concern, from 1969 on, that the old development model excluded at least 40 per cent of the world's population from its benefits, a concern leading to the 'absolute poverty eradication' and 'redistribution with growth' themes in IBRD and associated intellectual speeches, analysis and programming.

(9) The International Labour Organization's World Employment Programme, and the conversion of those most involved in it from a wage employment to a national strategy – working poor – full productive employment focus.

(10) A general revolt – especially by periphery participants – against intellectual overcentralism. One branch was a 'revolt of the periphery' against Eurocentric intellectual paradigms, and another a questioning of top-down analysis.

(11) The experience of several nations which did pursue strategies markedly

[1] Indeed, *What Now*? grew out of an initial UNEP request to the DH Foundation to do a global minimum-needs study. 'Grew out of', since *What Now*? followed another development away from the minimum material-needs starting point. See also W. H. Mathews (ed.) *Outer Limits and Human Needs* (DH Foundation, 1977).

unlike that of the pre-1970 development paradigm. China and Tanzania were central for the BHN advocates, Taiwan and South Korea for the more conservative BN modellers. Sri Lanka has been a source of fascination but doubt for both, because its BN approach was basically non-participatory, curiously random intellectually, only peripherally linked to primary redistribution, and neither economically nor socially self-sustaining.[1] These experiences were felt partly as expressed by the leaders and intellectuals of the actual states involved, and partly as experienced or observed by the other analysts.

Of these influences, the last was, and is, probably the most important intellectually, and certainly operationally. However, the UNEP–IBRD–ILO strands occasioned much of the particular analysis and writing leading to the present form of the BHN dialogue, and each of the elements was dominant for some of the early proponents.

II BASIC HUMAN NEEDS AND ASSORTED KINSMEN

The Basic Human Needs conceptual model sketched here is the full-blooded (radical social democratic or unorthodox socialist) one. This is not the only variant, nor necessarily the one most widely publicised or criticised, but it is the one which is most significantly divergent from the old development orthodoxy of the 1950s and 1960s. Three other 'versions' can be noted in passing:

(1) 'Minimum material needs' ('absolute poverty eradication'), which might be any of the following: an approach to limiting potential explosive pressures from the excluded; a means to satisfying conscience by technically programmed, means-tested global charity; or (and) a modern statement of the Ricardian–Marxian conditions for maximum sustainable exploitation in the service of rapid expanded reproduction, assuming either that full utilisation of labour is possible or that the reserve army should be kept at a level of full operational and reproductive subsistence. (One variant of this is Friedman's negative income tax for a guaranteed minimum income.)

(2) Technocratic 'basic needs' models, which assume that the problems are largely management gaps by élite decision-takers and lack of ability to grasp opportunities by 'the poor'. These may go beyond 'minimum material needs' in a production/distribution sense, but only on an

[1] See *Towards a Socialist Sri Lanka* (Centre For Society and Religion, 1977) and *Sri Lanka An Experience In a Need-Oriented Development* (Marga Foundation/International Fund for Development Alternatives, 1978). The perplexity of perception is shared by Sri Lankan participants not limited to outsiders.

implied 'welfare state' basis. Politically they are naïve: élite decision-takers do not develop management for the purposes posited because they perceive them as opposed to their (personal or subclass) interests rather more than because they are unable to understand what is proposed. Workers and peasants lack the power to enforce such a strategy on decision-takers.

(3) Social democratic 'basic needs' models (e.g. *Redistribution With Growth* in its more radical moments), which do begin to grapple with asset and power distribution, but in a rather hesitant, incremental and micro manner quite atypical of serious political economic paradigms or structural transformations. This is true even of the more radical models – e.g. Bariloche – if they are conceived of as protoplans and not destructive polemics against the present paradigm. In them the asset, institutional, income distribution, class power and state role elements are not merely not endogenous to the models, but are so implicit in the initial assumptions as to be virtually invisible and irretrievable. The most rigorous reading might be that of a call for 'global Fabianism' (i.e. the ultimate strategic victory over revolution to be won by a series of planned tactical defeats on specific reform measures) but, apart from its unworkability, that is probably unfair to the rather broader and deeper intent of many of the writers.[1]

III BASIC HUMAN NEEDS: CONCEPT AND STRATEGY[2]

As an organising concept for a development strategy, basic human needs – as the name implies – centres on human (primary community and individual) needs, and gives primacy of place to moving towards the satisfaction of those needs as perceived by workers and peasants. It rejects maximisation of the rate of growth of productive forces and, therefore, denies primacy to accumulation. The sacrifice of a decent (socially determined) standard of life for workers and peasants, to provide the 'incentive' for capitalist accumulation or the raising of socialist production forces, for the benefit of future generations, is also rejected.

BHN as a strategy turns on five broad target clusters:

(i) basic personal consumer goods: food, clothing, housing, basic furnishings and other socially defined necessities, whether 'material' or not (as, for example, a decent burial in the Chinese six guarantees);

(ii) universal access to basic services: primary and adult education, pure water, preventive and curative health programmes, habitat (environ-

[1] Cf. S. Cole and H. Lucas (eds.), *Models, Planning and Basic Needs* (Institute of Development Studies, 1978), especially Section 5.

[2] This section is largely a synthesis of the conceptual framework of *What Now?*, of *Employment, Growth and Basic Needs*, and of *Report* (Egham Meeting of the World Council of Churches' Unit Justice and Service, 1977).

mental sanitation, urban and rural community infrastructure) and communications (in both senses);

(iii) the right to, and reality of, productive employment (including self-employment) yielding both high enough productivity and equitable enough remuneration for each household with an able-bodied adult member to meet its basic personal consumer goods needs out of its own income;

(iv) an infrastructure – physical, human, technical institutional – capable both of producing the goods and services required (either directly, or indirectly through foreign trade), and of generating surplus flows adequate to finance the basic communal services and to provide for investment to sustain increases in productive forces needed to advance toward BHN fulfilment;

(v) mass participation in decision-taking and review, and in strategy formulation and control of leaders, as well as in implementation of projects and carrying out of decisions.

As a strategy, BHN is production-oriented – transfer payments in the sense of secondary redistribution of consumption power are very much secondary, not central:[1] Its emphasis is on primary redistribution – of income, assets and power – because it views separation of production and distribution as theoretically unsound and practically non-operational. The productive employment need is, therefore, both an end and a central means.

Indeed, one somewhat inconvenient characteristic of the model as now constructed is that each of the end clusters is also a means. In the case of participation the end is overcoming alienation but the means is power: mobilisation to enforce the strategy, and mobilisation to release resources not otherwise utilisable because their centralised exploitation is impracticable on technical or production relations grounds.

Similarly the production of basic goods is a means because it interlocks with the full employment and participatory power goals/means. The evident

[1] The counter view – e.g. T. N. Srinivason, 'Development Policies and levels of living of the Poor: Some Issues' (1977 Bellagio Workshop, World Bank) – is a clear misreading. The 1976 World Employment Conference *Declaration* underscores raising productivity and production and stresses primary (earned income) not tertiary (consumption transfer payments) redistribution as to the sources cited on p.91. Indeed BHN formulations tend to be rather austerely work-oriented, with a clear bias against subsidising any person capable of working (and a clear bias toward making his right to productive employment and adequate remuneration meaningful and operational rather than figurative and moral). The same appears to hold of national practice, e.g. China and Tanzania are quite clear about using consumption transfers as a last resort for a limited number of persons unable to work and /or special transitional situations (high-price grain imports dominating the latter category in both countries).

way for rural communities to meet basic food needs (achieve an operational right to an adequate diet) is to produce it themselves. On the one hand this would increase their power *vis à vis* employers and bureaucrats, but on the other it would normally require power either to enforce a prior land reform or (and) to prevent large landholder/bureaucratic demobilisation and diversion of the approach.

What degree of reduction of inequality – and of what types of inequality – is built in to the concept is not quite clear. For practical reasons (relating to resource limits) ceilings as well as floors are needed. How wide the acceptable floor/ceiling range would be appears likely to be country-culture-time-production relation specific; total equality and present degrees of inequality are limiting rather than likely target cases.

BHN uses 'socially determined' needs. The attainment or near attainment of one set of specific targets would be the cause for another, not for a feeling of arrival. Comparative not absolute poverty – exclusion – inequality is the basic target. This is a major divide from the 'minimum material needs' school, albeit one obscured by the failure to date to specify even a hypothetical BHN trajectory for a middle or high level polity/economy (e.g. Mexico, Singapore, Sweden).

Similarly BHN is not limited to material needs. A decent burial has little to do with production; universal adult education, including consciousness raising, is neither easily fed into a growth model nor self-evidently politically stabilising. The employment goal, at least to some proponents, rests on a belief that creative activity includes work and is not limited to leisure.

The global inequality implications of BHN have usually been glossed over or set aside – particularly in papers emanating from international organisations[1] – because they are so strikingly at variance with the *status quo* and any plasuible trajectory as to appear either non-operational or counter-productive. Further, the national experiences drawn upon have been operated rather separately from the international economic strategies of the states concerned, which have concentrated on exploitation of specific possibilities for marginal gains in the present international economic context; and on participation in NIEO-type state coalitions along international (not inter-personal or class) distribution of surplus lines.

IV BHN, ACCUMULATION, GROWTH

The divergence of the BHN conceptual model from the standard development model on growth is fairly wide but, at least on the one level, in the direction

[1] For example, ILO's publications beginning with *Employment, Growth and Basic Needs*, *What Now*? and the World Council of Churches *Report* do take a somewhat – but only somewhat – less cautious look at global equity implications, but neither seriously poses the potential ceilings for industrial economy real resource use (and presumptively consumption and accumulation) in any overall fashion that remotely approaches operationality.

of observed reality. BHN treats growth of productive forces as a means. However, its interest is in specific material embodiments of growth which directly or indirectly contribute to providing basic goods and services to those requiring them.

This does mean that maximum growth of GDP is not seen as either an end or a means. Equally it can create objections to technologies or modes of production which either produce the 'wrong' specific goods (e.g. brandy as opposed to milk, 'international'-type soap as opposed to low-cost washing compounds) or produce them in a way creating material and income distribution problems (e.g. grain on land held by commercial landowners rather than on peasant or communal holdings).

However, these are not divergences from the model unique to BHN, but aspects of BHN's closer adherence to general patterns of historic experience and less implausible views of decision-taker and class or community motivations. Decision-takers do not in some abstract sense wish to maximise GDP (or its growth rate) without reference to its composition. They have quite specific material priorities – tanks for their armies, butter for their tables, bread for their workers (or at least some of them), exportable commodities for their import needs. Nor are they indifferent as to technologies and sub-modes of production. Decision-takers interested in maximising independent defence capacity are not much interested in technologies raising light industrial productive forces except as they may make wage goods, and thus the wage cost of heavy industrial vectors ending in armaments, cheaper. Corporate managers do not choose technologies maximising output or labour incomes if these either reduce their surpluses directly or undermine their structural position by opening access to potential competitors.

BHN admittedly does not posit the same specific content of growth or technology or submodes of production as most present decision-takers choose. That, however, is a question as to its political feasibility conditions, not as to the plausibility of viewing growth in disaggregated terms and as a means rather than an end.

The accumulation aspects of BHN represent a rather more basic break with conventional wisdom. Its first aspect, the denial of any necessary link between inequality of income distribution and growth rates, is already empirically demonstrated,[1] at least in the sense of showing that there are considerable degrees of freedom as to inequality for any target growth rate.

The factor share distribution relationship to growth is equally not a very close one in the paradigm – or more critical here, its marxian variant – unless one assumes that capitalists neither have variable levels of luxury consumption nor export varying proportions of saving, that there are no savings out of labour (including professional) incomes and that saving/investment by petty

[1] Cf. e.g. Chenery *et al.* (eds.) *Redistribution with Growth* (Oxford University Press, 1975); A. Foxley (ed.), *Income Distribution in Latin America* (Cambridge University Press, 1976).

commodity producers is trivial. Even with these somewhat extreme assumptions, one would need to add relative homogeneity of technology and capital/output ratios on the investment side to complete a model in which there were not substantial degrees of freedom between factor shares and growth of productive forces.

More positively, the BHN conceptual frame at least implicitly takes savings available for domestic investment to be subject to institutional control. Outside petty commodity production and petit bourgeois family enterprises, discretionary personal cash savings are normally a small proportion of total savings. Private and public productive enterprise, state and schedule (insurance, pension) private savings are much larger and are clearly subject to institutional manipulation and/or control both as to savings and as to the share reinvested locally as opposed to that flowing abroad. The petty commodity and small enterprise savings can be influenced by a variety of policy measures including market rigging and market access controls.

The determining factors potentially under state control include technology and submode of production. For example if tree-crop agriculture is dominantly peasant – not plantation – then a high direct labour investment (saving) embodied in land improvement and plant (trees) can be secured; whereas under plantations the investment would be out of cash surpluses and the potential for direct peasant saving likely to be wasted. Similarly selective limitations on access of urban (local or imported) wage goods to rural areas and small towns (e.g. by high transport rates) is likely to make usable pockets of labour and natural resources otherwise rendered unusable by 'free competition', whereas the urban resources (especially the incremental ones) can readily be shifted to other lines of production.

State and public enterprise saving – at least at the macro level – is basically fiscally determined. Public enterprise sectors which states are determined to have achieve a surplus do so (e.g. Hungary, main-line Algerian enterprises, Tanzania) partly perhaps by more attention to cost control but also by price-setting (market rigging) consistent with achieving the broad macro surplus target. Treasuries whose decision-takers require a surplus of recurrent revenue over recurrent expenditure plus a variety of state savings schemes (e.g. National Provident Funds) to provide a steady financial flow to government-fixed investment are usually technically capable of meeting the broad target set. Similar possibilities are seen to exist on the linkage between savings and growth, i.e. the capital/output ratio is seen as less central and less fixed than in the simplified growth models which have actually influenced planning technicians and decision-takers. In the first place fixed capital is only a part of the contributing factors to growth. Albeit many of the remainder do require public expenditure, and therefore surplus collection and allocation (e.g. agricultural extension, rural roads, water), they are not included in standard growth models and – *per contra* – are usually to a substantial degree within the control of fiscal policy (i.e. they can be financed). Further there is some reason to suppose that a concentration on basic goods and, where reasonably practical, on decentralised, small-scale production using local products of labour and natural resources would lead to lower macro capital/output ratios even if there were not major changes in most micro cases. In some sectors – especially construction – micro changes towards labour and away from capital (especially imported capital goods) are feasible, given market rigging or in some cases simply better forward planning. The shift in specific capital inputs is not *strictu sensu* an alteration in the capital/output ratio, but labour and local materials directly embodied in capital by communal or private petty commodity production units, or communal public works schemes, are never credited in any serious way to savings and their output to capital stock (even when, as in some African countries, the tree crops and associated improvements may well be up to a half of true physical capital stock). The effect of institutional measures to augment such specific types of capital input would thus be to lower observed incremental capital/output ratios.

BHN presentations at conceptual level have, to date, not dealt with the accumulation linkages systematically. Even at national level – where articulated but perhaps less co-ordinated – attention has been paid to the types of saving/income and capital/output issues treated above detailed operational or theoretical statements appear to be lacking.

In the final analysis BHN advocates would normally accept some fall in the accumulation rate in return for a more rapid approach to initial BHN targets. However, for reasons related to the above institutional aspects of both the savings and embodiment sides of accumulation they would deny that there was any reason to link BHN with low accumulation, specific growth or even GDP growth rates. Indeed they may well go further – both Tanzanian and Chinese leaders do on occasion – and assert that in certain contexts BHN will produce more general growth of productive forces or GDP, quite apart from more specifically targeted growth of particular outputs. There is not a large enough sample nor long enough experience to test the latter contention; the 4–6 per cent growth trends in China and Tanzania are consistent with the first contention, and somewhat above those achieved by the least unparallel polities (India, Ethiopia) pursuing sharply different strategies.

V POTENTIAL FEASIBILITY – TECHNICAL

In principle, the impracticability of attainment of a social science paradigm or strategy should be a barrier to its acceptance. In practice this is not the case, but the realisation usually comes after the collapse of the paradigm – as with growthmanship/gapmanship. However, in considering a body of concepts for a potential place in a new paradigm it would appear prudent to consider the feasibility of their posited goals both in technical and political terms.

A problem arises immediately in applying any such scrutiny: if Basic Human Needs are socially determined and relative, and have a tendency to alter upward as initial targets are approached, then their total fulfilment becomes an eschatological state. Further, there is no logical reason to assume that a society – even if power rested in the hands of peasants and workers – could not have initial targets which were indeed technically unattainable because the requisite productive-force levels were unattainable. Therefore, any testing would need either to be empirical in a specific context or, if general, related to substantial improvements over the *status quo*.

Basic personal and communal consumption levels

Levels which are adequate in general physical terms could be reached on the production side by 2000 with 6–8 per cent annual growth rates, assuming fairly marginal income redistribution judging by the Bariloche, ILO and Leontieff (UN) models.[1] If anything these may overestimate. The author's back-of-envelope calculations for Tanzania suggest that if all additional goods and services were those included in what Tanzanian workers and peasants perceive as basic personal and communal consumption needs (and if the right mix of these goods and services were produced) a 25 per cent increase in per capita output – say 4.5–6 per cent a year (1.75–3.5 per cent per capita) for eight to fifteen years would potentially be adequate to meet the target. On either calculation the rate of increase of productive forces is not in absolute terms qualitatively different from attained levels. Most basic goods (and *a fortiori* services) are fairly practicable candidates for domestic production in most economies and the possibility of indirect production via exports is as open under BHN as under any other strategy. Thus a mismatch of gross output and particular physical requirements seems unlikely to prove a barrier to feasibility.

Full employment

With adequate productivity and remuneration to cover personal consumption needs, full employment, on the face of it, raises rather more serious technical feasibility problems. The fair renumeration issue is primarily a political one, but the productivity one poses real technical questions, which levels of consciousness (or will) cannot resolve in the absence of changes in productive forces of quite specific kinds.

These changes are attainable – European industrial socialist economies (other than Yugoslavia) and China achieved near full utilisation of labour time fairly quickly. Some of the utilisation, especially in private petty commodity and services production, may have had very low productivity and some larger

[1] Cf. discussion in Cole and Lucas, *op. cit*. The models are very rough – or in the Leontieff case not very closely linked to specific output breakdowns related to basic needs – but do in general demonstrate the feasibility of meeting initial BHN targets rapidly without insuperable real resource or trade constraints given substantial (but not in many cases revolutionary) income redistribution.

scale enterprises may have been seriously overstaffed. Indeed, in these economies the present problems are of increasing labour productivity and mobility because labour time has become a 'scarce commodity'.

Less rigorous transitions towards socialism do not appear to produce equally marked results: in Tanzania urban unemployment is of the order of 8–10 per cent,[1] and national 3–4 per cent, but the proportion of rural labour time which peasants would be eager to devote to even moderately productive artisanal capital works or agricultural effort, if they had complementary knowledge and inputs and a rigged-market structure ensuring they would reap the rewards, may be as high as 30 per cent rising to 50 per cent in some areas of peculiarly baleful ecological constraints. This is a particularly striking case because land reform would do little to alter the situation.

In most non-socialist peripheral economies the situation is substantially worse. Only Singapore (which is excessively atypical and operates a socially determined minimum material needs strategy of considerable sophistication and efficiency) seems close to meeting the employment test. Mexican land reform initially did create a situation which may have approximated relatively full employment at adequate productivity levels, but subsequent differential productive-forces evolution and market rigging, perverse from a BHN point of view but necessary as perceived by post-1940 Mexican decision-takers and the dominant subclasses, have eroded it beyond any probable chance of revitalisation.

These fairly superficial observations suggest that the technical feasibility of this need cluster cannot be considered except in relation to the political structure. It seems quite attainable in a rigorous transition to socialism context, less clearly so in a less rigorous one, and only fortuitously and transitorily possible within the parameters of peripheral capitalism.

Infrastructure

In the broad sense used in this paper infrastructure poses severe technical transitional problems for any strategy shift. Clearly an alteration in primary income distribution does alter the overall pattern of production required; alterations in relative incomes and (probably more critical) relative prices can cause problems in achieving desired micro levels and allocations of investible surplus. The institutional structures for a more rational, more equity-oriented economy are likely to need to be substantially altered from those of an open-export, import-substitution or labour-intensive manufacturing export-led economy.

However, the problems do not appear to be particularly insoluble at a technical level – even within the parameters of a mixed economy. Macro

[1] 1977 ILO Mission guesstimates. The position has been basically static in this respect since 1967; it appears to be significantly better (lower unemployment) than in other African urban areas.

efficiency in achieving and directing surpluses (even if with substantial micro inefficiency in production and allocation costs) is not all that unusual in peripheral economies. Institutional controls, including public enterprises, are hardly new nor unique to would-be socialist economies. Private enterprise actions can be significantly altered by state market rigging even in the case of TNCs. Transitional problems – i.e. new demand for basic goods appearing before new production and generating foreign balance patterns (e.g. Tanzania 1971–73) – can be substantial but hardly of an order of magnitude beyond the 'normal' shocks regularly facing peripheral economies from weather, industrial economy cyclical swings, etc.

Certainly inadequate efficiency in pursuit of a BHN strategy can destroy it – that is true of any political economic strategy. There is, however, a special technical problem – the staff of bureaucrats, managers, entrepreneurs, politicians and technocrats needed to operate the technical side of BHN are unlikely to be, or to see themselves as being, its principal beneficiaries. Therefore, a narrow path exists between aborting the strategy to maintain broad staff support (as some would accuse Tanzania and, *a fortiori*, Algeria of doing) and alienating and destroying the credibility of the staff to a degree which undermines the technical practicability of the strategy (one of the main charges against the Gang of Four). There is a contradiction in utilising élites to construct a non-élitist economy; and that contradiction is always in danger of becoming violently antagonistic, or of being rendered apparently non-antagonistic by *de facto* surrender to the élites.

Participation

Participation is perhaps not usefully considered primarily as a technical problem. It is ultimately political. A strategy based on equity and mass needs cannot succeed without growing mass control of, and disciplinary power over, the subclasses categorised as staff.

However, several technical issues are relevant. Totally centralised planning and administration is not consistent either with effective worker and peasant control over micro decisions, or with mobilising use of local pockets of labour and other resources to increase the frontiers of the productive force level. However, BHN's concern with equity and ceilings, and the reality of élite power to manipulate decentralised systems, requires a structure rather far from either total communal or work unit autonomy or 'free market' pseudo decentralisation. The mechanics of a coherent, partially decentralised, integrated system with national guidelines, parameters and key targets set by a participatory political structure but with a high degree of local decentralisation of micro decisions and of mobilisation to implement them is not very complex on paper. In practice, it requires detailed knowledge of the full context of the society, but probably no more so than the more widespread 'penetration' strategy institutional models.

VI POTENTIAL FEASIBILITY – POLITICAL

The most serious questions in respect to the full-blown BHN strategy are as to its political feasibility (power) conditions.

For a variety of reasons the course of emergence of the concept has hampered attention to this area, but despite this a few things can be said (partly, admittedly, to stimulate dialogue and more empirical research). At least a significant fraction of the dominant decision-taking coalition must be – or see themselves to be – responsible to and dependent on the classes or subclasses who would benefit from a BHN strategy. There must be a level of consciousness and of organisation among the would-be beneficiaries sufficient to sustain initial steps (keeping the decision-takers in power), and to provide a base for initial operation of both productive and decision-taking participation. The higher the degree of consciousness, mobilisation and organisation of those who would lose under BHN, the greater the level of consciousness, organisation and mobilisation of the would-be gainers needed to allow the initiation or sustain the trajectory of a BHN strategy. The initial redistribution of power and resource allocation needs to include changes in asset ownership and production relations, and also to liberate new productive forces and to create bases for mobilisation and consciousness raising in support of further measures.

While an initial revolution will assist in respect of some of the above points it is in itself inadequate; the greatest political difficulties are in the use, not the seizure, of power, and the construction of participation not the destruction of a particular structure of hierarchical exclusion – *vide* Algeria. Whether a start towards a BHN strategy can make significant progress without a violent revolution is unclear – the dangers of *immobilisme* or inadequate momentum to sustain progress, and the growing internal contradictions arising from limited initial worker and peasant mobilisation, are very real ones – *vide* Tanzania. Similarly, whether a commitment to a partial BHN strategy within a capitalist polity at middle or high productive-force levels would be structurally meaningful or would end in marginal reformism is also unclear – in a sense the most likely test cases may be Venezuela and Norway or Sweden.

In any event, a transition to a BHN strategy requires time – both because of the tension between productive-force and consciousness levels and between the historic context (even if past power structures are smashed) and the new goals – the relatively step-by-step approach of Chinese and Vietnamese decision-takers after the initial liberation struggle, and of Tanzanian ones after 1967, seem less unlikely to achieve a more participatory frame than the rather apocalyptic approach of the 1975–78 Kampuchean (and perhaps the 1976–78 Camerean) leadership. External pressures can co-opt or destroy a BHN strategy – e.g. Chile of the Unidad Popular – or reduce a state whose leadership might well seek to follow such a strategy to chaotic efforts to survive – e.g. Angola.

The political feasibility conditions are not fully separable from the technical. The weaker the balance of political forces for the strategy, and the smaller and less conscious its mobilised base, the greater the need to avoid major technical errors. Absence of basic consumer goods (or the means to pay for them) which were common before a strategic change is the speediest way to discredit the strategy and its proponents to workers and peasants, leading to coups, strategy reversals or reversion to coercion.

Similarly, centralisation/decentralisation and order (top-down)/mobilisation (bottom-up) pose technical as well as political tensions. The question is not either/or but the attainment of a succession of temporary, workable proto-syntheses.

The brevity of this section is not intended as an index of its importance. The basic political economic barriers to BHN strategy adoption are political, not technical. Further they are political economic in the sense of subclass interests and power, not political ethical in the sense of will. Two barriers prevent a more detailed exposition.

The first is the present state both of conceptualisation and of empirical work. The second is that the political feasibility conditions are capable of statement only in very general or very country-specific terms. To seek to derive the political feasibility pre-conditions for a BHN strategy in Malawi or Kenya simply by studying Tanzania, and assuming the national contexts were basically similar would not be a sensible exercise; and to seek to project from Tanzania (or China or Vietnam) to Venezuela or Norway would be even less likely to result in a set of propositions with any serious objective correlative.

VII NOTES TOWARD A PERSPECTIVE

On the positive side – at least as far as considering the possibilities and limits of a development strategy oriented to meeting mass needs with high priority given to present generation needs and to equity – it is possible to draw several tentative conclusions:

(1) Fairly wide degrees of freedom exist in setting the central wage rate and labour remuneration structure, the central rate and structure of surplus generation, the range of permitted inequality and relative price structures. The freedom is subject to one constraint of internal consistency and another of consistency with total real resources (productive forces) mobilisable.

(2) There is no particular reason to concentrate on tertiary (consumer transfer payment) redistribution. Most empirical evidence suggests secondary (public service) redistribution is more able to influence both production and effective equality of consumption positively at the same time. Primary (earned income) redistribution via asset redistribution or market rigging can be highly macro efficient (realising intended surplus levels, particular production patterns or alterations of income distribution) if specifically related to goals and contexts and carried out consistently, not piecemeal.

(3) Because the Paretian optimum (and indeed any market-dominated system) depends on income distribution (demand pattern), its productive efficiency statements are special-case ones, and a quite different set could be constructed for any consistent set of income-distribution targets subject to productive forces constraints.
(4) The limits of potential productive forces utilisable under different strategies are difficult to integrate into distribution theory but can radically alter results in any actual case. They are not determinate in principle – the Chinese rural and county industry strategy as applied extends the boundaries of productive forces but so do small private entrepreneurs in Japan and Kenya; the macrostrategy of 1930's Soviet material-balances planning may well have reduced the overall level of productive forces, but increased those available for building up an autonomous economic infrastructure for national defence.

VIII BASIC HUMAN NEEDS

A similar set of tentative observations on BHN as a development strategy with an internalised set of concepts as to distribution can be made:

(1) The BHN approach was conceptualised after the disintegration of support for the 1945–70 'maximum development by maximum accumulation for maximum growth' paradigm.
(2) Its intellectual and national operational origins are both substantially older and dominantly third world – in that sense it represents an intellectual revolt of the periphery just as some of the national experiences influencing it (e.g. China) represent a political economic action revolt of the periphery.
(3) The full BHN conceptual model is internally consistent although both the joint ends/means nature of its basic elements and the nature of its participation/power component render it considerably less easy to manipulate formally than standard models.
(4) Equity – defined in terms of increased equality as well as of absolute increases in access to basic goods and services – is central to BHN. It is in that sense result-(as opposed to opportunity-) oriented, but not committed to absolute equality or to total allocation of resources to artificially defined categories of people.
(5) Because of its intellectual and operational history, BHN is rather weakly articulated conceptually and highly context determined nationally.
(6) The conceptual flexibility is in some aspects – especially political conditions – a way of covering gaps; at national operational level it appears to be related to serious efforts to relate the necessary to the possible, and is not consistent with either a weak state or a high level of macro inefficiency.
(7) Technically there are no evident general reasons to question the

operationality of BHN. There are difficulties and constraints, but these are not in any sense different from those confronting other strategies.

(8) Political feasibility conditions for BHN strategies have not been articulated at all clearly. The degrees of freedom here are unclear. With the exception of Tanzania and perhaps Somalia (and for the most conservative BHN formulations, Taiwan) all the national cases appear to have come following armed revolution lasting for an extended period and greatly eroding the power base and mobilisation capacity of opponents; while a notable failed case – Chile – illustrates problems of a partial initial access to power with well-articulated internal opposition and external intervention able to capitalise on political economic efficiency miscalculations. On the other hand, an armed revolution is quite clearly not a political or technical sufficient condition – what happens after access to power is even more critical.

(9) In principle BHN is applicable globally, and for high and middle as well as low productive-force level economies. There is no serious prospect of global application because the equity constraints could not be met, and the international enthusiasm for support to 'the poorest' is at best very ambivalent and marginal support for existing national BHN efforts.

(10) Given the participation element in BHN the step-by-step approach needed to raise consciousness is likely to be both relatively slow and subject to considerable dislocations and temporary alterings of course.

(11) National application has been of more interest both to BHN practitioners and analysts than theory-building. While correct in one sense, this limits the level of dialogue and the development either of existing or new national strategic formulations and applications. It also means that BHN is a considerable distance from meeting the intellectual preconditions of a paradigm.

Because BHN is a revolutionary strategy based on an egalitarian and a communitarian view of society, it is unlikely to be accepted without struggle. Partial abstraction and 'reformulations' for use as palliatives or cheaper methods of suppression aside, it is not attractive to most dominant subclasses and their decision-takers. Its success, therefore, is dependent on whether the present context is one in which mobilisation in support of BHN is necessary and possible in a substantial number of polities. (Africa from the Equator to the Cape may be a relevant subregion in this context.) Certainly development strategy – not simply at the level of intellectual paradigms in any abstract sense but at the more basic one of results of decision flowing from such paradigms – is in a state of 'great disorder under heaven', a state which in Chinese tradition heralds the fall of a dynasty, a period of disorder and the re-emergence of an ordered state of affairs. BHN's contribution to the fall of the old paradigm is clear enough, its existence as one of the conflicting parties to the disordered struggle is real enough, its potential role in any new order is as yet much more problematic.

Discussion of the Papers by Professors Green, Morecka and Herer, and Dr. Sadowski

(Chairman: Professor J. F. Rweyemau)

Professor Hagemejer (Poland) opened the discussion with a summary of the three papers. He noted that they dealt with very different topics. Professor Green outlined a new strategy for development, for which the set of prescriptions was quite definite but the theoretical basis was still rather vague. Professor Morecka discussed the nature of social equality and its significance for socio-economic progress; and Herer and Sadowski investigated the impact of a change in the distribution of income on the pattern of consumption and hence on the growth of the economy. In this respect their approach was the reverse of that of Professor Morecka: they saw equality as an instrument, not as a goal; and would accept a higher degree of inequality if that would promote their objective of a more rapid growth of output.

Dr Streeten (UK) said that he wanted to make three comments on the paper about Basic Human Needs (BHN). First, he thought it was helpful to think of the meeting of basic needs as a 'public good' for those who wished to satisfy these needs. One could take the example of a family of adult brothers and sisters: if one of them had a large windfall gain there was no tendency for this to be redistributed, but if there was a 'basic needs' problem (e.g. a need for large expenditure for a child on health or education) then the members of the family would tend to rally round. It was thus possible to subscribe to the case for meeting BHN without fully accepting any utilitarian or egalitarian doctrines. Humanitarianism appeared to have a more useful claim than egalitarianism. This approach was reinforced by the tendency – shown in an opinion poll – for US taxpayers to be opposed to 'welfare' as an idea, but at the same time willing to support aid for specific needs such as food for undernourished children, or caring for the health of the old, and this public appeal was a significant feature of the BHN approach.

Secondly, Dr Streeten referred to the distinction made by earlier investigators, notably Seebohm Rowntree, between primary and secondary poverty. In the former case the family earnings were not sufficient to cover their basic needs. In the second case the earnings were adequate but the family was still in poverty because the money was not spent on basic needs but on drink, gambling, etc. or was wasted by inefficient housekeeping. The BHN approach (in contrast with the earlier income approach) in effect applied this concept of secondary poverty to the developing countries. For example it recognised that it was not sufficient to raise the real income of poor peasants (e.g. by encouraging conversion to more productive cash crops) without at the same time ensuring that supplies of food were available in the area that were at least of equal nutritional value to those consumed when the peasants were subsistence producers, and also that the cash earnings were actually spent on essential food and other basic requirements. The BHN thus led one to think much more clearly about direct ways of satisfying basic needs, e.g. by the provision of school meals to correct faulty intrahousehold distribution of income.

Dr Streeten's third point related to the possible trade-off between growth and meeting BHN. He thought that Professor Green's treatment of the issue was not entirely satisfactory. All strategies must have a time dimension; the BHN approach must be seen as dynamic and must not be regarded as an alternative to growth. In the first place, this strategy *required fewer* resources, because it permitted economies in expenditure on the non-basic needs of the poor and the better-off, and in investment expenditure on the provision of non-basic needs in the future. In the second place a successful BHN approach would tend to make *more* resources *available*. More would be produced because the composition of output needed to satisfy basic needs was likely to be produced more labour-intensively and this would raise both employment and production. Improvements in health, nutrition and education would improve the quality of the labour force and might well yield higher returns at the margin than some more conventional forms of investment in physical capital. Furthermore, it would help to remove the motives for large families and so reduce the number of unwanted births and this would also increase the available resources per head of the population. All these benefits were additional to the fact that the satisfaction of basic needs and the improvements in the quality of life were desirable in their own right. A BHN strategy could thus save resources, mobilise more resources and make these resources more productive, and after a period of time the rate of growth of consumption might actually exceed that achieved by a Stalinist-type high investment strategy.

Dr Kulig (Poland) noted that an important source of the BHN strategy was the concern for the environment and the search for growth patterns which were less resource-intensive, particularly for the developing countries. He hesitated to criticise the new approach because of its high moral content, but he did have a few reservations.

It was only a hope that the BHN strategy would be 'less capital intensive'. In certain intellectual ventures, e.g. the Bariloche model, the capital coefficient had indeed turned out to be lower than usual, but this was only a paper exercise. Capital intensities differed substantially, depending on production mix, consumption patterns, structural issues, resource endowments, etc. and there was no evidence to show that it would actually be lower under a BHN strategy.

For policy purposes, BHN should be treated simply as a set of suggestions for programming and orientation of planning, particularly for long-term plans. It could not claim to be a new development *theory*, and as such went far outside the confines of the present conference. It belonged more to 'social engineering' or social philosophy than to theory as such. For policy purposes it required primarily a sound development pattern from a social point of view, i.e. in particular a sound agricultural policy giving sufficient food supplies, and other essentials.

Green's view that BHN should aim at 'self-organisation' or self-employment etc. had very limited value, particularly for modern production processes (even if we thought only of medicines, or bicycles, not to mention computers, etc.). It could not provide a sound and realistic alternative to modern technology.

Dr Kulig also thought that there was an important relationship between the BHN strategy and the idea of the New International Economic Order (NIEO) to be discussed in the following session. The BHN approach provided a strong moral argument for aid and resource-transfers, and had already proved effective in various attempts by the IBRD to establish a new form of control over aid programmes. The NIEO might thus involve a sort of bargain between the developed and the developing countries: the NIEO would be implemented by the former provided the latter reorganised their development patterns in accordance with the BHN strategy.

This raised a further, and most important question. As formulated by Professor Green, the BHN approach would achieve a state of 'bliss' with full employment, egalitarian income distribution, full participatory democracy, etc. To whom was all this addressed? The BHN approach was usually understood as applying to the poorest countries. These, in turn, were more often than not also the most unequal and reactionary regimes. But here we came to Professor Seers' famous statement (in his 1969 paper on 'The Meaning of Development') that in these developing countries it was precisely the existing power élites which provided the strongest and most effective barriers to development. If this was the case, then who were the new strategies intended for? Certainly not for the prevailing élite. But here, however, the question of transition arose. How could one visualise a transition from the existing inequalities backed by their respective social and institutional structures, to the desired 'BHN bliss' without a full-fledged revolution of a socialist type? Could the author provide his view on this transition process?

Dr Kulig said that a subsidiary question must be the dynamic version of BHN strategy. As so far presented, it was essentially distributive. If the strategy was to be superimposed on existing realities, i.e. glaring inequalities, etc., a transition process must necessarily visualise a dynamic orientation of BHN implementation starting from the existing state of things. How would these new strategies be implemented by weak governments relying on foreign assistance? Unless these questions could be answered, the whole BHN strategy would simply amount to an instrument for the implementation of a particular pattern of aid from the developed countries.

Dr Desai (India) said that he wished to comment on a number of points arising from the paper by Professor Green.

With reference to Dr Streeten's discussion of Rowntree's study of poverty, it should be noted that in England poverty became a concern only towards the end of the nineteenth century, as in the United States it became a concern only in the 1960s. The eradication of poverty as a social goal had thus been achieved over a much longer span of time than was being envisaged now. We were compressing the time span quite drastically in our current urge to meet basic needs in the third world. This was of course because we lived in a much more democratic age.

He agreed with Professor Green that the BHN strategy was technically feasible. Taking the case of India, there was certainly adequate food and clothing *produced* to meet the population's needs, but it was *distributed* badly. Hence political feasibility was a much more difficult question than technical feasibility. The problem arose from the political difficulty of redistributing income. One might say that one should either produce a different vector of goods – eliminating wasteful, luxury goods or the same vector in different proportions. This required a more detailed 'value theory' in terms of how incomes, outputs and prices are decided than was tackled in this paper. In discussing the trade-off between growth and distribution, it had been readily assumed that growth took place in some homogeneous lump called income which was then available for distribution like a pack of playing cards. But growth took place in specific ouputs providing specific jobs at given wage rates. Redistribution could take place only by imposing taxes and subsidies on economic activities and outputs. These fiscal measures had to be voluntarily borne.

This led him to the problem of inequality *among* the poor. He thought that it was not enough to say, for example, that 40 per cent of the population was poor, because even in that group there were levels of poverty. This had been brought out by Professor Amartya Sen's[1] measure of poverty. It should be appreciated that the less poor may resent being taxed to meet the needs of the more poor. There was a conflict here which should not be ignored.

Dr Desai said that the detailed 'value theory' became important because one must make sure not only that goods are produced which are needed, but also that the poor had the incomes to buy them. This would not matter in self-employed families which produced their own output of needed goods, but even here families might not be self-sufficient as well as self-employed. For all practical purposes, incomes were needed to buy the basic goods. Professor Sen[2] had shown in his study of the 1943 Bengal famine, where many died, that the root cause was not so much availability of food as shortage of purchasing power (lack of 'exchange entitlement' as he called it) on the part of people who were outside food-growing activities.

He thought it was necessary to make a distinction between the provision of basic needs and the distribution of income. One might be able to provide for some basic needs, but that would not reduce income inequalities. The

[1] A. K. Sen, 'Poverty: An Ordinal Approach to Measurement', *Econometrica*, 44 (1976).

[2] A. K. Sen, 'Famines, Food Availability and Exchange Entitlement: The Case of the Bengal Famine', *Cambridge Journal of Economics*, 1 (1977).

experience of China could be cited here. In urban China, food, clothing and cooking oil were the three rationed goods which everyone had been guaranteed. (Prices of these goods were controlled but people still had to have the requisite income.) This might still leave a lot of earning inequality as between workers in different industries, or as between rural and urban areas, or as between a rich commune and a poor commune. This might not matter very much once basic needs were met, but these were two separate problems.

Dr Desai then raised a point which also concerned the paper by Professor Morecka. Observed income inequality in an economy where everyone was productively and fully employed might be primarily due to differences in family size, especially in the number of dependents, but such inequality was taken care of when the dependents grew up. Much more important was inequality in income where there was low income due either to lack of employment, or to low productivity even when the income earner was employed. This low productivity might be due either to lack of skills on the part of the worker, or to lack of complementary inputs in the enterprise or in the region where he/she was working.

A subsidiary point related to the reduction in family size. He said that Dr Streeten had rightly pointed out that people desire a large family size as insurance for old age or for periods of ill-health. This had the implication that a large family privatised the costs of care of the ill and aged. Those who urged reduction in family size should realise that this would *increase* the cost of health provision. Thus population reduction could be costly.

Professor Pajestka (Poland) said that the socialist countries could be considered to have pursued a variant of the BHN policy from the very beginning, i.e. the provision of food, housing, health etc. had always been the primary objective and they had never regarded the growth of GDP in itself as an objective. They now had a wealth of evidence about the consequences of such a policy. The main lessons of their experience were:

(1) The concept of needs changed extremely rapidly and the aspirations of all sections of the population grew more rapidly than the economy. This gave rise to acute social and political tension. It was thus necessary to place great emphasis on the socially conditioned and dynamic nature of basic needs. As soon as one level of needs was met there would be pressure for a still higher level and this was one of the engines of progress.

(2) A policy of full employment was very important but also raised great difficulties. For the sake of maintaining full employment Poland had introduced widespread subsidies, and this had destroyed the effect of th profitability principle and lowered efficiency. It also affected the distribution of income and had had major political consequences in 1956. In addition the high level of subsidies had implications for price relativities.

In the long run Professor Pajestka thought that the BHN policy as followed in Poland had had both positive and negative effects, and he regarded the possible conflict between economic efficiency and the egalitarian principle inherent in the BNH approach as the crucial issue. This was a matter which required constant reappraisal and there was no one sacrosanct rule.

Professor Malinvaud (France) said that Professor Green had stated in his conclusions that 'fairly wide degrees of freedom' existed in influencing income distribution. He could not agree with this statement if it was intended to apply to a *given social structure* (which specified in particular the structure of power and the distribution of property rights). Professor Green relied in particular on Sraffa's model: but it was quite clear that this was not a complete model of existing economies. Recent experience showed that reshaping the income distribution without changing the social structure was very hard indeed. However, this latter conclusion did not mean that he disagreed with the general tone of Green's paper.

Professor Malinvaud thought that once the importance of the social structure for the discussion of distribution was realised, it would be necessary for economic theory to consider this aspect of the question much more systematically than it had so far done. A much greater variety of social structures should be rigorously studied and their economic implications characterised. The *Journal of Comparative Economics* might be said to have been launched in order to fulfil this need, and he hoped that it would be successful.

He said that, as usual, the progress of economic theory should rely on both empirical or inductive studies and abstract reasoning. He had little to say here on the first type, except to voice a warning about the need for a very careful scrutiny of the statistical base used. (Being a statistician he knew a lot about the weakness of statistics, even in developed countries, and about the frequent lack of international comparability, particularly for income concentration.)

As for abstract reasoning, he saw signs that important progress might be forthcoming. A few theoreticians (e.g. Vanek and Weitzman) had started studying unconventional social structures in a way that seemed to be promising and should stimulate a new trend of research. It is noteworthy that this theoretical work fruitfully used the notion of general equilibrium, as distinct of course from competitive general equilibrium of a private ownership economy.

Finally Professor Malinvaud referred to the paper by Professors Herer and Sadowski. He said that they approached the difficult and important question of the relationship between efficiency and distributional equity. They insisted on the large import content of the consumption of lower income groups, hence on the obstacle to growth that a strong redistribution could imply. He wished to mention another relationship that has been extensively studied (notably by Atkinson) namely the fact that high taxation of the most able people might lead them to restrain their efforts, so that society did not reap the full fruits of their abilities.

Professor Seers (UK) pointed out that, as Professor Green's paper showed, the concept of 'basic human needs' (originally devised by Rowntree a century ago) provided a useful yardstick for assessing development policies and trends. A development strategy that left a large fraction of the population with unsatisfied needs for food and drinking water could hardly be considered a success. He was, however, against widening the concept to cover adult education, equality, participation, etc. which diluted priorities. There was, anyway, a potential conflict between popular participation and the technocratic listing of basic needs: people might well give a high weight to television sets and public order. To follow Dr Streeten's point, Rowntree had shown that fewer families were in 'primary' poverty, because their income was inadequate, than in 'secondary' poverty, because they 'misspent' it, from a technocratic point of view. Moreover, there could well be maldistribution within the family (an area to which practically no attention had been paid). Some family members, especially children, *did* need state intervention to save them from poverty: yet excessive intervention could be dangerous, not least because it implied the doctrine of 'false consciousness' – that bureaucrats knew the interests of people better than people themselves. The optimal balance depended on the country concerned. For many countries, the main state intervention, apart from the provision of 'public goods' such as water and education, should be to deliver milk and other necessities directly to children, leaving to wage and fiscal policy the task of providing people with enough income to satisfy their own basic needs as they saw them.

Professor Seers said that he agreed with the interjection by Dr Streeten at this point, that the State should also try to counterbalance forces such as advertising that shaped people's perception of their needs.

Dr Simonyan (USSR) said that in his view the BHN approach was very interesting, but was outside the sphere of economic theory. As he saw it the real problem was that of the distribution of income, and that could not be changed without a prior transformation of a country's social structure and the underlying property relations. He referred to Dr Desai's example of countries where total output was adequate to provide for everyone's basic needs but which failed to achieve this because of the existing social structure and consequent maldistribution of income. The history of his own country (Armenia) and of certain other republics within the USSR was an example of the opposite case, showing how the problems of redistribution could be solved.

Professor Urquidi (Mexico) said that in his opinion the question of basic needs must be seen in its overall context, and not as an approach that could be followed anywhere. The existing economic structure, especially the industrial base, was a limiting factor. An idyllic rural society could not be created where there was already considerable industrial development. It was not possible to go back to primitive technology as a general approach – the transistor radio and even TV had penetrated the rural areas of many countries, including China, and the growth in communications made it inevitable that new aspirations, requiring industrial technology, should emerge. There were also social and cultural factors to be taken into account which were peculiar to certain countries or to regions within them. Many countries were forced to assign priority to non-economic needs, e.g. defence. It would therefore be useful to distinguish the basic needs approach as between countries in different stages of development. The population growth pattern was also important, because excessive human fertility in rural areas led to migration and to the necessity of industrial employment. It was a different matter to meet the need for absolute essentials – e.g. water and drainage, health, education and housing – but this did not necessarily imply the basic needs approach as sketched out by Professor Green, although there was much merit in it. A further point was that the cost of a basic needs policy should be shown explicitly, since it involved subsidisation on a large scale.

Mr Kaser (UK) said that his comments related to the paper by Professors Herer and Sadowski, and to their discussion of the effects of wage differentiation. He thought that the experience of the socialist countries should be examined, as Professor Pajestka had done. In the 1930s the USSR had combined extremely rapid growth with income differentiation in a policy made explicit by Stalin's denunciation of egalitarianism. Similar policies had initially been followed in Eastern Europe after the Second World War (though as Herer and Sadowski had noted, there had been a marked levelling of income in Poland) but this had given way to a more equal distribution of income. One important aspect of this was that agricultural incomes had been brought much closer to those of non-farm workers: Mr Kaser thought that the relative level in the USSR had risen from about two-thirds to virtual equality. The one exception was Hungary which had in recent years experienced a widening of income disparities and was also the socialist country with the best growth rate relative to planned targets.

Professor Porwit (Poland) said that he wished to draw attention to certain aspects linking the field of rationality discussed earlier with that of income distribution and consumption patterns. In that context, he thought one should support the approach expressed by Dr Desai, i.e. an emphasis on rationality from the viewpoint of the whole system and its components as well as on the interrelations between these viewpoints. In comparison with the notions of macro and micro rationality this was not only a change in names, but an essential difference in the substance of meanings attributed to such notions. A system's behaviour could not be conceived except through the actions and interactions of its components. Similarly, the manner in which components behaved, the conditions for their rationality, depended heavily on the patterns and structures of the whole system's behaviour. Consequently one could not think about 'macro' notions of rationality as replacing those of 'microrationality' and diminishing the importance of the latter.

If we assumed a system-component approach then a basic question arose: in what manner did the viewpoints of the system and of its components mutually influence each other in the sense of perception of aims and constraints, formation of evaluation criteria, etc? In this sense the problems of income distribution (as well as of availability and distribution of 'benefits in kind') should be considered as important aspects in shaping the relations between the system and the components and, also, in the context of the notions of their respective rationalities. From the viewpoint of the whole system one might then look on such problems as relevant for creating motivations and attitudes of the components, which in turn would be either promoting or conflicting with the endeavours of the whole system to behave more rationally (i.e. also purposefully and efficiently).

Professor Porwit said that in this regard he would not support the views expressed concerning the inevitable controversy between equality and efficiency, and that he would prefer the approach taken by Professor Morecka in comparison with that chosen by Professors Herer and Sadowski. What was important in that respect pertained to the manifold ways in which components of the system were informed about the distribution of benefits and grasped a better understanding of links between their performance, the performance of the whole system, and the manner in which the outcomes were utilised. This involved such issues as the enrichment of analytical tools in terms of various socio-economic indicators; and more emphasis on teleological premises for choice at the levels of system's components, which must be based on corresponding *ex ante* calculations. To conclude, he emphasised those distributional aspects which were related to a process through which wider societal aims might be 'internalised' within the sets of aims of particular componentsof the system. Professor Porwit considered this an area where future research and more progress in theoretical conclusions was desirable.

Professor Morecka (Poland) said that she had found the paper by Professor Herer and Dr Sadowski very interesting, but there were some arguments with which she could not agree. Firstly, she thought their analysis of the impact of income differentials on the growth of consumption was one-sided since it was concerned only with the productivity of the means of production, and neglected the influence of income distribution on the productivity of labour. This was a much more complex factor than the authors suggested.

Secondly, she doubted whether it was possible to relate wage differences directly to the pattern of consumption. In practice what counted was the impact of changes in the distribution of income per person, not per wage-earner, and demographic factors could have a substantial impact on this, as had been the case in Poland. She would also want to give more weight to the level of income, rather than to its distribution, when considering the determinants of consumption.

Finally, Professor Morecka said that one got a very pessimistic picture of the possibility of solving the problem of consumption growth. If incomes were low, they pressed the raw materials equilibrium; if they were high, there was disequilibrium in export-import relations. She thought that more attention should be paid to the active shaping of consumption patterns (economising on raw materials and imported goods), thus permitting the growth of the consumption fund.

Dr Osiatynski (Poland) said that he would like to comment on the paper by Professor Herer and Dr Sadowski. He did not see any contradiction between their argument and the 'shift of emphasis from efficiency to equity', which was the theme of the present session. Herer and Sadowski measured efficiency in terms of consumption goods output which, in turn, determined the possibilities of reductions in income differentials. The trade-off they discussed was not between some abstract efficiency and equity; and the authors did not suggest that equity should be sacrificed for the sake of increased efficiency. Rather, they showed there was some trade-off between the composition of the wage-goods basket and the possibilities of reducing income differentials. They did not say that because such a trade-off existed one should not go for equity in income distribution. On the contrary, they were clearly for it, and in this they were in full agreement with Professor Morecka. Within the fairly narrow limits of their analysis, they showed that increasing equity in income distribution might involve costs, and asked what that cost was. He thought this was a legitimate question to ask.

Dr Osiatynski said that a further conclusion which could be drawn from the paper was that the possibilities of reducing wage differentials were the greater, the closer the composition of the wage-goods basket was to one which could be satisfied largely from local resources; i.e. broadly speaking, the smaller the demonstration effect of foreign consumption patterns. It was thus obvious that once the public could be persuaded to follow consumption patterns which involved relatively lower raw materials and/or import requirements than otherwise would be the case, this would result in a greater output of consumer goods and better chances of equitable income distribution.

He next wished to draw attention to an interesting relationship between this paper and some of the observations made in the previous session by Professors Seers and Pajestka. Professor Seers rightly noticed that the developing countries should import not so much the most sophisticated technologies but rather those which best suited their specific needs and local conditions. He also gave some illuminating examples of the causes for what may be called a 'technological demonstration effect'. Dr Osiatynski said that it was clear that the smaller both the 'consumption pattern demonstration effect' and the 'technological demonstration effect' were, the better were the chances of development *and* equity.

Professor Pajestka had discussed the feedback between economic efficiency and the pattern of objectives, and in this context he had postulated that the study of social and economic objectives should be included in the domain of political economy. Certainly, economic efficiency was a decreasing function of a discrepancy between the set of objectives desired by the people and the one which was actually pursued. If consistency in people's wants was assumed, then from Pajestka's argument it followed that the higher the participation ratio of the broad masses of population in formulating the pattern of social and economic goals, the better the economic performance of the country in question. He was thus brought back to the argument of Herer and Sadowski. For if the broad mass of the population could be persuaded to accept such a pattern of objectives, including, *inter alia*, objectives concerning the pattern of consumption which met the postulates of Herer and Sadowski's paper, and if these objectives could be achieved in accordance with the postulates mentioned by Seers, then not only economic equity but also economic efficiency goals could be achieved more successfully than in the absence of such acceptance.

Professor Morecka said in her reply that she had wished to show the need for *integrated* socio-economic goals and had taken the issue of social equality to illustrate this thesis. She had been interested in Mr Kaser's comments on wage differentiation and economic growth in the socialist countries. The position in Poland was that they had had a stable wage distribution for the past twenty years: the ratio of the average wage of the top decile to that of the bottom decile had been constant at about five. In her opinion, the distribution of wages could adversely affect the rate of growth as mentioned by Mr Kaser. However, this would be the result not of an egalitarian distribution but rather of one which was not appropriate for the specific conditions of the given labour force.

In his reply to the discussion, *Professor Green* said that he accepted that BHN was primarily a political economy concept, but most good economic theory had arisen out of political/economic debate and had been designed – implicitly or explicitly – to advance the cause of a party to the political economic confrontation underlying the debate. He saw no reason to treat a political/economic conceptualisation as irrelevant to (or not subject to criticism in terms of) theory.

He thought the question of participation was central to BHN both as a means and as an end. As an end it was justified by a view of the nature of human beings – a view related to rejection of alienation as an acceptable state. As a means, participation (in production and in decision-making) was critical to power to maintain the strategy. BHN was a conflict- – not consensus- – based approach, and could hardly be supposed feasible beyond initial reformist steps unless the beneficiaries had power based on their roles in production and decision-taking.

A pseudo-BHN strategy without either fully productive and fairly remunerated employment or mass participation in decision-taking was possible so long and so far as dominant classes saw them as serving their interests. But that was just as political as BHN.

He saw BHN in conceptualisation, and still more in application, as tied to *objective correlatives* and to ones intelligible to decision-takers (including workers and peasants). This was one of its strengths in political-economic terms as opposed to more abstract (e.g. redistribution with growth) or somewhat confusingly aggregated (quality of life) formulations. In this he agreed with Dr Streeten. However, it also raised a danger of descent into mindless, directionless marginal reformism. The individual targets (e.g. pure water or land reform, or the technological choice for a given plant) needed to be seen within, and tested against, the broader BHN frame of reference. In this he agreed with Professor Seers.

Professor Green said that he did not regard BHN as an attack on *growth per se*. As Professor Porwit pointed out, there was no general trade-off between equity efficiency and output efficiency – the requirement was to avoid creating contexts in which there was such a trade-off. What BHN denied was the legitimacy of growth/accumulation as overriding ends, not their frequent validity or even necessity as means. No basic need, however non-material or non-marketed its embodiment, was likely to be attainable without use of real resources – and by no means all would either automatically release new productive forces equal to those demanded, or be attainable by redistribution of existing productive forces.

He agreed that the 'who addressed?' question was relevant. However, the answer related to the context. It might be dominant decision-takers (say in the Namibian liberation movement) or a faction in an existing decision-taking coalition (say in Venezuela) or intellectual/technocratic individuals and clusters (say in Tanzania or, under quite different conditions, the Philippines) who might put BHN to use within an existing macro context as a means to systematic change.

In other contexts (and perhaps at least one of the countries cited) the basic audience was presumptively those who sought to change the system root and branch, and might wish to consider both articulation of why such change was necessary and, more relevant to BHN, a conceptual framework for organising change after armed struggle. BHN in many national contexts was revolutionary in its message.

Professor Green said that he accepted what Professor Malinvaud had said about the *degrees of freedom* in respect to distribution, accumulation and price determination possibly being quite limited in any actual context. He agreed with Malinvaud's interpretation of these limits as imposed by social and power structures. His point in the paper was not to deny this, but to argue that theoretically and empirically (looking at a range of different social and power contexts) there was little evidence to support technical or efficiency determinism of a type limiting feasible decisions to a narrow range. That was consistent with a wide range of practicable choices so far as economic theory and productive efficiency went, with actual contextual decisions being individually limited by social, power, productive submode constraints and with the actual decisions being sharply divergent from each other because the contextual constraints also diverged sharply.

Professor Green said that he could not accept interpretations of BHN which saw it as centred on *redistribution* defined as *transfer payments*, with the dominant form being that of consumption subsidisation. BHN as a conceptual frame stressed the impossibility of dividing the processes (relations) of production and distribution. Therefore it had an inherent distrust of personal consumption transfers as a central means because they did not alter production, power or participation relations. The one redistribution regularly appearing in BHN strategic formulations was land reform – a production redistribution – and the types of land reform posited were draconic (Japan of 1945 or China of the People's Republic) not marginal or partial (e.g. India or Egypt).

Professor Green said that he regarded the *absolute/relative* issue as critical. BHN had stressed relative and not merely absolute needs. BHN advocates would see absolute poverty eradication as a critical first step but not as an arrival.

PART FOUR
The New International Economic Order

8 Some Aspects of the New International Economic Order and the Developing Countries

J. F. Rweyemamu
UNIVERSITY OF DAR ES SALAAM

I GROWTH AND TRADE UNDER THE OLD ORDER

The Bretton Woods order was conceived during a world war that followed a world depression. It was also conceived when the majority of the developing countries were colonies who could therefore not participate in the formulation of that order. The architects of the Bretton Woods order wanted to ensure that the post-war period was freed from worldwide depressions and was geared towards economic expansion. There is little doubt that the last thirty years have been years of prosperity unparalleled in history. Between 1948–75 growth of world output was 5 per cent per annum, contributed by increases in population and productivity at 2 per cent and 3 per cent respectively. World trade in the same period grew at 7 per cent per annum. In order to appreciate the unprecedented nature of this growth, it is useful to contrast it with the growth record in the period preceding post-war expansion, 1913–48. During this period world output grew at 2 per cent per annum, contributed equally by increases in population and productivity while world trade increased at 1/2 per cent per annum.

Two features of this growth record, however, are worthy of note. First is the dismal record of the low-income developing countries during this period. The least developed among them grew by less than 1 per cent per annum. Secondly, the post-war expansion was accompanied by greater interdependence of the world economy, an interdependence that brought new challenges to economic policy-makers in the industrialised countries. As interdependence must be accompanied by the necessary discipline, and this was not well appreciated by the decision-makers, or perhaps more accurately the balance of power changed, the gains of the unprecedented post-war expansion were gradually eroded, beginning in the late 1960s, culminating in the stagflation, international monetary crisis and growing unemployment.

This brief paper will endeavour, though briefly, to examine the sources of this growth, paying particular attention to the factors underlying the meagre share of the developing countries in the benefits of the post-war expansion and the causes of the current recession in the industrialised countries. These latter issues are examined together because of the belief that they are interrelated.

Much has been written on the sources of post-war growth. I do not intend to review this familiar literature. Briefly, the post-war gains are largely a result of the Bretton Woods *order* – i.e. a framework of laws, conventions, regulations and *mores* that establish the setting of the system and the understanding of the environment by the participants in it. The Bretton Woods institutions provided an environment in which countries could pursue the mutual gains that trade offers. Technical progress embodied in greater specialisation and international division of labour increased the attractiveness of these relations. The GATT and IMF, in particular, were instrumental in smoothing out the chaos of the interwar years by introducing rules delineating permissible monetary and trade behaviour by creating a framework for the progressive reduction of tariff barriers and by stressing the principles of non-discrimination. These combined to create a degree of security and predictability in world markets that was unknown in the pre-war period and made possible the long-run commitment of funds to outward-looking investment.

II THE IMPACT OF THE OLD ORDER ON THE DEVELOPING COUNTRIES

In assessing the growth impact of the old order on the developing countries, it is needless to mention that the institutions created by the Bretton Woods order were primarily concerned with the interests of the industrialised countries. It would indeed be an extraordinary world if the asymmetries in military and political power were not reflected in asymmetries in economic relations. The International Trade Organisation (ITO) that might have regulated the world markets of primary commodities was not even set up. And yet the economic profession continued to preach the 'inviolability of the market forces' doctrine as if these mechanisms arose spontaneously and inevitably out of economic necessity. It failed to appreciate that markets were creatures of social and political systems. It is these systems that decide which markets should operate and how, which markets are encouraged and which are suppressed. Furthermore, the belief that free market conditions were the rule rather than the exception in commodity markets has hindered further progress in resolving the commodity problem in international negotiations. In the case of commodities of interest to developing countries, for example, most of the markets are either closed (bauxite, phosphates, iron ore, bananas) or have oligopolistic buyers (coffee, oilseeds, tobacco, cocoa, tea) or are otherwise controlled (sugar, beef, cereals). Moreover, these markets are such that supply and demand change constantly, often in unexpected ways. This does suggest that the search for the long-run 'equilibrium price' of these commodities is a will-of-the-wisp. For an equilibrium price that shifts every time there is a change in the assumptions on which it is based, cannot by definition be a 'long-run' equilibrium one.

The point of the above discussion is not to argue that economists should not be concerned with long-run equilibrium prices, or perfect competitive markets or elasticities. Rather, it is to point out that such agile exercises should not be performed outside the politico-social context in which the functioning of markets takes place. It is not, for example, the attributes of third world commodities as reflected in their price and income elasticities which account for the wide fluctuations and deteriorating terms of trade. Nor have these factors been critical determinants of which commodities have entered into international commodity agreements. Indeed, what evidence there is suggests that except for non-renewable commodities, especially oil, it is the attributes of the selling country rather than the attributes of the product, that are a crucial determinant of price. If one trading partner produces and trades in a *basic* good in the Sraffa sense, i.e. a commodity which either directly or indirectly is used in the production of *all* commodities in the economic system – while the other is unable to produce it, the former will obviously have the possibility of turning the terms of trade in his favour as he wishes. Nor is there any doubt that where a competitive commodity production regime with little market staying power is pitted against a financially strong oligopolistic buying regime with considerable possibilities of stock manipulation, wide fluctuations and deteriorating terms of trade cannot be avoided.

The foregoing discussion suggests that the nature of the productive structure of an economic system bears significantly on its trade gains. An economy without an endogenous wherewithal to reproduce itself is likely to be forced to sell on a falling market. Such a likelihood is even greater if it also lacks financial infrastructure to support its stocks in such periods. One of the theoretical implications of these observations is that a Walrasian equilibrium model is an inappropriate tool in analysing the problems of less developed countries. A theoretical model that assumes that coca cola is as important as machine tools in the evolution of an economic system must rest squarely on a fundamental misunderstanding of stocks and flows. This underscores the valuable work of Janos Kornai's *Anti-Equilibrium*. A second consequence is the need to appreciate the key role played by basic industries as defined by Sraffa in his 'Production of Commodities by Means of Commodities'. Some of these commodities resemble Ricardian 'corn' in that they are capable of producing other commodities and also themselves (e.g. engineering industries). The set of such goods in an industrial regime can be observed in a triangularised (capital) input-output matrix.

When one examines the workings of the international monetary system one is struck by the 'benign neglect' of the interests of the less developed countries. The US delegation at the Bretton Woods prevented the Articles of Agreement from making any distinction between developed and developing countries. Moreover, in 1946, the Executive Directors of the IMF provided an interpretation of the Articles of Agreement which viewed the IMF's purpose as that of giving 'temporary assistance in financing balance of payments deficits on current account for monetary stabilization operations'. Economic development was viewed as being purely incidental, and indeed the IMF actively sought assurances that such assistance as was given was to be used only for short-term stabilisation and not for reconstruction or development. In most of the debates of the 1960s that called for a reform of the international monetary system, the specific interests of the less developed countries were not so much ignored as regarded as irrelevant. For it was thought self-evident that the economic development and the trading prospects of the LDCs depended on the efficient functioning of the international monetary system which was determined by the policies and practices of the major industrial countries.

An evaluation of the Bretton Woods order must examine some of the implications of the above factors. A financial system was created that conferred seigniorage advantages to the reserve currency countries. In such a system the non-reserve currency countries extend credit to the reserve currency-issuing countries. Trade between a less developed country and a country issuing reserve currencies cannot therefore be based on 'equal exchange' as the latter need only issue IOUs for real goods. In addition, this type of seigniorage has conferred on those countries the ability to increase their international investments by the cumulative deficits in their balance of payments. It is therefore no surprise that no special international institutions were created to deal with long-term financing other than IBRD. And the rules of the IMF refer specifically to short-term liquidity only. Between 1948 and 1970, the US foreign assets increased from US$29.4 billion to US$166.6 billion. And of the total growth of world monetary reserves over the years 1970–76 (144 billion SDRs) less than 5 per cent has been invested in the less developed countries.

It is needless to mention that such an international financial system would have detrimental effects on the growth prospects of the less developed countries. Only recently, with the adjustment of the Bretton Woods order to accommodate the requirements of transnational corporations for increased, unsupervised liquidity, have some of the more developed countries taken advantage of private capital. For the majority of the poor countries, their dependence on the IMF has continued. It is indeed one of the asymmetries of international economic life that even the short-term IMF funds are tied to 'conditions' geared to maintain 'price stability' when the commodity prices of the developing countries remain unstable and their imports exhibit a rising price trend. It is a confirmation of the present power relations that although the broad characteristics of the developing countries are such as to impose greater adjustment burdens than would be the case in the more broadly based economies, this factor has not been taken into serious account in allocating liquidity to the developing countries.

III THE REQUIREMENTS OF A NEW INTERNATIONAL ECONOMIC ORDER

If the developing countries are demanding a new international economic order it is because they feel that the old one has not only been inefficient (as far as their interests are concerned), but grossly inequitable as well. They look towards an order that will ensure an equitable distribution of resources and power and an equal sovereignty. In such a search it would be helpful if the economic profession was to be a little more enlightened. Received economic doctrine has been particularly weak in its treatment of distribution issues. It may be impertinent to expect it to treat equity problems in a more adequate fashion. Yet the fact that this conference is being held perhaps heralds a watershed of great significance. In this context it is appropriate to suggest that we seek for at least a new basis for international exchange, i.e. one which implies a guaranteeing of financial sovereignty through the denationalisation of 'international' currency and the establishment of equitable trade on the basis of exchange of real value for real value. Such a scheme might require a necessary 'tidying up' of the old order in the form of a new Marshall Plan.

Let me also add that the developing countries look towards a new order because the old order is no longer appropriate even to those it was tilted to favour. As pointed out earlier the post-war growth was accompanied by a greater interdependence and hence a reduction of security or sovereignty for every participant in the system. As is well known, a high level of prosperity based on specialisation and exchange imposes a discipline which reduces each country's autonomy to pursue its own particular goals and policies. The constraints of national sovereignty, especially since the balance of power has gradually changed, make it impossible to deal effectively with problems which are essentially international. It is these difficulties of sustaining interdependence – an interdependence which plays a double role of both encouraging and confining the freedom of countries to act independently – which have resulted in disputes among the industrial countries between those in deficit and those in surplus regarding responsibility for balance of payments, deliberate exploitation by dominant currency countries to defray their current government expenditure abroad (as reflected in the doubling of world reserves between the end of 1969 and the end of 1972), etc. There is little doubt that such difficulties are at the heart of the current crisis. The developing countries are concerned about these trends as they prefer a growing demand for their goods, a less protective sentiment and a less cartelised front from the industrial countries.

9 Some Thoughts on International Economics and Problems of the New International Economic Order

Marian Paszyński
RESEARCH INSTITUTE FOR INTERNATIONAL MARKETS AND PRICES, WARSAW

I INTRODUCTION

The quest for a change in the structure of international economic relations stems from the reaction to the crisis of the 'old economic order', the main framework of which had been established as a result of the change in the power relations in the world that had been in evidence since the First and, especially, the Second World War. There are many causes of the said crisis but two among them are of particular importance: one, the growing contradiction between the internationalisation of the productive forces in the world embodied in the expansion of the transnational corporation, (TNC) and the national basis of the rules of the game in the 'old economic order'; second, the unevenness of the development process and growing disparities between countries predominantly in the industrialised world, including the emergence of the two groups of countries (developing and socialist) dissatisfied with the old rules of the game, either because they suited the interests of the already established economic powers, or because they fitted into the mode of operation of the capitalist economy and did not recognise the modalities of operation of the socialist one.

It would follow, that all groups of countries, albeit not to the same extent, are interested in the change of the 'old order' and in the building of a new one. The most comprehensive vision of such a 'New International Economic Order' (NIEO) has been put forward, however, only by developing nations.[1] We will therefore concentrate discussion in this paper

[1] Socialist countries established a new type of international economic relation only on a regional basis. They have not advocated its extension to the world as a whole though, obviously, it could constitute an inspiration for any attempt at reorganising the existing economic order or, at least, some of its facets. Socialist economic thought has always been centred upon the process of development of national economies and has devoted less attention to international relations.

upon the NIEO concept as presented by developing countries, though we recognise that any successful programme for restructuring international economic relations must be based upon recognition of the interests of all groups of countries, and must be aimed at remedying the underlying causes of the crisis of the 'old order' in a comprehensive way.

In considering NIEO we are bound to determine the exact framework for our discussion. It should be borne in mind that the concept of NIEO has not been founded upon a previously elaborated theoretical basis. Even now, international economics has not constructed a comprehensive theoretical system upon which the NIEO programme could well be based. The theoretical considerations related to NIEO are being undertaken *pari passu* with the practical efforts directed at its implementation. Even irrespective of these circumstances it would be proper to consider NIEO as a programme put forward by the governments of developing countries, this being our legitimate reference point. As we shall point out later on, the NIEO concept represents an attempt to change the international economic power structure, and should accordingly be regarded as the programme of the real actors in the international economic scene, not that of the economic thinkers. We should at the same time bear in mind that the postulates presented under the NIEO framework reflect the interests of the ruling élites of developing countries and only to a very limited extent express the aspirations of the working masses or the societies in these countries.[1]

We shall, therefore, try in this paper to analyse the gist of the NIEO programme as formulated by developing countries, and its relation to international economics. The task will not be an easy one, as it seems that international economics does not sufficiently explain the balance of power relations in the world economy; and it is even more inadequate in devising ways and means to alter the balance in question. There is a backward linkage between economic operation in the national and international spheres and, therefore, international economics alone cannot in many cases find an explanation for changes in international relations that are determined principally by national factors. It does not constitute an independent branch of general economic theory but, like foreign trade in a national economy, forms its subordinated element. Some NIEO issues relate not simply to international economics but also to development economics.

It is evident that a short paper cannot deal with all aspects of this vast issue. It will focus attention on certain problems only, and even these will not be discussed in detail.

[1] Sometimes, the stress put on NIEO, directing the brunt of social discontent towards the outside world, serves only to turn attention away from the failures of the domestic development policies. Furthermore, the growth of the TNCs means that some of the NIEO demands (e.g. access to the markets for manufactures from the LDCs) might be found to represent the interests of the TNCs.

II THE BASIC OBJECTIVES OF NIEO

The crux of the NIEO programme amounts to a shift in the position of developing countries in the world economy, and a concomitant alteration in the balance of world economic power. The NIEO concept of developing countries appears to be based upon four basic premises. First, that the sources of disparities in the levels of development are exogenous in respect of developing countries and that the causes of their retardation are primarily external. Second, that the world is basically divided into two groups of countries: developing and developed ones. Such a dichotomic vision of the world assumes that relations between developing and developed nations represent the main conflict in the contemporary world. Third, that because of an inequality prevailing in international economic relations, the rules of the game of NIEO should also be based on an inequality principle but in a reverse fashion; they should provide for preferential treatment of the weak and for discrimination against the powerful. Fourth, that in view of the existing inequalities a 'new order' should in fact be primarily distributive, leading to transfer of resources from wealthy to poor nations. In its extreme form it would amount to a vision of international economic relations as a zero-sum-game.

To achieve the expected change in the position of developing countries in the world economy, the NIEO programme provides for a multitude of instruments, not always cohesive, and sometimes even mutually conflicting. From the maze of the proposed instruments four can be distinguished which epitomise the whole lot. They may be grouped under two headings, representing the difference in the time-horizon of action.

First, action aimed at achieving results in a relatively short period. Here we may note two objectives and their corresponding instruments. One, the transfer of resources from developed to developing countries. This could be effected either by way of a change in the prices of commodities exported by the latter relative to the manufactures they import; or by simple financial transfers providing for a similar automaticity in the mobilisation of funds (e.g. development tax) and their transmission. Apart from the feasibility of the former mechanism there arises the question of its discriminatory features in respect of exporting countries;[1] as well as the question of its effects on the

[1] To be sufficiently discriminatory price increases for commodities should have been limited to developing country exports, a course of action hardly possible under the present structure of commodity trade. Moreover, general increases in commodity prices cannot be contemplated otherwise than in scarcity conditions. Any forced increase would be costly in terms of stocking requirements. As pointed out by Kaldor, even in the case of an increase in free market commodity prices this might be more than compensated by a change in the administered price of manufactures.

developing commodity importers.[1] Two, the short-term object of a change in the balance of power is also to be obtained through revision of the decision-making process in the international bodies that determine the rules of the game, so that developing countries achieve a decisive influence over the fixing of these rules.

Second, action calculated to bring longer term results and establish a more lasting basis for a change in the power structure. Here, we can point to the demand by developing countries for sovereignty over not only their natural resources, but also the operation of their economies. This would provide real economic (not only political) independence. The change in the position of developing countries in the international division of labour constitutes another demand under this heading. In both cases NIEO calls for international action to bring about the desired results (in the case of the change in international specialisation – aid to industrial development, transfer of technology and access to markets for industrial products from developing countries).

Under the impact of the deep recession in the capitalist world and the shock resulting from the collapse of the commodity boom, the developing countries' outlook on NIEO has undergone a considerable evolution in which short-term considerations play an ever growing role. Instead of orienting itself towards structural change, the evolution of NIEO puts growing stress on cyclical phenomena. Its mechanism limits itself, at present, to counteracting the effects of business cycle swings and to maintenance of the import capacity of the developing countries during the prolonged downward phase of the cycle. That is why the Integrated Programme for Commodities, debt rescheduling and the question of an automatic support for the balance-on-current-account deficit (primarily through a reform of the monetary system) came to the fore in discussions on NIEO.

Before we go further in analysing the relevance of economic theories to NIEO let us stress that NIEO as it has been conceived by developing countries leads to the transmission of development patterns from the already industrialised to the developing countries. Certain economists, especially from developing countries, contest this proposition. They attack the growth concept as a goal for development and counter it with the idea of satisfying the basic needs of the society.[2] Although one recognises the humanistic value of such ideas one cannot refrain from making certain comments in this respect. First, the basic needs concept reflects the distributive aspects of the NIEO formula on two counts. It stresses distribution on the domestic level and – at the same time – coexists with the idea of international distribution of wealth. However, these two are to some extent inconsistent, because the

[1] Developing commodity importers by the very nature of their less diversified economic structures cannot adjust to price changes as easily as developed ones.

[2] For an exposition of this approach see Chapter 7 by R. H. Green, above.

notion of closing the international income gap strongly implies the transmission of development, investment, technology and consumption patterns from the already industrialised to the developing countries. This represents one of the main contradictions of NIEO.

Second, distribution without growth leads to less welfare not more. And while one can agree that focusing attention primarily on growth, as was the case with the early development theories starting with Arthur W. Lewis, has not been justified, neglecting growth as a prerequisite for distribution is likewise wrong. The attack on growth represents a somewhat misplaced criticism. Growth does not by itself bear inequalities. What growth adversaries attack is in fact the social system that is unequal. Kuznets rightly turns our attention to the fact that, whatever its negative aspects, positive consequences of growth prevail in the long run.

Therefore, we cannot base our assessment of NIEO upon idealistic models of 'another' or 'endogenous' development. We must accept the realities of life, and the NIEO aim of 'catching up with the Joneses' implies the import of foreign development patterns. It might even lead to a greater dependence, because the transmission of development patterns overtakes the mastering of means of their implementation in a developing economy. That does not, however, diminish their attractiveness and, unfortunately, neither economic theory, nor the other social sciences have produced sufficiently enticing alternative development or consumption patterns which could counterbalance the existing external ones.

III THE CAUSES OF UNDERDEVELOPMENT

One of the main NIEO premises, namely that concerning exogenous causes of underdevelopment, calls for certain comments. Economic theory has not provided a comprehensive and consistent explanation of the phenomenon of economic retardation, and it probably requires more than the efforts of economists to arrive at a full and convincing interpretation of this phenomenon. Though colonialism without any doubt played an important role in impeding the economic advance of most of the countries of the 'third world', it cannot be taken as the only or even the primordial cause of economic backwardness. We are confronted here with a rather vicious circle of explanation of certain phenomena by their characteristic features (a tautology as such). This applies also to 'dependency' theories which try to define and explain inequalities by their very existence.

A similar approach is represented by ascribing to the concept of international division of labour social characteristics (appropriate to class relations) that transform it into an *independent* instrument of perpetuation of underdevelopment.[1] This may be considered as fetishism, as the present

[1] It calls for a great degree of imagination to decide whether the division of labour between socialist and capitalist countries represents a capitalist or a socialist division of labour.

international division of labour reflects and strengthens the existing unequal relations in the world, but was not the original cause of such a state of affairs. It is utilised by the stronger countries to solidify their superior position, but cannot be taken as the ultimate cause of such a position. If that were so, we might legitimately ask why other countries did not use this very instrument as a tool of their advancement. The deficiency of economic theory in this respect could be attributed rather to its inadequacy in explaining the present pattern of international specialisation and, in particular, the role of socio-economic and political factors. It is obvious that neither Ricardian nor Hecksher–Ohlin nor Keasing theories are sufficient and exhaustive as an explanation of the contemporary form of international specialisation.

That is why the 'interdependence' theories do not reflect the realities of life as well. The collapse of the 'transmission of growth' mechanism,[1] especially in the post-Second World War period, and the existing asymmetry in international economic links, makes the transmission mechanism operate in a reverse manner, with slower growth in the developed countries having more pronounced effects on growth in the developing ones. These negative effects are accentuated by the fact that it is more difficult for a developing economy to adjust to changes in the external environment. The inefficiency of the 'transmission of growth' mechanism in international relations resembles to some extent the weak linkages between the modern and traditional sectors in a dualistic economy with a clear indication of the need for modernisation of the traditional sector. It does not follow from the previous reasoning that the comparative advantage concept, especially in its dynamic form, has no relevance for the economic policies of developing countries. Arghiri Emmanuel's criticism of the Ricardian approach to international specialisation, based upon the unequal exchange theorem, seems to substitute the absolute (if at all measurable) magnitudes for the relative ones, making the two approaches hardly comparable.[2]

While we have pointed out obvious weaknesses in the explanatory power of 'dependency' theories, they nevertheless contain a grain of truth as descriptions. Once the world has been divided into more and less developed countries, the less developed are confronted with an unfavourable, if not totally hostile, external economic environment. The existing rules of the

[1] The concept of transmission of growth from the centre to a periphery (or Nurkse's 'trade as an engine of growth', *Equilibrium and Growth in the World Economy* (1961)) has come under criticism from J.B. Kravis, 'Trade as a Handmaiden of Growth', *Economic Journal* LXXX (1970). It seems, however, that the differences between Kravis and Nurkse are apparent rather than real; the acceleration of growth in the periphery is ascribed by Kravis to the diversification of its exports pattern, not to the expansion of its traditional exports.

[2] A. Emmanuel, *Unequal Exchange* (1972).

game always play into the hands of the stronger. That is why List's theories on protection have gained a new popularity in the context of discussions on NIEO. This reflects the comparative advantage produced by pre-modern trends which now act against the latecomers in the development process. While the existing industrialised countries of the West entered the path of modern economic growth from the vantage point of economic advancement over the rest of the world,[1] the developing ones cannot avail themselves of such an opportunity. They have a different and more difficult starting point for modernisation.[2]

The present obstacles to economic development that result from the existence of inequalities in international relations do not, however, explain the ultimate cause of these inequalities. To stick to a concept that attributes underdevelopment to the action of external environment has two important and dangerous consequences. First, it leads to neglect of the internal forces that are decisive in breaking out of the vicious circle of underdevelopment and – possibly – to a fatalistic attitude towards acceleration of economic advancement. Second, it might increase the dependence of developing countries upon the industrial ones. The underlying concept of NIEO implies precisely this sort of economic policy. If the original causes of underdevelopment are external, it is with the help of external forces that this state of affairs can be changed. And the prime instrument of such a change in the short run, namely the transfer of resources from the industrialised capitalist countries to the developing ones, could serve as means of perpetuating their dependence, and not as an instrument for gaining economic independence.

On the other hand, the idea of 'self-reliant' or 'endogenous' development may, at its extreme, especially in the context of 'dependency' theories, lead to a conviction that economic independence can be gained only by a complete breach with the external environment. The goal of delinking developing countries from the outside world, because participation in international exchanges enables the transfer of foreign patterns of development, is obviously as unproductive as the imitative policies it tries to counteract. Apart from its utopian aspects[3] it might lead to spurious

[1] It could even be claimed that since the British industrial revolution the industrialisation process could not be initiated in any country within the framework of free trade mechanism in international relations.

[2] The thesis that disparities in development levels might stimulate the rate at which the latecomers catch up does not apply to the third world countries as the disparities are now too wide for the thesis to hold.

[3] Satisfaction of nutrition requirements under conditions of population explosion (brought about by assuring one of the basic needs of society for better health and sanitary conditions) will require an industrialisation of agricultural production that would not materialise in isolation from the outside world. Quick improvement in housing conditions will similarly call for industrialisation of the construction sector.

independence at the cost of severely worsening the welfare of the society. The question here is not – as was aptly summarised by Streeten – whether the developing countries benefit or lose from their coexistence with developed ones, but how they can pursue policies that permit them to derive benefits from international economic co-operation without simultaneously exposing themselves to the detrimental effects it might entail.

That brings us back to the causes of backwardness. Though external influence, and in particular colonial domination, exerted a restraining effect on the development prospects of the present-day developing countries, the real and original causes of underdevelopment should be sought in socio-economic, institutional structures that had come into existence in these countries in the historical process of the evolution, and in the political and ideological superstructure of the mode of production that correspondingly evolved. Once the disparities in the levels of development were clearly established, the external environment acted negatively on the development prospects of developing countries. Therefore, the way out of the dilemma lies primarily in changing socio-economic barriers to economic expansion in the developing countries themselves. The change in question will simultaneously allow for partial mitigation of the negative effects on growth stemming from the external environment and will enable developing nations to draw greater benefits from international economic relations.

Strengthening domestic developmental capacities in developing countries might assist them in their drive to restructure international economic relations in such a way that the new rules of the game would favour their domestic development effort. By contrast, the stress on international reform isolated from internal changes might lead to a greater dependence upon the hostile external economic environment.

IV CRITICISM OF THE 'RICH-POOR' VIEW OF THE WORLD

The dichotomic view of the world as divided primarily into poor and rich countries also calls for a critical comment. First, such a view substitutes interstate relations for social or class ones. In this way it objectively camouflages the social and class contradictions which exist in the world, and cannot contribute to the institutional change that is a prerequisite of a successful drive against underdevelopment. It both neglects the existence of internal social contradictions between the working masses and the possessing élites in developing countries, and also disregards the class nature of the state, whether in developing or developed countries. On the other hand, it substitutes a 'poor-rich' relationship for the basic conflict between socialism and capitalism on the international level. It also overlooks the important social contradictions in the developed capitalist countries themselves. Its roots can be traced to the Trotskyist and Maoist theories depicting the developing or newly-emerging nations as a revolutionary village, and the developed countries (which the socialist ones are reckoned to belong to, at least by implication) as a reactionary town, the village taking the role of the new revolutionary proletariat of the world. The accent on external dichotomy, coupled with a distributive approach to NIEO, might even lead to strengthening of the internal maldistribution of welfare[1] in developing countries.

Second, it disregards the diversification within the developing nations, including that relating to the form and intensity of their links. There is a distinct lack of clear classification criteria allowing for the delineation of the developing countries as a group. The level of national product per head of population cannot serve as such a criterion both because certain developing countries are already within the high per-capita-product level or will reach this level in the relatively near future (in the time-span of two to three decades); and, further, because the differentiation within the developing countries is rapidly increasing, the gap between the poorest and the richest expanding threefold in the last twenty-five years. Therefore, the group of developing countries was established on the strength of geopolitical rather than socio-economic criteria. Because of the social and political diversity within the group such criteria are also misleading.

Third, if the differences in per-capita-product are to be regarded as the principal criterion distinguishing the developing countries as a group (on the strength of the income gap concept), it calls for elimination of the gap by income redistribution with all its effects in respect of independent development.

Fourth, a dichotomic view based upon 'dependence' theory also seems to be internally inconsistent because, as was realistically pointed out by Sanjaya Lall, the structure of dependence in the contemporary world is pyramidal rather than dichotomic, the dependency relations existing within both the developing and the developed world.

Therefore, the dichotomic view of the world as divided primarily between rich and poor countries[2] provides neither an appropriate description of

[1] Under certain conditions it might be contended that resource transfers postulated in the framework of a dichotomic vision of the world constitute a reversal of the well-known Marxian thesis on the workers' aristocracy. While in the nineteenth century surplus product extracted from the colonies served to corrupt a certain section of the working class in order to support the existence of the capitalist system, likewise, nowadays, resource transfers (the source of which is nothing other than surplus value generated by the working class in the developed capitalist countries) might be used to support ruling élites in the developing countries in order to preserve the capitalist system internationally.

[2] Once again it should be stressed that we do not question here the existence of the rich and the poor. What we object to is the exclusiveness of this vision of the world and the reduction of the international relations to such a crude simplification.

international economic relations, nor a tool for their restructuring. It does, however, point to the inadequacy of economic theory in working out criteria depicting the state of underdevelopment and measures of the degree of retardation which would allow a clearly defined group of developing countries to be distinguished. In my view these criteria and measures should refer to the concentration of bottlenecks to economic development, to the position of a country in the international division of labour and to the existence of structural deficiency of productive capacities in respect of demand (this is Kalecki's suggestion) rather than to the level of per-capita-product.

V INEQUALITY IN THE INTERNATIONAL DISTRIBUTION OF POWER

The distributive approach to change in the structure of international relations has two aspects, international and national. The latter is connected with the concept of satisfaction of the basic needs of society. We have briefly touched upon this aspect of the question previously. We have also stressed that to set the generation against the distribution of national product does not represent a creative approach to solving the development problems. As far as the basic needs concept is concerned, it could be considered as distributive both internally and externally as long as satisfaction of these needs is linked to the transfer of resources from abroad.

Again, the basic issue of the heterogeneity of the nations of the world, including the developing nations, should be mentioned. Until antagonistic classes or social strata no longer exist, one cannot contemplate the equal spread of welfare effects throughout the society, and the distributive approach to basic needs satisfaction is self-deluding. The same applies to transfer of resources from abroad, the effects of which will not permeate downwards but will only serve to enrich the élites.

As indicated earlier, one of the short-term goals of NIEO is a change in the decision-making process in world economic organisations that could, in turn, assist in altering the rules of the game in international economic relations. Such a change is deemed necessary primarily in view of the fact that the old rules, based upon classical economic theory, consider reciprocity to be the cornerstone of such relations. Reciprocity or, in other words, equal treatment leads in an unequal world to even greater inequality. Return to equality would require unequal treatment in favour of the weaker partners which have less bargaining power.

Inequality in the rules of the game has already been accepted but as an exception (even as an anomaly) to be granted or negotiated on a case-by-case basis. It should be adopted as a principle rather than as an exception on two conditions. One, that it is not coupled with a distributive approach to NIEO, especially with the extreme of that approach personified by a zero-sum-game concept which would result in less welfare for all rather than the elimination of the income gap at a higher level of prosperity. Second, that lack of equality of treatment is restricted to countries in obviously different positions as far as the balance of economic power is concerned.

VI THE INADEQUACIES OF ECONOMIC THEORY

As we have seen, economic theory is unable to explain fully the disparities among nations. It is even more inadequate in showing how this situation might be rectified. It has been already said that what NIEO is all about is the change in the power structure in the international economy that will favour developing countries. Such a change cannot be brought about by goodwill alone. International relations are not governed by philanthropic considerations, and any shift in the balance of forces can be effected only by means of tangible pressure. It seems, however, that NIEO is founded upon a basic contradiction in this respect. It aims at a change in power relationships and at the same time it is conditioned by such a change.

Economic theory cannot assist in resolving this contradiction. In the international domain, it is not in a position to forecast realistically the future of commodity trade. Nurkse and others pointed to the decreasing income-elasticity of demand for commodities. On this basis Prebisch and others developed a theory of secular deterioration in the terms of trade of developing countries. However, they did not anticipate the supply shortages which occurred at the beginning of the 1970s and which helped to underpin and to feed the catastrophic theories of resource exhaustion.[1] The economists did not contribute sufficiently to criticism of the stereotype of developing countries as the principal commodity producers and exporters.[2]

Though the commodity boom of 1973–74 collapsed and the spectre of resource scarcity has somewhat subsided it has been evident that inadequate investment in resource extraction could lead to supply shortages, at least temporarily in the future. And economic theory has not solved the problem of resource pricing that takes into account long-term supply considerations as against short-term market equilibrium pricing. The market mechanism is devised to deal with problems of short-term equilibrium, and must be assisted by outside regulation to solve the long-term problem.

Economic theory, likewise, has not dealt sufficiently with the other side of developed countries' interest in maintaining economic relations with developing ones, namely the problem of foreign markets as a condition for

[1] These theories transposed the Ricardian law of the diminishing returns to land to exhaustible resources. In a similar way they did not recognise the potential counteraction of technical progress (in respect of consumption as well as production) that might reverse the impact of the operation of the law.

[2] Similarly to the decrease in the percentage share of commodities (other than fuels) in world exports in the post-war period (1955–76), the share of developing countries in commodity exports (other than fuels) also declined substantially.

the operation of the capitalist economy. Rosa Luxemburg, as is well known, pointed to the expansion within the pre-capitalist environment (especially by the way of domination over colonial markets) as a condition for capitalist extended reproduction. The government interventionism and militarisation of capitalist economies, as well as the growth of trade in manufactures between the developed capitalist countries pushed aside for the time being the prospects of a collapse of the capitalist reproduction process. But the prolonged economic recession and the apparent impotence of the traditional instruments of government economic regulation to solve the problem of stagflation once again turned attention to the significance of outside markets. If the growing importance of developing countries as outlets for realisation of capitalist production could be substantiated by economic theory, these countries would gain an argument in their quest for NIEO which would probably be of greater value than commodity power.[1]

A new international economic order without a new domestic economic order will inescapably lead, as has already been pointed out, to more inequality in developing countries. However, a new domestic economic order is also called for as a prerequisite of strengthening the capacity of developing countries to exert pressure in their drive for restructuring international economic relations in such a way as to make the external environment more conducive to economic development, or to allow developing countries to benefit rather than suffer from international economic co-operation. The traditional approach of development economics founded upon the market-based resource-allocation principle does not serve the purpose well enough, especially when treated in the international context. A market-based allocation process accentuates internal and external inequalities. We have stressed earlier that developing countries are faced with a more difficult road towards modernisation precisely because of the existence of a more economically advanced environment. The flourishing theories of effective protection and the proposed methods of project appraisal (Little–Mirrlees) that in fact introduce an element of absolute, not comparative, advantage,[2] would make the industrialisation of developing countries in most cases unattainable. In fact, after the British industrial revolution export-based industrial expansion by any country would have been possible only in exceptional circumstances. Socialist experience of planned resource allocation and centralised mobilisation and disposition of economic surplus could be of advantage to developing countries in their drive for acceleration of economic development.

Traditional development economics, utilising somewhat abstract models

[1] Recent discussions on the need for a new Marshall Plan for the developing countries lend support to this sort of reasoning.

[2] Due to the fact that calculations of levels of protection are based upon the so-called international prices, reflecting price structure prevailing in developed countries.

of investment-growth relations, paid insufficient attention to bottlenecks in economic development. The essence of the contemporary development process boils down to overcoming such bottlenecks, and an important part of development economics should be the economics of bottlenecks. Therefore, it is material balances or input/output analysis rather than econometric models that are best suited to development economics.

It obviously follows from the above that the quest for NIEO must bear relation not only to international economics but to the economic theory as a whole, and in particular to development economics.

VII CONCLUSIONS: NIEO AND ECONOMIC THEORY

The following conclusions could be drawn from the preceding arguments. First, that the quest for NIEO has not been preceded by economic studies and its 'philosophy' is being elaborated simultaneously with the practical efforts aimed at its implementation. That might have contributed to the internal inconsistency of the NIEO programme as conceived by the developing countries.

Second, economic theory has not been successful in substantiating NIEO. It could not consistently explain the causes of the existing inequalities in international relations, especially the internal socio-economic and institutional roots of underdevelopment. It shows severe weaknesses also in formulating economic premises for a successful restructuring of international economic relations. Some economists analyse NIEO from the point of view of a moral imperative rather than the balance of economic forces, but the former approach is far from realistic.

Third, economic thought has not linked together in an explicit way the need for a parallel change in internal and external economic orders, without which NIEO would not be justifiable or even attainable. NIEO cannot be linked only to international economics, but should also be related to general economic theory and, in particular, to development economics.

Fourth, economic theories which were formulated in the context of an economic mechanism substantially different from that operating in a developing country[1] cannot be regarded as best suited for analysis of the problems of developing economies, nor able to serve as a guideline for policy recommendations.

Fifth, economists do not discuss NIEO in terms of the need for an overall change in the structure of international economic relations. Under the influence of developing countries they tend to concentrate upon the view of NIEO that has been conceived by the developing nations. However, an isolated NIEO, i.e. a restructuring of international economic relations in the

[1] Especially in respect of the structural deficiency of productive capacities in relation to demand in developing countries as distinct from the structural excess capacities in developed capitalist countries.

interests of the developing countries alone is not feasible even if it were justified, which it is not. To solve the great contemporary world problems a more profound approach to the establishment of a new system of regulation of the international economy is required. Some form of economic interventionism on a global scale must be devised as a cornerstone of a comprehensive NIEO. A spontaneous change, which is also possible, would probably be more costly and would not allow for avoidance of unnecessary tensions and crises. Spontaneous change might also lead to further regionalisation of international relations, which would not be advantageous for all. It might at the same time lead to a new order imposed upon the international community by global corporations, the least desirable outcome of spontaneous change in the international balance of forces.

Sixth, economic theory has not worked out methods and parameters for the classification of developing countries as a group, or for measuring their heterogeneity. In the absence of such classification tools, NIEO is being applied to all third world countries without distinction or modification, which is not sensible. That is, incidentally, the reason why NIEO represents a conglomeration of so many unconnected or even contradictory demands.

Discussion of the Papers by Professor Rweyemamu and Dr Paszyński
(Chairman: Professor V. L. Urquidi)

The discussion was opened by *Dr Kulig* (Poland). He noted that Professor Rweyemamu's analysis of the Bretton Woods order emphasised the extent to which the markets for commodities supplied by the developing countries were either closed, controlled or subject to oligopolistic buyers, and that this had important implications for the determination of prices in these markets. These implications were generally unfavourable for the developing countries, as were the monetary aspects of the existing international system. The demand for a new international economic order (NIEO) could thus be seen as a demand for a more equitable distribution of power and resources and for equal sovereignty.

Dr Kulig then summarised Dr Paszyński's paper and showed that it was essentially very critical of the programme for a NIEO put forward by certain of the developing countries. These criticisms were both theoretical and practical.

Dr Kulig said that in his view Professor Rweyemamu's paper did not adequately consider the relevance of economic theories and perhaps assumed too readily that theory was irrelevant. He also disagreed with the interpretation of '*interdependence*' given in the paper. He agreed with the statement in Professor Pajestka's paper that one could speak of interdependence only within the developed countries of the capitalist world or of the socialist world. Between the developed capitalist countries and the developing countries there was not interdependence but only the normal type of dependence.

He thought that Dr Paszyński's criticisms were related too narrowly to the current (1976–78) version of the NIEO programme. However, the programme had been evolving since the 1950s and this evolution had to be seen as a long-term historical movement. The recent version of the programme had in a sense been forced on the developing countries by the stagflation, unemployment and currency disorder which was the developed countries' response to the deterioration in their terms of trade, and was their method of attempting to reverse this trend. It was possible that earlier, more radical, versions of NIEO might in time reappear. He also thought that Dr Paszyński was too cynical about the moral aspects of the developing countries' campaign for equity. The moral face of the desire for equality was a painful factor which should not be dismissed.

Dr Streeten (UK) said that the campaign for NIEO came from two sources. The first was the case made by official negotiators at international gatherings. Their actual demands were not as great as their rhetoric would suggest and they would probably be satisfied with modest concessions. They accepted the existing framework of international relations. The second source was various groups of radical intellectuals; they were asking for something much more fundamental, for a restructuring of power relations. He agreed with Professor Rweyemamu that the existing international system had not helped (and may have harmed) the poorest countries, but many of the middle-income countries (e.g. Brazil, Mexico, Taiwan and Korea) had been greatly assisted by flows of trade and of private capital.

Dr Streeten said he agreed with the view that there were substantial biases or imperfection or exploitation in the existing order. He gave as examples discriminatory provisions in favour of migration of skilled workers and against unskilled; discrimination in location of plants for processing of raw materials; in shipping, access to technology, pricing of exports and imports, in anti-trust and anti-cartel legislation, and so on. This was also true in non-economic spheres, e.g. the collection and dissemination of news. But there were also imperfections and biases which worked the other way, such as OPEC and the fact that access to capital via official aid was actually biased in favour of the poorest countries. And some of the biases (e.g. in shipping) cut across the North-South divide and worked against some industrial countries. However, he recognised that on balance the biases worked against the developing countries and especially against the poorest.

Professor Furtado (Brazil) said he wanted to turn to the basic theme of the relevance of economic theory. Economic rationality was linked to a system of values: at the micro level there was the concept of the utility function, and at the macro level the concept of national interest. However, at the international level this conceptual framework was not available. In his opinion it was essential to introduce the concept of power, and it was the responsibility of economists to investigate the nature of economic power, in particular in its application at the international level.

Professor Furtado said that power was not abstract, it was based on the utilisation of resources. These could include military resources but in analysis of the international economic order it was not military power which was crucial. In his view there were five major sources of international economic power:

(i) control of markets, including control of the home market by protection;
(ii) control of finance;
(iii) control of scarce, non-renewable resources;
(iv) control of technology: this was the 'noble resource', a country which enjoyed this could overcome most other problems;
(v) control of labour supplies, particularly cheap labour.

This analysis had to be related to the role of the TNCs. They were today the engine of growth and it was necessary to develop a more adequate conceptual framework to cover the role of the TNCs in international trade and thus in economic growth. Professor Furtado said that in his view the present dissatisfaction with economic theory was explained by its inability to deal with the concept of power, not by weaknesses at a more sophisticated level.

Professor Malinvaud (France) said that he regarded Dr Paszyński's paper as an excellent discussion of the relevance of economic theory for the main challenge that the world would face in the decades to come. Economic theory had many deficiencies, but we should not develop an inferiority complex because sociological and political theories were certainly not more helpful in this respect, even though the challenge also concerned them.

He accepted all six conclusions of the author, but he wished to make brief comments on two of them. About the fourth conclusion, it was true that existing economic theories were not *best* suited to analysing problems of developing economies; but they should not be neglected altogether since some of them were partially relevant for some of the problems faced by developing economies. Concerning the sixth conclusion he considered that a start had been made in classifying developing countries and measuring their heterogeneity; but undoubtedly much more needed to be done before we had a typology that would be fully appropriate to future international arrangements.

Professor Malinvaud said that he would also like to comment on a secondary issue arising from section VI. He fully agreed with Dr Paszyński that the 'market mechanism is devised to deal with short-term equilibrium problems and must be assisted by outside regulation to solve the long-term ones'. But he disagreed with the preceding sentence. The theoretical problem of defining appropriate long-term resource pricing had been well explored and by-and-large solved to a very large extent. The factual knowledge might be very deficient by the standard of what was required, but that was another matter.

Dr Owosekun (Nigeria) said that with reference to Section III of Professor Rweyemamu's paper, the conditions specified by the IMF involved much more than 'price stability'. For example, in a recent case Zaire was effectively required to submit its entire economy to control by international organisations.

He thought that Dr Paszyński's paper was very useful and showed the lack of any theoretical foundation for NIEO. He was concerned that regional and subregional groupings generally comprised some of the least developed countries who constituted a liability rather than an asset to such groupings. It was unfortunate, he noted, that the 'exclusion principle' could not be applied to this category of countries. He also noted that the theory of economic integration did not help to explain how the least developed countries could be most effectively accommodated in regional or subregional groupings.

He said the new international economic order had a counterpart in a new internal order requiring the developing countries to concentrate attention on a number of critical areas. For example, the development objectives should be consistent with the resource base. In a world of ever-rising expectation but limited resources, there was the need to restrain the consumption pattern and since political stability was a prerequisite for economic prosperity, the developing countries should aim at maintaining law and order and at minimising external political influence. There was also the need to discourage excessive individualism in the management of enterprises. Internal sources of financing economic development needed to be improved.

Mr Lengyel (UNESCO) said he thought the economists were making a much better contribution to discussion of this topic than the other social sciences. He thought Dr Paszyński's paper was excellent and should get very wide circulation. He thought it was essential to appreciate that NIEO could not be obtained by confrontation – a new Order implied consensus not conflict, and if everything was challenged at once nothing would be achieved. It would simply reinforce the status quo. A new Order could not be demanded; it had to come out of a slow process of negotiation with appropriate theoretical underpinning.

Dr Desai (India) said that Dr Paszyński had analysed the NIEO using concepts of marxian economic theory, and this was welcome because so far the conference had been treating economic theory as synonymous with neo-classical economic theory.

The major contention of the paper was that those who demanded NIEO in the third world argued that the causes of slow development were exogenous. Marxian theory laid much more emphasis on the class nature of the society and the contradictions between forces and relations of production to explain underdevelopment. Indeed in Marx's work, growth was explained by and large without reference to international trade. Thus in discussion of balanced growth in extended reproduction in vol. 2 of *Capital* and of cycles in vol. 1 of *Capital* there was hardly any reference to trade. This lacuna was to some extent corrected by Rosa Luxembourg when she put Marx's theory in the context of the world economy. But even then, the integration of growth and trade in Marx's theory was an unfinished task. Such discussion as we had of an international context of growth in Marxian theory was entirely in political terms of neo-colonialism. But the concept of neo-colonialism denied far too strongly the quasi-rent to be earned out of political sovereignty even for relatively weak countries.

In any case he thought the analysis in Dr Paszyński's paper overstated the national as against the international dimension. His analysis was accurate for the larger LDC such as India but could not be extended everywhere. Dr Paszyński also somewhat neglected to discuss actual policy issues.

Dr Desai said that he would like to discuss these. To begin with it must be appreciated that the collapse of the Bretton Woods system came about without any reference to, or contribution by, the third world countries. It was caused by the unwillingness of some European countries, especially France, to hold surplus dollars instead of gold. This was the beginning of the end of the Bretton Woods. This was why there was no reference to the third world in the reform of the monetary system.

He then turned to the two short-term measures mentioned by the author:

changes in relative prices and financial transfers. It was clear that given the experience of development aid in the last twenty years, the prospect of international financial transfer was meagre. The taxpayers of the developed countries would be reluctant to agree to substantial transfer. There was much more prospect of changes in relative prices. But here there were qualifications to make. It was not true that the developed countries exported only manufactured goods, and that the developing countries exported only primary products. Many developed countries were large exporters of primary products as were some of the richer nations among the third world. As a result, distorting the terms of trade might not distribute the gains in an equitable direction. Similarly the differences among the poor countries meant that the exporters of manufactured goods among them would be reluctant to bear the tax to help other poor countries. For example, India would be reluctant to curtail jute production to help Bangladesh.

The best way to alter relative prices would be to stabilise a vector of commodity prices simultaneously with a buffer stock holding a portfolio of commodities in order to do so. Stabilising prices case by case would not help. But the profits of such a stabilisation scheme ought to be redistributed on a basis of some independent criterion of absolute poverty. Otherwise the most poor nations who had neither trade surplus nor economic surplus would not benefit from the NIEO.

Academician Mateev (Bulgaria) referred to the need to support theoretical analysis of the conditions for development by consideration of actual experience, and he thought the example of Bulgaria could be helpful. His country started from a higher level of development than that as yet reached by the majority of third world countries, but allowing for war damage and for the rural character of the pre-war economy Bulgaria in 1945 could be regarded as an underdeveloped country. By now she had come a long way.

The particular lesson he wished to emphasise was the close interrelation between the internal and external conditions for development. Internally, the major national objective was growth and accumulation and all factors were organised for the achievement of this objective. Accumulation represented 25–30 per cent of the national product. Externally the CMEA provided assured markets for exports (with stability provided by long-term planning) and thus financed the necessary imports. The system also enabled Bulgaria to specialise and thus to export to countries outside the CMEA.

Professor Urquidi (Mexico), commenting upon Professor Rweyemamu's paper as a participant and not as Chairman of the session, felt that it gave too little attention to recent developments in the international monetary area, such as the creation and use of Special Drawing Rights (SDRs) and the 'link' with development. He mentioned, for instance, Professor Robert Triffin's proposals for a new international monetary order in the RIO report and elsewhere. Professor Rweyemamu also did not take sufficient account of the role developing countries – particularly the Latin American – played at the Bretton Woods Conference in 1944 and during its preparatory period, in connection with both the IMF and the IBRD agreements. One example was the exchange restrictions clauses, and later, in the early years of the Fund, the multiple exchange rate policies; another, the emphasis on development lending in the Bank. The whole scheme became much more flexible, from the developing countries' point of view, thanks to negotiations led by developing countries. He had witnessed some of them personally at Bretton Woods as a member of the Mexican delegation and had followed developments at later times.

Turning to established theory about international economic relations, Professor Urquidi emphasised that the policies of the industrially advanced countries were still inspired by the classical theory of comparative advantage (costs), from which followed the nineteenth-century-type international division of labour, free trade, free demand-supply conditions in international commodity markets, factor flows, compensatory elasticities (determining the gains from trade), gold-flow adjustments, etc. – all the way from David Ricardo, through Hecksher–Ohlin to Harry Johnson and others who developed much theoretical refinement. But policies based on classical and neo-classical trade theory had led to international inequality, discrimination in export markets, terms of trade losses, instability, asymmetrical effects and, eventually, to protection in the industrially advanced countries; while the developing countries became dependent upon foreign savings and technology. A critique of traditional theory and its policy implications had been carried out at first mainly in the UN Economic Commission for Latin America through the work of Dr Raoul Prebisch and his associates, later in other parts of the world; and was the basis for the work of UNCTAD. Even in the discussion of economic integration schemes in Latin America, Africa and Asia, their theoretical foundation was brushed off by the neo-classical economists as 'second-best', and such schemes were at first strongly opposed on simplistic theoretical reasoning. It had taken ECLA a long time to obtain recognition for the structuralist approach to international economic relations but there was still resistance, as witnessed by the discussions on the New International Economic Order in recent years. It might be that there was not yet a sufficiently consistent body of thought behind the idea of the NIEO. Professor Furtado had cited the problem of power over resources as central, including technology. The gains from trade were also at the centre of the power struggle and consequently of the whole discussion. Through industrial power and technology the advanced countries dominated world trade and weakened the position of the developing countries.

The paper by Dr Paszyński contained a good many interesting ideas and was an important contribution. However, neither author had mentioned the work of Professor Tinbergen, especially the RIO report (Reshaping International Order) which he had co-ordinated, and which was more comprehensive in covering international relations with respect to food, science and technology, environment and other topics in addition to trade and investment. It was notable that *inter alia*, the RIO report pointed to the need for a *new* international division of labour, and to the potential deriving from world disarmament, international use of the sea-bed, etc. The authors of the papers did not mention the North-South dialogue and its failures on both sides, including the commodity and the external indebtedness questions. It was in such discussions that the absence of a new, coherent theory was particularly felt.

Professor Pajestka (Poland) asked why there was this longing for a general theory of a new international economic order. NIEO was a political movement and as such did not require a new general economic theory. He agreed with Professor Furtado's analysis of the elements of power, and thought the real force behind the NIEO, which started it, had been the power exercised by OPEC. However, their power had now been weakened by various factors, for example, the recession and inflation. These problems must be analysed by economists and this would be more helpful than some grand general theory.

Professor Seers (United Kingdom) said that he welcomed the note of realism in the paper by Dr Paszyński. The co-operation of governments of rich industrial countries in NIEO could be obtained on the basis of either a moral claim, fear or mutual interest. Because of the passage of time, the spare resources of such countries had declined, guilt over the colonial period had dwindled, and many formerly 'poor' countries had become much less so. Governments of rich countries were becoming less apprehensive about losing sources of materials through, for example, social revolutions. It was clearly too expensive for many Marxist governments to opt out of the world capitalist economy. There seemed no political basis for collective sanctions by the 'third world'. The bargaining power of most of their governments was weak (he would add food dependency to Professor Furtado's list of the determinants of power), and likely to become weaker because of the prospective world energy shortage in the 1980s and 1990s, which would hit them especially hard. So the only sound basis for some NIEO must lie in mutual interest: an expanding world economy would provide rich industrial countries with a dynamic impetus they at present lacked; and secondly they needed secure and growing supplies of various primary products. There was thus the basis for a bargain.

Professor Rweyemamu, replying to the discussion, said that his paper was prepared in the form of Notes for Discussion as time had not permitted him to write a full paper. He was grateful to Professor Urquidi regarding the historical framework of the New International Economic Order. The Latin American School was instrumental in the changes of perception by the third world countries on the functioning of the world economy.

He very much appreciated Professor Furtado's comments. As would be readily apparent he was concerned with two aspects of power – control of commodity markets and finance. He stressed these two aspects because he believed they were fundamental to the interests of the less developed countries. Of course, for the middle-income countries who now had access to private capital, control over technology took pride of place.

Professor Rweyemamu said that he would like to stress the following aspects:

(i) that since an economic order was a political proposition, we must begin shifting our emphasis toward political economy;
(ii) that our shift toward political economy must incorporate a 'rationality' that dealt with issues of global equity and distribution;
(iii) that the major political aspects which could assist in the analysis of international relations related to power, and he had selected those power aspects which had a particularly unfavourable effect on the poor countries and about which the international community could do something;
(iv) that received theory contained biases in presentation that hampered current and future negotiations between the 'haves' and 'have nots'; and
(v) that economic theory was also inadequate in its treatment of the functioning of a fragile economy; he had indicated some directions for further work in this regard.

Turning next to the specific comment of Dr Kulig, he wished to point out that the interdependence mentioned in the paper referred only to the industrial countries. As for the relationships with the developing countries there was no doubt in his mind that any theory of multinational economic relations which did not specify how the constituent national entities could maintain their economic and political sovereignties was a theory of imperialism.

Finally, Professor Rweyemamu said that even the sources of economic wisdom historically had not been independent of the prevailing power relations. If anyone had any doubt about this, the discussion just held must have dispelled it. Nevertheless, major social changes had taken place in defiance of prevailing conventional wisdom. Perhaps this would be the case with the movement towards a new international economic order.

Dr Paszyński made four points in his reply to the discussion:

(1) His point of departure was NIEO as formulated by the developing countries, e.g. at UNCTAD. There were other versions but this was the most important.
(2) NIEO must be an order for all. The collapse of the old system was due principally to the unevenness of the development of the industrialised countries (as pointed out by Dr Desai) though there were other factors.
(3) He was grateful to Professor Furtado for his helpful intervention, but

its effect was to make him pessimistic. Bargaining power lay with the developed countries, not the LDCs. The latter could exert only political pressure and that was why international economic relations were now so politicised. However, this approach required unity among the LDCs which could only be achieved for very general demands – this was a weakness.

(4) He entirely agreed with Professor Urquidi that he had not presented any consistent alternative, but this was precisely because of the inadequacy of the present economic thinking on this question. On this point he disagreed with Professor Pajestka and thought some theoretical background was essential if the NIEO were to be developed.

PART FIVE

Economic Theory and the Limits to Natural Resources

10 Natural Resources – a Shift of Emphasis from Best Utilisation to Conservation

Amilcar Herrera
LATIN AMERICAN FACULTY FOR SOCIAL SCIENCES, (FLACSO), MEXICO CITY

I ORIGINS OF THE ENVIRONMENTAL PROBLEMATIQUE

The present concern about the limitations of the natural resources available to mankind is part of a wider and deeper concern for the meaning and content of present economic growth theories, which are normally equated with 'development'.

In recent decades, particularly in Latin America and other third world regions, a critical analysis of growth theories and, above all, of their implications for the wider concept of development, has occurred. The theory of dependency, the concepts of basic needs and self-reliance, are some of the results of this new approach.

A most important contribution to this revisionist process – if not in the building up of a new conception, at least in helping to convert it into an intellectually respectable option – is the fact that for the first time since the Industrial Revolution the western world has started to have serious doubts about the soundness and rationality of its own way of development. As is well known, doubts about the intrinsic values on which present western culture rests have been expressed from inside in the past. However, those critical views were always restricted to individuals or small groups – artists, philosophers, dissident political groups – and never reached any kind of consensus in the society as a whole. What is new now is that these doubts extend even to the material basis of western society, and have reached wide sectors of the population, including scientists, politicians, intellectuals, and a considerable part of the informed general public.

If one looks at the evolution of ideas in the last few years, it seems apparent that the main cause of the re-evaluation of the western approach to its own development was the sudden revelation that humanity was probably exceeding the carrying capacity of its physical environment. A deeper look, however, reveals that the realisation of the environmental risk only triggered off fears and doubts that were more deeply rooted than the simple concern for physical survival.

In the first place it is interesting to see the evolution of the content of the 'environmental problematique'. When it began, a few years ago, its main emphasis was on the limitation of the physical resources ultimately available to mankind; and the main responsibility for the ensuing dangers was placed on the rapid growth of the population, particularly in the underdeveloped world. Typical of the literature on this subject were *The Population Bomb* (Erlich) and *The Limits to Growth* (Meadows, D. *et al.*). Despite its limitations, this approach contained two basic ideas that, although not new in themselves, were new in their global implications. Firstly the conception of a single humanity, in the sense of the interdependence of all human societies – 'the space ship Earth'; and secondly, the awareness that an indefinite increase in material consumption is in the long term a physical impossibility, as well as a doubtful social goal.

From those simple ideas, some of the sectors of what can be called the 'environmental movement' have developed a current of ideas that greatly transcends the original approach. It has incorporated the concept of 'human environment', not merely to denote the human material counterpart of the physical environment, but as a proxy to call in question all the basic values and goals of western society. To a certain extent, the environmental movement reflects the deep sense of frustration and lack of meaning and purpose that permeates, to a varying degree, all social strata of the western world.

Another fact that reveals the nature of the environmental problematique is that it is difficult to conceive that the revelation of the possibility of physical limits to economic development would have caused so much concern, had it taken place in the nineteenth century, or even before the Second World War. Until that time there was a general belief in the basic values of western society and, above all, a seemingly unshakeable conviction of the capacity of science to overcome all possible obstacles to an endless human material progress. In the last few decades this blind confidence in science – or perhaps more exactly, in technology – has, to a great extent, vanished; for the first time since the beginning of the scientific revolution, western man has started to question the aims and role of science in society. Some of the reasons for this attitude can easily be identified and refer to the awareness of the actual or potential dangers of some recent scientific developments: the atomic bomb; the real or imagined dangers of nuclear energy; the possible implications of the manipulation of the genetic code; the possibility of manipulation of the human mind through psycho drugs; the visible deterioration of the physical environment, etc; last, but not least, the insufficiency of current economic theories to cope adequately with the host of problems involved in the transition to a new world order. I am not referring specifically to the New International Economic Order, but to the process of change that is affecting the whole world and whose results – very difficult to foresee – will depend on the actions of the national and social actors involved.

The above considerations represent an effort – perhaps redundant – to show that the field of natural resources cannot be approached as a single economic or technological problem. It is a part of a complex 'problem situation' in which natural resources are only a component; after all, it is difficult to talk of an 'economic theory of natural resources', at least in macroeconomic terms. They have normally been treated just as inputs in growth theories; as for their availability, the concept of scarcity has been used in the relative sense of traditional economics.

The above does not imply that there is not a specific field of economics related to natural resources, but that it will be most important for the subject of this paper to explore, at least in general terms, the consequences of the new problematique of natural resources for other fields of economics.

In what follows I will concentrate basically on non-renewable natural resources, the main reason being that they are the ones that present most clearly the problems associated with natural resources. Besides, other natural resources – in particular soil, the most important – are, in a certain sense, also non-renewable, at least in the time horizon relevant for long-term socio-economic planning. I will divide the treatment into two main areas: (a) the problem of the ultimate exhaustion of non-renewable natural resources; (b) the problem of conservation.

I will not attempt an exhaustive treatment of the field. Firstly, because it would be impossible in the time available for the preparation of this paper and secondly, and more important, because I am not an economist myself, but a natural scientist concerned with natural resources and technology. If I accepted the task of preparing this paper, it is basically because I think it could be useful for professional economists to have an external view of how the tools provided by economics are viewed by people who have to use them in the area of natural resources.

II EXHAUSTION OF NON-RENEWABLE NATURAL RESOURCES

Before analysing the economic tools available to deal with the problem of absolute depletion or scarcity of non-renewable resources, it is necessary to say something about the nature of those resources.

In the first place, there is no such thing as a 'natural resource'. There are physical bodies in nature which, combined with a given amount of knowledge, can be used by man. The simplest definition of a mineral deposit is *that geological body from which it is possible to obtain economically one or more useful metals or minerals.*

This definition seems to give a relatively simple procedure for determining whether or not a geological body is an ore deposit. This simplicity, however, is only apparent, because the factors that allow economic exploitation are multiple. Some of them – such as the shape, size and grade – are of a geological nature and can be determined by adequate studies. There are two other factors, however, that are relatively independent of the characteristics of the ore deposit: the market conditions, and the available technology. These ultimately determine the cost of exploitation and with it, the very existence of something that can be called a resource. Both are time-dependent variables.

The existence of those time-dependent variables – fundamentally technology – means that any calculation of the amount of reserves of a given mineral resource available to mankind is only valid in the technological conditions of the moment when the evaluation is performed. In other words, any such evaluation represents a cross-section in time; cross-sections at different moments could give – and normally do give – completely different results.[1] A couple of well-known examples will serve to illustrate the point. A few decades ago the total amount of reserves of nitrogenous compounds for fertilisers was contained in the natural nitrates of some arid regions of the world, mainly northern Chile. Now, nitrogen is obtained from the air, so the total amount of reserves of that element available are those contained in the atmosphere. Also, until a few decades ago, the only source of aluminium was bauxite – a residual soil with aluminium hydroxides formed in certain special climatic and topographic conditions. Now, aluminium can be extracted – with little difference in cost – from high alumina clays and shales, whose total reserves are practically inexhaustible.

We can now analyse the hypothesis of scarcity of natural resources traditionally used in economics, and formulated in their general form by Malthus and Ricardo.

Malthus starts from the assumption of a fixed and known amount of resource (in this case the soil). At the beginning food production increases as the soil is gradually occupied; during this phase, in which part of the soil is still not utilised, the cost of production remains constant. When all the soil is under cultivation, a point is reached where each supplementary unit of production can only be obtained at a higher cost, until a further increase of the factors of production does not improve yields; this is the absolute limit of production.

Ricardo's hypothesis – which at first glance seems more appropriate for non-renewable natural resources – does not necessarily imply a predetermined amount of resources. It is assumed that the best resources from an economic point of view are exploited first, and that increasingly poorer resources are utilised as the best ones become exhausted or fully utilised. The cost of production starts to increase from the beginning of the exploitation, until a point is reached where it becomes socially unacceptable.

To what extent are these hypotheses of scarcity applicable to mineral resources? Let us first consider Malthus. His hypothesis is based on the existence of a known fixed amount of resources. As we have already seen,

[1] In order to simplify the treatment, we are implicitly assuming that the *total* reserves of a given resource in current economic and technological conditions are known. However, this is not the case; as exploration involves a cost, the reserves developed at a given moment are basically a *function of the demand*, and represent only an unknown fraction of the total possible reserves.

this condition, in the case of mineral resources, cannot be fulfilled, even if we consider only the total amount of resources available with the current technology. If the time variable is introduced, as the long-term evolution of technology is unpredictable, it becomes clear that *the total amount of resources eventually available to mankind is intrinsically unknowable.*

As for Ricardo's hypothesis, its assumption that the best resources are exploited first is untenable, even when considering current technological and economic conditions, for the following reasons: (i) the hypothesis requires as a precondition a complete knowledge of the total amount and quality of the available resources; as we have seen, this requirement cannot be fulfilled; (ii) historically, the first resources exploited were those more easily discovered, and closer to the centres of production, not the 'best' ones. If the first oil-producing wells were drilled in the USA it was not because those oil deposits were of better 'quality' than those of the Middle East, but because they were closer to dynamic centres of industrial activity.

When time-dependent technological change is introduced, it becomes impossible even to formulate Ricardo's hypothesis in intelligible terms. Each technological change modifies the criteria used to decide which type of resource is the most convenient from an economic point of view. Take the example already given of the nitrogen compounds: does it make any sense to say that the shifting from natural nitrates to those produced from the nitrogen content of the atmosphere represents a transition from a 'high' to a 'low' quality resource?

In conclusion, it is clear that the traditional hypothesis of scarcity used in economics cannot be applied to non-renewable natural resources. However, most of the predictions about the exhaustion of those resources in the relatively near future are based on one of those hypotheses or on a combination of both. The latter is true of the MIT model;[1] by assuming (a) that there is a known fixed amount of resources, and (b) that the best resources are exploited first, the model produces the collapse of the world economy at the beginning of the next century.

III A NEW APPROACH TO THE PROBLEM

The fact that the traditional hypotheses of scarcity cannot be applied to non-renewable resources does not mean that there is no problem in this domain; it only means that a new approach is necessary. It is not a question of ultimate depletion that can be predicted with any degree of certainty with present knowledge, but of increasing *risk* of creating situations that could have effects almost as dangerous for human development as partial or total exhaustion of non-renewable resources. The mechanisms through which these situations could emerge can only be described in general terms,

[1] Meadows, D. *et al.*, *The Limits to Growth* (Universe Books, New York, 1972).

as their inherent characteristic is the element of uncertainty or risk, to which we have already referred.

Historically, technology has solved the problems of actual or potential scarcity in natural resources by shifting from one source of a given raw material, to another more abundant or more easily recoverable. There are many examples of this process; the change from high-grade oxidised minerals to low-grade sulphides to extract copper; the extraction of sulphur from oil, anhidrite and gypsum which ended the dependence on the relatively scarce Frasch-type deposits of native sulphur; the transition, already mentioned, from sedimentary nitrates to the nitrogen of the air, etc.

In each case, the transition from one source of a raw material to another involved scientific and technological research, sometimes for a relatively long period. Until recently the rate of economic growth at world level, and with it that of the demand for raw materials, gave sufficient lead time to research to avoid the generation of serious economic bottlenecks in the transition. With the acceleration of economic growth and industrialisation at world level, coupled with the rapid increase of population, the demand for raw materials is growing at a rate never before recorded in history. As a consequence the lead time for research is continually decreasing, and the probability arises of temporary technological or economic bottlenecks that can seriously affect production.

The case of energy is a good example of a possibly dangerous bottleneck in the relatively near future. It is not a problem of absolute depletion of energy resources; the production of oil and gas will start to decline at the beginning of the next century, but the reserves of nuclear fuels – for fission as well as for fusion – and the potentialities of the so-called non-conventional sources of energy are practically inexhaustible. However, the transition to new energy sources is proving to have more technological difficulties than was formerly expected, and it is now doubtful whether the solutions will come in time to cope with the enormous demands of energy predicted for the next decades.[1]

Another dimension of the problem is the possibility of several bottlenecks occurring simultaneously, and reinforcing each other through a kind of synergic effect. All the bottlenecks do not need to be associated necessarily with depletion of resources; they can be side-effects of their exploitation and utilisation, as for instance the damage inflicted on the physical environment.

There is no need to elaborate further on a subject that is being amply discussed. The important point is that the exponential increase in the demand of non-renewable resources can generate problems – besides the possibility of absolute depletion – that can have very disruptive social and economic effects.

How is economic theory and practice prepared to cope with these

[1] See, for instance, Foley, G., *The Energy Question* (Penguin Books, Harmondsworth, 1976).

problems? Let us consider first the problem of uncertainty itself. As is well known, the subject of decision-taking under conditions of uncertainty has been rather extensively explored, but mostly in the area of resource allocation and under highly restrictive conditions. In the field we are concerned with, the problem is complicated by the following elements: (i) it is difficult to know in advance the real consequences of the possible bottlenecks or combinations of bottlenecks; (ii) the problems are worldwide and, therefore, are conditioned by long and complex chains of decisions not necessarily interconnected; (iii) the time horizon is much longer than the one normally considered in social and economic planning.

It is obvious that a situation of risk of that nature cannot be faced solely in terms of economics theory, as it involves also social, political and technical elements which are closely interwoven, and whose interrelationships are poorly understood. As there is an unavoidable risk,[1] however, a wide frame of reference should be defined within which a strategy at world level could be devised.

The first step to build up that frame of reference is to define what should be considered an 'acceptable risk'; otherwise we will fall into the concept of absolute risk very common in current literature. This considers, implicitly or explicitly, that if there is a risk that could endanger the future of humanity, it should be avoided at any price, even if it means the deliberate sacrifice of a considerable part of mankind. The other position poses the problem in its relationship with the basic values of our civilisation; the concept of acceptable risk is substituted for one of absolute risk. The definition of acceptable risk in this context is not simply an economic or technical problem, but a moral one.

Although it is very difficult to make long-term forecasts on which to estimate the minimum acceptable risk, there are certain elements which are sufficient as a wide base for a policy on natural resources. The most important is that the world population will surely reach about ten billion by the first half of the next century, before stabilising; the second, is that each one of those future human beings has the absolute right to a life worth living. With those two premises, we can now define what is the minimum risk humanity should accept: it is the one incurred to ensure that each future human being will have his basic needs satisfied, in such a way that he can enjoy a full and productive life.

The above definition is, admittedly, a very wide frame of reference, but it is enough, at least, to elaborate the basic elements of a strategy on natural resources. As we have already seen, the problem is not one of absolute depletion, but rather one of, given economic growth, enough flexibility to be able to cope with sufficient lead time with possible disruptive economic or technical bottlenecks.

[1] I use the word 'risk' in the commonly accepted meaning, which includes elements of uncertainty as defined in economics.

I will not attempt to elaborate the elements of a detailed strategy to obtain the proposed flexibility, but I believe that it should be built up around the following central objectives: (1) To develop methodologies to identify possible future bottlenecks in the availability of natural resources, in order to orient research in the appropriate direction; and to be able to recommend adequate socio-economic measures to cope with the consequences of the new situation. (2) To ensure the optimal use of natural resources, in order to avoid waste and irreparable damage to the physical environment. This includes everything from recycling to a complete revision of the current patterns of consumption, and of the technologies of production. (3) To reduce gradually the rate of growth of the global demand for natural resources. This is a very controversial subject, but it seems obvious that the current exponential rate of growth of the consumption of non-renewable natural resources is, in long-term projections, a material impossibility, and a doubtful social goal. It implies, in the not distant future, the necessity of reducing the rate of economic growth. This reduction should be selective, taking into account the unequal standard of living of different parts of the world.

I will try to analyse, very briefly, some of the implications for economic theory of the three general objectives stated above.

IV THE IDENTIFICATION OF FUTURE BOTTLENECKS IN THE AVAILABILITY OF NATURAL RESOURCES

Long-term forecasting, in its most general form, is almost as old as history. However, in a systematic form it is a recent activity, and has been mostly based on the development of mathematical models. The treatment of natural resources in those models, however, is rather poor. One of them,[1] as we have already seen, predicts the absolute depletion of mineral resources by applying the classical theories of scarcity. Most of the others[2] consider that there is no danger of critical scarcity in the foreseeable future, but forecast (more on the basis of intelligent guessing than on any empirical evidence) considerable cost increases in the next decades. The Latin American World Model,[3] on the same assumption of no danger of absolute depletion, proposes a very general strategy to cope with possible bottlenecks.

[1] Meadows, *et al.*, *op. cit.*

[2] Mesarovic, M. and Pestel, E., *Mankind at the Turning Point* (Dutton Readers Digest Press, 1974); Kaya, V. *et al.*; 'Global Constraints and a Vision for Development'–II, *Technological Forecasting and Social Change*, Vol. 6, 371–88 (1974); Leontief, W. *et al.*; *The Future of the World Economy* (Preliminary Report, United Nations, N.Y., 1976).

[3] Herrera, A. O., *et al.*, *Un Monde Pour Tous* (Presses Universitaires de France, Paris, 1978).

It is clear that a new approach is required in this area, and it should be based on a combination of technological forecasting and economic thinking. Economists are rather hesitant at getting involved in long-term forecasting, for the good reason that they know by bitter experience the dangerous pitfalls of this kind of exercise. However, by their very nature, the basic problems now faced at national or world level cannot be solved on a short-term basis.

This collaboration, or interdisciplinary research between natural scientist, technologist and economist, although it cannot be expected immediately to identify accurately future bottlenecks, will allow, at least, the identification of 'areas of danger' and recommend certain preventive actions. A careful follow-up of the situation will make it possible gradually to evaluate the risk, and to devise adequate strategies to cope with it. As a central by-product of this kind of exercise, there may also be valuable contributions to economic theory.

V ALTERNATIVE APPROACHES TO THE OPTIMAL USE OF NATURAL RESOURCES

The first question here is obviously the following: what is the meaning of 'optimal' use of natural resources? Instead of trying to give an *a priori* definition of the concept, I will try to identify its meaning – explicit or implicit – in the main currents of economic thinking.

Let us consider first the approach of welfare economics, based on neo-classical principles. I am not going to enter into a discussion of the general approach, but will consider briefly some basic points relevant to our subject.

Pearce, referring to allocation of exhaustible resources, writes: '. . . a perfectly competitive economy will allocate resources in such a way as to secure a Pareto optimal. The basic result also holds when we extend the analysis to include time. Consequently, if resource owners behave competitively, and if the rest of the economy is also competitive we could argue that the free play of market forces will secure an optimal allocation of resources over time . . .[1] Pearce further analyses the facts which interfere with perfect competition, and those that make it very difficult in practice to obtain optimal allocation of resources in a medium to long-term perspective. The corrections suggested, however, do not essentially modify the theoretical framework.

The main points concerning optimal use of resources in the neo-classical approach are the following. (1) As is well known, a Pareto optimal is obtained when a given allocation of resources makes some people better off, while making no-one worse off. It is not concerned with the *absolute level*

[1] Pearce, D. W., *Environmental Economics* (Longmans, London, 1976), pp. 149 *et seq.*

of demand for resources, but only with their distribution, regardless of the pattern of consumption – wasteful or at the level of survival – of a given society.

It can be argued that the price mechanism will also determine the optimal absolute level of use of resources. Leaving aside the well-known imperfection of market prices, these react only to clearly identified constraints in a relatively short time horizon, and are not able to cope with the type of risk we had referred to. The current energy crisis is a clear example; it has nothing to do with *cost* of resources (the rise in the *price* of oil is not based on problems of scarcity). Up to a few years ago economic planners were making provisions for exponential increases in the demand for energy, apparently unaware of any possible impending crisis. (2) The Pareto optimal position is indifferent to income distribution, in other words, to the amount of natural resources consumed by each social group within a society.

In conclusion, in neo-classical economics optimal use of resources has only an economic meaning, in the restricted sense, and not a social one. Moreover, it does not offer adequate tools to deal with the long-term global problems in the field of natural resources we are referring to.

It is possible that this brief analysis does not do justice to the many economists who have tried to introduce a wider social dimension into neo-classical economics but, in my view the basic approach is still unchanged.

We can now look, also very briefly, at the marxist approach to the problem. I will refer only to the two points that are of special interest to the consideration of the subject: the approach to the problem of global scarcity (which we have stated in terms of possible bottlenecks), and the problem of optimal use of resources.

As for the first point, there are no essential differences between marxism and classical economics. In both cases the position regarding the use of natural resources was born out of the Industrial and Scientific Revolution, and the implicit assumption was that those resources are just an input of production and, in practical terms, virtually inexhaustible. What has been said about the inadequacy of economic theory to deal with the problem of absolute depletion, is equally valid for the marxist approach.

On the second point – the optimal use of resources – the situation is different. In classical or capitalist economics, the driving force is competition in the search for profit; there is no *explicit* effort to achieve an egalitarian distribution of the benefits of the use of resources. In a socialist economy, a central objective of economic planning is to distribute those benefits to the whole population on an essentially egalitarian basis. A net result is that the essential needs of the population can be satisfied with a much lower *per capita* consumption of natural resources, than in a free market economy.[1] We

[1] It is obvious that above basic needs the consumption of a society is determined by its conception of quality of life. It is doubtful whether, at the present time, there is much difference in this respect between capitalist and socialist countries, at least on the material side.

will come back to this point in the next section, when dealing with income distribution.

In general terms it can be said that, although socialist economies have not developed a systematic, coherent approach to deal with the new problems in the area of natural resources, they are in a better position to face those problems than the capitalist economies for the following reasons: (i) a better *social* use of natural resources results in a lower overall demand to satisfy the same basic needs; (ii) the centralisation of economic and social planning facilitates the implementation of any strategy to face possible global bottlenecks of the type already described.

The above comparison between the two economic systems is necessarily schematic, as we are dealing basically with theories. In practice, the picture is somewhat modified – for instance there is some economic planning in most capitalist countries, and some mechanisms to reduce income inequalities – but the central elements of the comparison are still valid.

VI REDUCTION IN THE DEMAND FOR NATURAL RESOURCES

This point is intimately linked with the previous one, but I prefer to treat it separately, because it involves two very important subjects: the rate and characteristics of economic growth, and the unequal distribution of non-renewable natural resources among countries.

The need to diminish the rate of economic growth in a not too distant future – at least in its present form, and in the developed countries – underlies most of the discussions going on about the present world problematique. In a medium or long-term perspective – two or three decades – this need to reduce the rate of economic growth can hardly be discussed. What has been said previously about possible bottlenecks, and the strategy required to deal with them, is enough for the purpose and possibilities of this paper.

The selective reduction of the rate of economic growth or consumption is obviously not a simple matter of producing less of the same commodities or services. It involves the building-up of a society intrinsically compatible with its physical environment, which means a revision of the values underlying present social organisations.

In the countries of the third world, the concepts of basic needs and self-reliance are the nucleus around which a new conception of development is evolving.

Those subjects are being amply discussed all over the world, so there is no need to elaborate them here. I will refer only to distribution of income, because it has a great influence on any strategy oriented to reduce the demand for natural resources.

In the Latin American World Model[1] calculations were made to establish

[1] Herrera, A. O., *et al.*, *op. cit.*

the average GNP per capita that would be necessary for the basic needs of each person in the world to be satisfied, on the assumption that the current income structure is maintained for the countries considered. The calculation was made on the basis of the following premises: (i) it was considered that the basic needs of all inhabitants are satisfied when the least privileged 20 per cent reach an income level permitting fulfilment of these needs; (ii) the minimum income level – or GNP per capita – necessary to satisfy basic needs is calculated on the basis of the assumptions made for the standard run of the Model (which assumes egalitarian distribution of income). Calculations were made for the fifteen regions into which the world is divided in the Model built by Leontief for the United Nations.[1]

The results of the run show that in the developing countries the GNP per capita required to achieve the satisfaction of the basic needs with present distribution of income, is three to five times greater than that needed in the case of homogenous income.[2] If it is assumed that the consumption of natural resources is approximately proportional to the GNP per capita, this means that the amount of resources required to satisfy human needs can be reduced several times by modifying the income distribution. Even considering that the results of the model are no more than approximate, they are enough to demonstrate that changes of social organisation are more important for the conservation of resources than any amount of technical preventive or corrective measures.

Although very little advance has taken place in the last decades in the understanding of the mechanisms of income distribution within a capitalist economy, two facts have become clear: (i) economic growth does not automatically bring about a positive redistribution of income; (ii) the policies of redistribution of income attempted have up to now been, on the whole, rather ineffective.

There is nothing to be surprised about, in the fact that economic growth does not bring about equality. After all, economic growth theory, in its prevalent form, does not have the explicit objective (in operational terms) of creating a more equitable society, or even of satisfying needs in the context of human social and individual aspirations. This is not simply a problem of economics, but of social philosophy, and it requires a completely new approach to development. The main effort in this direction, as has already been said, is being made in the third world countries.[3]

[1] Leontief, W. *et al.*, *op. cit.*

[2] In the capitalist developed countries the GNP required is three times higher. In socialist countries it is two times higher (we have no data for China).

[3] See, for instance, *Another Development, Approaches and Strategies*, M. Nerfin (ed.) (The Dag Hammarskjold Foundation, Upsala, 1977).

VII THE INTERNATIONAL DISTRIBUTION OF NON-RENEWABLE NATURAL RESOURCES

The problem of the international distribution of natural resources, and its implications for international trade and for the relationship between the industrialised and the third world countries has been amply discussed in recent years; however, it does not seem that it has had much influence on economic theory or practice. This is not surprising, as the terms and conditions of international trade have been determined historically as much by political power as by economic factors.

There are two points in this area that deserve special attention: the first is that the availability of cheap natural resources from the developing world is due, to a great extent, to the use of inexpensive labour and to the control of the market by the big powers. The second is that, to a certain measure, the third world is a big exporter of natural resources because it is a very poor consumer. It is to be expected that this situation will change in the following decades as the poor countries, with a rapidly growing population, strive for a better standard of living, and a far greater degree of autonomy in social and economic decisions.

Here again, the problem of how to use rationally and equitably the natural resources of the earth at the international level cannot be solved solely in economic terms, given the multiplicity of factors – economic, social, political, technical – involved. However, economic thinking can greatly help, at least to pose the problem correctly.

VIII CONCLUSIONS

I have tried to review – or more properly to pose – the main problems confronted by economic theory in the field of non-renewable natural resources. Many areas of economic thinking relevant to the subject, such as the microeconomics of the exploitation of resources, the study of externalities, and evaluation of technologies, were left aside. Obviously, in such a selection there is a strong element of subjectivity, but this is unavoidable, as social and human problems are not important in absolute terms, but within the frame of reference of a set of accepted values.

The conclusion – or rather *my* conclusions – could be summarised in two points: (i) the economic tools at our disposal in the field of natural resources are still not adequate to cope with its new problems; (ii) the problem of conservation of natural resources – in particular non-renewable resources – cannot be dealt with solely in terms of traditional economics, even in theory. The possible contribution of economics requires the definition of a new approach to development, based on a revision of the predominant social philosophy.

11 The Use of Natural Resources: Worldwide Problems and Socio-economic Aspects

R. R. Simonyan
INSTITUTE OF WORLD ECONOMY AND INTERNATIONAL RELATIONS, MOSCOW

I THE GLOBAL PROBLEMS

The vital importance of such issues as the problem of raw materials, energy, food supply, ecology and the World Ocean is characteristic of the development of the world economy and international relations in the 1970s. Different in scope, in form, in extent and the way they affect the economy and policy of a country, these problems have one thing in common – they are all connected with the use of natural resources, or viewed in a wider sense, with the relations between society and nature.

At present the problems of utilisation of natural resources directly (due to the universal nature of the environment) or indirectly (because of international economic relations) influence the economic, social and other aspects of life in all the countries of the world, thus being really global in scope.

The events of 1973–75 have clearly shown that under certain social and economic conditions these problems can seriously change the pattern of economic development, adversely affecting such spheres of economy as trade and foreign currency.

Just how acute the problems of the use of natural resources are in the 1970s can be seen from:

(i) the danger of inevitable exhaustion of the natural resources and the increasing scarcity of raw materials, energy and foodstuffs;
(ii) the increasingly negative consequences for nature of man's activities, and the threat of irreversible degradation of the environment;
(iii) the intensification of contradictions between non-socialist countries in the use of natural resources in the world economy and the widening of the gulf between industrial and developing countries.

The fact that the problems of resource use are very complicated, and that the economic and political interests of different countries vary greatly, has given rise to extreme contradictions in the interpretation of these problems, in the evaluation of their influence on the development of world economy and also on the ways and means proposed for solving them.

The crucial situation in the world markets of raw materials in the first half of the 1970s has led some scientists to the conclusion that there is a deep crisis in the relations of man and nature, evident in such fields as raw materials, energy, food and ecology. In their opinion, the sharp changes in the prices of raw materials in the world market in 1973–74 made it clear to all that the main outcome of the crisis was to bring to an end the 'era of cheap raw materials' and to ensure rising prices in the future.

There is also a different point of view based on the assumption that what happens to mankind as a whole, and to individuals in particular, at a given moment is something exceptional. That is why the problems of natural resources are artificially dramatised, though as a matter of fact, these problems are not new ones, and events like the crisis of the first half of the 1970s have taken place before. In principle, no changes of a qualitative character have taken place and a market economy has its own means and measures for regulating the situation (if not entirely automatically, at least with the aid of the government) which enables the temporary difficulties that have occurred in the course of economic development to be solved.

Scientific analysis of problems having a worldwide significance should make a distinction between the global aspects involved, and those typical for certain socio-economic systems.

We believe that the natural-historical reasons for the origin of the problems of natural resources include:

(i) the growing amount of natural resources required in the economy;
(ii) the relatively limited supply of natural resources available for satisfying world demand at the present level of knowledge and of technology for the utilisation of natural resources;
(iii) the disparity in the geography of natural resources and the location of productive forces.

The factors mentioned above are global in scope and are typical for modern economies regardless of the social system of a country or group of countries. They are closely related to the general laws of development of the relations between productive forces and nature.

II INCREASING DEMANDS FOR NATURAL RESOURCES

The growing population and production demand an increasing supply of foodstuffs and raw materials, which inevitably exerts an ever growing pressure on the resource potential of our planet. This influence is known to proceed in two directions: through the extension and intensification of the utilisation of natural resources on the one hand, and environment pollution with by-products and waste of economic activity, on the other.

During the post-war period only, that is, during the last 25–30 years, at least as large an amount of mineral resources was utilised as during the whole previous history of mankind. In the non-socialist countries during 1950–76, when there was a general growth of industrial production by 3.5 times, the average annual consumption of primary sources of energy (oil, natural gas, coal and uranium) increased by 2.6 times, use of metals increased threefold, of chemical raw materials 3.5 times. In the USA alone, industry annually mines about 2.5 billion tons of ore and waste – the equivalent of about six Panama Canals. These figures do not include fuel or large amounts of stone, sand and gravel.

Until recently the results of man's influence upon nature have in general had a local effect, and have not led to any serious disturbance of equilibrium in the biosphere. But nowadays, man is exerting an influence upon global natural processes. Many kinds of bio-resources, particularly fish and timber, are now threatened by irremediable damage. The influence on the environment in one region can often lead to a change of natural conditions in very remote places. The chemical composition and physical state of the atmosphere and World Ocean are changing under the influence of human activity. The exchange of matter and energy between nature and society, in the opinion of many specialists, has reached such dimensions that a further uncontrollable influence, exceeding the ability of the biosphere to self-recovery, would lead to an irreversible disturbance of global equilibrium.

The growth of production, necessitating the expansion and qualitative renewal of its natural basis, and the intensification and change of technology for the utilisation of natural resources, aggravate the problems because at every given moment the opportunities for their utilisation are limited by the level of the development of productive forces.

It is well known that the productivity of arable land could be, for example, considerably improved; large territories of now unused semi-desert and desert land, and deposits of natural resources, could be utilised. At the same time it is quite evident that at any given moment the limits of expansion of the natural basis of production are rather strictly determined from an economic point of view. Society has no possibility of abruptly increasing the expenditure of capital and utilisation of labour in order to use natural resources, without a serious change in the economic system as a whole. It is also relevant to the problem of overcoming the negative consequences of pollution: at the present level of development of productive forces the economic opportunities of achieving effective measures for the protection of nature are far from being unlimited.

A relative scarcity of natural resources, the utilisation of which is profitable at the existing level of knowledge and technology, and under the conditions of the growing scope of their use, could undoubtedly aggravate the problems. However, it should be mentioned that the relative scarcity of natural resources should not be taken for an absolute shortage of natural resources, or for an inevitable physical exhaustion.

Let us consider the case of the mineral resources used in industry. Thus, according to the data of the USSR All-Union Geological Fund, the ratio of the gross amount of known mineral reserves to the average annual level of their extraction in the non-socialist world by the middle of 1970s was as follows: iron ore – about 150 years; nickel – 100; aluminium – 70; copper – 55; coal, natural gas and oil – 600, 40–45 and 30–35 years, respectively. Taking into account the exponential growth of extraction during the post-war period, this ratio is essentially lower. If, for example, the ratio of the reserves to the current level of extraction is 35 years, then these reserves would be exhausted in 20 years provided the rate of growth of extraction is 5 per cent per year, and in 15 years if it is 10 per cent per year. Just this circumstance is often used as evidence of the impending rapid depletion of mineral resources of the highest quality and as an argument in favour of the inevitable rise in prices of raw materials once deposits of lower grade ores are exploited.

III RESERVES OF RAW MATERIALS AND THEIR RELATIVE PRICES

If the index which characterises the ratio of the reserves to extraction is considered statistically then the exhaustion thesis is supported. But the picture changes completely if this ratio is considered dynamically.

Analysis shows that during the post-war period the rate of growth of practically all kinds of reserves, both as a result of geological exploration and of scientific and technological progress in mining and metallurgy, exceeded, as a rule, the rate of growth of extraction of corresponding kinds of raw materials in the world non-socialist economy. As a result of this, the availability of the reserves in 1950–76, for the majority of mineral resources, not only did not decrease but, on the contrary, increased. The increase in the economic ore reserves during this period, taking into account the proportion extracted, exceeded by several times the total amount of resources of similar category discovered by the beginning of the 1950s.

In general, the trend towards the growth of discovered deposits of mineral resources by rates at least comparable with those for extraction is not only a characteristic of the post-war years. During the whole period of existence of the mining industry there never was a long period when the availability of world mineral resources was steadily decreasing. This is true even for oil, although many specialists would agree that reserves of oil would really be exhausted if the present trends in its consumption are maintained in the foreseeable future.

We should not ignore the fact that maintaining the reserves at a stable level relative to their extraction may involve the necessity of utilising lower grade ores, or of 'going further, digging deeper'. This could result in an increase in the cost of extraction and higher prices of raw materials. However, it is known that the content of the useful component in some of the ores that are extracted, for example in iron and copper ores, has been steadily decreasing for many years. Furthermore it is characteristic that the utilisation of lower grade ores and the exploitation of new deposits in remote areas (especially in Canada and Australia) which do not have any developed infrastructure, has not, so far, been accompanied by a growth of real costs of output, i.e. costs compared with a general price index.

The absence of a long-term rise in relative prices of mineral, non-energy, raw materials during the period of observation, indicates that the main factor, leading to industrial exploitation of lower grade ores, was technological progress rather than the lack of high-quality ores and favourably located deposits. Their utilisation in the non-socialist world was usually achieved only when conditions were provided for profitable exploitation of lower grade deposits as the result of the perfection of existing technology and the development of new methods. By these means they received extra profits within the existing price system even when unexploited deposits of higher quality were available. Therefore, it is not right to connect the decline in the cut-off grade in ores directly with an inevitable exhaustion of natural resources. On the contrary, the utilisation of lower grade ores has resulted in a considerable growth of reserves without an increase in real costs and prices.

It must be also taken into consideration, that the total known mineral reserves can be essentially augmented both in territories that are comparatively less explored and in well-known areas.

Accordingly, it may be concluded, there are no fundamental reasons for pessimism in respect of mineral reserves as a whole. (However, such a conclusion cannot be made without reservations as far as oil is concerned.) This does not mean that the abundance of natural resources *per se* can solve the problems connected with satisfaction of the economic requirements for minerals. The most important problem is the increasing time-lag between making the decision to organise production and beginning actual production. That lag increases with the rising scale of exploitation and the growing utilisation of lower grade ores and less accessible deposits. According to some estimates this time-lag already amounts to more than 10 years. While the demand for minerals is growing, further reduction of elasticity of supply[1] under conditions of low short-term elasticity of demand (characteristic for the mining and smelting industries) tends to increase the possibility of serious disproportions between production and consumption. This is especially likely when extra demand cannot be satisfied by means of available inventories and an increase in the use of existing capacity.

The negative consequences of such a situation may result in sharp price rises and a lack of some kinds of raw materials during the period necessary to develop new deposits.

[1] I mean short-term elasticity, because in the long term supply may be increased to any extent necessary for normal functioning of the economy.

IV DEVELOPMENT AND POSSESSION OF NATURAL RESOURCES

The problems of natural resources utilisation are aggravated by the increasing disparity in the geography of natural resources and the location of productive forces. Moreover, in the course of increasing international division of labour the dependence of the development of productive forces on natural resources is weakening. It is likely to acquire the character of interdependence, inevitably arising from specialisation within the world economic system.

However, it must be emphasised that, together with the general tendency towards a reduction in the importance of direct possession of natural resources for economic development of individual countries and areas, the role of world economic relations (such as trade, credit, financial, scientific and technological links, etc.) in the sphere of natural resource utilisation is increasing considerably.

Thus, in the non-socialist world, well-provided with mineral resources as a whole, some regions, especially industrially developed countries, are in deficit. Though this group of countries remains a leader in mining and processing the greater part of mineral resources, it is done mainly by intense exploitation of deposits in Canada, Australia, the USA and South Africa.

The tendency in the main centres of the non-socialist world towards reducing their supplies of raw materials of their own production may be observed quite clearly. As a result their dependence on deliveries of raw materials from external sources, including developing countries, is growing. For example, the USA is now importing more than 40 per cent of liquid fuels consumed (without taking into account their latent import in energy-intensive products). Many other industrially developed countries depend almost completely on external deliveries of crude petroleum and other energy resources. The majority of developing countries, in their turn, run a deficit of foodstuffs and depend on deliveries from industrialised states. This is due to the lack of land suitable for effective agricultural production, aggravated by the lack of financial and material resources, knowledge, techniques and qualified working power. The dimensions of this dependence are growing.

V THE BASIS FOR A SOCIALIST SOLUTION OF THE PROBLEM

The imbalance between production and consumption of raw materials and foodstuffs in several areas, as well as unsettled questions of international law connected with exploitation of the World Ocean resources are two of the key factors determining the tremendous influence which international economic and political relations exert on the state, development and solution of the problems of natural resource use.

Thus, a deeper understanding of the laws governing the relations between society and nature; and, based on this, the regulation and rationalisation of the processes of natural resource utilisation in the interests of the development of all mankind represents the necessary condition for the successful and timely solution of the global problems of natural resources.

It is obvious that a planned socialist economy has all the necessary possibilities for conscious regulation of the relations between man and nature. However, this does not mean that there are no problems in this field. For instance, there is the problem of overcoming the utilitarian approach to nature. This has been prevalent for ages, and its solution is not simple even for a socialist state.

The complex planning activity of socialist states is aimed at the extension of the natural resource base of production by active prospecting for mineral resources, improvements in the technology for utilisation of natural resources, rationalisation, and the most favourable distribution of productive forces (taking into account all the possibilities and limitations of the environment).

VI THE PROBLEMS FOR CAPITALISM

A worldwide problem can develop into a crisis only when mankind is unable to solve the problem in a given period of time, either because it does not possess the necessary scientific and technological knowledge, or for socio-economic reasons. Here we approach the specific character of the problems of natural resource utilisation under the conditions of the capitalist mode of production, i.e. a market economy.

The essence of the natural resource problems of modern capitalism lies in the contradiction between the rising needs for raw materials and food (considering the relative scarcity of world natural resources and the disparity in their geography and that of productive forces), and the social and economic conditions of the capitalist utilisation of natural resources. The socio-economic relations and, in particular, the property relations peculiar to capitalism are the conditions which can lead to a crisis. In the process of capitalist reproduction these problems appear from time to time, whether in the form of relative overproduction, or of a shortage of raw materials and food, as well as in the irrational use of natural resources and degradation of the environment. In the sphere of the world economic relations of capitalism the problems of natural resource utilisation reflect the contradictory character of relations between industrial and developing countries, between developing countries and multinational corporations.

Due to changes in the old mechanism of resource use, which was formed in colonial times, and to sharp aggravation of the contradictions between the 'centres' and the 'periphery' of the world capitalist economy, the raw materials problem (including the energy shortage) and the problems of food and, to some extent, of the World Ocean, have resulted in a crisis. It is this that is new in the evolution of the problems of utilisation of natural resources in modern capitalism.

Thus, the crisis of natural resource use in the non-socialist world is, first of all, the crisis of the present system of capitalist division of labour; and this crisis can be overcome only through radical reconstruction of the world capitalist economy, and by changing the character of international economic relations. It assumes the settlement of numerous questions, such as the financing of development, transfer of technology, activities of multinational corporations, etc. One of the most important tasks of modern economic science is to work out democratic ways and means of solving the problems of natural resource utilisation, taking into account the interests of all the states; and to determine the prospects for international co-operation in the field of natural resource use.

In the Report of the Central Committee to the XXV Congress of the CPSU it was said that: 'Global problems such as primary materials and energy, . . . environmental protection . . . and the utilization of the resources of the World Ocean are already sufficiently important and urgent. In the future they will exercise an increasingly perceptible influence on the life of each nation and on the entire system of international relations. The Soviet Union, like other socialist countries, cannot hold aloof from the solution of these problems which affect the interests of all mankind.'

The following issues, in my opinion, are of primary importance for research connected with solving the problems of natural resource utilisation:

(i) thorough study and simulation of the interrelations between the world economic system and its natural resource base;
(ii) investigation of the long-term prospects for world demand for raw materials, energy and foodstuffs;
(iii) analysis of the carrying capacity of the biosphere, and its capacity for self-recovery;
(iv) study of positive changes in the structure of the world economy and international relations, taking into account the interests of all the states.

Realisation of the proposals of the socialist countries, jointly put forward at the Fourth Session of UNCTAD, can serve as an important practical contribution to the solution of international economic aspects of the problems of natural resource utilisation. These proposals include:

(i) expansion of the practice of concluding long-term agreements in the field of complex development of natural resources, in particular, compensation agreements;
(ii) normalisation of international trade in raw materials and limitation of the effect of spontaneous market forces and the negative influence of multinationals on the development of the world markets of raw materials;
(iii) creation of a co-ordinated system of international stabilisation agreements of a new type which could stimulate the economic growth of developing countries.

Discussion of the papers by Professor Herrera and Dr Simonyan

(Chairman: Academician T. Khachaturov)

Professor M. Ostrowski (Poland) introduced the discussion of these two papers. He noted that they were more optimistic about the problem of natural resources than some earlier commentators and thought that their work provided a more balanced approach to the issues. This turned on the increase in the risk of danger from the relative scarcity of particular non-renewable resources rather than on the problem of ultimate depletion. It thus raised the question of the mechanism by which this situation of increasing risk would emerge and of the difference in the degree of risk faced by particular countries.

This new approach via the notion of risk of scarcity had important consequences for economic theory. For example, it would require a different approach to the factors of production, and it would also have implications for the concept of rent and the rules of pricing.

Concern about natural resources was thus concern about the degree of acceptable risk, and Professor Ostrowski noted that attempts were being made in Poland to develop new ideas on these lines. He welcomed Professor Herrera's suggestions about the strategy for dealing with possible bottlenecks but observed that reducing growth rates and the consumption of resources was not a costless process – it required investment to provide alternatives.

Finally, Professor Ostrowski said that the third world countries were large exporters of natural resources because they were low consumers. This would not last. The problem of natural resources was thus, above all, of a political character.

Professor Malinvaud (France) said that it was unfortunate that Professor Herrera was not able to attend the conference. His paper provided a particularly good introduction for the discussion but Professor Malinvaud did not agree with the last sentence. There were many good reasons for changing present social philosophies, and in particular the predominant one (whatever it was today!); we must also recognise that the foundations on which our approach to development was based were too weak. But it would be too easy to say that economics could not contribute to a better management of natural resources unless a new approach to development was introduced.

Turning to the substantive parts of the paper, Professor Malinvaud said that he would not dwell at length on what was said of positive economic theory and of the real dimensions of scarcity of natural resources. It was indeed true that Ricardo's hypothesis was too simple, as also was Hotelling's hypothesis on exhaustible resources. However, economic theory had been developed in the directions suggested by Professor Herrera; and though further progress was certainly needed, there should not be any basic difficulty in this respect.[1]

[1] See in particular the paper by G. Heal in E. Malinvaud (ed.), *Economic Growth and Resources*, Vol. 1 (Macmillan, 1979).

The problems of normative economic theory, i.e. of resource allocation, were much more formidable. Professor Herrera was right when he pointed to risk as the major component in the field he considered. Indeed, in Professor Malinvaud's view, the problem was even more dramatic than was apparent in the paper. The management of exhaustible resources was the major case (we could even say, neglecting a few special situations, the only case) in which long-term consequences of our present decisions were of major importance. It was only under the favourable circumstances in which there would not be, after all, any significant physical limit to natural resources (and to our future technological knowledge) that the problem would be mild.

But he would claim that economic theory had recently done a lot to clarify how exhaustible resources should be managed. In this respect Herrera's section on 'the optimal use of natural resources' was rather weak. The quotation from D. W. Pearce was certainly not the best one to give and he would not himself subscribe to it. Moreover, Professor Herrera seemed to believe that 'neo-classical economics' advocated only the market system, paid no attention to long-term horizons and was dependent on a narrowly economic definition of 'optimal use', as opposed to a truly social definition. None of these points was correct, unless we meant by neo-classical economics a very old type of economics, which was not the one in which modern theoretical contributions would find their place.

Professor Pajestka (Poland) disagreed with Professor Malinvaud's criticism of Professor Herrera's comment on social philosophy in the last sentence of the paper. He thought the pattern of development of science and technology should be approached from this point of view, and that the concept of global long-run rationality previously discussed should be extended to cover this development of science and technology.

Mr Kaser (UK) asked Dr Simonyan whether he foresaw a rise in the price of natural resources relative to labour and capital. His paper (pp. 165–6) was not clear. He would also have liked Professor Ostrowski to clarify his comments on techniques for charging for the use of resources.

Dr Desai (India) welcomed the fact that both these papers rejected the pessimism about supply of exhaustible resources which used to prevail not many years ago. When forecasts of eventual shortage of resources were made, the economic profession's first reaction was to rely on the possibility of substitution, the ability to *economise* in face of higher prices as an antidote to eventual exhaustion. This reaction though conservative had proved to be correct. But at the same time, the challenge posed by exhaustibility had inspired research.

He discussed the problem of risk brought out in both the papers. There might be different types of risk:

(i) certainty of eventual exhaustion of a certain resource;
(ii) uncertainty of exhaustion due to the possibility of future discoveries of new reserves or new substitutes;

(iii) uncertainty of exhaustion due to the possibility of technical change which might economise on the use of the exhaustible resource or which might develop substitutes.

These problems had been discussed by economic theorists. (See especially the recent special issue of *Review of Economic Studies* on Exhaustible Resources, Symposium, 1974) and the forthcoming book by Dasgupta and Heal.[1]

The answers which had been reached by theorists, albeit using abstract models, had concerned the social rate of discount which should be used and the rate of extraction of the exhaustible resource. Some progress had been made in this field.

Dr Desai noted that Professor Herrera's view implied that economic theory provided restrictive economic solutions rather than a social solution (p. 158). This might mean that theory concentrated only on short-run private profit-maximising solutions. If so, this was untrue. Much of the discussion had been in terms of *society's* preference function taking into account *social* benefits and costs. It might be objected that the framework was often utilitarian since an integral of discounted social utility was usually the maximand. But this was a technical problem which could be tackled in other ways.

Both authors mentioned the uneven geographical distribution of natural resources. In a system of nation-states, a country sitting on a reserve of natural resource could extract the quasi-rent from this ownership. Its actual ability in bargaining with the country or TNC supplying technical or financial inputs would depend on many local factors, such as the character of the ruling élite, but the potential for extracting such quasi-rent existed.

Professor Urquidi (Mexico) recalled that earlier statements by Dr Herrera, e.g. in the so-called Bariloche Report, had been less cautious about non-renewable resources, assuming that there was no cost in digging miles and miles below the earth's crust to obtain every kind of mineral. However, in his paper and that of Dr Simonyan, there was still not enough emphasis on real cost factors, especially for the developing countries. Therefore the idea that there were unlimited supplies of non-renewable resources was not a very realistic one, nor one that could help the developing countries to assess their development potential and allocate resources from this point of view, because of competing demands.

Professor Niehans (Switzerland) confessed to being somewhat disappointed that both of these papers failed to take account of the literature about exhaustible resources which had grown up over the years. He wished to make five comments which were explicitly related to Professor Herrera's paper, but to some extent applied also to Dr Simonyan's paper.

First, when the problems of natural resources began to appear more and more urgent, economic science, in fact, responded vigorously and rapidly. The

[1] P. S. Dasgupta and G. M. Heal, *Economic Theory and Exhaustible Resources* (Cambridge Handbooks, 1979).

result was a vast and still growing stream of contributions written from many points of view, considering a large and varied number of problems and using many different approaches. While even a partial bibliography would have the size of a small volume, topics included (with a few names added for illustrative purposes) the optimal depletion of resources (Gordon, Koopmans), resources in optimal growth (Anderson, Stiglitz, Hauri and Hung), the optimal exploitation of replenishable resources like fish (Gordon, Scott, Crutchfield and Zellner, Smith, Quirk and Smith, Cliff and Vincent, Plourde), the efficiency of resource use under competition (Stiglitz), the influence of monopoly (Weinstein and Zeckhauser, Stiglitz), intergenerational equity (Dasgupta, Solow), the influence of uncertainty about demand and future technology (Dasgupta and Heal, Weinstein and Zeckhauser), investment in resource industries (Burt and Cummings), cost-benefit analysis for resources (Fisher and Krutilla), recycling (Weinstein and Zeckhauser), interactions between resource depletion, population and capital (Niehans), environmental economics (see survey by Fisher and Peterson), water resources (Kneese), energy policy (Nordhaus), uranium reserves (Manne), and systems analysis of world dynamics (Forrester, Meadows *et al.*).

Second, he thought Professor Herrera's discussion of Pareto optimality was less accurate than it could be. Pareto optimality, in fact, required that *nobody* could be made better off without somebody else being worse off, and it was very much concerned with the absolute level of the demand for resources. It was generally known, on the other hand, that the Pareto criterion did not provide a complete ordering of possible allocations, so that other criteria were needed to select the optimal allocation.

Third, precisely those who felt that free markets failed to provide an optimal allocation of natural resources should find it profitable to turn to economic science, because the possible causes of market failure were one of the main topics in this area.

Fourth, concern with limited resources was not a recent fad, but could build on a strong tradition. In classical economics it took the form of the Malthusian concern about the limited availability of land. With Jevons, a protagonist of neo-classical theory, it became a concern for the exhaustion of coal, and his pessimistic predictions were similar to those we now heard for petroleum. The work was later extended by Gray and Hotelling, who in 1931 described the problem very much as we would today.

Finally, and more generally, Professor Niehans said that he was not sure what 'neo-classical economics' was supposed to include. In many respects, particularly with respect to exhaustible resources, it seemed to be virtually identical with economic science. In any case, it was by far the largest available body of relevant scientific contributions on natural resources, and it was relevant irrespective of whether we preferred a free market or centralised planning.

Professor Hagemejer (Poland) said that existing economic theory dealt with short-term problems and that a different set of measures would be necessary to solve the long-term problems. In his view it was important for economists to concentrate on this rather than on questions of social philosophy. He noted that Dr Simonyan was relatively optimistic about the future but other countries were not as richly endowed with resources as the USSR and so might face a more difficult situation. He agreed, however, with the main points of the paper.

He also referred to Dr Desai's observation that ownership of resources could be a source of quasi-rent, and said that the giant corporations had taken over the role of the old colonial powers and possessed a monopoly of technical knowledge. This affected the distribution of the gains from raw materials and it was necessary to stress this.

Professor Furtado (Brazil) said that there was an important problem of demarcation: one should not blame economic theory for the existence of all problems, and Professor Hagemejer expected more from economics than it could offer.

He also pointed out that neo-classical economics did not imply that non-renewable resources had to be privately owned. The market system and the use of prices could operate with public ownership, though where resources were privately owned this influenced the time horizon for price decisions and technical progress, and as a result there could be tremendous waste of resources. Fundamentally, however, he saw the problem as a global one with the same implications for socialist as for capitalist countries. They shared the same technology and the same constraints of time horizons.

Professor Seers (UK) said that simple calculations brought out the energy problem which was correctly highlighted by Dr Simonyan. The US consumption of energy per capita would be approaching 30 tonnes of coal equivalent (tce) at the end of the century. Hypothetically let us assume that in the year 2050 a world population of 9 billions enjoyed this living standard. It would require a total energy use that year of 252 billion tce, or about 25 times the current level. Moreover, to reach that figure exponentially would require a total energy use of 10,000 billion tce in the intervening 70 years,[1] or more than 6 times the total known reserves of fossil fuels (a figure which might well be increased by exploration and technical changes, but one must allow for the environmental costs of extracting all the reserves, especially of coal). The lead time in non-conventional sources of energy would be very long, especially in the fusion process of nuclear power. Moreover, unless technical advances were dramatic, capital requirements would be beyond the capacity of most countries. Even in the industrial countries, the development of nuclear power could well be jeopardised by a major nuclear disaster, which would send them back into the narrowing market for oil. Another risk was a change of depletion policy in Saudi Arabia. Governments with responsibility for their

[1] *World Futures: The Great Debate*, (eds.) Chris Freeman and Marie Jahoda (Science Policy Research Unit, Sussex University: Martin Robertson, 1978).

people's living standards would need to shape their policies accordingly, introducing into cost-benefit calculations unquantifiable factors such as national security.

Dr Streeten (UK) said that the movement from the original Club of Rome report to the subsequent work of Leontief (Bariloche), Herrera, Tinbergen (RIO) and others represented a reaction against excessive emphasis on physical exhaustion of natural resources and high costs of combating pollution, and an attempt to allow for economic, social and political constraints. He was not sure which was more pessimistic: to assume that the limits were physical and technical, or social and political. Was it easier to discover substitutes for coal and oil, or to prevent strikes of coal miners and embargoes by OPEC?

Professor Ostrowski (Poland) replied to Mr Kaser's question about pricing policy. He and a colleague had proposed that a 'prudence premium' should be incorporated in prices as a reflection of uncertainy and of the real cost which society was paying for a variety of policies to increase reserves. A more radical proposal would be to base all prices not on actual costs (including the prudence premium) but on anticipated costs. This would lead to economies in the use of resources at the micro level.

In practice, however, prices were not much used in Poland for this purpose, and the Government influenced decisions in other ways. Regional policy played an outstanding role in this respect.

Professor Z. Sadowski (Poland) said that he was far less optimistic than others about the optimum allocation of resources and the extent to which the problem had been solved. He thought that Professor Herrera's paper showed what the answer might be at a global level but the full solution to the problem of optimum allocation could only be found at the national level. This had not yet been done, and he was doubtful whether it could be done, i.e. he did not think that it was possible to find a proper basis for a set of criteria for decisions on the optimum allocation of resources. It was technically possible only on the basis of so many rigid assumptions that it was of doubtful relevance.

It was necessary to develop a method of flexible adaptation, of trial and error; and this was a task for economists because no other discipline could undertake it.

Professor Malinvaud (France) said that he wanted to clarify one issue. He did not want to leave the impression that he considered the future management of exhaustible resources to be an easy problem. He merely claimed that economic theory had, for its part, provided a set of analytical tools and models that were relevant for the treatment of the problem.

The difficulties did not result from a deficiency of economic theory but from inadequate factual knowledge and from the inadequacy of the political process. On the first inadequacy he mentioned as an example the erroneous information that was given to the economists by energy specialists in 1974, namely that, at a price of more than 6 dollars a barrel of crude oil, production of shale oil would be undertaken at a profit. The second inadequacy basically came from the fact that our fellow citizens refused to be explicitly confronted with major choices involving risk and trade-off as between generations. We must recognise that the political debate on the management of exhaustible resources was at a very low level.

Professor Porwit (Poland) said that one of the interesting points in Professor Herrera's paper was his observation of a growing discrepancy between the scope and rate of changes in demand, and the possibilities for coping with such changes, especially from the viewpoint of the so-called technological lead time. This might be considered as a symptom of a more general issue of dynamic interrelations between the size and frequency of changes induced by exogenous and endogenous perturbations and reflected in the behaviour of socio-economic systems and – on the other hand – systems' capacitics of adaptation. In that context Stafford Beer made a remark (in his book *Designing Freedom*, London, 1975) that '. . . relaxation time becomes on the average longer than the average interval between perturbations with the result that the institutional system is permanently unstable'. He added that similar tendencies were observed in the field of regulatory processes (dealing with information and organisation). In terms used by system analysis and cybernetics one spoke about the 'proliferation of variety' within socio-economic systems and the difficulties involved in ensuring regulatory mechanisms able to cope with such tendencies. In this context remedial measures of two types were considered. One was to reduce the scope and rate for the proliferation of variety in order to make the situation more manageable. It seemed that the examples of this approach could be seen in arguments for checking the rate of growth, for harnessing autonomous technological development, for limiting the impact of imported consumption patterns and technologies. The other type of measure related to amplification of the capacities of regulatory processes, i.e. producing better and more suitable information, strengthening organisation, improving regulatory mechanisms in a wider socio-economic sense. In this area significant progress could be noted in econometrics and decision-making sciences as well as in the area of studying economic and financial mechanisms.

Measures of the first type appeared to be unrealistic if they were only general postulates and did not follow out of the manner of the system's behaviour. Within the second group we were getting much significant instrumental knowledge which was certainly relevant for coping with practical problems, but this did not answer the question for whom, for whose sake and benefit, in what manner, the instruments might be used.

Professor Porwit thought that even if better and more comprehensive information was ensured some conflicting issues were still likely to emerge. Information might be a source of power which might give various components of the system uneven possibilities to use it. Possibilities of flexibility in adaptation, of devising and implementing anticipatory measures, depended not only on information but also on the really existing domain of freedom for choice and action, which might be constrained. There were conflicts between the perceived necessity to engage on large long-term projects (such as those related to the so-called offensive technological strategies and to more distant aims involving structural reconstruction) and – on the other hand – the scope of decision potential existing at present, with additional determination to keep some potential for unforeseen but inevitable adaptations in the future. Symptoms of such issues might be observed within particular national economies and also at an international, global level.

From the viewpoint of the main topic of the conference, Professor Porwit considered that we had developed relevant scientific tools for analysing general tendencies in systems' behaviour, always based on certain assumptions abstracting from some features of reality. On the other hand there were powerful tools for concrete quantitative treatment of definite situations, tools for diagnosis or decision-making, if such situations were sufficiently and correctly identified. One should not underrate these possibilities, but there was perhaps a gap in between, related to understanding the complex pattern of interactions between numerous agents and components of the system, especially looked upon as being in motion. This was perhaps an area where future research should be concentrated.

He said that against this background he would be inclined to introduce some qualifications to the words of critique levelled at the stream in economic theoretical writings based on formal mathematical apparatus. There were certainly many examples of essays in which economic notions were used only as a framework for an analysis of a formal nature, with conclusions distant from economic reality. However, there was also a great number of examples of the utmost significance and relevance. Probably the feelings of dissatisfaction were expressed because the complex, multidimensional features of dynamic interactions within the system seemed too difficult to be modelled, although they were of crucial importance for present-day society.

Professor Niehans (Switzerland) made a comment arising from Professor Seers' remarks on energy supplies. He said that economic history showed, and economic theory confirmed, that adjustment mechanisms invariably came into operation to prevent the disasters predicted by simple extrapolation of past rates of growth. These adjustments might, for example, work through prices or through the growth of population.

Professor Ostrowski (Poland) said that there was a universal problem of management (or mismanagement) of natural resources. The role of economic theory was to give some approximate guidance between the various options including improved technology to increase supply and changes in consumption patterns to reduce demand.

Dr Simonyan, replying to the discussion, emphasised two points. First, in his view the supplies of natural resources would not be an insurmountable constraint on the future growth of the world economy, or of the economies of particular countries, subject to normal development of international economic relations. Nor would the emerging scarcities lead to a long-term trend to higher costs of raw materials, especially of non-fuels, relative to those of other commodities. In the past the process of 'going further, digging deeper' had not raised relative costs and in his view (which was not shared by many other Soviet economists) the position would not be essentially different in the future. This was only a general rule, however, and there could be specific exceptions. It would be a major function of investment policy and technical progress to prevent such future bottlenecks.

Secondly, he wanted to underline his agreement with the view expressed by Professor Seers that the problem of natural resources was above all a political and social issue. The full utilisation of existing reserves would depend on a transformation of the existing national and international conditions in the non-socialist countries.

PART SIX
Economic Development: Theory and Policy

12 Development: What have we Learned?

Paul Streeten
THE WORLD BANK, WASHINGTON, DC

I interpret my task as being to survey development theory critically, in the light of its realism and relevance to the problems of development, to discuss the case for interdisciplinary studies, to separate ideas that have been discarded from those that have withstood the test of time and to point to promising new departures.

I A WHIRLWIND TOUR OF THE THEORY OF DEVELOPMENT POLICY

One often hears that the objective of development has been GNP growth maximisation. This, of course, is complete nonsense. No self-respecting economist ever advocated growth maximisation. GNP consists of consumption and investment. To maximise GNP growth would mean tightening our belts so as to reduce consumption to the bare productive minimum, to accumulate a vast stock of capital until doomsday and, just before the world comes to an end, to indulge in a vast consumption orgy. Since GNP growth has costs in terms of foregone consumption, a more sensible objective would be to maximise the current value of the flow of consumption (or welfare), appropriately weighted for different income groups, and appropriately discounted over time.

Growth was never a sensible objective, but it was accepted as a principal performance test of development, usually on one of three assumptions. First, some assumed that GNP growth would have a tendency to spread rapidly to all social groups. The mechanism of this tendency to 'trickle-down' was thought to be rising demand for labour, growing productivity reflected in relatively lower prices of consumption goods or higher wages of workers, upgrading and acquisition of skills, etc.

An alternative assumption was that growth may not have a tendency to spread automatically to the poorer groups, but government, through social services, progressive taxation, and other measures will correct the tendency of the benefits of development to be highly concentrated.

A third assumption was that, while there is neither automatic trickle-down, nor government action that corrects gross inequalities, inequalities and even the perpetuation of poverty must be not only tolerated but positively encouraged, for without these development cannot proceed.

Models like those of A. W. Lewis, and the use and abuse of the so-called Kuznets curve encouraged this view. Galenson and Leibenstein argued that capital-intensive methods were to be preferred to labour-intensive ones, because they generated profits and profits are the source of savings. In other words, the savings had to be squeezed out of the poorest groups, the unemployed, who, if they were given jobs, would consume more and frustrate the accumulation of capital.

It is clear that the early writers did not neglect distribution, as is often maintained. They thought either that distribution will look after itself, or the government will look after it, or nobody should look after it.

In the light of the experience of the last twenty-five years, none of the three positions is tenable, at least universally. There has been no universal tendency of trickle-down, though some countries, with appropriate 'initial conditions' (in the form of land distribution and education) and correct policies, have succeeded in combining high growth rates with a high degree of dispersion of benefits. Government, normally recruited from the same groups that benefit from concentrated growth, did not usually show willingness to adopt policies that would spread these benefits to the poor. And the third assumption, that things would have to get worse before they get better, and that inequality and even poverty are necessary conditions for growth, was contradicted when it was seen that small farmers were more productive than large farmers in terms of yield per acre, and often even of yield per unit of all inputs, that savings ratios did not necessarily decline with lower incomes, and that there was productive potential in the urban 'informal' sector, about which more below. In any case, it became clear that the strategy 'grow first and redistribute later' was not a politically realistic option.

The Lewis model had led us to expect that the rural poor would gradually be absorbed in the modern, urban, industrial sector and that, though inequalities might increase for a time (as the low-income, low-productivity subsistence farmers and landless labourers are absorbed by high-income, high-productivity modern industry, assuming that the differential between inequalities within agriculture and within industry does not exceed a critical size), after a relatively short period the whole labour force would be in the high-income, high-productivity sector and the golden age would be ushered in, in which growth is accompanied by equity. For a number of reasons, such as high rates of population growth, trade union action and minimum wage legislation keeping urban wages high and providing incentives for the use of capital, and the nature of modern, capital-intensive technology, this process of absorption of rural labour was extremely slow or absent, and dualism between town and country, and between industry and agriculture, instead of diminishing, grew. More particularly, unemployment in the towns and underemployment in the country appears to be recalcitrant. The emphasis shifted from growth to employment. The ILO mounted an employment programme and sent missions to Colombia, Sri Lanka, Kenya, Philippines, Iran, Sudan, the Dominican Republic and other countries to recommend action.

The missions brought back a mass of useful evidence and analysis, but one of their conclusions, also emphasised possibly at excessive length in Myrdal's *Asian Drama*, was that 'employment' and 'unemployment' are not concepts appropriate for the analysis of poverty in poor countries. It is an example of the transfer of an inappropriate intellectual technology from one setting, where there are labour markets, a trained and willing labour force, information about job availabilities, labour exchanges, etc. to an entirely different setting, where the dimensions of labour utilisation depend on much more than creating demand for labour (reducing Keynesian unemployment) and providing co-operating factors like machines (reducing Marxian unemployment). Demand could easily be expanded and capital was grossly underutilised, to an even greater extent than in developed countries, where capital is more abundant. Yet labour remained grossly underutilised.

A full analysis of labour utilisation raises complex issues. In many poor countries higher consumption of the labour force would raise its productivity. Better nutrition, health and education of the labour force contribute to more output. And a sole emphasis on employment may conflict with more efficient labour supply, as when dairy farming creates more jobs but reduces the growth of subsistence crops like millet or maize or sorghum and lowers the quality of the diet. Labour utilisation is also determined by attitudes, such as caste membership or aspirations for white-collar jobs created by overeducation. And it depends on institutions like labour exchanges, and on land ownership, tenurial laws, credit for mechanisation, etc.

Some of the ILO missions also 'discovered' the 'informal' sector in the towns, the 'working poor', the carpenters, blacksmiths, sandal-makers, builders, lamp-makers, who, far from being unemployed, work very hard and very long hours, but often unremuneratively and at low levels of productivity. Indeed, it was said that in order to be able to afford to be unemployed you have to be quite well off. The truly poor cannot afford unemployment.

The employment concept, it was soon found, suffered from other limitations, in addition to ignoring the multiple dimensions of labour utilisation and mobilisation. It does not deal with the unemployables. Even if jobs were available for all who can work, there are those who cannot: the sick, the old, the disabled. Are they to be entirely neglected? They may comprise as many as 20 per cent of the population of many poor countries.

A third limitation of the employment concept is that it does not tell us anything about the provision of and access to public services. Income gives purchasing power over goods and services sold in the market, but health, education, water and waste disposal, all essential to the poor, are not normally sold. While private income may be an essential condition for access to these services, it certainly is not sufficient and an employment and income approach ignores this whole domain.

Fourthly, employment can aggravate both inequalities and unemployment. Those fortunate enough to get jobs in modern industry belong to the highest income groups in many developing countries. And Harris and Todaro have shown how the creation of extra jobs can attract additional migrants from the country, swelling the ranks of the urban unemployed.

The discussion then turned to the 'working poor' and more specifically to the way in which their productivity and incomes can be raised. This naturally focused attention on distribution, redistribution (of both assets and income) and on the links between redistribution and growth. How does redistribution affect economic growth? And how, in turn, does growth affect income distribution? Is there a dilemma, are there trade-offs, or does redistribution accelerate growth? Are there ways in which growth can be conducted so as to spread its benefits widely?

The literature on the analysis, the measurement, and the cures of inequality proliferated. 'Redistribution with growth' or 'redistribution from growth' attempted to combine growth with equity, by advocating instead of the politically 'difficult' redistribution of existing assets, especially land, redistribution of increments of income. But, like the employment approach, the redistribution approach, although it threw up many interesting lessons, was found deficient. Incremental redistribution is politically as difficult as non-incremental. In addition, its results are extremely meagre. A simulation model showed that channelling 2 per cent of GNP into public services for the poor would raise the incomes of the bottom 40 per cent after forty years by 0.5 per cent p.a., that is $1 out of an income of $200.

It was also found that redistribution as an objective is somewhat irrelevant if we have widespread poverty. Measures of inequality such as the Gini coefficient tell us about the whole range of incomes, whereas we are not very interested in what happens to the middle 40 per cent. Even for purposes of reducing inequality, we are more interested in comparing the bottom 30–40 per cent with the top 10 or 20 per cent. How do the landless labourers fare and what can redistribution do for the urban poor, who have no assets and cannot readily acquire any? Where are the areas of deprivation – which members of families, which age groups? Gini coefficients do not illuminate these questions.

The final step in this evolution has been a zooming in on the eradication of absolute poverty, on meeting the basic human needs of those who still live a subhuman life. Basic Needs, apart from being a powerful organising concept, has the advantage of being more positive and operational than 'eliminating poverty' or 'reducing unemployment' – both of which are two negatives. In addition, it focuses on ends rather than means. A focus on the proper end, far from neglecting means, draws attention to the proper means. And since Basic Needs has a time dimension, and we must heed how growth is composed, whom it benefits and how it is measured, in space as well as in time, growth is the ***result***, not the *objective*, of a basic needs approach to development. Basic Needs liberates us from commodity fetishism and puts man in the centre of things. It may well require higher growth rates than past strategies, but such growth will be differently composed and distributed (and measured).

Thirdly, Basic Needs follows the evolution of our experience and thinking in being a further step in the march from the abstract to the concrete, from the general to the particular. It goes behind concepts such as money, income, employment, all of which are necessary but too aggregative. We have been following a path of growing disaggregation: from GNP and its growth to employment and distribution, to the unemployment of specific groups, like school leavers and recent migrants, to the needs of the small farmer without water. Basic Needs zeroes in on specific deficiencies – calories, health, content of education – of particular deprived groups, women, young children, ethnic groups, and treats their satisfaction as a public good, both nationally and internationally. People give higher priority to reducing malnutrition in children than to redistributing income, and my satisfaction in doing this does not detract from yours.

II THE MEANING AND PURPOSE OF INTERDISCIPLINARY STUDIES

With almost monotonous repetition, we hear calls for interdisciplinary studies, or, more accurately, for the breakdown of boundaries between disciplines, at conferences, in papers and in books about the problems of development in the third world. Yet relatively little is done to achieve this breakdown. This is partly due to lack of clarity about what is meant by the plea and partly due to the fact that the only forum where interdisciplinary studies in depth can be conducted successfully is under one skull, and that such skulls are scarce.

There are three quite distinct reasons for interdisciplinary, multidisciplinary, transdisciplinary or supradisciplinary work.[1] Each has different methodological implications. First, a practical problem like improving nutrition, instituting a mass rural health service, introducing new varieties of crops, controlling population growth, reducing pollution, planning a town, may call for drawing upon and applying several disciplines. In the co-operative effort the disciplines are not transcended but brought together to solve a particular set of practical problems. The prevalence of planning at all levels has contributed to the co-operation between different disciplines. The planner has to draw on all relevant knowledge and skills. This practical need to bring all relevant methods, data and information to bear on the solution of a specific problem does not affect the methods used in the contributing disciplines. On the contrary, it is just because they are specialists in their fields that the different members of the team have a contribution to make to an integrated solution. We might think of them as members of a Royal Commission investigating problems of controlling environmental

[1] Some people object to terms like 'multidisciplinary' or 'interdisciplinary'. It is true that they sound somewhat pretentious and abstract. I have not been able to think of a better expression for this type of work.

pollution, deciding upon a family planning programme or meeting basic needs in a particular country. The attempt to meet basic needs might, for example, call upon the skills of engineers, doctors, educators, nutritionists, development administrators, political scientists, anthropologists, sociologists, and even economists, whose job it might be to explore externalities, linkages and social cost benefit analysis.

Second, it may be the case that certain assumptions, concepts or methods, hitherto applied only to one sphere of activity, yield illuminating results when applied to another, previously analysed in quite different ways. There has been some invasion by economic concepts and methods into the territory of political scientists and sociologists. Thus, the assumption of maximising behaviour has been fruitful, up to a point, in analysing the behaviour of consumers, firms and farms. Its success has encouraged its application to political activities such as voting and party formation. It has also been applied to the exploration of politically feasible income distributions. Calculations of economic returns have been extended from profit-making investments to education, health, birth control and the allocation of time between work and leisure and of leisure time itself. It has even been extended to family relations, to the desire for children, to marriage, to extra-marital affairs, to criminal behaviour and to other fields. Occasionally, though much less frequently, concepts used in political theory have been applied to economic problems. Albert Hirschman's use of 'voice' as an alternative to 'exit' is an interesting example.[1]

There is a third, and deeper, reason for interdisciplinary work. It may be that for a particular time or region the justification for a discipline consists in the empirical fact that between the variables encompassed by this discipline and those treated by another, there are few interactions and the effects of any existing interaction are weak and damped. Only then are we justified in analysing causal sequences in one field, without always and fully taking into account those in others.

We may all agree that society is a system and that all social variables are related, but with growing differentiation of functions and standards, some relationships are stronger than others. This justifies us in separating, say, business responses from family responses, or economics from anthropology. As Michael Lipton has argued in a stimulating and valuable article, the need for interdisciplinary studies does not arise because people in underdeveloped countries, particularly in subsistence households, perform many functions normally separated in rich countries, but because there is interdependence between variables normally analysed separately. 'Lack of specialization among the people being studied in no way justifies lack of specialization among the students. A student of Michelangelo could well confine attention to his sculpture, while caring little for the architecture and painting in which

[1] A. O. Hirschman, *Exit, Voice and Loyalty* (Harvard, 1970).

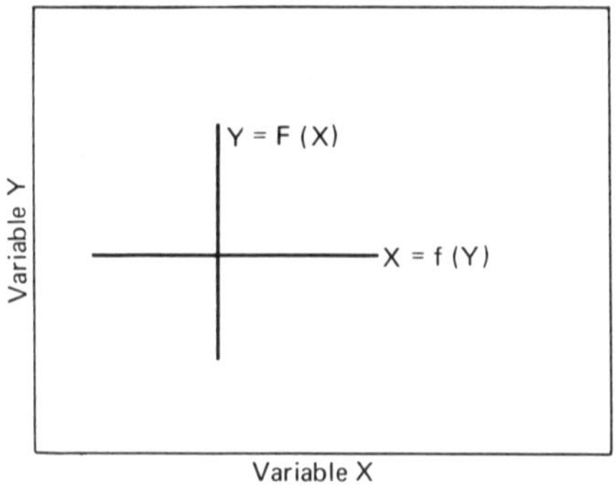

Fig. 12.1 Non-interdependence

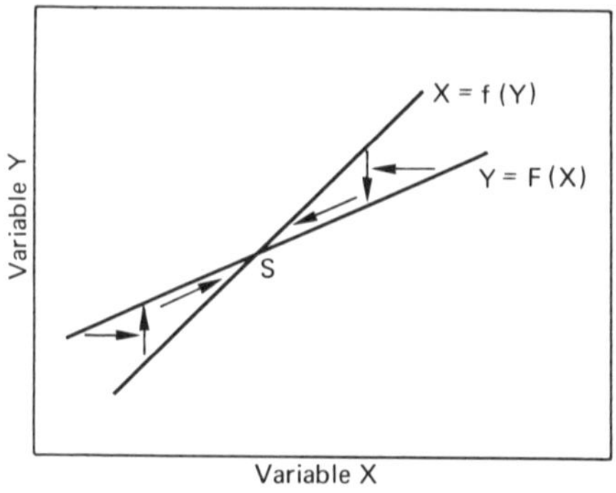

Fig. 12.2 Damped interdependence

Michaelangelo also excelled.'[1] The fact that functions in underdeveloped societies are less differentiated does, of course, have a bearing on the interdependence.

The situation can be illustrated diagrammatically. Figure 12.1 depicts the absence of interdependence between the variables X and Y. Figure 12.2 shows interdependence, but it is weak and damped, so that if one variable diverges from the stable equilibrium point S, the system will tend to return to it. Whether we are justified in neglecting such interdependence will depend upon the size of the reaction coefficients, the comparative slopes of the lines, and on the time lags in the adjustment process. Figure 12.3 shows a cumulative process away from the unstable equilibrium at U. Clearly, we must not neglect such interdependence in our studies. Figure 12.4 shows

[1] Michael Lipton, 'Interdisciplinary Studies in Less Developed Countries', *J. Development Studies*, 9 (October 1970).

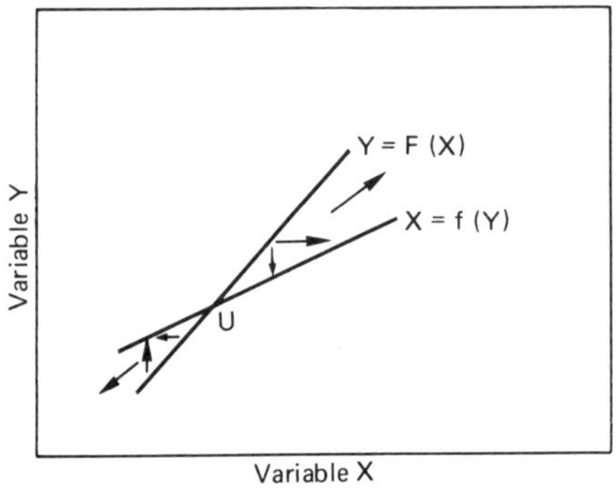

Fig. 12.3 Explosive interdependence

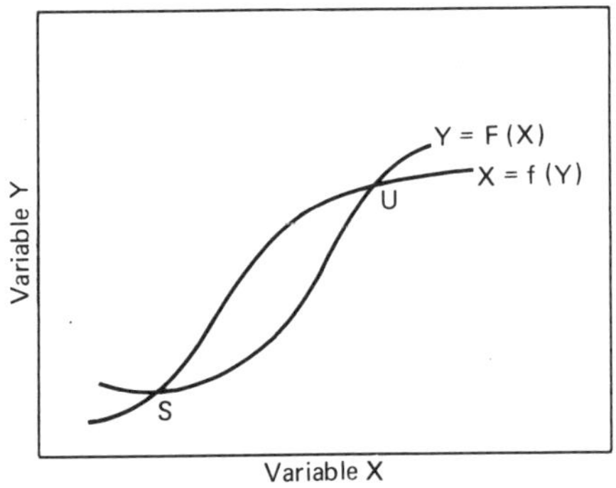

Fig. 12.4 Non-linear interdependence

that stability and instability may be the function of the size of the move, so that for small moves interdependence is damped and for large ones explosive. Theories of the large push or the critical minimum effort are based on such non-linear relationships.[1]

There are numerous illustrations of such interdependence in the field of development studies. One is the relationship between income per head and population growth. High rates of population growth may be presumed to reduce income per head and higher income per head may be presumed, in certain conditions – but only in those conditions – to reduce population growth.[2] Or take the relationship between the level of living of a deprived minority group, for example a low caste or a racial minority, and an index of

[1] The model is the same as that used by N. Kaldor to analyse the trade cycle. 'A Model of the Trade Cycle', *Economic Journal* (1940).

[2] See H. Leibenstein, *Economic Backwardness and Economic Growth* (John Wiley, New York, 1963).

prejudice against it. Prejudice will be a function of the level of living – the less educated, the less healthy, the stronger the grounds for prejudice – and the level of living will be a function of prejudice – the stronger prejudice, the stronger discrimination in jobs, education, and so forth.[1]

Or consider the relationship between productivity per man and the investment/income ratio. The higher the productivity, the higher will tend to be the savings and hence the investment ratio, but the higher the investment ratio the more capital per worker and hence the higher productivity. There is also interdependence between the quality of interdisciplinary studies and the quality of the scholars they attract. One can continue.

If interdependence between variables normally studied separately is strong, or, though weak, if reaction coefficients are large, or though small, if they change size for moves above a critical level, there is a case for breaking down the boundaries between disciplines. This is sometimes called transforming parameters into dependent variables. Family ties and economic calculus, land tenure and responses to incentives, religious beliefs and commercial motivation may interact in this way. Where interdependence of this kind occurs and where the interdependent variables belong to different disciplines, there is a case for interdisciplinary work.[2]

It is possible to draw two quite different conclusions from such interaction. First, it might be said that what is called for are not interdisciplinary studies, but a new discipline that constructs concepts and builds models appropriate to the conditions of underdeveloped societies. In this case, we should have to discard concepts like employment, unemployment, underemployment, income, savings, investment and construct altogether new terms.

Second, and less radically, the existing concepts and models may continue to be used, but their content may have to be changed or their definition modified.

The difference can be illustrated with the concepts 'capital' and 'investment'. Conventionally, 'investment' is defined as the addition of physical pieces of equipment, plant or stocks in order to raise the future flow of products or services above what it would have been otherwise. 'Capital' is the stock of these productive items that has resulted from past flows minus depreciation through use and obsolescence.

Now it is possible to enlarge this concept so as to cover all forms of expenditure that lead to a larger flow of future output, not only those that result in physical items of machinery, construction or inventories. This would

[1] See G. Myrdal, *An American Dilemma* (Harper, New York, 1944).

[2] An important attempt to discover which variables and interactions may be appropriate under which circumstances is to be found in I. Adelman and C. T. Morris, *Society, Politics and Economic Development* (Johns Hopkins Press, Baltimore, 1967).

include 'investment in human capital', such as education, health and, at low-income levels, nutrition; possibly expenditure on birth control, if we are concerned with raising income per head; it would also include investment in productive knowledge that is not incorporated in machinery or in people; it would further include expenditure on building social institutions and on shaping human attitudes that raise productivity.

All this can, in principle, be covered by an enlarged concept of 'capital' and 'investment', as long as one condition is fulfilled: there must be a fairly systematic connection between the devotion of current resources, that might otherwise be used for unproductive current consumption, and the resulting flow of extra output. These resources need not be the only condition for the enlarged flow of output, but they must be systematically linked to this output by a fixed set of technical coefficients, or at least by a range that is not too wide.

But if the link between the devotion of current resources and extra output is only tenuous, so that a given result can be achieved with widely varying inputs, or the same inputs can lead to widely varying results, or if the results can be achieved without using any current inputs, or if in spite of large current inputs, no results can in principle ensue, the notions of 'capital' and 'investment' become inapplicable and we have to focus on those factors on which the outcome systematically depends.[1]

The output of a factory may be within wide limits a function of the degree of capacity utilisation which, in turn, will depend upon the quality of the management; the result of a family planning programme may be only tenuously linked to the money spent on clinics, doctors, nurses and contraceptives, but largely depend upon changeable economic, social, cultural and religious attitudes of couples. The quality of the administration, the system of land tenure, the solidarity between different classes, the ethnic origin of the entrepreneurs, their power over the workers, the history of the country may be more important determinants than the amount of resources. If this is so, no new wine can be poured into old bottles, the bottles themselves must be changed.

In either case, in the process of analysing social phenomena in underdeveloped countries, we may incidentally gain new insights into those in advanced industrial countries. Studies of the caste system in India may illuminate trade union behaviour and demarcation (jurisdiction) disputes in England or the role of women in Western Europe; scrutiny of the capital/output ratio may change our view of the production function. Research into small-scale, intermediate technology may be useful for reducing environmental damage in advanced countries; research on the social services may teach us how to improve our own; a wider concept of capital

[1] 'As Voltaire said, an incantation will destroy a flock of sheep if it is accompanied by a sufficient dose of arsenic', A. Marshall, *Official Papers* (Macmillan, London, 1926), p. 40.

may throw new light on our own problems of industrial management. If this happens it will be a bonus over and above what we had bargained for. Research can thus be made not only co-operative but also mutually enlightening.

Let us illustrate how this would work out between, say, economics and anthropology. In the first case of interdisciplinary work – the team approach – anthropologists will be used for their traditional training. If a land reform or a birth control programme or a tourist project or even a research project is proposed, they will be able to point to 'constraints' in the beliefs and *mores* of the people, or they will be able to point to beliefs or institutions that can be mobilised and on which the proposed reforms or projects can be built. Nothing new or radical is required here.

The second case is more interesting. I suspect that economic method could illuminate some anthropological work and probably the converse too. While I know of some cross-disciplinary work of this kind between economics and political science, I do not know of any between economics and anthropology.

The most interesting possibilities are opened up by the third case, whether in its reformist or radical version. It is quite clear, for example, that an agricultural production function in many underdeveloped countries should count among its inputs, not only the conventional factors, land, labour, fertilisers, water and power, but also levels of education of the farmers, nutritional standards, distance from town, health, systems of land tenure and of family kinship. All these variables are likely, in some societies, to be systematically related to agricultural production.

Still, while we adhere to the notion of a 'production function', a status-conscious anthropologist will complain that he is being used only to provide ammunition for the canons of the economist. A self-respecting anthropologist might refuse to have all the important questions asked by the economist and to be reduced to a handmaiden, supplying low-class empirical material for the high-class analytical structure of another discipline. Questions of status and precedence are, of course, not of concern to serious scholars, who are concerned not with anthropological problems or economic problems, but with problems. John Maynard Keynes looked forward to the day when economists would have become like mechanics, when they could 'get themselves thought of as humble, competent people, on a level with dentists . . . '.[1]

But it may turn out that the whole notion of a production function is wrong or misleading. Perhaps there is no systematic relationship between inputs, whether of fertilised, irrigated land, physical capital, or of educated farmers, human capital and crops. It may be that output depends upon variables that have been constructed and analysed by anthropologists: the

[1] J. M. Keynes, 'Economic Possibilities for our Grand-Children'. Reprinted in *Essays in Persuasion* (Macmillan, London, 1931), p. 373.

relationship between majority and minority groups; religious beliefs, the Protestant or Confucian ethic; or kinship systems.

Or again, at a different level of discourse, it may be that large increases in output beyond a decent minimum are not a crucial component of development either at this stage or ever. The society may have opted for an alternative style of development, in which the ever growing production of material goods is rejected. It prefers containment of wants and aspirations to increasing production to satisfy ever growing wants and infinite aspirations. Or, through a shift in valuations, unemployment may be converted into leisure, or, in Ivan Illich's words, to 'useful unemployment'. If this is the case, the crucial questions will have to be asked by the anthropologist or the sociologist. He has to construct the concepts and it may be that it is then the economist's turn to fill the boxes constructed by the anthropologist. Which of these possibilities should be realised, will depend partly upon empirical conditions, but ultimately upon valuations and the choice of a style of life.

What is the conclusion for policy-oriented research? The first case, a team of members from different disciplines solving a practical problem together, presents no problem. Teams can be, and have been, assembled who put their heads together to solve a particular problem, each member bringing his expertise with him. Interesting organisational, managerial and administrative problems arise about the levels and the forms in which the heads should be brought together, and about the relative weight to be given to each in the light of possibly controversial objectives, but this is not our concern here.

The second and third cases (extension of methods to other fields and changing concepts and models to include 'outside' variables) are much more difficult. The only solution is to back individuals and groups of individuals who are interested in and excited by this work, who read each other's drafts and discuss their ideas among themselves, and who are sensitive to the limits of the techniques in which they were educated, in spite of having acquired a certain vested intellectual interest in them. I suspect that such backing will be more successful than backing chairs, institutes or projects that declare, programmatically, that they are committed to interdisciplinary work, though institutional change clearly must accompany psychological change.

A modest practical proposal is to give grants to scholars for the purpose of reading and catching up in fields outside their narrow professional expertise, so as to familiarise them with what has happened in these fields. Problem-oriented survey articles, critically summarising the literature and pointing to gaps, without respect for the traditional boundaries between disciplines, can also be a help initially in introducing outsiders to the work done by groups of workers.

Interdisciplinary work raises some of the same issues as collaboration between scholars from different countries, as is shown by our use of language: the 'frontiers' of development economics, 'poaching' on other people's territory, intellectual 'imperialism' as an attempt to extend the 'frontiers', etc. Here, as for international collaboration, considerations of sovereignty, status, power and legitimacy are out of place. The language of research should be quite different from the language of diplomacy or power politics and should have no room for 'legitimacy' or 'sovereignty'.

Applied development economics clearly is a service discipline: it draws its inputs from engineers, scientists, agronomists, technologists; it delivers its output to policy-makers. It is noteworthy that research on the 'inputs', essentially research in the natural sciences, has been more readily welcomed by the developing countries than the research at the next stage of processing. This is so because, as we approach the final use of the product, namely policy, both valuations and biases are more likely to colour the analysis. Problem-oriented, applied, usable research can overcome these objections, not by emulating the natural sciences in being 'value-free', but by making the valuations explicit.

Economic analysis has found certain assumptions convenient. Among these may be included optimising behaviour of atomistic units; convexity, for example, absence of increasing returns and of indivisibilities, diminishing marginal utility; constancy of certain determinants such as tastes, knowledge, institutions; absence of uncertainty or the construction of certainty equivalents or of 'contingent commodities', the prices of which are all known; fragmentation of power, hence inability of any one unit to affect the behaviour of other units and therefore exclusion of problems of bargaining, alliances and interdependence.

These assumptions, while convenient for yielding determinate equilibrium solutions, have been criticised and have occasionally been relaxed. Some of these relaxations amount to breaking down the barriers between disciplines, for example stepping from atomistic behaviour into bilateral monopoly, from economics into politics. The only criterion for this must be the realism and relevance of the resulting research and, beyond that, direct and indirect implementation of the results of research for the benefit of mankind.

III DISCARDED IDEAS

The elements in earlier thinking on development which have largely been discarded can be briefly summarised.

(1) Analysis and policy were originally dominated by the experience of the rapid recovery from the war, supported by Marshall Aid, of the industrial countries of Western Europe, by the high post-war rates of economic growth and the scientific and technological triumphs of postwar reconstruction. The problem of development is, however, in some respects fundamentally different from the problem of reconstructing war-damaged advanced economies.

(2) Priority was given to industrialisation and infrastructure (power and transport) which came to be almost synonymous with development.

Hence also the strong emphasis on capital accumulation as the strategic variable in development. The savings ratio and the capital/output ratio together were thought to determine the rate of growth of output, which was either the main objective or the performance test of development. It was found, however, that capital often accounted for only a relatively small portion of growth, that capital was as much the result as the cause of growth, and that growth was not the same as development.

(3) Central government planning from the top down and the need for a 'big push' dominated thinking and policy-making, and the limitations of administrative capacity, of human and institutional constraints, and the need for participation, decentralisation and mobilisation of local labour were not sufficiently recognised.

(4) Policies were dominated by the reaction to colonialism. The governments of many newly independent states wanted to do what the colonial powers had neglected to do. This reinforced the desire for planning, for industrialisation and for import substitution. It also fed the desire, after the achievement of political independence, for economic independence, which, however, was often equated (wrongly) with a high degree of economic self-sufficiency, mistaken for self-reliance. Latin American countries, which had been politically independent for a long time, felt that economic independence, which did not follow from political independence, was elusive.

(5) Thinking was deeply influenced by foreign trade pessimism, which led to the formulation of two-gap models. Pessimism about export prospects and the terms of trade reinforced policies of import-substituting industrialisation, which in turn created strongly entrenched vested urban interests that resisted efforts to liberalise trade.

(6) There was a belief that high average growth rates of production will lead to reduced poverty either as a result of trickle-down or of government policies: that the best way to attack poverty was indirectly, by supporting growth poles, and that the spin-offs would, after a time-lag, benefit the poor.

(7) The rate of population growth and the problems generated by it were underestimated and diplomacy ruled out the topic for the agenda of both bilateral and multilateral development agencies.

(8) The goals, or at any rate the performance tests of development were defined narrowly in terms of GNP and its growth, and other goals, such as greater equality, eradication of poverty, meeting basic human needs, conservation of natural resources, abating pollution, and the enhancement of the environment, as well as non-material goals, were neglected or not emphasised sufficiently.

(9) The contribution by the developed countries was seen too narrowly in terms of capital aid and technical assistance, instead of as the impact

of all policies pursued by the rich countries (and by other poor countries), whether or not they were pursued with the express purpose of assisting development efforts: these would include science policies, the thrust of research and development expenditure, policies towards transnational companies, migration policy, monetary policy, regional policy, trade and employment policies, agricultural policy, as well as foreign policy and military alliances generally.

(10) The 'third world' was considered monolithically, as an area with common problems, whereas it became increasingly clear that some of the differences within the group of developing countries were at least as great as those between them and the developed countries.

(11) Development was considered exclusively as a problem of underdeveloped countries becoming less so. In contrast development is now beginning to be viewed as a problem common to the whole world: it gives rise to problems that are shared by the rich, overdeveloped and by the poor, underdeveloped, with some interests in common, others in conflict.

IV THE NEW STRATEGY

The new development strategy may be summarised in the following way.

(1) We must start with meeting the basic needs of the majority of the people who are very poor. These needs are more and better food, safe water at hand, security of livelihood, health, sanitation, education, decent shelter, adequate transport; in addition there are 'non-material' needs like self-confidence, self-reliance, dignity, capacity to make one's own decisions, to participate in the decisions that affect one's life and work, and to develop fully one's talents, all of which interact in a variety of ways with 'material' needs.

(2) Meeting the basic needs of the billion poor people requires changes not only in the income distribution, but also in the structure of production (including exchange and foreign trade). It calls for increases in basic goods bought in the market, as well as in the purchasing power to buy them, and for an expansion in public services. To ensure that these actually reach the poor, restructuring public services will be necessary, as well as greater participation at the local level, better access to these services, and an appropriate delivery system.

(3) Since the majority of the poor live (and will continue to live for some time) by agriculture in the countryside, priority has to be given to growing food for domestic consumption. Agriculture has been the lagging sector; it has been holding up development and its produce has been unevenly spread. Agriculture also forms an important potential mass market for industrial goods. Its productivity growth

is a condition for successful industrialisation and gains from foreign trade.[1]

(4) In order to meet the needs of the rural population, credit, extension services, fertiliser, water, power, seeds must be made available so that these reach the small farmer. He must also be given security of tenure or secure ownership of his land, often consolidation of scattered holdings, and a guarantee that he gains from the improvements that he makes. He needs inputs, including information, appropriate institutions and incentives.

(5) The small farmer must also be provided with access to markets in market towns and regional cities through feeder roads and marketing facilities.

(6) A group of smallholdings should be serviced by modern centres of processing, marketing, financial services and extension services, but this must be done in a way which does not call excessively for scarce managerial resources.

(7) Efforts should be made to develop efficient labour-intensive technologies or, more accurately, technologies that economise in the use of capital and sophisticated skills and management, and are appropriate for the social, cultural and climatic conditions of the masses of poor people in developing countries, especially in farming, processing and agro-industries, as well as in exports and import-substitution. Construction with appropriate building materials also offers opportunities for creating efficient work.

(8) The rural towns should provide middle-level social services, such as health and family clinics, secondary schools and technical colleges.

(9) The new structure will reduce the rush to the large cities, economise in the heavy costs of certain services, and will increase the scope for regional and local participation.

(10) The whole process should embrace human and social, as well as economic development. More particularly, hundreds of millions of people will not be more productive, for some time to come. They need social help.

All policies, such as price controls, allocation of inputs, financial and fiscal measures, credit control, foreign exchange controls, etc. should be scrutinised with respect to their final impact on the specified goals. Although some increase in inequality may be inevitable in the early stages, as long as it does not impoverish the poor, those measures whose incidence is to benefit the rich at the expense of the poor should be abandoned or redesigned.

[1] See W. Arthur Lewis, *The Evolution of the International Economic Order* (Princeton, 1977).

V GENERAL CONCLUSIONS

No doubt there were errors, false starts and dead ends in the development story of the last three decades. In accounting for these, there are Keynesians and Marxians. Keynes attributed (at least in a much quoted passage in the *General Theory*) the errors of 'practical men, who believe themselves quite exempt from any intellectual influences' to 'some defunct economist'. He thought 'that the power of vested interests is vastly exaggerated compared with the gradual encroachment of ideas'. On this interpretation it was the mistaken doctrines of Nurkse, Prebisch, Singer and Rosenstein-Rodan that led governments to subsidise industrial capital equipment, support high urban wages, overvalue exchange rates, raise the costs of farm inputs by protecting domestic industry, lower the prices of farm outputs and generally neglect or, worse, exploit, agriculture and the rural poor.

Marxians believe that it is the power of class interests that is reflected in ideas. The above-mentioned doctrines, on this view, are merely an ideological superstructure, reflecting the powerful vested interests of the urban capitalists and their privileged workers.

But there is a third way of looking at the succession of problems and difficulties: there is a Hydra-like aspect to development (and perhaps to all human endeavour). Many of the difficulties encountered in the path of development were neither the result of economic errors, nor attributable to vested interests, but were the offspring of the successful solution of previous problems. Scientific confidence asserts that there is a solution to every problem, but history (and not only the obstructionist official) teaches us that there is a problem to every solution.

The solution of one problem creates a series of new ones. Success in manufacturing industry has brought out the lag in agriculture. The need to expand the production of food for domestic consumption became so acute partly because of the remarkable growth of industrial output. The seed-fertiliser revolution has spawned a litter of new problems about plant diseases, inequality, unemployment and the other so-called second-generation problems. The need for birth control arose from the successful attack on mortality through cheap and efficient methods of death control. Growing unemployment is (partly) the result of the high productivity and its growth of manufacturing investment. Education raises excessive aspirations and contributes to the movement to the cities and the consequent unemployment of the educated, and to the brain drain. The success and the attractions of urban development have shown up the need to accelerate rural development, which, however, by the turmoil it creates, may further accelerate the migration to the cities.

This Hirschmanesque generalised doctrine of unbalanced growth cannot, of course, be used to justify and legitimise errors in development thinking and policy. Of these there were plenty. But on the other hand, not all difficulties are the result of past mistakes, and some are the consequences of the successful solution of preceding problems.

'Hydra' is the wrong metaphor, for it suggests the hopelessness of all endeavours. 'Second-generation' problems, on the other hand, may be too optimistic a term. The question is whether, in spite of the subsequent emergence of new problems, the series converges to, or diverges from, a solution to given problems. While some solutions are worse than the problems, others represent progress. It is important to bear in mind that solutions are not readily transferable between places and periods.

Another lesson is what more sophisticated colleagues like to call 'the counter-intuitive character of systems analysis'. Things are not necessarily true because they are paradoxical, but in development studies, as in other fields, commonsense does not always lead to the correct answer. Job creation may cause more, rather than less unemployment; import substitution may call for more, rather than less foreign exchange; import restrictions and physical allocations, intended to reduce inequalities, may strengthen monopoly power; a strategy that sacrifices economic growth of consumption in order to create more jobs may require faster, not slower, growth; policies designed to help the poor may benefit the middle and upper classes, and so on. As these illustrations show, the implications of this view can be profoundly conservative or startingly revolutionary. In a given power structure, attempts at piecemeal reform *may* be self-cancelling and the system will then tend to re-establish the initial wealth and power distribution. Only a deep, structural change *may* enable reform to take root.

On the other hand, piecemeal reform *may* trigger off pressures that lead to further reforms, whereas revolutionary change, as the many revolutions that failed show, may fail to achieve its objective.

A third lesson is that in many areas only a concerted, properly phased, attack on several fronts yields the desired result and the application of some measures without certain others may make things worse. 'Correct' prices in a society with a fairly equal distribution of assets and available appropriate technologies may raise efficiency and reduce inequality, but to use 'correct' prices in a society with very unequal ownership of assets may only change the manifestation of inequality and poverty.

Not only are there Myrdalian cumulative processes, but the processes require packages; the causation is cumulative and joint. The appropriate metaphor is the jigsaw puzzle, the fitting together of different parts, not the toothpaste or the sausage machine which respond to pressures with homogeneous flows. To do something in a certain sequence, together with other things, brings success; to do it in isolation may be worse than doing nothing. A programme of education without employment opportunities will only accelerate the brain drain. What is needed is a range of interrelated, properly phased, measures. There are no simple remedies. The solution of underdevelopment is not to be found in making the soil more, and women less fertile, in a combination of fertiliser and pill (the technocratic solution);

nor, for that matter, by staging a revolution (the revolutionary solution), or implementing a radical land reform (the radical solution), nor by 'getting prices right' (the economist's solution), though each, in conjunction with the others, may have something to contribute to a total solution.

A fourth lesson is that few problems are narrowly economic ones. The difficulties often lie with human attitudes, social institutions and political power structures, more than, or as well as, with scarcities of productive inputs and their correct allocation. Scarce inputs – capital and skills – will probably also be needed to attack social and political obstacles, but the link between resources and outcomes is a tenuous one: there are no fixed capital coefficients between resources spent and an effective land reform, or between money and a successful birth control campaign.

Finally, the response of the rich countries to the challenge of development is not to be found in development aid alone, whether it consists of capital, skills or brains, even if it were 2 per cent instead of ⅓ per cent of GNP, or in freer access to the markets of the rich countries. It is the *total* relationship,[1] the impact of *all policies* of countries on one another, that is relevant, and that has to be our concern, if we are serious about international co-operation.

[1] The term, the idea and its elaboration are due to Dudley Seers.

13 Development: Theoretical and Conceptual Considerations

Celso Furtado
UNIVERSITY OF PARIS

I THEORETICAL ANTECEDENTS

Having originated in economics, where emphasis is laid on its quantitative aspects in the form of *growth*, the concept of *development* inevitably goes beyond this context, penetrating into the domain of other social science disciplines, in cases where growth cannot be visualised as a homothetic process, or cannot be understood in the absence of a system of values which the economist is unable to integrate into his conceptual frame. This ambiguity gives rise to a whole series of problems which have led economists to draw a distinction between *development* and *growth*, assuming to the first of these concepts, even when qualified by the adjective 'economic', a breadth which perforce transforms it into an interdisciplinary subject.[1]

The sources of the notion of development may be detected in three currents of European thought in the eighteenth century. The first of these arises from the philosophy of the Enlightenment, with history being viewed as a gradual advance towards the supremacy of reason. The second is linked to the idea of the accumulation of *wealth*, in which it is taken for granted that the future holds out promise of increased wellbeing. The third is related to the idea that the geographical spread of European civilisation means access to superior modes of life for the other peoples of the world, considered as being more or less 'backward'.

[1] An extensive bibliography on theories of *economic growth* is to be found in F. H. Hahn and R. C. O. Mathews, 'The Theory of Economic Growth: A Survey', in *Surveys of Economic Theory* (London: Macmillan, 1965). For a more selective bibliography, see the introduction by Amartya Sen to *Growth Economics* (New York: Penguin Books, 1970). The bibliographies available on theories of *economic development* are less comprehensive. See the select bibliographies listed by Benjamin Higgins in *Economic Development* (London: 1968); Charles K. Wilber in *The Political Economy of Development and Underdevelopment*; and Henry Bernstein in *Underdevelopment and Development* (New York: Penguin Books, 1973).

In the eighteenth century, the emergence of a philosophy of history – a secularised view of the development of society – takes the form, with the *German Enlightenment*, of a search for a 'subject' whose essence is achieved through its own historical process. The *faculties* ascribed by Kant to the conscience of a transcendental subject constitute the starting point of an overall view of history: that of the transformation of chaos into rational order. With Hegel, mankind assumes the role of the subject, as an entity which reproduces itself in accordance with a logic that aims in the direction of *progress*. This optimistic conception of the process of history, which allows a glimpse of the 'possible future' in the form of a more productive and less alienating society where today's antinomies have been outstripped, leads to the quest for a propitious agent – the working class, the entrepreneur, the nation, the State – a 'negativity' capable of sifting contradictions and precipitating the future, in other words, a vector of *progress*.

The publication of the *Critique of Pure Reason* was preceded by five years by that of the *Wealth of Nations*, which set out to prove that the pursuit of self-interest is the mainspring of the common good. The harmony Kant claimed to have discovered in the heterogenous faculties of the human mind, in the form of *commonsense*, is seen, in Adam Smith's social order, to be the work of an *invisible hand*. Adam Smith argues, however, that this harmony presupposes a certain amount of institutional order. The wealth appropriated by the feudal baron was of little value to the community, since it was spent on entertaining his commensals, or rendered unproductive. It is only in a society where obstacles to the flow of goods and to the exercise of individual initiative are reduced to a minimum, that the harmony in question can come into being. Viewed thus, progress does not necessarily stem from the 'logic of history', but is within men's reach, and the way to achieve it is known. The main point is to have institutions which enable the individual to develop his abilities to the full.

With mercantilism and colonialism, foreign trade was considered as an imperial activity, hence, inseparable from the power of the nations engaged in it. This doctrine came under fire from the middle of the eighteenth century onwards, and was gradually replaced by liberal ideas during the first half of the nineteenth century. International specialisation made it possible to carry still further the division of labour, its positive effects on productivity being obvious in each country. According to the liberal doctrine, international trade leads to a better use of productive domestic resources, and the resulting increase in productivity is of benefit to all. A corollary of this doctrine was that, in forcing other countries to fall in with its lines of trade, Europe was performing a *civilising* mission, thus helping to increase the welfare of peoples enslaved by obscurantist tradition.

II THE HISTORICAL BACKGROUND

While in the second half of the eighteenth century European thought was advancing, on a number of different fronts, towards an optimistic view of history – a view summed up in the idea of *progress* – contemporary social reality was by no means reassuring. The rise of commercial capitalism over the previous five hundred years had had relatively little effect on social organisation. Agricultural products from a still feudal land tenure system, articles manufactured by the guilds, and sometimes colonial products, found their way into the commercial channels and strengthened the financial power of a bourgeoisie whose involvement in politics became daily more noticeable. Here the appropriation of the social surplus reflected the strong position of the bourgeoisie, which controlled trade channels, *vis-à-vis* the landowners, the members of the trade guilds and other subagents of production. A fundamental change took place when the traditional structures controlling production were dismantled (as in the case of the guilds) or reduced to the role of passive agents (landlords who became rentiers).

In this way the pattern of trade, previously based on an exchange of finished or semi-finished products, became also vertical, a part of the structure of production: the elements or factors of production, being converted into merchandise. Thus both land and labour gradually came to be regarded as commodities. This process, which led on from commercial capitalism to industrial capitalism, had two main results. On the one hand, substantial new possibilities were opened up for the social division of labour, in particular in the manufacturing sector. Specialisation at the level of the product, or of an important stage in the production process, was replaced by the dividing up of work into simple tasks, which increased the possibility of using machines. On the other hand, the party with which the capitalist had to deal was no longer either an element in the dominant social structure or an entity with inalienable rights, but had become an isolated worker, who could easily be replaced, given the simplicity of the task he performed.

The penetration of capitalism into the organisation of production can be interpreted as a broadening of the social space governed by criteria of instrumental or formal rationality. The capitalist who had formerly dealt with landowners, guilds invested with privileges, or similar bodies, now had to deal with 'production factors' which could be regarded in the abstract, reduced to a common denominator, and were quantifiable. From this point onwards the 'sphere of economic activities' could be considered as apart from other social activities. But the progress of 'rationality' is neither more nor less than the widening of the area of social relations governed by the criteria of mercantile organisation. The growing subordination of the vision of the social process to the criteria of instrumental or formal rationality brought about substantial changes in social structures. In agriculture, for example, it led to the depopulation of the countryside and the drift to the towns or to new colonial settlements, sometimes on other continents. The price revolution, caused by more effective manufacturing processes, speeded up the decline of artisanal forms of organisation in areas where the conditions did not exist for creating new types of employment.

Thus while the accumulation resulting from the progressive injection of market criteria into organisation of production gathered speed, social structures entered on a stage of radical change. Some of the visible forms of this change – the chaotic growth of towns, the disintegration of community life, mass unemployment, the conversion of human beings (including children) into merely a labour force – made contemporary observers deeply uneasy.[1] This accounts for the pessimistic way in which the more clear-sighted economists, in the first half of the nineteenth century, viewed the future of capitalism, which appeared to them to lead inexorably towards a 'stationary state'. Their central concern was the process whereby the social product was appropriated, and indeed how income was distributed. Given the sharp rise in population which followed on the rapid growth of towns, the 'Population Principle' formulated by Malthus appeared to them to be obvious: any increase in real wages would be cancelled out by the population growth generated thereby.[1] Again, the law of decreasing returns, which prevailed in agriculture, and the pressure to raise land rents which accompanied agricultural expansion on poor quality soil, combined to reduce investment potential, thus slowing down the capacity of the system to create employment. This idea of a trend towards long-term stagnation, which it was argued could be deduced from the logic of capitalist economy, was presented in different ways by classical economists, and was to play a basic role in Marxist thinking. Marx, however, far from drawing pessimistic conclusions from this so-called trend of the capitalist system towards a loss of impetus, saw in it a clear indication that the 'internal contradictions' of the system would inevitably grow worse. On Hegelian lines of thought, these contradictions can be presented as harbingers of a higher form of society in the making, one which will be more productive and less alienating. Thus at a stage when the social cost of the process of accumulation was particularly high, criticism of capitalism directly contributed towards maintaining the view inherited from the Enlightenment, whereby such accumulation would open up the way to universal improvement.

III. ACCUMULATION AND TECHNICAL PROGRESS UNDER CAPITALISM

In identifying accumulation with a *wages fund*, or in other words with a stock of current consumption goods (*corn*, in the language of Ricardo) and in claiming that it could be measured in homogeneous units of *simple labour*, classical economists created considerable obstacles to an understanding of the

[1] Sismonde de Sismondi, who described the beginning of the introduction of criteria of 'rationality' into agricultural activities in Italy and England, has handed down to us an invaluable account of the impression made on his contemporaries by the subordination of the social process to economic criteria. See his *Nouveau principes d'économie politique*, first published in 1819.

[2] In this way there was ascribed to a biological law, what in reality were the external signs of the transformation which had taken place in the system of social domination.

part played by the development of technology in capitalist society. Technological progress came to be regarded as a means of economising a scarce production factor (land, labour or capital), which could be clearly defined in a microeconomic setting. This way of viewing technology, through the prism of an isolated productive unit, was at the root of the difficulties later encountered by economists in adopting a dynamic approach to economic processes rather than comparing static situations. A large number of the most significant forms of what is called technological progress – namely economy in the use of non-renewable resources, economies of scale, external economies, changes in the pattern of demand as a result of the introduction of new products, etc. – can be fully grasped only by means of an overall view of the social system, and of the nature of its relations with the physical environment it controls and with the outside world.

Technological progress is a vague expression which, in the sense most commonly used, covers all the social changes which make it possible for the process of accumulation to continue, hence for capitalist society to reproduce itself. By 'accumulating' is meant transferring to the future the ultimate use of resources available today. In capitalist society, the action of accumulation brings in a return, with the result that the reproduction of social structures makes it necessary for accumulation to generate an increase in the overall productivity. But in default of changes in the availability of natural resources, technology or the composition of final demand, accumulation inevitably tends towards saturation point. Changes in the distribution of income on egalitarian lines may open up new outlets for accumulation, but do not prevent saturation point being reached. The same may be said of the discovery of better quality or more abundant natural resources, and also of the positive effects of opening up new channels for foreign trade. None of this alters the basic context, which is that of the trend towards diminishing returns as soon as there is overaccumulation. The group of factors which alters this basic context is what we call technological progress. This assumes visible form mainly in two ways: (a) greater efficiency of production processes; and (b) the introduction of new end products.

Technological progress by means of the adoption of more efficient production methods, if unaccompanied by the introduction of new products, would not be sufficient for the accumulation process to continue without encountering major obstacles. After a certain stage, accumulation could continue only if social inequality were reduced, or the labour force made use of it to a lesser degree. Moreover, accumulation based solely on the the introduction of new products (without any change in the efficiency of production processes), where this is technically possible, entails growing social inequality. Briefly, the social changes implicit in the concept of development fall into two main groups: an increase in the efficiency of production techniques, and a growing diversification of the final product. Let us consider what are the social forces behind these two processes, and what basic relationships exist between them.

Capitalist society, which bears the seeds of the type of the material civilisation which is predominant almost everywhere today, when reproducing itself generates a process of accumulation which tends to outstrip population growth. There is no need here to seek the historical reasons underlying this pattern of growth; it will suffice to recall what has been said about the social disorganisation which occurred in the period when accumulation gathered speed, and to refer to the position of strength of the countries which became industrialised when the system of the international division of labour was becoming established. Once a certain pattern had been set for the appropriation of the social product, the behaviour of the ruling classes was directed towards their self-preservation, which meant that certain levels of accumulation had to be ensured.

This ineluctable rule of intense accumulation is the root cause of the instability which is characteristic of capitalist society. One must put down to the absence of any global theory of accumulation the fact that the science of economics, far from moving on towards an explanation of overall social processes, tended to restrict its field of observation, confining itself to studying the rationality of isolated agents. Neo-classical economists saw in the instability of capitalist society a reflex of 'adjustment' to, or oscillation around, a 'position of equilibrium' which could be strictly defined only by adopting as a postulate the absence of accumulation. The fact is that the perception of an economic situation, taken out of its overall social context, is possible only in a strictly synchronous analysis, that is to say assuming that there is no real accumulation. Although Keynes remained true to the tradition of *pure economics*, he adopted an approach which was static only in appearance. His followers were not slow to understand that a congruence could be obtained only between the parametric role of the stock of capital and the flow of net investment, by restricting the analysis to a consideration of situations of underemployment. At the macroeconomic level, net investment perforce signifies accumulation.

The *models of growth*, which have been the subject of a major part of the theoretical work of economists in the last three decades, are a by-product of attempts at a dynamic approach to the Keynesian model. The bulk of this work follows along two lines: on the one hand, renewed contact with the classical tradition, linked to a pattern of institutional distribution of income, and on the other, a continuation of the neo-classical tradition founded on the concept of the production function with flexible coefficients, linking the return on the factors with their respective marginal productivity. This theoretical work had only limited significance for the progress of ideas on development, both in the highly industrialised countries and in the so-called underdeveloped countries. The inability of growth models to account for major structural changes – i.e. the interplay between the 'economic' and the 'non-economic' – and to record the complex relations which arise at the boundaries of the economic system (the relations with other economic systems and with the ecosystem) stem from the very conception of the science of economics on which they are based. The more sophisticated the model, the more remote it is from the multidimensional reality of society. It was for this reason that the most important changes – caused by the gathering speed of accumulation in the last quarter century, and the advent of transnational structures with an ever growing role in the allocation of resources, the creation of liquidity and the geographical distribution of income – have taken place without the theorists of growth having grasped their impact at the level of national economic systems. The inability at present shown by the governments of the great capitalist nations to reconcile the aims of their respective economic policies is in great part due to the direction taken by the *theory of growth*, and its considerable influence on the elaboration of these economic policies.

While it is true that the reproduction of capitalist society generates a substantial potential for accumulation, it is also true that such accumulation can be achieved only through delicate and continuing alterations to social structures. It is thus necessary to consider how the reproduction of structures of privilege succeeds historically in blending in with the need for change. The ruling classes, who control the strategic points in the decision-making system, direct their policies towards preserving the privileged position they occupy. In so doing, however, they trigger off a large-scale process of accumulation which gives rise to a demand for labour in excess of population growth, and promotes social tensions. While in the early stages – when artisanal structures were being dismantled – accumulation proceeded under conditions of an elastic supply of labour, in time it came up against a growing inelasticity of supply, necessitating population movements, mobilising the potential of female labour, etc. The reproduction of a capitalist economy is inconceivable without such social tensions which have been resolved by directing technological progress so as to offset any rigidity in the labour supply. Those who claim to have discovered in the logic of capitalism an inexorable trend towards stagnation, the aggravation of social antagonisms, and self-destruction, underestimate the potentialities of technology for generating new power resources. The agents who direct or supervise economic activities in capitalist society seldom form part of a system having objectives explicitly established beforehand. In reality such agents compete for position, triggering off a process of accumulation which produces pressure to increase the share of labour in the social product. Thus in competing with each other, these agents unleash forces which are conducive to reducing the space for which they are competing. This situation favours agents who innovate with a view to economising labour.

Social antimonies, and the constant outstripping of the tensions resulting therefrom, generate the sweeping social changes which characterise the development of capitalism. On the one hand, substantial accumulation, and on the other, the concentration of economic activity are conducive to making the individual worker an element in structured social groupings, and give rise to new forms of power, all of which tends to transfer social conflicts to the political level. Thus the driving force specific to capitalist society is above all a result of the fact that the reproduction of its built-in structures is based on technical innovation. In other words, the advance of technology is given every facility to succeed by this society, precisely because it ensures the perpetuation of the privileges of the ruling classes. However, the assimilation of technological progress in a competitive society implies substantial accumulation, which in turn generates social pressures for a reduction of inequality. Thus the combined action of technological innovation and accumulation makes it possible for the privileges to continue, and to exist side-by-side with the social forces which challenge it.

So long as a capitalist economy succeeds in keeping growing, the expectations of agents with antagonistic interests can be satisfactorily met: real wages increase, and the share of capitalists and other privileged groups in the social product tends to be maintained. A superficial observer would see only a field of class conflicts, and antagonism between members of the same class. Since accumulation and the penetration of technological progress bring about continual changes in relative prices, speed up the installation of new equipment to replace that which has become outdated, continually eliminate certain goods from the market, alter the distribution of income both in space and in time, and concentrate economic power, etc., the field is extraordinarily unstable, and appears even, from a certain angle, to be chaotic. But from a wider viewpoint it can be seen that thanks to this mutability (in which Marx claimed to have discovered *anarchy*) capitalist society reproduces itself and maintains its basic class structure.

IV INTERPRETATION OF THE CONCEPT OF DEVELOPMENT

The concept of development has been used in two cases with reference to contemporary history. The first concerns the evolution of a social system of production which, by means of accumulation and technological progress, becomes more efficient, or namely increases the productivity of its labour force as a whole. Concepts such as *efficiency* and *productivity* are, of course, ambiguous when applied to complex production systems in which *inputs* and *outputs* are heterogeneous, and vary with time. It can, however, be admitted as self-evident that the social division of labour increases efficiency of manpower, and that accumulation is not only a transfer in time of the ultimate utilisation of a resource, but the means whereby the division of labour takes on a diachronic dimension. The possibility of intensifying the division of labour is considerably increased, when tasks which are carried out simultaneously are supplemented or replaced by others which can be spread out over periods of varying duration. The worker who uses a tool shares the work with others who previously contributed, directly or indirectly, towards making the tool concerned.

The second case in which reference is made to the concept of development relates to the degree to which human wants are satisfied. In this case the ambiguity is even greater. There is a first level at which objective criteria can be used: the satisfaction of basic human needs such as food, clothing and housing. The life expectancy of the population – bearing in mind certain distortions due to social stratification – is an indicator of the degree of satisfaction of basic needs. As we move away from this first level, reference to a system of values becomes proportionately more urgent, since the very idea of a *need*, when unrelated to essentials, becomes obscure outside the cultural context to which it belongs.

The concept of development can accordingly be approached on the basis of three criteria, which have a complex interrelationship: the criterion of an increase in the efficiency of the production system; that of the satisfaction of the population's basic needs; and that of the attainment of the objectives sought by various groups in a society, which are linked to the use of scarce resources. The third criterion is certainly the most difficult to define, because what represents wellbeing for one social group may seem a mere waste of resources to another. That is why the *view of development* held by a society is not unrelated to its social structure.

An increase in the efficiency of production – commonly defined as the main indicator of development – is not an adequate prerequisite for the fuller satisfaction of the population's basic needs.[1] We cannot rule out the possibility that the deterioration in the living conditions of the population at large is due to the introduction of more 'efficient' techniques. Furthermore, an increase in the availability of resources and a rise in living standards may occur in the absence of any change in the production process when, for example, the pressure on reserves of non-renewable resources is increased. The current view of development overlooks the fact that in the capitalist system the creation of economic values entails a greater cost than that which is shown in either private or public accounting systems. Man's *productive activity* increasingly involves irreversible natural processes such as dissipation of energy, which tend to increase universal entropy.[2] The stimulation of forms of technology based on a growing use of energy (the outcome of the short-term view engendered by the private appropriation of non-renewable resources) aggravates this trend, making of the economic process something which makes increasing inroads on resources as time goes on.

In the process of the reproduction of capitalist society, technological progress fulfils a dual role: it reduces the pressure for social equality, and keeps consumption by middle and high-level income groups growing. Thus, the orientation of technological progress governs the evolution of the entire production system, the structure of which must be such as to ensure the social diffusion of products originally reserved for high-income minorities. For

[1] It is only in relation to the satisfaction of basic needs (which can be defined objectively) that one can speak of measuring the efficiency of a society's production system.

[2] In this connection, see the work of the pioneer Georgescu-Roegen, *The Entropy Law and the Economic Process* (Cambridge, Mass.: 1951).

example, the mechanisation of the individual transport of high-income minorities, and the subsequent search for economies of scale in the production of automobiles leads to spread among the general public of the habit of using the same kind of transport, even though this entails substantial social costs.

The subordination of technological creativity to the objective of reproducing a social structure which is largely non-egalitarian, and where accumulation is at a high level, is the root cause of some of the most paradoxical aspects of contemporary civilisation. Even in countries where the accumulation process is the most advanced, a proportion of the population (between one-tenth and one-third) has not reached the level of real income required to satisfy what are regarded as basic needs. Cases occur in which an increase in wages is part and parcel of a process which includes both an increase in the coefficient of waste inherent in expenditure by high-income groups, and the spreading throughout middle-income groups of more and more sophisticated forms of consumption. Thus the elimination of 'poverty in the midst of plenty' may become more difficult as accumulation proceeds. Now it is precisely in terms of the values of this civilisation that an awareness has been born of increasing inequalities in living standards among nations, of accumulated backwardness, of *underdevelopment*. And it is with reference to the problems involved in international inequalities that the concept of development has grown up, as a central concern in this time.

The geographical concentration of economic activities, for the benefit of a small number of countries, was one of the most striking consequences of the intensification of the accumulation process. Adam Smith had already observed that the opportunities created for the social division of labour are much greater in manufacturing than in agriculture.[1] The division of work into tasks in manufacturing subsequently opened up unprecedented possibilities for accumulation, and gradually changed the structure of manufacturing, in which the separation between production processes tended to prevail upon product specialisation. Thus the interdependence of manufacturing activities began to increase both synchronously and diachronously. The idea of productivity, which could be grasped at the microeconomic level in agriculture and handicrafts, gradually became inseparable, as industrialisation proceeded, from the degree of development attained by industrial activities as a whole. In addition, since technological innovation – both in production processes and in the composition of the final product – is conducive to the appropriation of the surplus by those in its vanguard, it is easy to see that a structural tendency exists in a capitalist economy towards a concentration of income which benefits urban areas (where manufacturing activities are grouped together) and countries exporting products which incorporate the most sophisticated technology.

That these problems were recognised is shown clearly in the great debate

[1] Cf. *The Wealth of Nations*, edited by Edwin Cannan, vol. 1, p. 7.

which took place in the second half of the nineteenth century on free trade versus protectionism. The reaction against the doctrine of free trade was based on the idea of the complementarity of economic activities, and was to lead to the concept of the *national economic system*. The spread of industrialisation, which produced in the second half of the last century a whole constellation of independent economic centres, took place for the most part in the context of national protectionsim. From then onwards the concept of development became clearly bound up with the idea of *national interest*.

V DEVELOPMENT THEORY SINCE 1945

From the end of the Second World War onwards, reflection on *development* had as its starting point awareness of the economic backwardness of certain countries in relation to others, assessed by the differences between levels of productivity and/or of consumption. Other indicators of a social nature were soon added thereto, such as infant mortality, the incidence of contagious diseases, the degree of literacy, etc., thus contributing to the confusion of the concepts of *development, progress, social welfare* and *modernisation*, all seen as giving access to life-styles created by industrial civilisation.

This reflection began by taking the form of a political concern, which was the fruit of the major changes brought about by the Second World War, such as the dismantling of colonial structures and the appearance of new forms of dominant international interests, based on the mastery of technology, and on ideological manipulation. During this first stage, a major catalytic role fell to the new international institutions – the United Nations, its regional Commissions and Specialised Agencies – whose Secretariats carried out the first empirical studies with a view to defining these new problems.

The fact is that for the last three decades, reflection on development has remained directly related to problems in which the political dimension has been decisive: the deterioration in the terms of foreign trade, the fact that the price system was ill-suited for use in orienting investment, the insufficiency of accumulation in societies exposed to the *demonstration effect*, the inadequacy of traditional institutions when faced with the new functions of the State, the unsuitability of imported technology to cope with the potential supply of factors and the dimensions of the domestic market, outdated agrarian structures, the tendency for income to be concentrated, structural tensions reflected in chronic inflation, continuing disequilibrium in the balance of payments, and so on. This complex group of questions was broached without any appropriate attempt at theorising in advance, and almost always in a totally inadequate conceptual context.

With its primary emphasis on an overall view of economic decisions, where inadequate co-ordination was responsible for unemployment, the work of

Keynes gave great impetus to the theory of economic policy.[1] Keynes' analysis gave rise to a theory of the co-ordination of economic decisions, which set considerable store on decision-making centres at the national level. But if the elimination of unemployment required action by the State in directing the economic system as a whole, what about the structural modifications essential in order to overcome underdevelopment? This approach led to emphasis being laid on the political aspects of economic problems, and to the concept of development as the fruit of deliberate action, not the effect of spontaneous generation.

In taking an overall approach to economic problems, development specialists are led to resume contact with the tradition of historicist thought which contributed towards the criticism levelled against international liberalism in the middle of the nineteenth century. With neo-classicism, the theory of production was limited to an abstract study of the individual enterprise, and of its cost equation, in a context which was regarded as neutral. But the social antinomies inherent in capitalism, which are inseparable from the driving force behind it, cannot be apprehended from a study of isolated agents. The first step towards formulating a theory of production is not taken until one has grasped the interdependence of productive activities, which makes it necessary to start with the idea of a *system*. The historicist tradition had produced, with Friedrich List, the concept of a *system of productive forces*, which was to be used extensively by Marx.[2] This concept shed light on the complementarity of productive activities, which are regarded as a social process, not as an aggregate of isolated entities. In this way *external economies*, which are of considerable importance in the study of development, can be included in the theory of production. Thus the inadequcy of microeconomic criteria of rationality for defining a model of social productivity becomes obvious.

Possibly no concept has had so much significance for the advance of studies on development as Raul Prebisch's concept of the centre-periphery structure.[3] Though Prebisch's main concern was the international propagation of the business cycle – the diversity of behaviour of economies which export primary products by comparison with economies which export industrial products – the concept was based on an overall view of the capitalist system, and opened the way to a perception of its structural diversity, a knowledge of

[1] The first edition of the work of J. M. Keynes, *The General Theory of Employment, Interest and Money*, came out in 1936. The first attempt to make the Keynesian model dynamic was by R. F. Harrod, in 'An Essay in Dynamic Theory', *Economic Journal* (March 1939).

[2] Cf. Friedrich List, *Das nationale System der Politichen Oekonomie*, first published in 1841.

[3] The ideas of Raúl Prebisch were presented for the first time in *El desarollo económico de la América-latina y algunos de sus problemas* (United Nations Economic Commission for Latin America (ECLA), Santiago de Chile, 1949).

which is essential in order to understand the special character of underdevelopment. The elaboration of this concept by Prebisch himself, and by the group of social scientists which met at ECLA (The United Nations Economic Commission for Latin America) – a group known as the Latin American structuralist school – gave rise to a trend of thought which has had considerable influence.[1]

Prebisch's starting point was a criticism of the system of the international division of labour and the theory of international trade based on the concept of comparative advantages, the validity of which was still uncontested in the academic world. One of the corollaries of this theory was that international trade not only provided an 'engine of growth' – it enabled all participating countries to make more rational use of their own resources – but was also a factor in reducing inequalities in living standards as between countries, since it eliminated some of the negative effects brought about by the lack of complementarity of the available factors. Yet the empirical data on the long-term behaviour of prices in international markets by no means confirmed these forecasts. Such evidence as existed was the other way around, i.e. it pointed towards the concentration of income in the hands of countries having the highest level of income. Prebisch brought the problem out of the abstract context of theorems of comparative advantages (an exercise in logic in which the conclusions are implicit in the premisses) into the context of social structures, within which costs are worked out and surpluses appropriated. The difficulty of bringing down money wages in industrial economies was pointed out by Keynes, who ascribed it to the vigour of trade unionism. But the situation was different in countries which exported primary products, a theme which was shortly to be linked to the theory of the structural surplus of labour. Thus there is a structural tendency in the capitalist system towards concentrating income in benefit of countries which have a more advanced form of social organisation. Disparities in the rate of accumulation, due in part to the system of the international division of labour and its impact on social structures, have produced a structural heterogeneity in the capitalist system which cannot be ignored in any study of international relations. Thus underdevelopment came to be regarded not as a stage on the road to development, but as a permanent structural feature.

Another idea of considerable importance, brought to the fore by the Latin American school in the early 1950s, was that of the harmful effects of the types of technology incorporated in equipment imported by late developing countries.[2] Bearing in mind the fact that these types of technology are bound

[1] A number of aspects of Latin American structuralist thought, and a bibliographical guide, are presented by Celso Furtado in *Economic Development of Latin America*, 2nd edn (Cambridge University Press, 1976).

[2] The first approach to the problem of the relationship between imported technology and underdevelopment is to be found in the study prepared by the ECLA team in 1951, *Theoretical and Practical Problems of Economic Growth*, Santiago de Chile.

up with prevailing social relationships in countries with advanced accumulation, it is easy to understand why it causes an ever increasing concentration of income in countries where accumulation is in its early stages, and frequently creates an incompatibility between the maximum profits sought by private enterprises and the social objectives of development policies. This subject subsequently aroused considerable interest with the debate on *urban marginality*, the choice of techniques, *labour-intensive* techniques, technological dependence, etc. The work of the Latin American structuralists evolved towards an interdisciplinary approach to underdevelopment, considered as corresponding to a type of society in which the relations of external dependence interjected into the structure of the society influence the reproduction of the society itself.[1]

VI SUMMARY AND CONCLUSIONS

Let us try to sum up. The process whereby the world economic system was formed, had, from the outset, two quite separate aspects. The first relates to radical changes in production methods, i.e. the destruction, in whole or in part, of family, artisanal, feudal and guild forms of organisation of production and the gradual establishment of markets for production factors, such as labour and the natural resources appropriated by man. These radical changes resulted in greater opportunities for the division of labour and technological progress, which explains the heightened pace of accumulation.

The second aspect relates to the upsurge of commercial activities, i.e. the interregional and international division of labour. The regions in which accumulation first began to gather speed tended to specialise in activities in which the contemporary revolution in production methods opened up greater possibilities for the progress of technology, and became centres which generated technological progress. However, geographical specialisation also brought about increased productivity, that is to say a more efficient use of available resources. These increases in productivity, the results of foreign trade, acted as vectors which transmitted the innovations of the material culture reflecting the acceleration of accumulation. *Progress* – the assimilation of the new life-styles produced by innovation in the dominating culture – became the universal ideology. The *modernisation* of models of consumption – the imitation and adaptation of large fragments of the material culture – was able to make substantial progress without markedly interfering with social structures, which explains how in many parts of the world foreign trade was activated in the context of pre-existing forms of the organisation of production, including slavery.

[1] For a sociological presentation of ideas on *dependence*, see F. H. Cardoso, 'Les Etats-Unis et la théorie de la dépendance', *Revue du Tiers Monde* (October–December 1976). See also Celso Furtado, *Théorie du développement économique*, 2nd edn (Paris, 1976).

The dissemination of capitalism was much swifter and more widespread as a *modernisation* process than in bringing about relevant changes in production methods and social structures.[1] Development and underdevelopment are thus historical processes which stem from the same initial impetus, i.e. they have their roots in the acceleration of accumulation which took place in Europe at the end of the eighteenth and the beginning of the nineteenth century. For an understanding of the causes of the historical persistence of underdevelopment, it is necessary to observe it as part of a whole which is in movement, as an expression of the driving force behind the world economic system produced by industrial capitalism.

The industrialisation of countries which have been caught up in the underdevelopment trap takes place in competition with imports, not with artisanal activity. It thus tends to be subordinated to the *modernisation* which precedes it. Far from being a reflection of the level of accumulation reached, the evolution of the production system is a simple process of adaptation, in which the dominant role falls to the external and internal forces which determine the profile of demand. This is the basic reason why the social structures of countries of belated industrialisation are so different from those which grew up in areas where industrial capitalism developed as an independent process.

The mechanisation of infrastructures, and the transformation of agriculture provoked by the drive to export and also by developing trends in internal demand, together with the impact of industrialisation in cases where artisanal activities were important – for example in sectors such as food, textiles and clothing – set in motion a long drawn-out process of destruction of traditional employment structures. The tremendous and chaotic spread of towns, to be found in all underdeveloped countries, is only one of the most visible signs of this complex process of disintegration of social structures. The concept of *disguised unemployment*, introduced by economists in the early 1950s, was the first form of an awareness of this problem, but it was the studies on *urban marginality* carried out in the subsequent decade by Latin American sociologists which made it possible to apprehend it in all its complexity, and to bring out the special character of the social structures in countries with dependent economies.

Populations deprived of their traditional occupations by changes in the forms of production tend to move into urban cultural subsystems which have only sporadic links with markets, but have a strong potential influence on them as reserves of labour. *Marginalised* populations, which are largely independent in reproducing themselves, are an expression of a type of social

[1] On the general subject of *modernisation*, although it is approached from other angles, see S. Eisenstadt, *Modernization: Protest and Change* (Prentice-Hall, 1966); and Marion J. Levy, Jr., *Modernization and the Structure of Society: A Setting of International Affairs* (Princeton University Press, 1966).

stratification which has its roots in *modernisation*. The *technological mismatch* referred to by economists has been reflected, from the sociological point of view, in the two extremes of *modernisation* and *marginalisation*. The attempt to find common theoretical ground leads to the theory of dependence, which is based on an overall view of capitalism as an expanding economic system and aims at apprehending the heterogeneity, in time and space, of the process of accumulation.

These studies, which bring out the basic links between the external relations and the internal forms of social domination in countries which have been caught up in underdevelopment, have highlighted other subjects of equal importance, such as the nature of the State in these countries and the role of transnational corporations in controlling their economies.

Where modernisation has been based on the exploitation of non-renewable resources (the case of the oil-exporting countries, though an extreme one, lends itself most easily to analysis), the surplus kept by the country of origin tends to be taken over by a central system of power. In this way, links with the outside world come to play a basic part in the evolution of the power structure, leading to its centralisation and reinforcement. This process, coinciding with the disintegration of social structures, confers on the State characteristics which are only now begining to be recognised as unique. As the State is primarily an instrument which appropriates the surplus, the evolution of social structures tends to be strongly influenced by the way in which the State directs the utilisation of the resources it controls. It is thus in a country's relations with the outside world, and in the process of accumulation, that we find the bases of the power system, whose action intervenes in the restructuring of society which accompanies the spreading out of capitalism.

The situation of countries which are linked with the outside world through the exploitation of non-renewable resources, and in which the State is the primary, almost the sole, instrument of accumulation controlled from within, is obviously an extreme case. However, in other underdeveloped countries political trends are moving in the same direction: the strengthening of the State machinery being the general rule, as well as the emergence of new forms of social organisation under its guardianship. Investments in infrastructure and basic industries depend directly on the public authorities, or the guarantees given by the latter to foreign groups. Local saving, to a large extent compulsory, would not exist without deliberate action by the State, which assumes growing responsibilities in the production field itself, where the enterprises it establishes operate with a considerable margin of independence. In the face of these trends, it is no longer possible to apply traditional criteria to differentiate government activities from private ones. That is why Weber's concept of *bureaucracy*, linked with the forms of power that are based solely on instrumental rationality, is of little value in accounting for the new realities of power to which we are referring.

The study of development, by leading to a gradual rapprochement of the theory of accumulation with the theory of social stratification and the theory of power, finds its place at a strategic point where the various social science disciplines converge. Early ideas on *economic development*, defined as an increase in the flow of goods and services which was more rapid than population growth, have been gradually replaced by others, which are linked to a complex of social changes that acquire meaning with reference to an implicit or explicit system of values. Measuring a flow of goods and services is an operation which has specific meaning only when such goods and services are related to the satisfaction of objectively defined human needs, that is to say which can be identified independently of existing social inequalities. Ambiguity will, however, always exist in any attempt to reduce to a common denominator expenditures by the different groups of a non-egalitarian society, or in any attempt to compare increases or reductions in inequalities. The postulate of the homogeneity of consumption expenditures is incompatible with the idea of *social welfare*, which, in one way or another, is comprised in the concept of development, since the hypothesis of an egalitarian society is excluded. The controversy on this point – apparently only a technical one – has led to a criticism of the types of society implicit in development projects.

It is easy to see why this controversy arose originally in underdeveloped countries, since the type of society in question *already exists* on account of these countries' backwardness and dependence. Thus the type of traditional thinking about 'obstacles to development' seemed likely to be replaced by another, which fed the controversy on the 'limits of growth', 'development styles', 'types of society', and 'world order'. An in-depth analysis of international relations of domination – dependence and their effect on social structures – has given a clearer insight into the nature of the forces which ensure the permanence of underdevelopment. In addition, criticism of the 'logic of markets' has thrown light on the impact on the ecosystem of a type of society which encourages accumulation, at the same time as it inevitably reproduces inequalities.

The fruitfulness of critical reflection stimulated by the theory of development is most certainly due to its interdisciplinary nature. And the horizons it has opened up may well have contributed towards enriching man's view of the contemporary world.

Discussion of the Papers by Dr Streeten and Professor Furtado
(Chairman: Professor D. Seers)

Professor S. Tsuru (Japan) opened the discussion with a reference to the historical experience of Japan. He noted that Japan had succeeded despite many handicaps, including a limitation on the level of tariffs, lack of foreign capital, external control of much foreign trade and transportation and an overvalued currency. He attributed the initial success of Japanese economic development to two principal aspects of policy: the Matsukata deflation of the mid-1880s, which was an ordeal but which established the discipline of the market and enabled private enterprise to flourish in the succeeding years; and the land tax reform of 1873 which assisted the monetisation of the economy, created a surplus in the hands of landowners which could be channelled into productive investment and at the same time helped to create a supply of wage labour.

Turning to the question of multidisciplinary approaches to economic development, Professor Tsuru drew a distinction between an approach which combined a number of separate disciplines including economics, sociology, psychology, anthropology and politics, and one – which might be called political economy – which had a unified and systematic methodology of its own. He cited Marx and Rostow as examples of the latter approach and said that he thought that Professor Furtado's paper would also come into that category, and this was, he thought, the better approach.

Finally, Professor Tsuru expressed his views on the irrelevance of much economic theory to the problems of development, and gave the Mahalanobis model of 1955 as an example of modelling based on unrealistic assumptions.

Dr Desai (India) said that he agreed with Professor Tsuru that the promise for the future in development studies lies not so much with interdisciplinary studies as with political economy. But he saw difficulties. In eighteenth- and nineteenth-century political economy, economic theory was always the backbone. This was true of Adam Smith as well as Karl Marx. Marx chose not to denounce capitalism as earlier socialist writers had done on grounds of exploitation, but he provided a value theory to support his theory of the dynamics of capitalism. The problem with modern political economy was that as yet it lacked a coherent economic theory. The modern political economist was unhappy about what he believed was the message of the static, competitive theory of resource allocation; he believed it was *status quo* reinforcing and that it neglected the political dimensions of unequal exchange. The new political economy believed that the international division of labour which took place in the context of unequal power relations led to a transfer of economic surplus from the poor to the rich countries. If this was true and quantitatively important, as he agreed it was, then we still needed a theory of the transfer mechanism. The task was by no means easy. It was as difficult as was the value price transformation problem in Marx.

Dr Desai said that an added difficulty in modern political economy was that the practitioners emphasised the monopolistic aspects of modern capitalism. The transition from the competitive to the monopolistic phase of capitalism was dated around early twentieth century. In Adam Smith and Marx, the competitive forces – not perfect competition – were emphasised, and competition rendered the task of building up the value theory easier. Monopoly elements made the task harder. However, a coherent value theory was still needed to underpin the transfer mechanism. What existed today was a mixed bag of empirical results with Keynesian, Marxian and neo-classical concepts.

Referring to the paper by Dr Streeten, Dr Desai noted that over time the priorities of less developed countries had changed: at different times the emphasis had been on growth, on employment, on distribution and on basic needs. This had happened partly because earlier results created new problems; partly also because of political changes in the character of the ruling class. What was initially an urban, westernised class was in some countries replaced by groups more representative of small-scale and rural interests, and this led to changes in values and in economic policies.

Finally, Dr Desai said that he wanted to draw attention to the original and important contribution to political economy made by the late Stephen Hymer in his work on transnational corporations. This should not be overlooked.

Dr Streeten (UK) asked whether Dr Desai was saying that the new approaches to economic development were non-western and indigenous. He did not think this was the case. Much of the new thinking was based on the writings of Schumacher, Colin Clark, Ivan Illich, Johan Galtung and others who reflected western traditions, and he thought the only significant exception to this was the model developed at ECLA by Prebisch and others.

Professor Green (UK) said that he wanted to raise two questions. Firstly, he wondered whether there was not a deeper difference among the three ways of looking at the succession of development cited by Paul Streeten than Marxian–Keynesian–Hirschmanesque. The first two – as used in the Streeten paper – assumed linear, balanced development to be possible and desirable. The third was based on the premise that development was necessarily zigzag or spiral in nature and followed a moving disequilibrium path.

He thought that the latter perception of development and development strategy was valid. However, this approach raised very real conceptual and policy problems which were not tackled in the paper by Streeten. If the trajectory of development was a series of zigs and zags, each of which led away from equilibrium, how did one define the conditions for such a series converging on an equilibrium solution? At an applied level how did one determine criteria for testing when and whether a zigzag should be reversed or a new area of concentration selected? Both premature alteration of course and inertial failure to switch from imbalance building to rebalancing were costly. Both the theoretical and the practical problems were heightened if the process of development altered the pattern of goals from those initially envisaged.

Dr Green's second question related to Professor Furtado's three criteria (page 208). He doubted whether these were entirely adequate for Furtado's political economic system. The first appeared to take the efficiency of the production systems to be in some sense independent of social and production relations and technological processes. There was, however, no 'balancing' fourth criterion to cover these. Thus, as stated, the first criterion – while correctly recognising that levels of productive forces were important – appeared in danger of foreclosing the model against factors which were at least equally critical to the underlying political/economic matrix.

At a different level, he thought the empirical measurement of basic needs along the lines proposed was beset with problems. First, non-material and non-physical subsistence needs (e.g. a decent burial in many societies) were not adequately classed as group objectives but nor were they physical or subsistence needs. Second, basic needs – e.g. cleansing, eating – did not easily correspond to actual goods, services or expenditures. For example, expenditure on soap had to cover the costs of advertising, etc. Similarly, most actual food consumption mixed amenity services (e.g. in a restaurant), taste preferences (individual, class or social) and other factors with the basic nutritional need element. Thus the criterion – as now stated – ran the risk of being too narrow and too little operational.

Professor Kabaj (Poland) said that in his view economic theory was largely irrelevant for the developing countries. The number of unemployed in these countries was already very large and would increase, and he thought this would be one of the major problems of the next two or three decades. Economic theory put too much emphasis on scarcity of capital, too little on the low rate of utilisation of available capacity which was a feature of many of the developing countries. He cited some statistics to this effect for Pakistan and Nigeria.

Professor Pajestka (Poland) expressed his agreement with Professor Tsuru's views on the methodological question of political economy rather than multidisciplinarity. He also said that he thought Professor Green claimed too much for the Basic Needs approach and that he preferred Dr Streeten's view which emphasised basic needs as applied to the poorest countries, but did not put it forward as a general theoretical prescription for all cases.

Mr Lengyel (UNESCO) said that multidisciplinarity had become a slogan, but in his view it was extremely difficult to make it operational. Economics must not be allowed to ignore important social or political factors but at the same time it was necessary to maintain a coherent and intellectually satisfactory approach.

Dr Owosekun (Nigeria) discussed three major issues arising from Dr Streeten's paper. First, with respect to the relationship of economics to other disciplines he wished to stress the importance of sociology rather than anthropology. Many of the major problems facing his country had an important sociological component. Second, he expressed reservations regarding the Basic Needs strategy. He thought it was rather simplistic and could not solve the problems of the developing countries. Finally, he said that he would want to add to the list of points summarising development strategy on pp. 195- of Dr Streeten's paper. It was also important to recognise the many costs and sacrifices which development imposed and the fact that the type of development that was desired could not be achieved in a relatively short period of time.

Professor Malinvaud (France) said that the conference should be grateful to Professor Furtado for his contribution because he had given an excellent lesson on what could be done by using an interdisciplinary approach to the theory of development. Drawing on the results of economic and sociological analysis and observation, we could today obtain a much more accurate description of modern development than we could in the past.

He saw as Furtado's main thesis the view that in order to avoid falling into stagnation, the capitalist system needed on the one hand intense accumulation with accompanying (endogenous) technical progress, on the other hand the reproduction of non-egalitarian social structures. The thesis went beyond pure description in as much as it stated an objective necessity. He said that he was not opposed to this thesis, but would like it to be specified and, if possible proved, more rigorously. For instance, to substantiate a notion such as 'the subordination of technological creativity to the objective of reproducing a social structure which is largely non-egalitarian', he would like to see an analytical model which would show how this subordination came about, and which could be empirically tested.

Professor Malinvaud said that his main concern was what was implied by the paper on the general issue of the 'relevance of economic theories'. Professor Furtado had not dealt explicitly with the subject, except by some side comments whose implications were not always clear. But some readers would probably have the feeling that Furtado rejected most of our existing economic theories as irrelevant. If these readers were right, there would be a clear conflict with Professor Malinvaud's own paper where he stated that a good many of our theoretical efforts had been and were relevant.

One possible explanation was in the meaning given to the adjective 'relevant'. For a narrow group of people, nothing was relevant if it did not deal directly with the choice of the societies in which men should live, all other problems being negligible in comparison with this one. He had, of course not taken such a definition and he did not imagine Professor Furtado would accept it either.

Professor Malinvaud said that he would like, therefore, to obtain from Professor Furtado answers to the two following questions, in which he understood 'theory' in the broad meaning given to this word in his paper. Which of the present economic theories were directly or indirectly useful for specifying and substantiating his main thesis? Did he agree that economic development within the capitalist system could take many different forms, which were not equivalent for the people living them, and hence that many important problems required the attention of economists, beyond the global and qualitative description to which he devoted his attention?

Commenting upon Dr Streeten's paper, particularly pp. 193–5, *Professor Urquidi* (Mexico) agreed with most of the suggestions, and wished to emphasise the following: first, the problem of producing food for domestic consumption had not been given enough thought, and there was a vast difference between the macro and global problem and that facing the individual farmer; second, we did not know enough about the relative merits and effects of industrial versus agricultural subsidisation in promoting development; third, the whole question of the introduction of capital-saving technologies was neglected in thinking on development; fourth, systems analysis was a necessary adjunct or tool of development theory; fifth, the notion of a concerted attack was a valid one; sixth, what was the role of nationalised or socialised economic activities, i.e. public sector output? Regarding the first and second points, it was strange that industrialisation was not mentioned as a basic requirement for development; there could be too much emphasis on agriculture and rural areas.

Professor Furtado said in his reply to the discussion that he had linked his approach to interdisciplinarity rather than political economy because the latter had not been listed as one of the themes to be discussed at the conference. Furthermore, he wished to avoid being trapped in the specific conceptual framework created by the historical origins of European political economy in a particular theory of value. He felt that a wider conceptual framework was needed which would incorporate the experience of Japan and other countries.

He stressed the phenomenon of *Power* and said that this was always present, whatever the issue under discussion, and must be integrated in the basic conceptual framework. In his view it was necessary to start from the way in which power was exercised in society, and the theory of power must be part of the theory of the social structure. Inequality was the expression of a surplus and power was the mechanism by which the surplus was extracted.

Professor Furtado then turned to the question of capital accumulation. He noted that it was not necessary for accumulation to be linked to the development of the productive forces; as in the case of Brazil, it was possible to have substantial outlays on, for example, the beautification of cities, without any expansion of productive capacity. He was interested, therefore, in studying how the advanced capitalist countries had expanded their capital and wanted to see whether this could be applied to the developing countries. He did not think economic theory was either useless or irrelevant; but in its present state it could not cope with the problems that he was concerned with, and needed to be further developed along the lines indicated in his paper.

Finally, Professor Furtado said that he would reply to Professor Malinvaud's questions during the following session.

Dr Streeten (UK) replied first to the points made by Professor Pajestka. He said that his understanding of Basic Needs was that it was not a strategy but an adjunct to other strategies incorporating what had been learned about development, it was a way of supplementing the 'income generation' approach which placed all emphasis on the increase in the productivity of the small farmer and the informal urban sector, without regard to other, equally important, aspects. It was even possible that the higher output might be achieved at the cost of basic nutritional needs where, for example, it involved the substitution of cash crops for the crops previously grown for the farmer's own subsistence, or of women's earnings for breastfeeding. Other ways in which the income generation approach had been found to be inadequate included its omission of efficient, low-cost public services, of the crucial issue of intrahousehold income distribution, its inability to deal with the problem of the unemployables, and its failure to consider non-material needs which could not be provided via the market. The Basic Needs approach did not necessarily show how these problems could be solved but it was helpful to have them emphasised.

In reply to Professor Urquidi, Dr Streeten said that a full analysis would take far too long but he had been influenced by two recent books by W. Arthur Lewis.[1] These showed that it was not a question of agriculture versus industry, but that improvements in domestic agriculture for food were a necessary condition for successful industrialisation.

[1] W. A. Lewis, *Growth and Fluctuations 1870–1913* (George Allen and Unwin, London, 1978), and *The Evolution of the International Economic Order* (Princeton University Press, Princeton, 1977).

14 Positive Economics and Development in Industrial Countries

Edmond Malinvaud
INSEE, PARIS

INTRODUCTORY

At the present time a highly critical view prevails both on what economic development has done for the people of the world and on the significance of our growth theories. This 'crisis of development' concerns practically all countries and all schools of thought. Hence, we must welcome this IEA roundtable in which, with due concern for the problems that seem acute to our fellow-citizens, we shall ponder over our present theories and suggest new avenues to scientific knowledge.

Our conference runs two opposing risks, of which I shall try to be aware in dealing with my subject. No useful purpose would be served here if we should either simply echo the current dissatisfaction about existing theories, or dwell on new marginal improvements to these theories. Constructive evaluation and criticism of the main laws of analytical models should be our motto.

Considering the positive theories of growth raises a large number of issues, even when attention is limited to their relevance for developed countries; actually the whole of economics may come into the picture. By necessity, because this paper should not be long and because my knowledge is limited, I shall stick to the central part of growth theories. Even so, I am conscious that some of my statements may be found mistaken because of ignorance, lack of good judgement or poor logic on my part.

For dealing with my subject, I believe it is advisable to start from the present concerns, inquiring how they could find scientific answers in economic theory (section I), then to examine what has been achieved by the work of all those who tried to build theories from the systematic observation of facts (section II). The relevance of the abstract theories will finally be considered against this background (section III).

I WHAT KIND OF A SCIENTIFIC RESPONSE IS NEEDED?

When people of industrial countries express dissatisfaction about economic growth they may articulate one or other of the four following protests: a too slow development, a too costly development, a too unequal development, a too unstable development. Scientists should explain first why this happened, second whether and how better performances can be achieved in the future.

(1) *Normative questions*

In their attempts to play their part, scientists face many questions that are at times purely positive (how can such and such facts be explained?) but that often also have normative content (to speak of a too slow, too costly, too unequal or too unstable development implies implicit reference to a norm on the appropriate speed, cost, equality or stability of growth). Since this paper is concerned only with positive theories, it may be proper at the start to give a quick look in the direction of normative questions, which will not be discussed again here.

The two main normative questions are: what should be the objectives of economic development? How can economic development be controlled?

One could argue that the study of objectives does not belong to economics, or even to political economy, but rather to social philosophy. Economists concerned with growth and development have often stated this principle, but very often just to transform themselves later into social philosophers. In this conference we may wonder why economists went outside the confines of their discipline and whether their contributions were then relevant. My own quick answer is that, because they had to study precisely growth and development, economists were more aware than others of the difficulty of deciding about objectives; moreover they had to consider the actual implications of the choice of such or such objectives and this in turn made them better equipped for a reflection on the exact meaning of these objectives.[1] I think the final aims of economic activity are better discussed by economists than by other scientists and, though on such a delicate subject opinions vary and progress toward a lucid consensus may be judged much too slow, some steps are being made in the right direction.

The question of how economic development can be controlled is obviously addressed to economists and may well be the most challenging of all those we shall consider. The time has passed when a large proportion of economists claimed an active economic policy to be useless or even detrimental. But the time has also gone when some economists could consider the planning of development to be an easy operation; even within particular countries long- and medium-term economic policy or planning raises difficult problems which basically follow from the multiplicity of agents and from the fact that information and operations are dispersed, the difficulty is much increased by

[1] The necessity of a feedback from the characteristics of an optimal growth programme to the characteristics of the objective function defining it has been well argued by T. Koopmans in a lecture given in Warsaw in September 1966. See 'Objectives, Constraints and Outcomes in Optimal Growth Models', *Econometrica*, (January 1967).

the international character of the development problems faced by the modern world.

Some economic theories are intended to clarify particular aspects of the control of growth. I consider that very significant progress has been made in this respect during the past three decades: activity analysis, the theory of decentralised planning, the theory of optimal growth, the study of externalities and public goods, all seem relevant in one respect or another. I should argue this statement if my paper had to deal with normative issues. I should then point out that our main weakness lies in our inability to help significantly with the resolution of conflicts between social groups or nations that have partly opposing but also partly convergent interests.

(2) *Positive questions*

However, the purpose of my paper is to scrutinise the positive theories intended to explain economic growth as it is observed. Following Simon Kuznets,[1] I may view the aim of these theories as being to indicate the factors in the development of advanced industrial countries, to frame the factors so that a testable analysis of obstacles to economic growth becomes possible, finally to consider the operation of these factors under various institutional regimes.

A first classification of the factors of development leads Kuznets to distinguish: (i) population growth, about which we should know in particular how fertility and mortality are related to economic and social conditions, (ii) the accumulation of technological and other knowledge, which should be better understood both in its speed and in its direction, (iii) the adaptations of societies to the growth potential resulting from their population and their technological knowledge, (iv) the relations between nations, relations which, either peaceful or combative, play their part both in the growth capabilities of each country and in the international propagation of modes of organisation and development.

The bulk of the investigations by economists bears on the third group of factors, those concerned with the adaptations of societies to their growth potential, and I shall restrict my attention to them here. Among those factors the accumulation of capital has a central position, but we should try not to forget two other important ones. On the one hand, we should explain how socio-economic behaviour is determined and how it affects growth; particular attention should then be given to 'entrepreneurs', i.e. to all those who innovate, promote productive activities, or assume responsibility for their organisation. On the other hand, we should relate economic development to structural transformations, which permit it or result from it, such

[1] Simon Kuznets, 'Toward a Theory of Economic Growth', first published in 1955, reprinted in S. Kuznets, *Economic Growth and Structure* (W. W. Norton, 1965).

transformations concerning not only the production sphere, but also its social and institutional environment.

Even after we have restricted the positive theory of growth to explaining such adaptations of societies to their growth potential we must repeat the verdict stated by Kuznets in 1955 for the broader conception of this theory: 'Such a theory of economic growth of nations may never be within our reach. Obviously we do not have it now' (p. 4).

But I do not think we could go on as he then did and write: 'What is more important, we are not yet ready for it. The very concern about economic growth is recent, and it is hardly an exaggeration to say that since the mid-nineteenth century, when the Classical and Marxian schools had already formulated their economic theories of the long run, no significant theoretical work has been done in this field, excepting the attempts to revise Marxian theory in the light of subsequent events'. On the contrary, during the past twenty-five years, the theory of growth has been the object of many contributions and of heated debates. But the question may well be raised: were all these efforts relevant to help us better to understand the motive forces of development?

(3) *What do we mean by a positive theory*?

In order to approach the challenging question on the relevance of our present theories we must, in one way or another, survey them. But our survey must be different from the ones usually found in the professional literature. Not only should it be much shorter, but it must also be geared in a different direction. This is particularly clear when we look at the famous survey by Hahn and Matthews.[1] The authors then stated that their 'central concern was with *models* of economic growth' (my italics) and that 'this approach to growth theory is . . . different from that which would be used if the *immediate* purpose was to provide the best available explanation of the variety of historical growth experience' (p. 779, their italics).

For our purpose, a theory should not be identified with the model that may formalise it. (Indeed, such an identification is too frequent nowadays and may be held as responsible for some imbalance in the allocation of the collective efforts of economists as between abstract formalisation and inductive research.)

By a theory we mean a general representation of some facts or phenomena, i.e. a representation that, intended to be applicable to a well-defined class of observations, has both explanatory and predictive value within this class. Following Kuznets, we may equivalently say that a theory is 'a statement of testable relations among empirically identifiable factors, such relations and

[1] F. H. Hahn and R. C. O. Matthews, 'The Theory of Economic Growth: A Survey', *The Economic Journal* (December 1964).

factors having been found relatively invariant under various conditions in time and space' (p. 4).

When we keep such a definition in mind, we realise that our theories of growth are often still in the making. Not only can they not claim to grasp the whole phenomenon of the adaptation of societies to their growth potential and are they more modestly intended to represent some parts of it, but also they often have not yet reached complete maturation: the definition of the 'factors' is still imprecise or the statement of the 'relations' not yet well articulated. However, some relevant improvements in our scientific knowledge has been achieved during the past twenty-five years.

I shall argue this conclusion in the next part of this paper, where I shall also point to the enormous gaps that still remain and on which we have not made progress. I shall then be in a position to evaluate against this background, in the third part of the paper, the relevance of the abstract theories, which I do not want to dismiss, as you may well imagine.

II BUILDING THE POSITIVE THEORY FROM FACTS

The systematic collection of data, the computation of aggregates, indices or indicators, the setting up of accounts have been pushed ahead to such a scale during the last few decades that much better preconditions for building objective theories exist now than at the end of the nineteenth century when the German historical school failed in its attempt to produce a theory of capitalist development. Moreover, the processing of data by precise quantitative or econometric methods has attracted a large number of economists who can now bridge the gap that existed during the major part of this century between institutionalist historians and abstract theoreticians.

Surveying here all the work done and scrutinising, piece by piece, its relevance would require a much longer inquiry than I can pretend to undertake. But we may take a very broad view of recent achievements and of our present knowledge, limiting ourselves to factors of growth as opposed to phenomena concerning business fluctuations.

The first manifestation of economic growth is the increase of labour productivity. It is then natural and sound to accept the present approach that starts from the proximate factors of productivity changes and tries to go up the causal chain towards more remote, and probably more fundamental, factors. This methodology may be long and painful, but the example of natural sciences shows that it is likely progressively to achieve its purpose. At the present stage it is also a good antidote against the inclination of economists and social philosophers towards sweeping but unwarranted generalisations.

(1) *Proximate factors of productivity*

In order to discover which factors directly react on productivity and by how much, it is natural to relate past changes in productivity to past changes in its would-be factors. For instance, in order to know by how much investment will increase income per head in the long run (indeed a relevant question) one has to consider how, in the past, changes in the capital stock have been associated with changes of productivity. This apparently simple operation raises, as every economist now knows, important methodological issues to which I shall come back in the third part of this paper. But no sensible and informed person could pretend that methodological difficulties make useless or insignificant the systematic scrutiny of simultaneous past changes in productivity and its would-be factors.

The main factors that were so explored are investment, education of the labour force, transfers of workers and capital from low- to high-productivity sectors, technological research and development. On the study of each one of them a full branch of economic research has grown: econometric analysis was and is being made on many data bases consisting either of micro data on firms or individuals, or of aggregate data for whole industries or regions; appropriate formalisations have been looked for, more complex models replacing those that were found unduly simple; spurious factors have been identified and studied (such as the selection effect in the length of schooling).

When taking a perspective view of this work, as I must do here, the conclusion emerges that it is debated and incomplete, but relevant.

No one should be surprised to realise the existence of scientific debates in a field that has been grasped only recently, that covers complex phenomena and that must be analysed by the use of data whose limitations are serious. Such debates reveal the liveliness of the subject and the interest that is found in it by strong personalities. Actually it is noteworthy that the results could look reliable enough to permit a systematic numerical decomposition of the growth rate of output in as many components as there are factors of productivity, each component relating to one factor. The work of Denison in this respect was certainly bold in 1962 when its first results were presented; but one must recognise today that the large bulk of econometric studies performed since then showed none of his main estimates to be much off the mark.[1]

The study of the proximate factors of productivity is, of course, still incomplete. This is made quite apparent in the growth-accounting exercises 'à la Denison' by the presence of a substantial residual, covering the impact of all factors that were not individually identified. One may suspect that, among those factors, the two following ones play dominant roles: the

[1] This does not mean that I accept all of them; I still have strong doubts on what he calls 'economies of scale'. See E. F. Denison, *The Sources of Economic Growth in the U.S.* (Committee for Economic Development, New York, 1962); *Why Growth Rates Differ* (Brookings Institution, Washington, 1967); *Accounting for US Economic Growth* (Brookings Institution, Washington, 1974).

intensity of work by both employees and entrepreneurs, the structural efficiency of the organisations within enterprises and within the country. For the time being, these factors escape quantification and even objective characterisation. I am afraid I cannot make any useful suggestion for their study here.

But what has been achieved is quite relevant for the answer to policy questions that are at the same level of aspiration: the impact on output of a reduction of the working week; the medium-term forecast on the growth of productive capacities etc.

(2) *Capital accumultion*

After the study of proximate factors of growth we must consider more fundamental causes that could explain differences in the speed of investment, education, intersectoral transfers or technical progress. We economists put great emphasis on capital accumulation, broadly understood. Capital accumulation concerns savings and investments. But it is strongly correlated with the importance of innovations, technological research and development, interindustrial transfers. Hence, explaining capital accumulation would be making a major step in the explanation of most proximate factors of productivity.

A good deal of econometric work has been devoted to it. Surveying this work now would now be a major task. Indeed, we know much more about saving and investment than thirty years ago. Such research as has concerned for instance the life-cycle hypothesis has direct implications for the theory of growth (the relation between population growth and economic growth in this instance).

But we must recognise that the econometric work on investment demand is much more useful for the study of short-term business fluctuations than for the understanding of long-term economic development. This is not surprising; differences in orders received by producers, as between years or firms, are so important a factor of investment that it has first to be correctly accounted for, before the impact of any other determinant can be seen; and the great heterogeneity of the set of firms obviously makes any econometric work on investment particularly difficult and uncertain.

Notwithstanding this remark, the consideration of whatever results are now available rather confirms and should progressively make more precise an idea that is fairly natural, has long been entertained in economics and can even be called the 'classical law of capital accumulation' (Marx accepted this law, of course): investment is related positively to the rate of profit and negatively to the cost of capital, hence in particular to the long-term rate of interest.

The question that remains open, and on which we made too little progress during the past decades, is to know how to explain differences, as between periods or countries, in the excess of the rate of profit over the long-term rate of interest. Again, short-term fluctuations are becoming better known as a result of econometric work on prices and wages. But this is not very relevant to our subject.

Before leaving the subject of capital accumulation, I must mention a related field of econometric research that is active and should bring a block for the inductive building of growth theory, namely the research on industrial structures and their performances.[1]

(3) *Inequality and development*

An old idea about differences concerning the rate of profit, as between countries or sectors of a dual economy, is that they result from the respective power of the various countries or sectors and that their explanation must therefore be found in political rather than in economic analysis (in this respect one cannot help thinking today of the relations between OPEC and OCDE countries). In particular the past growth of the major industrial nations would be due to imperialism, i.e. to the exploitation of the rest of the world.

This same notion, namely that political forces determine respective economic advantages, is also extended by many people to the whole range of income distribution, within countries as well as between countries. Since income distribution reacts on saving and investment, it would follow that any complete explanation of economic growth should result from an integrated social theory, in which economic analysis would go hand in hand with political and sociological analysis.

As a methodological claim, this last statement cannot be disputed. We must recognise that, if our present theory of growth has only limited relevance, this in part follows from its lack of integration into a more global social theory.

Should we feel guilty in this respect? I wonder. The case may well be argued that social scientists always hurry too much and tend to imagine global theories too quickly without going through the painstaking stage of detailed empirical analysis. Hence, it may turn out later to have been a very wise research strategy in the long run for economists to accumulate data and to see how far they could go by themselves in explaining them, as they did during the last thirty years. Such a strategy will appear retrospectively as having been justified if, in the coming decades, economists succeed in filling the present gap between their purely economic theories and a broader explanation of social phenomena.[2]

[1] The classical reference now is F. M. Scherer, *Industrial market structure and economic performance* (Rand McNally, Chicago, 1971).

[2] Any prediction as to the chances of such a success would be too risky. On the one hand the challenge appears as very difficult, when we realise how limited our economic theories of growth still are and how complex are global social phenomena. On the other hand, we may now already witness in various special fields progress of economic theories towards an analysis not only of economic but also of broader social phenomena: in the abstract theory of choices where political decisions are not ignored, in the theory of public goods, in labour economics, in the theory of individual behaviour.

Whatever role should be recognised for political power, purely economic analysis may still reveal itself as very useful for a relevant, even if incomplete, explanation of inequalities in development. The empirical study of the performances of alternative development strategies, in particular of inward-looking as against outward-looking strategies, is a very significant contribution to our understanding of economic growth; it helps in explaining how capital accumulation, interindustry labour transfers, on-the-job training and similar proximate factors of productivity can be promoted.

As for the shifts in income distribution within an economy, we must recognise that we made relatively little significant progress during the past decades.[1] This arises, I believe, from two causes. First, it is a major statistical operation to build a reliable data base for an empirical analysis of the factors explaining the inequalities in personal income distribution. At present serious discussions still exist as to what are the facts: whether there was a trend towards a greater equality or inequality within a given country, or whether inequality is larger in one country than in another.

Second, whatever shifts took place were rather slow and smaller than was anticipated. The great expansion of education did not bring a sharp reduction of wage differentials between educated and uneducated workers. Deliberate policies of social transfers had perverse effects, which somewhat counteracted their immediate impact. We certainly learned from observing these facts and analysing the reasons for them. But the simple schemes we had in mind before must now be seriously questioned.

(4) *Economic growth and human development*

A positive theory of economic growth should also consider whether and how the growth of production contributed to the satisfaction of human needs and to a better fulfilment of men's aspirations. One may well argue that, until quite recently,[2] it was a neglected subject and that no consideration was given to quite relevant questions in this respect. One may even claim that the explanation of how societies adapted to their growth potential cannot be complete if the end result of growth for human satisfaction is not considered; indeed, surely some feedback exists from

[1] At least such is my own conclusion after reading the proceedings of the IEA roundtable on personal income distribution (see W. Krelle, ed.) and the papers presented on this subject at the IEA congress in Tokyo (see in particular E. Bacha, 'The Kuznets Curve and Beyond: Growth and Changes in Inequality', in E. Malinvaud, ed., *Economic Growth and Resources*, Proceedings of the 1977 Tokyo Congress (London, Macmillan, 1979).

[2] The new concern for 'the costs of economic growth' has already stimulated the appearance of a few serious theoretical studies. Particularly revealing in this respect is F. Hirsch, *Social Limits to Growth* (Harvard University Press, Cambridge, 1976).

human satisfaction to such factors of productivity as the intensity of work effort or entrepreneurship.

Most economists more or less implicitly accepted the view that economic growth would automatically lead to better and better individual and social satisfaction. We now realise that such a view was much too simple. But economists are not the only ones, not even the first ones, to be blamed for this fault. When the dominant social philosophy praised the priority to be given to economic growth, economists could hardly resists the temptation to accept the prominence given to their field of study.

But this social philosophy has now gone and economists will have to consider how they can contribute to the emergence of a new one, in which the relation between human needs or aspirations and the socio-economic environment will be seen in a new perspective.[1]

III ABSTRACT GROWTH THEORIES

During the past twenty years we have seen the publication of many abstract models intended to concern the positive theory of growth. But we have also witnessed heated theoretical discussions about the conclusions of these models or between proponents of alternative models. The debate between the two Cambridge schools is present in the mind of every economist. What should we think of all that when we question the relevance of our economic theories?

I shall answer here that quite significant results were obtained, many of them being negative but nevertheless important to know.

Before I do so, let me however deplore the tone in which scientific debates occurred in this field and the dramatic misunderstandings that surround their interpretation. Anyone who has fully mastered the main results achieved by the various schools (probably no one can claim to master all the details, many of them being purely scholastic) knows that they have no ideological

[1] The need for a new social philosophy is the message to be read in a recent book: C. Mendes (ed.), *Le mythe du développement* (Le Seuil, Paris, 1977). For instance: 'Non seulement la croissance économique ne résoud pas quelques-uns des problèmes les plus fondamentaux des êtres humains, mais c'est aussi qu'elle suscite et développe, si l'on peut dire, un sous-developpement moral, affectif, psychologique. Elle développe, en temps que des possibilités d'épanouissement humain, des carences qui précisément minent cet épanouissement' (E. Morin, p. 249). 'On croyait à un développement harmonieux, où tous les sous-systèmes devaient évolver ensemble, où les développements économique, social, culturel et politique devaient se faire facon synchrone. Il est clair maintenant que cette conception n'était pas nécessaire, car on a pu voir presque toutes les combinaisons possible possibles' (C. Mendes, p. 190–1). 'La crise du développement . . . est surtout la conscience obscure et inquiète d'un épuisement de la volonté, de l'imagination et des mythes qui ont inspiré le progrès.' (J. -M. Domenach, p. 20).

connotation by themselves. The type of presentation that is often given to them reveals the lack of scientific maturity of many economists, and perhaps of economics itself.

(1) *Aggregation and the logic of growth accounting*

A first objective of abstract theory is the consolidation of applied and empirical works. Under which conditions are the conclusions derived from these works valid? In particular what is the meaning of the theory of growth that is being currently built up through the accumulation and processing of data? First of all, can we define between aggregates measuring the volumes of the various categories of inputs and outputs a production function that would depend only on the technology of production?

To this last question the answer is no, except under very special theoretical circumstances that have no chance of being met in reality. The relation that is observed between the conventionally measured volume aggregates reflects not only technology but also other conditions of production. If these latter conditions change, a shift in the relation is to be expected.

Such a result is unfortunate for statisticians and econometricians, but they have to live with it. One cannot even say that it is a new situation for them. They have known for a long time that, as a measure of the changes in the cost of living, no consumer price index can be logically perfect; but this does not detract from the relevance of the currently computed indices. Similarly the currently estimated production functions have a relevance even if that relevance is less simple than one might have hoped, a relevance that must be studied both empirically and theoretically. Indeed, the theory of aggregation, which can deal with the various aspects of the present problem, may go a long way in giving us insight about the meaning of such estimated functions. There is no reason why the theory should stop at the negative answer when it can clarify the impact of the non-technical conditions of production on the relation between the main aggregate inputs and aggregate output,[1] a relation that cannot be ignored, neither in our historical analysis of path growth nor in our projections concerning future development.

The second main question on which abstract theory must provide consolidation to the inductive study of growth is how observed relative prices and remuneration rates can serve for the estimation of marginal productive contributions.

It has been clear for a long time that this crucially depends on the nature of competition ruling the various markets. One might have hoped that progress in abstract theories of 'imperfect competition' or of 'monopoly capitalism' could provide some guidance on how to infer productive contributions from remuneration rates. Such guidance appears particularly

[1] I hope to convey this message with convincing arguments when I teach macroeconomics to my students.

needed because experience with the econometric study of growth has shown that one cannot go far if one forbids inference from the price system to marginal productivity or rates of substitution.[1]

I think it is fair to say that modern abstract theory has so far failed to provide in this respect a better guidance than the rough one already existing forty years ago. Whether it proceeds from the theory of games or from the marxist theory of exploitation, it does not help us today to do anything better than intuitively guess the 'degree of monopoly'. This lack of relevance is undoubtedly due to the difficulty of the theoretical challenge: classifying and modelling the various forms of market structures in such a way as to come to clear conclusions about their impact on observed prices and remuneration rates.

(2) *Capital and the interest rate*

Assuming from now on perfect competition on the various markets we must note that, during recent decades, abstract theories have brought a negative answer to another relevant question that has concerned economists for a long time: namely whether, given the technology, an inverse relationship necessarily holds between the 'rate of interest' (or equivalently under perfect competition 'the rate of profit') and a simple global physical characteristic such as the volume of the capital stock per unit of labour input or the average period of production. Many believed that the existence of such a relationship[2] could be proved by purely abstract arguments. We must now give up this hope in the same way as we gave up long ago the hope of proving that demand curves are necessarily downward sloping. It is partly an empirical question and not purely a theoretical one to want to know whether, in the absence of technical progress and under competitive conditions, capital accumulation should bring a decrease of the rate of interest.

A quick look back to the theoretical developments during the past three decades may be instructive here because it shows how abstract thinking has permitted the answer to a difficult question. Two preconditions were required.

In the first place, the nature of the question had to be made precise. Since the rate of interest in general depends on the choice of the numéraire, attention had first to be concentrated on stationary or proportional growth evolutions, in which this dependence disappears. Similarly, while a precise definition of the physical characteristic involved was required as long as a

[1] One must remember in particular that apparently innocent analysis, such as simple-minded productivity assessments by accountants or economic statisticians, often implicitly depends on such an inference. Econometrics has only made the reference more explicit and less crude.

[2] I wonder whether stating this existence should not be considered as *the* neo-classical proposition.

postive answer was looked for, general formulations had to be found later for proving that no relevant definition could lead to such an answer.

In the second place, formal models were needed in which the development of productive activity through time under given technological constraints could be represented. The von Neumann model of economic growth and the activity analysis methodology then played a crucial role. The debate on the theoretical possibility of reswitching was then made possible, and this debate played an important role even though reswitching is not a necessary feature of examples showing that the inverse relationship does not hold.[1]

(3) *Intertemporal efficiency*

Thirty years ago, when discussing the efficiency of resource allocation in a perfectly competitive market economy (certainly a relevant question), many economists used to say that, even neglecting external effects, this efficiency only applied to a static and sure situation. They then meant that the theoretical proof of efficiency was crucially dependent on the absence of time and uncertainty, two essential features of economic growth. Work in mathematical economics since then has definitely clarified the issue.

On the one hand, the abstract models of the microeconomic theory of efficient resource allocation has been generalised to include proper consideration of time and uncertainty. Roughly speaking, the efficiency property of the sure and static competitive equilibrium has been generalised to a similar efficiency property of competitive growth under uncertainty.

On the other hand, this generalisation revealed possible sources of inefficiency. While most of these revelations seemed to fit nicely within prior intuitive ideas, the whole problem was made much more precise and much better understood.

Perhaps the most striking discovery was the possibility of permanent overcapitalisation. Since economic growth has no definite time horizon, it should be represented by models with infinite time. One then finds the existence of inefficient growth paths that meet all the formal conditions usually associated with perfect competition, such paths being dominated by others that use less capital. Of course such an inefficiency may *a fortiori* occur under imperfect competition.

A less striking feature of the generalisation was to require a tremendous number of markets that cannot be considered to exist in the real world: one market should deal only with the delivery that will be made of a specific commodity, at a specific date and if a specific combination of (*a priori* unknown) events occurs; there should then be as many markets as there are commodities, dates and possible combinations of events. Since only a much

[1] The best reference for our conference seems to be E. Burmeister, 'On the social significance of the reswitching controversy', *Revue d'économie politique* (March–April 1977).

simpler structure of markets actually exists, the interplay of individual economic behaviour can lead to inefficiencies. In particular, shortsightedness and inappropriate risk-taking are to be feared. This is of course particularly serious for those decisions that are irreversible or have long-lasting consequences, such as those concerning the use of exhaustible resources.

In the absence of a complete system of forward and contingent markets on which all future consequences of present individual plans would be confronted, firms and households must form their own expectations as to future economic and non-economic conditions. Intuition suggests that inefficiency is reduced if some central planning is organised in such a way as to collect all the information that concerns a large number of agents simultaneously, as to enlighten individual expectations, and as to proceed to a number of consistency checks between individual decisions that do not find appropriate markets for their confrontation.

Similarly, theoretical exploration of the problems raised by resource allocation over time and under uncertainty has led economists to realise why some productive operations are better assumed by the public sector than by private firms, why direct prohibitions or obligations may be required in some cases, why some interference with the price system may be wise.

(4) *Growth and stability*

Speaking of relevant issues, we should not fail to consider what is called by some people the stability of growth in market economies and by others the instability of capitalist development. Three views are offered: the neo-classical one shows a rather harmonious long-term progress, the marxist one foresees the collapse of capitalism, the keynesian one sees the chronic recurrence of difficulties and unemployment problems.

Abstract economic theory can obviously not prove the truth or error of any of these visions: economics itself would not suffice, since sociology and politics should also come into play; abstract thinking in social sciences is not yet, and perhaps will never be, able to grasp such global questions; it must operate at a much more analytical level.

I see three questions that bear on the broad issue of stability and can be approached by economic theory.

(1) Is competitive growth with perfectly flexible prices stable? Mathematical economics has provided some answer by studying an economy with a sequence of periods, in each one of which prices and interest rates are competitively determined. With the most aggregated model allowing for capital-labour substitution, economic growth appears as harmonious.[1] But it has also been found that when

[1] Capital-labour substitution plays some role. But the Kaldorian theory of income distribution, which is quite consistent with the mathematical economic theory here discussed, gives the same harmony to the growth path in the strict complementarity Harrod–Domar model.

there are several capital goods and some conditions are met, which do not look *a priori* pathological, the growth path may develop along strongly diverging lines for various productions and prices, hence may lead to a development that cannot be indefinitely sustained.[1] This is a consequence of the shortsightedness of an economy operating through a sequence of markets.

Everybody should agree that such a theoretical result is significant. Its actual implications for economic policy are still somewhat obscure, but it gives support to those advocating planning as a supplement to markets for enlightening long-term decisions.

(2) How does an economy with imperfectly flexible prices behave? This question, which introduces a complication with respect to the preceding one, is now being considered more and more seriously. The relative stickiness of some prices and wage rates is well established by econometric studies and plays an important role in the study of short-term equilibrium and short-term economic policy. Intuition suggests that its presence also affects medium- or long-term growth and may, under some circumstances, make it difficult: indeed, the present income and price policies in Western Europe aim at curbing real wage stickiness and this with an objective that goes beyond the immediate short run. It is my belief that we are now ready for a theory that will make this intuition more precise and that will therefore help with the answer to relevant questions.

(3) Is an industrial structure with important oligopolistic sectors a stable one? The question is indeed relevant for any long-term forecast as to the future of capitalist countries. But it seems to me that abstract economic theories do not at present help with its answer. The gap is still too big between the theory of games and its application to industrial structures. Moreover, we must recognise that the progress recently achieved by this theory does not go in the direction of reducing the gap.

Surveying the various questions raised by economic growth and evaluating the relevance of present theories for answering them, I have tried not to forget anything of importance. I am conscious that my evaluation will be found subjective in places; I hope it will not be found dogmatic.

A rather mixed picture appears. On the one hand, a lot of relevant work has been done and should not be forgotten. On the other hand, the answers to some pressing questions do not make any real progress, a situation that explains the irritation sometimes voiced against economic theory. Particularly noteworthy is the lack of proper theories for dealing with the interactions between economic and social developments. The challenge in this respect is not addressed only to economists.

[1] For a survey see in particular E. Burmeister and A. Dobell, *Mathematical Theories of Economic Growth* (New York, Macmillan, 1970).

15 Some Observations on Economic Theory and Technical Change[1]

Victor L. Urquidi and Alejandro Nadal
EL COLEGIO DE MEXICO

INTRODUCTION

The question of the relevance of economic theory to present-day society is particularly important when we come to the issues surrounding changes in technology. However loosely we define technical change (say, as changes in methods or processes of production as well as in the products themselves), the fact that it affects every aspect of social life undoubtedly justifies a close examination of the way in which economic theory tries to grasp this very complex phenomenon.

It is true that the relevance of economic theory (and of social theory in general) can be judged from various perspectives and according to different criteria. Two of the possible criteria which, at first glance, are obviously important are a theory's explanatory power over past and present events and the degree of predictability it offers over future events. These criteria are in turn dependent on various factors, of which internal logical consistency and external coherence (i.e. its coherence with real world conditions) are the most important. Without any pretension of exhausting the subject, this paper is an attempt to examine in general terms some aspects of these two factors in relation to the economic analysis of technical change.

In the first section we shall discuss some of the main problems related to the way in which technical change is articulated or integrated into the general framework of economic theory. We shall concentrate exclusively on neo-classical theory, and, anticipating our conclusions, we may say that in spite of progress in some areas, others remain in relative darkness. In the second section we shall examine some issues surrounding the question of the relevant 'facts' that must be taken into account if an acceptable degree of external

[1] The authors wish to acknowledge the comments received on earlier versions of this paper from G. K. Boon, Raúl Conde, Pierre Ewenczyk, Eduardo A. Guimarães, Patrick Maurisson, Alfonso Mercado, Carlos Roces and José Tavares. They have also benefited from the discussion at the round table.

coherence is to be attained. In this second section we shall focus our attention on the particular reality of less-developed countries (LDCs) but some references to similar problems in industrially advanced countries will be made. As can be seen, these two sections, although apparently difficult to articulate, for they seem to belong to different levels of conceptualisation, do in fact complement each other, at least in the limited sense that there has been in the past a trade-off between theoretical rigour and realism. This paper has the aim of pointing to some issues that are at the crossroads of this trade-off. In a broader sense, the aspects of internal consistency and external coherence cannot be fully separated, at least as long as abstract models have an economic content. A third and final section offers some concluding remarks and discusses some policy implications, especially for the LDCs.

A final introductory remark must be made. As has been already pointed out, this paper will be limited to what we shall continue to call 'neo-classical' economic theory for the sake of simplicity.[1] We shall do so because it can correctly be described as the dominant economic theory at least in the sense that, by and large, higher education curricula are biased towards it and that long-term economic policy is often blueprinted after the premises and assumptions of neo-classical theory in the so-called market economies. Although specific references will be made in some cases, this paper is not a survey of past and current work on technical change and this is why some issues may be found missing or dealt with in very general terms. It is the explicit purpose of this paper to launch a discussion which more often than not is lacking in the literature.

I THE ANALYSIS OF TECHNICAL CHANGE AND ITS LIMITATIONS

Neo-classical theory starts from a series of central assumptions, and if technical change is to be analysed within it it must be defined in a manner consistent with the initial framework. Therefore, we may be able to explain a lot about the evolution of the analysis of technical change by taking into consideration the initial neo-classical assumptions. For example, technology (and for that matter, science) is for neo-classics an exogenous variable, quite independent of the action of the economic system. Normally, when there is a reference to the issue of choice of technique, the situation is described as if the particular economic agent faced a series of possible alternatives from which he may proceed to select one. This comes as no surprise if we take into account that

[1] By neo-classical theory we shall mean the set of conceptions which have, from the first marginalist theories (Jevons, Menger) to their present-day continuators, adopted a value theory based on the dualism of 'utility-scarcity'. We will therefore not refer to one author in particular (although scattered references will be made), but rather to a theoretical tradition that sees in the resource allocation properties of the market mechanism the very foundation of economic theory.

Walras and the authors of the Austrian school started their analyses with 'given' supplies of productive factors whose services entered the exchange process by commanding a price. The price of each factor was determined by its productive contribution and the supply-demand of each of them in the factor markets; for the Walrasian model, prices in final equilibrium must equal cost of production with a simultaneous determination of product prices and prices of productive services. Of course, distribution in the classical sense (Ricardo's 'principal problem in political economy') was substituted by a problem of allocation of resources. This leads to the question of what precisely is to be taken as given from the supply side: in particular, is technology a datum for economic theory?

But perhaps even more interesting for our discussion, the sphere of production itself became a special application of the more general laws of exchange. For a representative author like Pareto, the notion of production is formed by a series of exchanges of productive services. And this leads to a second question: in what precise sense is 'technology' (and consequently, technical change) to be defined in a particular theory of production in which in fact production is reduced to a series of exchanges between economic agents? This problem goes to the core of the issues examined here since if technology (i.e. presumably a catalogue or 'book of blueprints' containing all *known* methods of production) is a given datum, then it becomes an exogenously determined variable. But at the same time, it becomes a boundary of the field of analysis (in this case, economic theory) and therefore remains unexplained by it. A disquieting conclusion could be that economic theory has nothing to say about how this book of blueprints ever came into existence and that the problem should be referred to engineers and other participants in the division of intellectual labour. As a consequence, economics would have very little to say about changes in technology.

Putting these questions temporarily aside, what we wish to emphasise here is simply that it would appear normal that if a conception of technical change had to arise from these views, it would logically have to define the entire problem as a choice between already existing alternatives. This means that economic agents would be faced *ex ante* with a schedule of methods of production, instead of conceiving agents creating *ex post* such methods (or adding new pages to the book of blueprints). This poses a serious problem for the conventional explanation of technical change in terms of economic forces, namely, the adjustment by one type of economic agent (entrepreneurs) to variations in the relative price of factors. First, this type of explanation has already received decisive criticism from authors such as Salter, Samuelson and Kennedy,[1] since under perfect competitive conditions it is incorrect to say that

[1] See for example, W. E. G. Salter, *Productivity and Technical Change* (Cambridge University Press, 1960); P. A. Samuelson, 'A Theory of Induced Innovation along Kennedy–Weisacker Lines', *Review of Economics and Statistics* (November 1965); and C. Kennedy, 'Induced Bias in Innovation and the Theory of Distribution', *Economic Journal* (September 1964).

market forces induce the adoption of labour-saving techniques because the entrepreneur is concerned with reducing total costs and not a particular type of costs. But a second question arises which may be more important: if we introduce the additional hypothesis that technology is not given exogenously, an explanation will have to be provided for the allocation of resources needed for generating technical knowledge. As Nathan Rosenberg[1] has pointed out, why should a society where the price of capital is low relative to that of labour have available detailed information about labour-intensive techniques of production? In other words, how is the market mechanism supposed to operate in order to allocate resources for the generation of techniques which reflect factor combinations that are not warranted by present factor proportions? If no adequate explanation can be given of this process the obvious alternative is to assume that the book of blueprints originates in the general evolution of science or other extra-economic factors. It is interesting to note that this position is not without its parallel in the field of philosophy of science with authors such as Polanyi.[2]

Another example of the problems that arise when trying to integrate an analysis of technical change within the general framework of neo-classical theory is the following. For a long time neo-classical authors were troubled by the question of taking into consideration cost-reducing technical change (as well as economies of scale) within their framework without introducing at the same time disturbing effects on competitive structures (i.e. without introducing effects that would drive the different market structures to imperfect conditions of competition). Consequently, technical change had to be assumed to have uniform and generally undisturbing effects on competitive structures; access to the book of blueprints (which continued to be provided exogenously by the general evolution of science) had to be assumed to be uniform or 'equal' for all agents. The contradiction between empirical observation and basic neo-classical assumptions led authors like Marshall and Wicksell to design formal schemes in which any potentially disturbing effects would cancel each other out, preventing cumulative disturbances on competitive structures and thus making possible the conditions of equilibrium. (These formal schemes were vigorously criticised by Sraffa[3] in his 1926 article.) Of course, the theories of imperfect competition (developed basically within the framework of partial equilibrium analysis) were designed to refine the analysis and to lead neo-classical theory out of this impasse. However, there is a justified general dissatisfaction with these efforts as many problems of integrating marginal price determination with imperfect competition

[1] N. Rosenberg, *Perspectives on Technology* (Cambridge University Press, 1976). p. 63.

[2] Michael Polanyi, 'The Republic of Science: its Political and Economic Theory', in E. Shils (ed.), *Criteria for Scientific Development* (MIT Press, 1968).

[3] P. Srafta, 'The Laws of Return under Competitive Conditions', *The Economic Journal* (December 1926).

hypotheses remain to be solved (so it is no surprise that enthusiasm for perfect competition hypotheses is still going strong).[1]

In this context it is rather astonishing that the general perspective of Schumpeter's analysis (in which technical change is a weapon of competition in the hands of the entrepreneur) should have dropped into darkness. It has recently been pointed out that inability to take into account the relation between technical change and *other* channels of competition has been a major handicap in studies of the rate of diffusion of industrial innovations.[2] In some cases, quite satisfactory adjustments are obtained taking into account only the specific characteristics of a particular innovation; such is the case with many of Edwin Mansfield's studies,[3] but because the dimension of technical change as a weapon of competition is ignored, no meaningful interindustry comparisons can be arrived at. (And in fact, interfirm comparisons sometimes lead to all firms remaining outside the rationale of a choice of technique model being considered as 'resistant to change', or simply as irrational precisely because channels of competition are not brought into the picture.) Against this context it is interesting to observe that cost-plus theories of price determination (which belong to a trend to draw away from neo-classical theory of prices) give a very important place to technical change in their formal schemes. But in spite of the fact that technical change is seen as a channel of competition, its origin remains largely unexplained.[4]

The notion of 'neutral' technical progress is another case in point of the limited way in which neo-classical theory tried to tackle the problems posed by the analysis of technical change. The definition of neutral technical change proposed by Hicks in his *Theory of Wages* was more concerned with the need to explain the general historical constancy of distributive shares. For him, a neutral invention would be one in which the marginal product of labour would rise in the same proportion as the marginal product of capital with a given set of factor proportions. Here, two different trends would offset each other in order to attain this result: the share of capital would tend to decrease with capital accumulation relative to labour, but the increase in the relative price of labour would induce inventions 'of a particular kind' as Hicks pointed out, i.e. inventions with a labour-saving bias. As stated before, the critique of Salter,

[1] See for example, G. J. Stigler, 'Perfect Competition Historically Contemplated', in E. Mansfield (ed.), *Microeconomics: Selected Readings* (New York, Norton, 1975).

[2] See the developments and criticisms to these studies in J. Tavares, (ed.), *Difusão do Inovaçoes na Industria Brasileira*, Rio de Janeiro (IPEA/INPES, 1976).

[3] E. Mansfield, 'Intrafirm Rates of Diffusion of an Innovation', *Review of Economics and Statistics* (November 1963).

[4] P. Sylos Labini, *Oligopoly and Technical Progress* (Harvard University Press, 1969); J. Steindl, *Maturity and Stagnation in American Capitalism*, 2nd. edn. (Monthly Review Press, 1976).

Samuelson and Kennedy was decisive. A different type of neutrality was defined by Harrod in order to develop his theory of equilibrium growth. Here an invention would be neutral if for a constant rate of interest it left the capital-output ratio unchanged. (These two definitions do in fact coincide in the case of a macroeconomic one-commodity production function of a Cobb–Douglas type.) But what is interesting for our discussion is that first, in these formulations technical change is still exogenously given (as someone said, by God and/or the engineers) and is somehow left out of the central preoccupation of the models even though it plays an important part within them. And secondly, these attempts at classifying technical change are more related to the formal preoccupation of maintaining the essential properties of the production function as a correct representation of the neo-classical laws of distribution. Since the production function cannot represent these laws correctly unless the entire product is exhausted amongst the intervening factors (see Wicksteed's proof using Euler's theorem), technical progress is qualified to allow us to respect these qualities of the production function. The overall conclusion is that the characteristics of technical change as an exogenous element are reinforced by these qualifications of 'neutrality'.

In this context it is interesting to examine some of the implications of the controversy over capital theory of the past years. This controversy produced a series of criticisms of the orthodox conception of factors of production and their role within the production function. As we shall see, the controversy is still raging at least over its implications for the entire body of neo-classical theory (the non-neo-classical authors themselves seem to be in disagreement over this point). The discussion had the positive effect of leading to a series of clarifications which invalidate some widely held simplistic views on the problems of choice of techniques. In fact, it had become commonplace in the literature on development economics to say that technical change in developing countries was capital-intensive in spite of the relative abundance of labour partly because factor-price distortions were introduced by various economic and social policies. This of course follows the tendency to equate technical change with simple substitution between factors (which is in turn related to the assumption of exogenously given schedules of techniques or methods of production). In a recent article on the problem of choice of technique, Pasinetti, one of the main participants in the controversy, writes that 'the main result of the debate of the last years on the reswitching of techniques has been to unmask the confusion, maintained for more than one century in economic theory, between the concept of choice of techniques of production and the concept of choice between the proportions of factors of production'.[1] As a consequence, an examination of the main issues of the

[1] L. Pasinetti, 'Le Choix des Techniques et les Theoriés du Capital, des Prix et de la Répartition du Revenu', *Revue d'Economie Politique* (March–April, 1977). (Our translation.)

controversy seems to be relevant to our preoccupation, and in the following paragraphs we shall highlight these main issues.

In order to define marginal productivity of capital we must be able to determine the quantity of capital. The problem that faced neo-classical economists is that this quantity depends not only on the addition of all physical means of production, but on their relative prices as well (and since they are produced commodities, these prices vary as the rate of profit and the rate of wages vary). Therefore, the value of the means of production cannot be determined independently of the conditions of distribution, and by way of consequence, the relation between capital and output cannot be a unique one.[1] In other words, if we keep labour constant and measure capital in terms of value, the relation between the quantity of capital and that of output is not a unique one: since the value of capital is not independent of the rate of profit, the same technique of production can appear to be compatible with several 'quantities' of capital (these quantities of capital differ according to the rate of profit used to determine the value of the stock of physical means of production). Or, if we keep this stock unchanged we could still say that it is compatible with several techniques of production according to the different rates of profit used to determine the value of these means of production. This means that the concept of marginal productivity and that of the production function are seriously affected: first, the marginal productivity of the factor 'capital' is undetermined; second, it can be stated that to a given spectrum of techniques of production may in fact correspond as many production functions as rates of profit used to evaluate (i.e. to establish the value of) the physical means of production used as capital. (As a matter of fact, when we consider capital in value terms, the notion of a production function implies not only the description of a known spectrum of techniques, but the relation between this spectrum and the conditions of distribution.) It is quite clear then that the implications of this problem for the neo-classical theory of distribution cancel any hope of being able to state with J. B. Clark's casualness that the laws of distribution are in any sense 'natural' and therefore supra-institutional.

One way out of this impasse was seen in the assumption of 'perfect malleability' of capital, considered as an inevitable simplifying assumption by Solow.[2] It was implied by this that it was possible to proceed with the analysis of an economy treating capital *as if* it were a homogeneous and malleable substance. In order to emphasise the arbitrariness of this type of simplification, to Meade's statement ('all machines are alike, they are simply a ton of steel'), Joan Robinson responds that we might as well use the word

[1] This impasse is not overcome by the Böhm Bawerk and Wicksell solutions which have to assume a rate of interest or profit in order to determine the value of capital goods.

[2] R. M. Solow, 'A Contribution to the Theory of Growth', in A. K. Sen (ed.), *Growth Economics* (Penguin Books, 1970).

'leets'.[1] Others will fancy other terms such as meccano sets, putty clay and the like. Under these conditions, the production function could be considered to define correctly the relation between a quantity of the commodity used as capital and the produced quantity of the same commodity: the relation between capital and output would be independent of the relative prices of commodities and therefore independent of the conditions of distribution. The analytical value of the production function would be safe and the initial premises of the neo-classical theory of distribution would remain untouched. However, it is important to note that the Austrian and Walrasian models involved multiple commodities and heterogeneous means of production, and therefore it is not a small change to transform the problem into a one-commodity world. Aside from certain criticisms which we might consider as details (for example, Joan Robinson has justly pointed out that there is no room left for the distinction between long and short run, and any possibility of introducing imperfect competition disappears), it is justified to state that the concept of relative prices itself loses much of its meaning, and with this in mind we are entitled to ask what becomes of exchanges and of the market economy as a whole.[2] Finally, if we were to judge the relevance of this solution on the basis of its degree of realism, we would have to accept that it fails even a quite elementary test.

The dilemma of neo-classical production functions has been elegantly phrased by Garegnani: 'Either a single commodity is produced in the economy and no problem of aggregation arises, or different commodities are produced and no "aggregate production function" exists'.[3] The dilemma is a crucial one since only if heterogeneous capital goods are reducible to a single quantity of capital, can a meaning be assigned to the proposition that to a fall in the rate of interest there will correspond a technique of production in which the capital-labour ratio increases (i.e. more 'capital-intensive' techniques will be substituted for the more 'labour-intensive' ones). However, it is this property of the production function (its ability to represent the ordering of the techniques of production in accordance with the proportion of capital to labour) that has been seriously called into question and disproven. The possibility of the 'reswitching of techniques' phenomenon has been demonstrated and generally accepted by neo-classical authors: no uniform relation exists between movements in the relative price of factors of production and variations in the capital-labour composition of techniques of production, since to a rise in the price of one factor we may associate a technique in which that same factor is used in a more intensive way. The now famous controversies

[1] J. Robinson, 'Capital Theory Up to Date', in E. K. Hunt and J. Schwartz (eds.), *A Critique of Economic Theory* (Penguin Books, 1972).

[2] See C. Benetti, *Valeur et Répartition* (Presses Universitaires de Grenoble-Eds. Maspero, 1974).

[3] P. Garegnani, 'Heterogeneous Capital, the Production Function and the Theory of Distribution', in *A Critique of Economic Theory, op. cit.*

over capital theory have produced the following result: it is not possible to order a spectrum of existing techniques according to their proportion of capital to labour because any such attempt will be affected by relative prices and distribution.[1]

The concept of the 'surrogate production function' advanced by Samuelson did not provide a way out from this entanglement with circular reasoning. It has been shown that the rate of profit at equilibrium does not correspond to the marginal productivity of the corresponding quantity of capital (again we find here a consequence of the impossibility of measuring capital in value terms independently of the conditions of distribution). Only if uniform ratios of means of production to direct labour are assumed throughout the economy can it be shown that the surrogate production function has an unambiguous meaning. Under different assumptions (i.e. when the individual factor-price frontiers are concave or convex to the origin) the variations of the capital-labour ratios may be in the same or a different direction as the rate of interest varies, without it being possible to assign any systematic pattern to this behaviour.[2] It is interesting to recall Maurice Dobb's remark that the straight lines depicting the individual techniques of production under the assumption of uniform capital-labour ratios correspond to the case in which Marx's transformation of values into prices of production excludes any divergence between the two systems, namely the case of equal composition of capital in all industries.[3] Once again we are left wondering if too much realism has been sacrificed for the sake of the initial assumptions which can only be preserved with parables of the Samuelson type.

The validity of these criticisms is generally admitted today by neo-classical theoreticians. However, there still seems to be wide disagreement over the implications of the controversy, and it is only fair to mention some of the contrasting views. For Kaldor, for example, there does not exist one single and exhaustive objection to 'orthodox economic theory, even if some Cambridge critics believe that the indeterminacy of the marginal productivity of capital is enough to dismantle the entire edifice of neo-classical theory'.[4] To other authors, it is only an argument to invalidate certain versions of neo-classical theory. Such an outspoken critic as Alfredo Medio is representative of this view: 'The statement according to which *all versions* of neo-classical

[1] For a comprehensive review of the controversy see G. C. Harcourt's account in *Some Cambridge Controversies in the Theory of Capital* (Cambridge University Press, 1972).

[2] Samuelson's concept was presented in 'Parable and Realism in Capital Theory: the Surrogate Production Function', *Review of Economic Studies*, 39 (1962). Garegnani's article makes a critique of this concept (see footnote on p. 245.

[3] M. Dobb, *Theories of Value and Distribution since Adam Smith* (Cambridge University Press, 1973), p. 256.

[4] N. Kaldor, 'What's wrong with Economic Theory', Conference at Harvard University, 29 April 1974.

theory are based on the idea that the rate of interest and wages are governed by the supply and demand of capital and labour does not rest on a solid base. The theory of general equilibrium in its modern versions has never assumed the existence of simple relations between the rate of interest (or of wages) and certain pseudo-technical characteristics of the system (such as the "scarcity of capital" or the "capital intensity"). That may be true for Samuelson but it is not true for Malinvaud or Debreu'.[1]

On a different type of disagreement we find the position according to which the whole problem of the 'Cambridge criticism' is of limited theoretical importance, and its nature is more empirical or econometric depending on the degree of substitutability there is in the system. In this case, the problem should be referred to econometricians until they provide an answer. This position has been criticised by several authors in the sense that econometric work based on the notion of an aggregate production function is already undermined by this criticism so that we may be asking too much from econometricians.[2]

But as we have already stated, whatever the theoretical implications are, at least a very beneficial effect is that some underlying issues surrounding the problems of technical change have been clarified and simplistic views have been invalidated. In particular, some of the popular notions held by many development economists have been proven to be groundless. There remains however the question of the validity of the neo-classical production function at the firm level. According to D. M. Nuti, at the microeconomic level the conditions necessary for the validity of neo-classical theory could hold, although difficulties arise in the case of increasing returns to scale.[3] But to return now to our problem, a production function is supposed to describe a set of technical possibilities of production within a given state of technology and therefore the origin of these different possibilities must remain unexplained.

II SOME QUESTIONS REGARDING THE 'RELEVANT' FACTS

We come now to the second level of questions pertaining to the relevance of the analysis of technical change. This level is related to the factual universe that is to be considered by the analysis if a degree of social relevance is desired. That positive theory as a scientific experience must build from

[1] A. Medio, 'Néoclassiques, Néoricardiens et Marx', in G. Faccarello and P. de Lavergne (eds.), *Une Nouvelle Approche en Economie Politique* (Paris, Economica, 1977). (Our translation.)

[2] This is essentially the criticism addressed to C. E. Ferguson's *The Neo-classical Theory of Production and Distribution* (Cambridge University Press, 1969), by Joan Robinson in her article quoted in footnote 1 on p. 245.

[3] D. M. Nuti, ' "Vulgar Economy" in the Theory of Income Distribution', in *A Critique of Economic Theory, op. cit.*

observed reality warrants a discussion of what facts are to be considered as relevant. Needless to say, this problem is not the only one concerning positive economics. The observation and measurement of 'relevant' facts is a necessary but not a sufficient condition to achieve an acceptable degree of realism (or in the terms of our introductory remarks, of external coherence); obviously, internal logical consistency must be maintained if explanatory power is to be achieved.

A second point is that the selection or determination of facts is not an entirely neutral process. Following the observations of Maurice Dobb on this, it is not possible to claim for this process the same degree of neutrality we claim to be a property of some of our analytical tools.[1] The very problems we define and the facts we observe (as well as the ones we ignore or choose to leave in the dark) are very much conditioned by what Schumpeter in his *History of Economic Analysis* calls the 'vision' of the analyst, i.e. the way in which the analyst sees and wishes to see the complex reality before him. Of course, this vision is a relative factor which depends on a variety of historical circumstances.

In this second section we will concentrate on those aspects of observed reality in less developed countries which we think must be included in a relevant analysis of technical change. These questions will most probably not solve the problem of how to turn technology and technical change into endogenous variables and integrate them coherently into the framework of economic analysis. For this task we must recognise that there is a lot of theoretical work to be done.

Perhaps the best way to start on this second section is to consider the attempt of Jacob Schmookler to analyse inventive activity as any other economic activity.[2] This may well be one of the most important attempts to treat technology as an endogenous variable, and in turn has inspired many studies on evaluation and selection of research and development projects at the firm level.[3] Through a painstaking effort of collecting empirical data, Schmookler tried to show how demand-side factors are the key element that determined changes in the allocation of inventive activity among different industries. As has been pointed out by Rosenberg,[4] the entire approach tends to overestimate the weight of demand-side factors (particularly in the consumer goods industries in which modifications in consumption patterns are seen by Schmookler as the factors determining inventive activity). But we

[1] M. Dobb, *op. cit.*

[2] J. Schmookler, *Invention and Economic Growth* (Harvard University Press, 1966).

[3] This is the starting point of R. R. Nelson's paper 'R & D, Knowledge and Externalities: An Approach to the Puzzle of Disparate Productivity Growth Rates Among Manufacturing Industries', presented at the Fifth World Congress of the IEA, Tokyo, 1977 (Macmillan, 1979).

[4] N. Rosenberg, *op. cit.*, p. 263.

may put forward a different question which may sound rather naïve: how far did we advance with this type of explanation? In other words, the entire approach was synthesised by Schmookler in the following terms: if we start from a certain point in the evolution of an economy in which a certain basket of goods is produced and consumed, and then introduce capital accumulation, technical progress, education, etc., we will observe a variation in per capita income, which will cause shifts in final demand patterns, which will in turn bring about a reallocation of resources for inventive activity. But are we not begging the entire question when we introduce technical change in this fashion? How did this technical change ever originate, or how are we to account for the inventive activity that gave rise to it? Somehow we are left with a flavour of some sort of circular reasoning in all this, since changes in the global composition of demand patterns are themselves a function of growth, capital accumulation and technical change: is it valid to put technical change both as a variable explained by a reallocation of inventive activity brought about by shifts in demand patterns due to growth, and at the same time as a variable that plays an important role in the overall growth process? To put things in a slightly different perspective we could ask ourselves if 'market opportunities' are somehow observed by inventors (i.e. in terms of pay-off periods for alternative R & D projects) or if they are 'created' by some inherent need of capital accumulation in the classical tradition? These are questions for which we shall not attempt to provide even an approximate answer in the hope of stimulating debate.

In any event, let us now contrast this study with our particular 'vision' of real world conditions in less developed countries. The first question that would come up in this comparison would relate to the unit of measurement of inventive activity chosen by Schmookler: after discussing the advantages and disadvantages of using patent statistics, he decided in favour of patents as a surrogate unit for measuring inventive activity. The issue that comes up is the following: as has been well documented in the past, the great majority of patents granted by LDCs are foreign-owned and the share of transnational corporations (TNCs) appears to be dominant. For instance, 87 per cent of patents granted in Mexico between 1950–70 were foreign-owned.[1] This example serves to illustrate not merely that the relevance of such a unit of measurement would be extremely limited but also to show that there are structural differences which should be considered in an analysis of technical change in LDCs. The question of an appropriate unit of measurement would lead us to the problems of the weakness of the scientific and technological systems of these countries, whatever the set of criteria we use to evaluate their scientific and technological capabilities (for example, percentage of GNP expenditure on R & D, number of scientific workers, etc.). Moreover, the

[1] See Anthony D. Tillet, 'Patents, Innovation and the Transfer of Technology in the Mexican Manufacturing Sector, 1950–1970', Mexico, 1975 (mimeographed).

scientific infrastructure that is already in existence (and which is expanding rapidly in many cases due to public expenditure) is poorly linked to industrial activities. In fact, in some instances there is a strong bias towards basic research and this may be a sign of a closer linkage with scientific centres of advanced countries.

The other side of the coin is of course the enormous weight of imports of technology by productive units in LDCs. Here too the growth of overall payments for embodied and disembodied technology imported by LDCs has been the subject of close scrutiny (at the international level, UNCTAD has carried out the most comprehensive studies on direct and indirect payments). The most interesting implications for our problem of analysing technical change arise from Vaitsos' pioneering work in which he showed how the determination of prices in international operations of transfer of technology depends essentially on the weight of each of the parties in the bargaining process.[1] What this means is that since the cost of producing a particular technology by the recipient party may be very high and the cost of transferring it will most probably be very low for the owner (say, a TNC), the operation may be and is frequently used to recover overhead expenses of the head firm, for example R & D expenditures on projects which do not necessarily represent an element in the transaction. On the other hand, the entire package may be used to transfer resources from the wholly owned subsidiary to the head firm when the particular technology is the object of a licensing agreement within the transnational corporation. Many more implications arise from an analysis of these operations (for example, restrictions on exports imposed on the recipient, changes in technology or pricing procedures, obligations to buy capital goods or intermediate products from an exclusive source, etc.). The most important point for our discussion is the following. As Vaitsos has shown, transfer of technology operations are used as a mechanism for the preservation of monopoly rents originated during the early phases of the product's cycle. In order to achieve this, the operation is linked to elements such as trademarks (which incidentally are included in the majority of licensing agreements) or the sales of different types of inputs. The monopoly characteristics of new technologies (whether they be related to processes or products) are thus extended to other non-technological elements. The results offered by Vaitsos would seem to reinforce the argument in favour of recovering some of the old Schumpeterian heritage and proceeding to study technical change within the context of channels of competition.

Coming back to Schmookler's work, whatever the criticisms that can be directed to his approach, one basic idea comes out strongly, namely that structural modifications in the direction of inventive activity were the result of an evolutionary process embracing a rather long period of time. Shifts in the allocation of inventive activity gradually came about as a result of changes

[1] C. Vaitsos, *Intercountry Income Distribution and Transnational Enterprises* (Oxford University Press, 1974).

in the economy's output mix. One may be tempted to say that inventive activity had sufficiently long delays to adapt to these changes. But what would be the result of a comparison with the situation in LDCs?

Taking Latin America as an example, the problem of identifying a gradual process in the evolution of consumption patterns leads to a picture of very fast and radical changes resulting partly from the way in which LDCs have been integrated into the international economic system. The enormous disparities between the consumption patterns of social groups connected with the activities that happened to be related to this integration, and of the rest of the population, would be the first stage of the process; this would be followed quickly by the establishment of a consumption pattern conditioned by an intense concentration of income. At the present moment, the disparities in consumption patterns may be greater than ever, with those of the affluent minority contrasting strongly with the traditional (or even subsistence) patterns of a large percentage of the population. Obviously, what we can say about the orientation of inventive activity according to a gradual shift in the global pattern of demand in this context will be of very limited value. (But on the other hand, we would have to answer negatively to the question of whether the distribution of gains from technical change, imported or locally generated, was uniform and helped to reduce the system's heterogeneity.)

But the contrast does not end there. It is normally recognised that whatever the degree of industrial concentration in advanced countries, it was the result of an evolutionary process which became more intense towards the last third of the nineteenth century. (In fact, this is normally seen as the passage from a competitive stage to a non-competitive one in the development of capitalism.) Unfortunately, the role of technical change is seldom discussed in this context, even though the interrelation between competitive strategies (basically through prices) and cost-reducing technical change had a lot to do with the entire process. Here again the comparison with the situation in LDCs results in a marked contrast because within them, industrial structures have been born with very high concentration ratios (whatever measure we use to determine concentration). Many factors are frequently invoked to explain this, of which the limited size of markets and industrial development strategies are very popular among economists; but the point we want to stress is that technical change must undoubtedly play a radically different role in this situation. For example, the question of access to technology has to be revised in the light of its implications as a 'barrier to entry': it has been shown[1] that for the subsidiaries of a TNC technology may not be a significant barrier since the technology developed by the head firm (or other subsidiaries within the group) is already available. However, for local firms the obstacle may appear as an unsurmountable barrier, and they must frequently yield to pressure from the owners of technology to grant them equity participation as

[1] F. Fajnzylber, 'Oligopolio, Empresas Transnacionales y Estilos de Desarrollo', *El Trimestre Económico* (July–September 1976).

part of the overall agreement. The general effect on market structures would appear to be the intensification of concentration, but the role of technical change is not the same as before in this process (just as the channels of competition and their relation to technical change vary).

As a summary of this section we can say that we are not striving to present a catalogue of items that should be taken up for further research. What we have attempted to put across was that with a particular 'vision' focused on the realities of less developed countries, the analysis of technical change cannot ignore the dimensions of a weak scientific and technological system, the impact of transfer of technology operations. radical and sudden changes in consumption patterns and high industrial concentration ratios *ad initium*. If improper attention is given to these dimensions, the analysis of technical change (its sources, impact and different orientations) will most probably turn out to be irrelevant.

III CONCLUSIONS AND SOME POLICY IMPLICATIONS

An overall evaluation of studies on technical change was not the purpose of this paper and so there may be important contributions that were left out unwittingly. Our aim was rather to raise a series of questions related to the general theme of this conference. The purpose of setting the questions on two different levels of conceptualisation was to put internal consistency ('theoretical rigour') and external coherence ('realism') in a relationship which we hope will not imply a trade-off between the two. We hope we have contributed something to this conference even in this limited sense.

Since this paper raises a series of questions and provides no answers or solutions, there is the risk that we project the impression that all is dark on the horizon and that no relevant progress whatsoever has been achieved. There has been progress in many areas, but in spite of this much conceptual and empirical work remains to be done in order to treat technology as an endogenous variable. The recent controversy over capital theory has shown how important it is to revise long-time accepted concepts which led in many cases to simplistic and groundless views on the determinants of technical change. This must be seen as an advance and not as a retrogression.

Having said this, the main conclusion can be expressed in the following terms. In order to treat technology as an endogenous variable we must think about a set of seemingly naïve questions we usually consider as having already received adequate answers. For example: What must be the economic definition of technology and technical change? What is the relation between technical change and competition in a capitalist economy? (In fact, this question will lead us to the issue of *what is* competition in the first place.) On the other hand, we must take into account a series of real world conditions which are extremely important for our problem, in particular, in the case of less developed countries some of the realities mentioned in the second part of this paper.

Despite the shortcomings of economic theory in dealing with technical change, and in particular the difficulty of conceptualising such change under oligopolistic market conditions (which are the reality in advanced market economies) the notion is prevalent that technical change is induced by market signals. Thus presumably if the price of an industrial or even an agricultural commodity were to rise on a long-term basis, reflecting either a 'permanent' increase in cost or a substantial and enduring demand-induced scarcity, forces are set in motion that lead to new research and development, the success of which is judged by its ability to reduce cost (i.e. increase profit expectation). In the process labour, which is the relatively scarce factor, is saved (although it is also possible that technological innovation will save capital per unit of output). The oligopolistic producer thus acts rationally from the point of view of the firm.

The above entails two consequences. The first and most obvious is that a change in technique, a technological innovation, is only introduced if it improves the firm's long-run oligopolistic position (where other than purely economic considerations also play a role). This means that science and technology are not directed to solving society's problems – in spite of the allegedly altruistic motives of certain corporations. Much technology will remain on the shelf or research will not be pursued to the implementation stage because it may not suit the competitive strategy of the corporation. It is true that there is independent research and development, particularly in areas like agriculture and health, but it will not reach application in an advanced market economy except through the private firm. There is thus a basic conflict between societal aims and the private pursuit of profit. Hence the inundation of the consumer markets – and producers' markets as well – particularly in the very high-income countries, with socially useless products and even socially harmful ones which nevertheless happen to be profitable for the individual firm or for a whole manufacturing branch given the imitation of products, the product differentiation or the interlocking licensing arrangements and marketing methods of groups of corporations.

Implicit in the above remark is also the idea that there is room for much socially directed technological innovation, and the R & D behind it, that could be pursued for its own sake and which need not be necessarily market-induced, although it could in any event yield a profit for the enterprise. This would imply a certain measure of planning of research, a difficult matter in any economy. It could operate at least in a negative way, namely, a minimum regulation of harmful technology (e.g. insecticides, pharmaceuticals, toxic chemicals). But the problem is of course deeper, in as much as there is good reason to question the motives of some R & D; or to put it more positively, to ask if there is some means through education and the media to motivate researchers and the corporations behind them differently. Again, a planning process would see to it that, given scientific and technological knowledge available to the public sector, certain orientations and directions could be given to R & D and product development to help meet societal needs.

The second consequence has to do with the LDC world to which some reference has been made before. Here is a situation where historical-institutional factors and the manner in which the developing countries have inserted themselves in the world economy through agricultural, mining or industrial activities developed under foreign investment control, have led to a technological dependence as part of the overall economic and sometimes political dependence. Research carried out in recent years throughout the LDCs has shown quite clearly that the science and technology effort of the LDCs is minimal (with a few exceptions such as India, Brazil, Argentina or perhaps Mexico)[1] The educational systems hardly support scientific and technological development. The formulation of a science and technology policy is frequently lacking, even in the most elementary manner, and there is no co-ordinating or overall agency or institution in charge of policy, much less with the responsibility of promoting R & D. The latter is true even in the more advanced LDCs, to the extent that science and technology does not enter sufficiently in the development planning process, and has a low priority in public sector budget allocation and management. Isolated efforts are made through certain R & D institutes, especially in agriculture, occasionally in an industrial branch such as electronics. Basic science is carried out in universities and independent institutes but in a limited manner. Information services for science and technology are only in an early stage of utilisation, in spite of the rapid growth of computer availability.

Thus in LDCs, even the more advanced ones, technology is imported, mainly through licensing agreements and know-how packages between foreign transnational corporations and their subsidiaries in the LDCs or independent domestic enterprises, or is obtained embodied in capital equipment. Such a transfer of technology is carried out mainly also under onerous conditions involving transfer pricing, restrictions on local innovation or research, restrictions on exports, etc. over which most governments have little or no control or regulation. At the international level, attention is beginning to be given to this problem to protect the interests of the LDCs; hence the proposed Code of Conduct on the International Transfer of Technology being considered at UNCTAD. It should be noted also that transnational corporations operating in LDCs usually do not make any contribution, direct or indirect, to the expansion of local R & D.

[1] See 'Draft Introductory Statement for the World Plan of Action for the Application of Science and Technology to Development. Prepared by the Sussex Group' (in *Science and Technology for Development*, UN. ST-ECA/133 according to this statement, 98 per cent of R & D expenses at the world level correspond to highly industrialised countries (centrally planned economies were excluded from the estimate based on data from OECD, UNESCO and the Pan American Union).

Could it be said that this type of technological innovation in the LDCs is a reflection of market forces, as it is alleged to be in the oligopolistic markets of the advanced market economies in the industrial countries? The answer seems to be in the negative. In the LDCs the subsidiaries of the TNCs, and the local enterprises utilising foreign technology under licensing agreements (including trademarks), operate under narrow oligopolistic conditions and sometimes under virtual monopoly, usually behind a strong protective tariff barrier. In addition they obtain substantial fiscal and other incentives from the local public sector, sometimes including subsidies, whether direct or implicit. Given the structural conditions, the licensee enterprises are unlikely to be threatened by locally developed technological innovation, unless there is a particularly strong local competitor, either private or public. As shown before, the general trend seems to be in the direction of total dominance by the licensee and franchised enterprises, as they take over technologically backward local independent companies. To the extent that there is a dynamic though highly protected domestic market, it is in the TNC's and its local licensee's interest to introduce innovations in process or product technology to the extent that there may be some competition between rival TNCs within the market; also to the extent that the products may be exported to neighbouring countries, other regional markets or even overseas back to the advanced country market. There is besides the question of 'keeping up' with the image of technological innovation projected in the countries of origin through new products, advertising, etc. The higher the local tariff protection, and the tighter the import controls, the greater is the incentive to smuggling (e.g. in a country such as Mexico); hence the 'latest' consumer goods of the high-income countries are soon produced from component parts in the LDCs.

But the basic fact is that under the conditions described above, technological innovation in an LDC is merely a reflection of the innovation generated in the developed country. It may have nothing to do with the real needs of the LDC society or even the limited market available. Moreover, and here lies the essential point, it is likely to be an innovation which is labour-saving and/or highly capital-intensive, so that it does not reflect the prevailing factor proportions in the LDC. Thus a basic tenet of the theory behind technological innovation – that technical change may take place, from the microeconomic point of view, to substitute the abundant for the scarce factor – fails to correspond to reality in the LDC economy. It is true, however, as recent studies have shown,[1] that in the LDCs pursuing rapid industrialisation the use and application of explicit and implicit instruments of science and technology policy are strongly biased toward capital-intensive technology, even in the face of obvious present and prospective labour surpluses. This is part of the dependence syndrome, and responds to imitative strategies and models of

[1] For example, the Science and Technology Policy Instruments (STPI) Project supported by IDRC, Ottawa.

development, as well as to local pressures from the private sector in favour of encouraging its own investment or association in investment with transnational corporations in such a way that the technology levels and standards of the TNCs are duplicated. In addition, it should be remarked that given the imperfect knowledge and the technology market imperfections in an LDC, the local entrepreneur frequently has little choice but to enter into licensing agreements and purchase technology packages of a capital-intensive nature. It should also be noted that in LDCs with a rising trade-union movement there is a further bias on the part of the firm in favour of capital-intensive technology, even automation, as a means of dealing as little as possible with large union membership.

Such trends in technological innovation in LDCs run counter to present factor proportions and, in countries with high rates of growth of population and consequently of labour force – in many, above 2.5 per cent per annum and even above 3 per cent – there is the presumption that the introduction of new technology is contributing to permanent unemployment and to worsening of the structural problems.

It is frequently stated that there is much technology available on the shelf which is less capital-intensive or more employment-creating. In the LDCs there is a suspicion that such technologies are obsolete, be they called 'intermediate' or 'scaled-down', or by any other name, e.g. 'appropriate' technologies. An essential condition is that they should be efficient in micro-economic terms, but in the LDC market economies it is unlikely that they will be abundantly used because of the other conditioning factors – mentioned above – which favour capital-intensity.

Nevertheless, to the extent that LDCs succeed in defining their science and technology policy and that the concept of technological autonomy advances – meaning the capacity to take technological decisions in the national interest, encompassing choice and transfer of technology and support for local R & D and the necessary human resource development – it may be possible gradually to move in the direction of more employment-creating technologies. This has to do with the product-mix, of course, and implies a higher degree of co-ordination in development planning. Such a process will also be helped by better regulation of private enterprise activities and by the spread of public sector enterprises (under conditions of efficiency). Overall, such a development must be essentially part of a general strategy directed to meeting basic needs. To meet basic needs, simple technologies, which frequently happen to be labour-intensive, are required. Much study is under way in various parts of the world to design such technologies. The example of China is much quoted and there are isolated examples in other parts of the world of successful applications of labour-intensive or scaled-down technologies. Attention is being given internationally to the problem, as well as to the introduction of capital-saving or employment-creating technologies in the industrial field.

One final word on future work on this subject. One must be ready to recognise that it is highly probable that a great many of the questions we may ask about technical change will not be explained in purely economic terms. Over the past years there have been a great many references to the need for interdisciplinary work and here we have a field in which this is urgently required. On the other hand, the analysis of technical change according to some of the guidelines mentioned above requires that proper attention be given to structural factors. For the present time, we must recognise the fact that an economic theory of technical change for the LDCs is obviously lacking.

Discussion of the Papers by Professor Malinvaud and Professor Urquidi and Dr Nadal

(Chairman: Professor Sir Austin Robinson)

The discussion was opened by ***Dr Desai*** (India). He said that both these papers addressed themselves directly to the question of the relevance of economic theory (defined as neo-classical or general equilibrium theory) to present-day problems. Urquidi and Nadal took up the theory and policy of technical change, and Malinvaud addressed a number of normative and positive theoretic questions about economic growth.

Both papers took a common view of the criteria of relevance. They were the explanatory powers of a theory in terms of past and present data, and its predictive powers with respect to future changes; either to actual changes or to hypothetical changes in the parameters. In other words, the internal logical coherence of a theory and its external coherence or its agreement with real world conditions.

Urquidi and Nadal began with the statement that technology and technical change were exogenous. Endogenising technical progress led to the introduction of disturbances to competitive structures. Schumpeter emphasised technical change as a weapon in competition but his work had been ignored.

Urquidi and Nadal then took up the notion of neutral technical change and its definitions in Hicks and Harrod. Dr Desai said it was important to remember the background against which these theories were advanced. Paul Douglas had shown that for USA income shares were roughly constant if productive inputs were grouped into capital and labour. Bowley substantiated this for UK. The aggregation of inputs into two broad categories was made in order to span both interclass distribution and the factor share distribution. Thus capital and labour could be thought of as inputs and as classes. Many problems arose from this conflation.

Constancy of factor shares was not only an interesting statistical fact to explain but also bore on the issue of the falling rate of profit. Contrary to classical and marxian predictions, the rate of profit had shown no discernible downward trend by the 1920s. At the same time real wages had risen in the USA and UK. In a static isoquant context these were difficult to reconcile unless there was a shift in the isoquant. Neutral technical change was invented to explain these stylised facts with a very simple extension of existing theory.

Thus neutral technical change was an extension of an isoquant which was defined at the aggregate level. This was an added simplification taken from prior measurement by applied economists. Thus theorists were assuming the existence of aggregates because measures had already been made.

But the isoquant at the level of the firm, or at the lower level of a homogenous output producing activity, could be drawn from technical information alone. Thus the spectrum of techniques would yield a (continuous or discontinuous) isoquant giving input combinations which produced the same quantity of output. At this stage only technical information was needed, not market information. But aggregate measures of an input could only be derived if heterogenous physical components could be compared. If this were done by taking inputs as proportional to their money value, it was assumed that their productive contribution was proportional to their prices. Thus the marginal productivity, factor price, proportionality was prior to the derivation of an aggregate input measure. Therefore, aggregate measures could not be used to test, confirm or rationalise the marginal productivity theory of distribution.

Dr Desai noted that the impossibility of deriving aggregate input measures independently of market information had been interpreted variously in terms of its consequence for economic theory. To some participants in the capital theory debate it meant not only an index number problem but also a challenge to the legitimacy of a return to capital. Thus the rate of return to capital as an intertemporal accounting price (relevant for capitalist and socialist economies) was contrasted with the rate of return as income of a class. These participants wanted to derive from capital theory the conclusion that the income from ownership of capital was not a function of the productivity of the input but was due to property relations very much in the way that Ricardo showed for rent. Thus the demolition of the logical basis of the marginal productivity theory of distribution was thought to be a demolition of the legitimacy of profits. Unfortunately economic theory did not yield such powerful results. What was more, the general equilibrium theory did not need an aggregate production function. An aggregate production function was needed to explain stylised facts about distribution. Thus its principal concern was not input-output transformation but aggregate income distribution. Dr Desai said that Urquidi and Nadal mentioned that econometricians should now be left to decide between rival theories. But this task was not simple since the data the econometrician would use had been shown on *a priori* grounds to influence the hypothesis tested.

Dr Desai then discussed the empirical relevance of reswitching. If reswitching required a change in the real rate of interest of say between 5 and 20 per cent then the reswitching question had no relevance but if the range was narrower then we had to worry about it. More work was needed here which would clarify the input-output structures which could yield quantitative estimates of surfaces which exhibited reswitching possibilities.

Dr Desai then introduced the paper by Professor Malinvaud. He said that this was confined mainly to the positive theory of economic growth. He thought that Professor Malinvaud was, in general, positive about the achievements of economic theory, although he recognised certain gaps and weaknesses.

In the positive theoretic explanation of growth, Professor Malinvaud took up Kuznets' criteria and his classification of factors of economic growth. The task of theory was to explain past experience, especially with a view to identifying obstacles to economic growth, and to consider the influence of different institutional arrangements.

Dr Desai said that the methodology that Professor Malinvaud proposed was to search for the proximate factors explaining the growth of labour productivity. One such factor was capital accumulation broadly defined. Then the next step was to look for factors to explain capital accumulation. Travelling up the levels of explanation we might arrive at a satisfactory explanation of fundamental causes. This was a long but sure route for scientific research.

Research on capital accumulation had been concerned mainly with business cycles rather than growth but it had confirmed the classical law of capital accumulation that investment was related to the difference between rate of profit and the cost of capital. It was, however, necessary to explain the persistence of intersectoral and intercountry differences in the gap between profit rate and long-term interest rate. One explanation was that it was inequality in industrial concentration or unequal political relations which caused the difference. There was nothing much we could say systematically about this as the theory needed to be integrated into a global social theory.

Finally, Dr Desai referred to Professor Malinvaud's views that abstract growth theories had clarified a number of questions. The capital theory debate had made the conditions for defining aggregate factor measures explicit. The aggregate production function might be a poor instrument for testing distribution theory when we did not have reliable volume aggregates, but it was still an adequate statistical description of the correlates of the growth process.

There still remained the difficulty that capital stock, however measured, was not monotonic in the rate of interest. This was independent of the possibility of reswitching. Theory had also thrown light on questions of inter-temporal efficiency, especially the consequences of myopia and of market failure when a full set of markets did not exist. The last set of questions related to growth and stability. We knew now that heterogeneity of capital goods might lead to Harrodian instability even when prices were flexible. On the other hand, lack of perfect flexibility in prices led to discussion of short-run dynamics, e.g. stagflation. Here there had been a spate of work developing general equilibrium and temporary equilibrium models of rationing.

Academician Khachaturov (USSR) expressed some disappointment at the paper by Urquidi and Nadal. He thought they had confined their discussion to the place of technical progress in neo-classical economic theory, but failed to consider the question in relation to the economic theory of the socialist world or the significance of technical progress to the economies of the USSR and other socialist countries. The economics of technical progress was in fact a very important part of the political economy of socialism. Technical progress was the main determinant of the productivity of labour, and at the same time the development of the economy was a condition for the promotion of technical change. In recent years the USSR had increased the proportion of the national income devoted to research and development and had also raised expenditure on education – a further important condition for economic growth.

Professor Khachaturov said that there were still several topics in this field which called for further research. For example, Professor Malinvaud had referred to the study of the factors determining the rate of growth of labour productivity and this was a matter which needed further investigation, including research into the relationship between new techniques and the setting of prices, and between new techniques and the cost of labour. It was also necessary to examine further the theory of the choice of capital investments in relation to the use of new technology. However, it could be said that the existing theory was well tested and relevant for practical use and this should be taken into account in assessing the contribution of economic theory.

Professor Furtado (Brazil) began by referring to Professor Malinvaud's comments at the previous session, when he had said that he would like Professor Furtado's thesis 'to be specified and, if possible, proved more rigorously' (see p. 220 above). Professor Furtado's response to this was that he did not think it required proof – it was evident for all to see. His hypothesis was that technical progress played a major role in enhancing the inequalities of capitalist society and for this reason he treated it as a form of power. He considered it to be a fact that inequality was not increasing in advanced capitalist societies, and the basic reason for this was the countervailing power exercised by organised labour.

He then went on to say that his primary interest was not in the position within the advanced countries but in the reasons why the same process was not successful at the international level. His basic answer was that it was because there was no countervailing power sufficient to offset the power of technical progress which was largely a monopoly of the advanced countries.

Professor Furtado said that all economic theories were linked to the concept of rationality at either the micro or the national level, but the problems he was concerned with were not encompassed by these theories. For example, he knew of no theory which could explain the determination of long-term commodity prices or the actions of transnational corporations. It was necessary, therefore, to look for another paradigm and this was what he was attempting to do. This did not imply that all existing theories lacked relevance – they were relevant to some situations but not to the one he wished to analyse.

Finally, Professor Furtado commented on some other issues raised by Professor Malinvaud, when he asked what was meant by a positive theory (see p. 226). The issue of relevance in connection with theories in the social sciences raised a number of fundamental questions, and he thought there was a deep epistemological difference between their two approaches. What, for example, were 'facts' in the social sciences? Malinvaud had quoted Kuznets, an outstanding empiricist, and referred, for example, to investment. But investment was a factor, a concept, it was not a fact, and it was necessary to be extremely careful in moving from concepts to facts. In order to define investment it was necessary to specify a social context and in a different context one might need a different concept.

Professor Niehans (Switzerland) said that he wanted to make three comments on the interesting paper by Professor Urquidi and Dr. Nadal; these were not meant as a criticism, but as supplementary notes.

His first point was that it was, of course, correct that Schumpeter's ideas had faded away, at least for the time being. He believed that Schumpeter was a tragic figure in the history of economic analysis; to use his own terms, he had a rich and potentially fruitful 'vision' of the process of innovation, in which entrepreneurs would transform the continuous stream of new ideas, inventions and discoveries into the cyclical pulse of the capitalist economy. However, Schumpeter was unable to implement this grand vision by an adequate theory. He could provide suggestive description, but not analysis; his theory was simply not up to his vision. Were his ideas 'relevant' today? Relevance was tested in the free market for ideas by a process of the survival of the fittest. Living organisms constantly produced new mutations, few of which survive. Similarly, new ideas were constantly offered, few of which stood the test of time. Schumpeter's ideas, though widely acclaimed, seemed to have been incapable of further development and thus dropped into the background. It was different with the theory of production – the authors called it 'neo-classical' though it was simply the production theory of economic science. It had been under constant critical attack throughout the history of economics, but in Professor Neihans' view it had survived, becoming richer and better with every round of controversy, and was today as 'relevant' as ever.

His second point was that although Urquidi and Nadal were correct in saying that production theory treated technical change, by and large, as exogenous, it should not be forgotten that certain elements of an endogenous theory were available. One of them was Arrow's concept of 'learning by doing', which stimulated a series of further contributions. While this approach tended to link technical progress to labour, other approaches rather linked it to capital investment. In particular, in what might be called the 'Jorgenson research complex' there had been careful and detailed efforts to separate technical progress from the capital investment with which it was associated. Furthermore, there was an extensive body of analysis about decision-making under uncertainty which was immediately relevant for the endogenous explanation of research and development inputs. Oil prospecting, which had been studied by Adelman and others, might be regarded as the paradigm of this class of problems.

Thirdly, Professor Niehans stated that while the lack of a completely endogenous theory of technical progress might be deplored, it might turn out to be very hard, if not impossible, to correct. A completely endogenous theory would imply that we could, in principle, predict today what would be discovered tomorrow. But this was inherently impossible, for whatever could be predicted today could no longer be discovered tomorrow. Technical progress was a game against nature. We knew our cards and the cards nature had played in the past. From this we could develop an endogenous theory about the card we were going to play next. However, we never knew nature's cards nor the way they would be played. As a consequence, nature's moves would forever remain an exogenous element in our understanding of technical change. This was a barrier the theory of long-term economic growth might never be able to surmount. As a consequence, no matter what economic theories we used, neo-classical or otherwise, economic growth would retain a large element of unpredictability.

Professor Z. Sadowski (Poland) expressed agreement with Academician Khachaturov's view that assessment of the merits and demerits of economics must take account of the experience of the socialist countries. He regarded this as particularly important in relation to the role of the state since this was so different under socialism and under capitalism. Two sets of questions could be distinguished. Firstly, there were those relating broadly to the logic of choice (e.g. theory of planning and optimum allocation of resources) – these were questions addressed to the state and dealt with control over the process of development.

Secondly, there were questions related to the actual process of decision-making – these were questions about how aims and goals were set. As soon as one left minimum subsistence standards it was impossible to find objective criteria for goals. For this reason Professor Sadowski said he felt it was necessary to consider the socio-economic context of decision-making and to analyse the actual machinery. He regarded all this as being definitely within the province of traditional political economy. His conclusion was that what was necessary was not only an analysis based on the logic of choice but also on examination of the social and economic conditions which affected the outcome.

Professor Sir Austin Robinson (UK) said that macroeconomists and growth theorists tended to talk about movements of resources and structural changes on far too large a scale. There was a great need for a study of microeconomic dynamics and of the limits to change. He thought that too little was known about many important constraints, and this accounted for some of the main deficiencies in economic theory. For example, in the employment of human resources inadequate attention was given to the time needed to create the relevant skills; to the problem of the transferability of skills from one set of activities to another; to the durability of skill; or to the unwillingness of those who possessed high levels of skill in one sphere to see those skills superseded and to relinquish the advantages they had derived from their skills.

Professor Robinson added that it was important to remember that overall growth was only one of the elements in structural change. There were also changes in tastes, in income distribution, in the pattern of international trade, etc. all of which required structural change.

Professor Green (UK) said that it was necessary to consider the relationships of theory to policies and to institutions, in a more articulated way. There was necessarily never a one-to-one read-off between abstract theory and particular practice, nor one-to-one generalisation from description (no matter in how great depth and detail) to a broad, abstract theory. However, there was a role for what could be termed intermediate theory to help bridge this gap.

This need had been illustrated in several papers – that of Łukaszewicz on separate and partially conflicting rationalities within a system, that of Paszyński on the analytical slightness of many NIEO proposals, that of Malinvaud on the limited success of abstract theory in illuminating institutional (e.g. oligopoly) and bargaining/conflict resolution processes.

The use of the same theoretical model did not necessarily lead to similar policy positions if two actors perceived themselves as having divergent real interests as posited by the theory. Similarly different theoretical models need not prevent an operational agreement, although they did make identifying a route to it harder. Different time horizons also led to divergent positions relating back to similar theoretical starting points.

Any political/economic operational position was influenced by several factors: a general socio-political world view, specific contextual and historic problems and possibilities, a general theoretical economic or political economic frame of reference (paradigm), particular analysis of perceived issues. These could not – taken together – form the basis for general theory. They could be treated at a level of political analysis well beyond description or case-by-case 'problem-solving' – that was what he meant by intermediate theory.

Intermediate theory should be critical to more informed decision-taking. It could help in the following:

(1) Interpretation of the process of economic change (with special reference to conflict and its negotiated resolution) and inclusion of institutional elements in that interpretation.
(2) Analysis of the means to resolve conflicts, build coalitions, achieve accommodation among partially conflicting and partially complementary interests. Theory to date – despite the formal elaboration of game and negotiating theories by several disciplines – was not a very helpful tool in this area because it either abstracted rigidly from contexts or used so many assumptions as to lose either applicability or (literally) portability. No directly usable pure general model was forseeable, but intermediate principles, guidelines, tools of analysis useful within certain contexts did seem to be attainable.
(3) Identification of key issues and institutions about which to negotiate, e.g. in the NIEO case 'Bretton Woods System' was a symbol which could mislead. That system was largely outside international institutions or joint management, either in detail or by more than a handful of capitalist industrial states. Therefore, debating fixed versus floating rates, or altering IMF voting power, missed the real issues and institutional instruments if a more managed, more participatory system was sought rather than Bretton Woods Mark II. Intermediate theory should have the cutting edge to identify key issues and

institutions and to relate them to each other (e.g. how would less unfavourable stability and price conditions for commodities and fewer barriers to market access for manufactures affect peripheral economy patterns of production, power structures, institutions, external dependence, self-reliance?).

To call for intermediate theory was not to deny the value of pure theory or of case-by-case work. It was to argue that there was an area between these two extremes which was now less well served than either, e.g. formal model building or individual project analysis, and which should be of concern to political/economic theorists if they were really committed to extending their relevance to present-day society and its decisions.

Professor Malinvaud (France) said that he wished to intervene at this stage just to comment on the one issue of Professor Furtado's view of positive science. He did not believe that there was, in fact, a sharp epistemological conflict between them.

Professor Malinvaud said that the question was indeed important; we must not be surprised to see that it emerged in our examination of the issue of relevance. This importance explained why he tried to define briefly in his paper what he meant by positive theory. But this definition was difficult to express and he was apparently misunderstood.

Before anything else he wished to say that he did consider as epistemologically correct the political economy approach adopted by Professor Furtado in his paper. If he asked for further elaboration of this theory, it was only because he thought the link between technological decisions and the reproduction of social structures was not fully proved, and Professor Furtado seemed to agree on that. (He was, of course, aware that inequalities existed and that some of the processes for their reproduction had been convincingly established by sociological research.)

Professor Malinvaud thought that the difficulty came from his use of the adjective 'general' in the definition of a theory; he wanted to oppose it to 'contingent'; he meant 'of some generality' and specified 'intended to be applicable to a well-defined class of observations'. He said that he knew that the generality of economic theories was always limited, and that abstract concepts, such as those identified as factors of growth, might be appropriate in some cases and inappropriate in others. (The same was fundamentally true for the natural sciences.) Hence, he fully agreed with Professor Furtado's statement according to which relevance was not an inner property of a theory. Relevance of an abstract representation to a concrete situation always posed to the scientist a difficult problem and required a good deal of judgement.

Professor Malinvaud concluded by saying that in this respect it should be noted that he was careful to mention in the title of his paper that it concerned 'industrial countries', at some places he stated 'capitalist countries'. The reader should understand that he claimed nothing for developing countries, on which he was not well informed. However, he suspected that development of those countries often required quite different tools of analysis than those appropriate for France or other industrial countries.

Dr Nadal (Mexico) said that he wished to refer to the exchange between Professor Malinvaud and Professor Furtado. He suspected that part of the issue underlying their viewpoints was related to the way in which each conceived abstract theory. Professor Malinvaud had said (p. 233) that 'A first objective of abstract theory is the consolidation of applied and empirical works'. He would like to ask if there were other objectives, and if so, what were they. Personally he found this one objective too narrow, too limiting. It was also necessary to ask whether it applied only to abstract growth theories or to all economic theory.

Turning to Professor Furtado's approach, Dr Nadal said that it was closer to the marxian tradition, and it would be desirable to recall Marx's criticism of economists: that they started their analysis from a series of categories derived directly from experience (competition, profits, wages, markets, etc.), and in this way the object of economic analysis was necessarily limited to an explanation of the way in which these categories interacted with each other and how they operated. But these categories were in themselves a problem which Marx thought *relevant* to investigate in the sense that they must be somehow explained in order to enable us to understand the process which assured the production and reproduction of the social relations that were the foundation of these categories. Dr Nadal said he thought Professor Furtado's approach could be fitted more or less into this line of thought, and Professor Tsuru's remarks (in opening the previous session) that his approach was not merely an interdisciplinary one were quite correct.

Professor Urquidi (Mexico) welcomed Dr Khachaturov's remarks, since in effect the paper by Dr Nadal and himself did not take into consideration technical change in the economic theory of socialism, but mainly neo-classical theory and its relevance to conditions in developing countries. However, Professor Urquidi assumed that given the factor proportions prevailing in most socialist economies, and other related conditions, technical change occurred in much the same way as in industrially advanced western societies and Japan. It should not be forgotten that the USSR had an important science base even before the Revolution (which is not the case in most developing countries). The USSR, however, at first imported technology and made adaptations, and then developed science-based local technology to achieve a transition to technological autonomy in a large sector of its economy. Defence and space exploration obviously explained a good deal of technological innovation in the USSR. Competition in export markets and import substitution must be strong guide lines. Consumer needs required technology as they were progressively met. And it could be assumed that much technical change was connected with a relative labour shortage, i.e. was labour-saving, which was the opposite to the basic situation in the developing countries.

Turning to the more general questions, Professor Urquidi said that he was inspired to contribute this paper with Dr Nadal as a result of much recent questioning about science and technology policies in LDCs, and because at the Tokyo IEA Congress there were papers affirming that technical change was essentially market-induced, with little regard for structural problems in the LDCs. This had led him and Dr Nadal to examine neo-classical theory to see how technical change was explained or treated. They felt that, as Dr Desai had said, economic theory was probably not meant to explain technical change (and therefore growth). Nevertheless, much technical change took place in the advanced market-economy countries among large corporations, operating under oligopolistic conditions in order to economise on labour and/or to guarantee survival of the firm. To this extent it was market-induced, but it was increasingly being questioned as to its social purpose and desirability, its impact on the environment and its relation to military expenditure. Recent studies such as the Harvey Brooks report to the OECD highlighted the need for a new social orientation of technology.

Unfortunately, the LDCs absorbed the technology developed by the advanced countries without adaptation to factor proportions or to social needs. Technological dependence was structurally induced, as Professor Urquidi tried to show in the paper, and such technical change as took place was merely a reflection of that undertaken by transnational corporations, transferred to subsidiaries and domestic LDC firms through onerous licensing agreements. In the LDCs there was a case for capital-saving or labour-intensive technologies, not as an overall solution but in certain areas and specific industrial tasks. For this there was need for local R & D and for appropriate government policies and entrepreneurial attitudes. R & D in LDCs would yield its results slowly, but there were many successful instances of research directed toward local needs and conditions. But it was not through market signals that such technical change was bound to occur.

Professor Łukasiewicz (Poland) said that the paper by Professor Urquidi and Dr Nadal had shown that reliance on market forces would have little hope of achieving technical progress in less developed countries. But accepting the need for planning still left a number of important questions; it was also necessary to decide, for example, what fields should have priority, what sequence of action should be envisaged in the development plan and what combination of internal and external technological possibilities could be adopted.

A second point which was, he thought, of great importance was that imported technology had to be absorbed and not just installed. In practice there were often barriers to absorption and it was necessary to investigate more closely the various forces which hindered this process. Among the many factors which would be relevant here, he thought the one of crucial importance was economic sovereignty. Technological progress could only be successful in the long run if there was an identity of interest between those initiating the changes and those who derived the benefits from it.

Dr Simonyan (USSR) said that in the USSR economic theory was thought of as being principally directed to the solution of practical problems. He therefore found the discussion too 'pure'. He had found Professor Malinvaud's paper very stimulating, but he thought it important to emphasise the differences between the social systems which now existed. It was not possible to have a global theory for the world as a whole – it was too divided, too heterogeneous, to be treated as a single system. What was rational for one country or group of countries might be irrational at a global level.

Dr Simonyan also commented on the classification of the factors of development given by Professor Malinvaud (see p. 228 above). The third factor was the adaptation of societies to their growth potential resulting from their population and their technological knowledge. He thought this was indeed an important factor but wanted to stress the extent to which the adaptability depended on a country's socio-economic structure and thus on the character of its property relations. He also thought that the international environment and the relations between nations was a factor of increasing importance which needed further study.

Professor Hagemejer (Poland) thought that economic theory was in disarray. He referred to the well-known problems of capital theory, growth theory, and so on. There was no theory of profits in general equilibrium theory. In the very long-run quasi-rents on capital goods would tend to equalise, leading to some rate of profit; but that was very unrealistic and something better was needed for practical purposes.

It was not possible, said Professor Hagemejer, to compare situations across different equilibrium positions. Capital values in money terms did not give a sensible time series under these conditions, because the shift to a new position of equilibrium used the common monetary unit.

Academician Mateev (Bulgaria) said that he found the discussion too abstract. Economists were not philosophers. He thought it was very clear that the real difficulties of the developed capitalist countries, especially the major current problem – stagflation – could not be explained by the orthodox Keynesian and neo-classical theories.

He also wished to ask Professor Urquidi what, in his view, was the main factor responsible for technical progress in the socialist countries. Professor Mateev said that he thought the main factor was the intensive pattern of development which characterised the current phase in the growth of the socialist economies, i.e. the attempt to raise the productivity of labour via technical innovation.

Professor Tsuru (Japan) observed that if one was discussing the relevance of growth theories to present-day advanced countries it was just as important to scrutinise the contents of *output* growth as to analyse the factors determining the changes in *input*. Contrary to what Professor Malinvaud said (on p. 232), if prominence were given to the economists' field of study by the dominant social philosophy praising the priority to be given to economic growth, that should be precisely the reason for economists to scrutinise 'the view that economic growth would automatically lead to better individual and social satisfaction'.

Professor Tsuru said that the concern for the costs of economic growth was actually quite old. It took the form of examining the components of society's economic activities long before economists began speaking in terms of GNP or national income. As an example he quoted John Ruskin's lecture to manufacturers in 1859 at Bradford; and Marx's dictum to the effect that criminals enhance national wealth by 'producing crimes'.

He would like to have seen a better balance in Malinvaud's paper in this regard.

Dr Desai (India) said that he disagreed with some of the criticisms which had been made of economic theory. It was wrong to say that no decisions could be made about the choice of technique or that nothing had been learnt about stagflation.

Professor Niehans (Switzerland) also responded to Academician Mateev's remarks about stagflation. He said that if an outside observer followed the debate on economic policies in newspapers and magazines, he might easily get the impression of frustration, dissension and bafflement. This impression was misleading. In fact, the recent debates about monetary and fiscal policy were an instructive example of the way in which free and sometimes aggressive controversy could lead to scientific progress.

At the beginning of the debate, economic policy was dominated by Keynesian ideas, characterised by a short-run perspective. Monetarism brought essentially a renewed emphasis on the classical long run, while Keynesian economics retained its relevance for transitory states. While it was true (or at least highly probable) that in the long run we were all dead, over the years the long-run results of Keynesian policies became increasingly manifest. Historical experience began to support economic analysis. The result was an emerging synthesis in which both Keynesian and classical elements had their proper place.

Professor Niehans said that the nature of this synthesis might be described by sketching the dynamic adjustment of an economy to a change in monetary policy. The instantaneous effects would be concentrated on the prices of existing assets like shares, bonds and real estate, and thus in interest rates and yields. In the next stage, monetary expansion would produce an increase in output and employment, while prices and wages remained relatively rigid; this was the Keynesian short run, which would typically last several quarters. Gradually, however, prices and wages would begin to rise, while output and employment would have passed their peak and begun to decline; during this phase, casual observers would diagnose 'stagflation', and if their textbooks were written from a Keynesian point of view, they seemed to need rewriting. Ultimately, employment would have returned to its initial level, prices would have risen approximately in the same proportion as the money supply, but there might be some lasting real effects depending on what the money was spent for. There seemed to be broad agreement about the successive stages of this process. The duration and strength of the various phases, however, was less clear; these were the topics on which the debate continued. Looking back it was easy to see that the protagonists in this debate at times appeared unnecessarily dogmatic, but this was part of the dialectics of a fruitful debate. Stagflation might have been baffling to the economists of the late 'fifties and early 'sixties. Today it appeared as a normal phase in the chain of effects of monetary policy – certainly a highly relevant result.

In his final reply to the discussion of his paper *Professor Malinvaud* said that the discussion showed very well that he had left out of his paper a number of important issues. He did not deal fully with what he called 'normative theories': what in earlier sessions of the conference were called theories of 'economic rationality'. If he devoted two pages to them, it was because he could not refrain from making two points, even though they were outside the scope of the subject to be covered.

He did not intend to approach the broad sociological questions raised by Professor Sadowski as to the 'analysis of the process of decision-making'. These questions lay outside his field of study. On the other hand, he did not speak of stagflation because he was used to considering this phenomenon within discussions on short-term economic regulation and not on economic development, though he agreed that this classification was disputable.

He recognised that he should certainly have given some consideration to technical change, and was glad that Professor Urquidi and Dr Nadal covered the question much more fully than he would have been able to do. Their contribution, as well as several papers presented at the Tokyo Congress of the IEA (to be published in the volume edited by C. Bliss and M. Boserup), showed that some interesting work had recently been done in this respect.

Professor Malinvaud said that he was probably not clear in section III.1 of his paper when he stated that an objective of abstract theories was the consolidation of empirical work. It was certainly not the only one. It was often also to provide a general framework for applied work. It might also be to provide foundations for 'intermediate theories', about which Professor Green spoke.

Finally, coming to the points of substance, Professor Malinvaud made two comments. Firstly, he agreed with Professor Hagemejer that capital values in money terms were difficult to compare between two distinct equilibria and that the comparison was ambiguous. But he referred in his paper to volume indices of capital, and these were a little less deceptive for the analysis of factors of productivity.

Secondly, he certainly recognised that power relations were important in economic life and must often be explicitly taken into account in applied work. But the question was to know whether the presently existing theories might help in this respect. His feeling was that, unfortunately, they were of little assistance.

In his reply *Dr Nadal* referred to the remarks by Professor Niehans on the attempts of Arrow, Solow and others to endogenise technical change. In his view that work was vulnerable to the Cambridge critique of the aggregate production function. The problem was a very complex one and in attempting to deal with it economists had been forced to introduce a series of assumptions which were unrealistic.

Replying to Dr Mateev, *Professor Urquidi* recalled that he had mentioned explicitly labour shortage as a factor explaining technical change in the socialist economies to raise productivity per worker.

He also added that in the LDCs technical change should be viewed as part of the development planning process, and as Professor Furtado put it, as integrated into social theory. To that extent, it was doubtful that we have today a theory of technical change. There was no doubt, however, that we needed one, and economic theory had little to say in this respect.

PART SEVEN
National Economic Planning

16 Economic Planning, Forecasting and Regulation

R. Belousov
ACADEMY OF SCIENCES, USSR

I INTRODUCTORY

The steady advance of the Soviet economy is a consciously planned process reflecting a major form of implementation of theory in social practice. The development of the methodology and of a functioning system of national economic planning is a breakthrough in twentieth-century social sciences equal to the most important discoveries of the present-day natural sciences.

A shrewd master never thinks only of today. He always looks and thinks ahead, striving to co-ordinate his efforts and resources in such a way as to ensure smooth running and an overall turn for the better for many months and years to come. In a socialist economy the society as a whole, and not individual masters, formulates clear-cut, long-term goals, directing and harmonising the efforts of many millions of people towards their achievement. A distinguishing feature of the last five-year plan periods in the Soviet Union has been a direct economic drive to raise quickly the welfare of the Soviet people, to improve their working and living conditions and to make considerable progress in health protection, education and culture.

II BASIC METHODOLOGICAL PREMISES

A quarter of a century ago the very idea of planning world industrial production would have seemed fantastic. Yet the Soviet Union today produces roughly as much as all the other countries of the world manufactured in the early 'fifties. And this vast mass of products, investments, and numerous co-operative, commodity and money relations is planned with utmost effect for society.

In theory and practice there are two approaches to the choice of criteria in appraising the efficiency of planning activities. The first is to appraise efficiency from the point of view of the degree or extent to which the goal (objective) set has been achieved. If the goal is achieved then planning is functionally efficient. The second approach is based on judging the efficiency of planning from the extent to which the economic potentials of the country, republic, industry or enterprise have been realised.

These criteria describe the quality of planning activities from different angles. Changes in criteria follow those in the objectives and conditions of economic growth. For many decades the main economic objective of the country and the people has been to gain time in economic competition with capitalism, i.e. to close the gap in developing the key economic sectors. The extent to which this objective was reached characterised the operational qualities of our planning system. The objective itself, namely, to gain time in economic development, was preconditioned by outside factors: the break in the capitalist system had occurred in a relatively weak link. To consolidate the victory of the revolution and survive in a hostile surrounding it was necessary to build up as quickly as possible our economic and defence potential.

If this criterion is used to appraise the results achieved one can see clearly that the Soviet system of centralised economic planning and management has proved most effective and efficient. The following statistics are proof of this. In 1913 Russia's industrial production comprised only 13 per cent of that in the USA. In the following years the percentage grew as follows: 1950, 30 per cent; 1965, over 60 per cent; and 1977, 80–90 per cent. In the current quinquennium our industry will close up on the American one, and exceed it in construction activities. Thus, the objective which for many decades was regarded as the principal one has been in the main attained. This gives ground for saying that our centralised planning, which made it possible to concentrate efforts and resources on the key sectors of the national economy, has proved a very effective and efficient tool of socialist construction.

At the present stage the objectives of planning are changing, and so are the criteria for appraising its quality. Now the immediate aim of production is fast growth of the population's real incomes to meet to the maximum the material and spiritual requirements of man. This aim warrants a full and diversified use of the entire economic potential, i.e. a very high efficiency of social production.

(1) *Democratic centralism*

It is obvious that an empirical approach based solely on experience cannot be adequate in raising the functional efficiency of such a complex system as the Soveit Union's national economy. A solid methodological base is needed for the planning agencies' complicated and multifarious activities. The principle of democratic centralism in organising national economic planning is the first one to be mentioned among the basic methodological premises. Centralised planning means uniform planning for the whole national economy as an integral system. As is well known any complex system must be controlled from one point, i.e. centrally. It is absurd, for example, to have two or three control towers working in parallel at a large airport, or to let each station master draw up his own train schedule. Stronger centralisation does not mean that central bodies are supposed to be involved in decision-making on a mounting number of economic problems. On the contrary, the latter should be fewer, but the decisions must be more substantiated and effective.

The economic need for a centralised approach as an effective means for an orderly economic pattern comes from 'below', from the working people. As proprietors of the means of production they are vitally interested in uninterrupted supplies of all the necessary resources to each enterprise to increase production. This universal interest in a well-adjusted and smoothly operating system of planning and supply expresses the democratic nature of socialist production relations.

One of the practical forms of achieving democratic centralism in economic planning is the state's control over the predominant part of capital investments, money for science and culture and the public consumption funds. This form of appropriation, distribution and use of the huge material resources, approximating to two-thirds of the country's national income, is socialist ownership in action.

Centralised funds constitute a material prerequisite for uniform scientific, technological and social policies throughout the whole national economy. The society as a whole is responsible for qualitative changes in the productive forces and for proportional and full employment at all times. The public consumption funds provide equal economic opportunities for all citizens in the field of education, medicare and social security, irrespective of occupation, family status, or the historical peculiarities of the regions where they reside.

(2) *Long-term and short-term plans*

Another important methodological principle of planning requires a long-term approach to the solution of large-scale scientific, technological, economic and social problems and, correspondingly, a prospective plan for a long period of time. This principle is translated into reality in the form of a three-sectional system consisting of long-term, five-year and annual plans.

Long-term plans make possible a broader use of mission-oriented methods of tackling national economic problems. Two factors are known to be taken into account in planning – the available resources and the goal (mission). In the final analysis the goal and the means of its achievement must be harmonised. In a short period of time (up to five years) it is not always possible to provide for the practical accomplishment of large-scale missions. A long-term approach designed for fifteen to twenty years begins with analysing prospective needs and substantiating scientifically the socialist society's development goals. They pinpoint the main trends of national economic growth on which qualitative changes in the society's social pattern are primarily contingent. The goals mapped out express the socio-economic concept of society regarding its future and determine one of the main aspects of the state planning strategy.

Its other aspect is determined by the possibilities of production and accumulation, and the proportions between various forms of the social product's flow – physical, material, commodity and money. Therefore, special intersectoral and interregional programmes providing for a balanced solution are drafted to substantiate the means and ways of accomplishing large-scale missions.

These programmes serve as the basis for elaborating a consolidated plan for fifteen years. The plan disregards possible effects of fortuitous, temporary factors, concentrating all efforts and attention on translating into reality the fundamental, long-term goals of the economic strategy.

Long-term plans are broken down into three five-year periods. Quinquenniums are becoming the main form of planning production on the nation-wide scale and in individual sectors, regions, associations and enterprises. A five-year plan makes it possible to particularise the economic policy and to ensure a proportional, balanced process of extended reproduction with due account of the more specific needs of society and the realistic potentialities of the given stage. Transition from the country's general five-year plan of economic development to the five-year plans of specific ministries, associations and enterprises means transition to ever more concrete and detailed plan assignments. Thereby each management agency is enabled to see clearly what are the prospects of its growth, what products it is expected to turn out in the next few years, what inputs are involved and what technical level is required.

The five-year targets are broken down into annual assignments specifying who is responsible for manufacture, accumulations, scientific and technical programmes and capital construction. The annual plan as part and parcel of the five-year plan is a working instrument of the latter's realisation.

It is the forefront of national economic management, where economic policies come into contact with man and his daily interests and concerns. In this connection it should be emphasised that the enhanced role of long-term planning in no way means the shifting of current planning to the background. On the contrary, a turn towards longer-term prospects and broader knowledge about the distant future is aimed, *inter alia*, at raising the quality of specific economic management and linking it closer to the main tendencies of economics, science and engineering. It is the objective need to foresee the implications of the current measures in a longer term perspective, and to prepare in good time for the solutions to be accepted after many years, that underlies long-term planning; not the subjective desire to solve today what is to be solved in several years. Experience indicates that the ground for these solutions must be laid beforehand through the current development of the economy in such a way as to create the necessary prerequisites for raising and handling in a longer term perspective more complicated and larger problems.

(3) *Sectoral and regional planning*

Another important methodological premise of national economic planning is the unity of the sectoral and territorial approach to the solution of production and social problems. In the system of all-people's co-operation of labour the sectoral aspect has priority, ensuring the carrying out of uniform technical policies in the manufacture of certain types (groups) of products. These policies are materialised in sectoral specialisation and need centralised capital investments within the framework of the respective ministries. This, however, does not belittle the significance of correct regional interlinkage of specialised enterprises with local infrastructure, and the problems of social development of towns and settlements where the former are located; on the contrary, their significance becomes greater. And here a complicated problem arises of how to interrelate the production activities of such enterprises with each other and also with the peculiarities of territorial labour division. A practical solution of all these problems presupposes, firstly, redistribution of sectoral capital investments related to the development of infrastructure, housing and social and welfare institutions, and their pooling on a regional or district level. Secondly, a need arises to strengthen local management agencies and extend their functions, rights and duties to enable them effectively to co-ordinate economic and social relations developing within the framework of individual regions. Further efforts to develop territorial and industrial complexes and industrial conglomerations are very important for the organisational solution of these problems in the Soviet Union. Among these the following complexes can be mentioned: the Kursk iron-ore mining complex; the Orenburg gas condensate deposit; the oil fields of Western Siberia; and the hydropower developments in Sayani, Bratsk and Ust-Ilim.

III THE NEED FOR SCIENTIFIC FORECASTING

In the context of a rapidly changing situation (historically), and the need to reconstruct in good time the relatively inert system (like any other large structure) of the national economy, forecasting of economic growth must be very exacting.

Scientific forecasts reveal the dialectical cause-effect relations between the past, the present and the future. A model of the national economy or its individual elements is built on the basis of comprehensive date about all the varieties of those material, political or ideological factors which have manifested themselves, or will probably do so in a longer term perspective, and which will have a regulatory effect on extended socialist reproduction.

For instance, the birth rate this year predetermines the level of labour resources in eighteen to twenty years to come. Enterprises under construction today to a great extent predetermine the volume and pattern of manufacture of individual groups of products in five to ten years, whereas the economic effect of the projected capital investments will manifest itself in ten to twenty years. Usually, it takes fifteen to twenty years to develop large new deposits of minerals, and data of geological surveying and prospecting are of great value for predicting the location of productive forces.

Four to eight years are needed to translate into mass or serial production the results of applied research, while fundamental breakthroughs take fifteen to twenty years. For example, the next five to ten years will be characterised by rapid growth of the atomic industry due to important successes in this field of science. Fundamental research in quantum electronics gives grounds for predicting that towards the end of the twentieth century comparatively cheap and highly reliable laser devices will be mass-produced. This will revolutionise the technology of many other industries, the techniques of communication, long-distance transmission of energy, outer space explorations, etc.

Humanity is creating and shaping its future by its present activities. It is only necessary to see the shoots of the new, to select what is really important for the development of productive forces and social relations, to brush aside erroneous ideas and correctly to systematise and generalise the scattered data. Of great importance here is the correct understanding of interrelationship between science and practice. The experience of the twentieth century indicates that science progressively tends to play an increasingly important part in developing technology and production. In our times progress in productive forces and economic relations is preceded by advances in the natural and social sciences. In this connection several fields of scientific knowledge can be mentioned which form the framework of economic forecasting of the 'past–present–future' functional dependences. These are as follows:

(1) Analysis of the system of economic laws and pattern-shifts in social requirements and production; substantiating qualitative changes in the mode of life of human beings, their professional and cultural level; finding out prerequisites for raising the economic and cultural standards of all nationalities; substantiating conditions for closer cohesion of social groups and stronger unity of society; and moulding a new attitude towards labour.

(2) Detection of the peculiarities of population reproduction, changes in the age, sex and nationality patterns, and also general educational and professional training of personnel. Various demographic tendencies predetermine both the quantitative parameters and the qualitative characteristics of a future working man. At the same time the growth of population and its changing pattern are treated as factors affecting not only the dynamics of the labour force, but also that of the consumption fund.

(3) Determining the main trends of scientific and technical progress, and an overall estimation of its economic effect in social production stemming from improved technical and economic parameters of the existing designs of machinery and know-how (evolutionary process); and also from designing and developing radically new implements of labour, sources of energy and raw materials as well as more progressive technological processes.

(4) Analysis and estimation of the future dynamics of mineral and water resources and of their possible economic uses in the prospective period.

The tendency in this field is that the most favourable deposits are being depleted and relatively worse ones have to be developed, often incurring higher costs despite technological progress in extracting industries. The problem of fresh water to meet industrial, agricultural and human needs also becomes increasingly acute with every decade.

(5) Study of the process of extended reproduction including the turnover of productive and non-productive assets. The growth of the socialist economy depends not only on how much is saved, but also on how intensive and effective is the use of these assets. Therefore, it is important correctly to appraise the qualitative aspect of capital investments, i.e. their effectiveness, on which to a great extent depends the way in which the national income will be broken down into the accumulation and consumption funds, as well as its rate of growth. In their turn, the level and pattern of capital investments, the dynamics of incompleted construction and the co-efficient of relative capital intensity predetermine the prospective volume and pattern of productive capacities, and, consequently, the principal parameters of manufacture, as well as employment and the growth of the population's welfare.

(6) Knowledge of the intra- and intersectoral relations is an important prerequisite for forecasting the rates and ratios of growth in individual lines of production interrelated through the comparatively stable technological coefficients of the relative inputs of primary materials, fuel and energy, as well as the amortisation of the fixed assets. Using these data to define the future requirements and the probable volume and pattern of the nation income (final product) it is possible to estimate, with a very high degree of accuracy, the prospects of growth of the leading industries and the overall pattern of the national economy.

(7) Research into the expanding volumes, trends and patterns of foreign economic ties. The role and significance of international labour division as a factor of economic growth is continuously enhanced. At the same time new forms of economic co-operation between the socialist countries come into being which conduce to higher rates and better ratios in their national economic development.

IV THE TASKS AND METHODS OF FORECASTING

The specific feature of forecasting as a process of cognition is, in the first place, that it deals with limited information of a probable nature. Partial uncertainty arises because it is impossible to characterise accurately all peculiarities of the scientific and technical progress as well as other factors which affect the longer term development of the national economy. Irrespective of the period for which forecasting is made, in the mental concept of the future economy there are always some 'white spots', i.e. unclear processes and phenomena that might pop up. The task of forecasting is to reduce uncertainty to a minimum.

This presupposes the development of special methods which can be roughly grouped as follows, depending on the aim and scope of research into the regularities of prospective economic growth: (a) analytical and computational; (b) normative and estimative; and (c) comprehensive, consolidated.

The methods of the first group are used for a qualitative and quantitative analysis of individual elements of the mechanism of objective laws which directly affect the rates of growth and patterns of the social product, the national income and other economic parameters at the base period, and their projection into the future with whatever corrections are required. Use is made in this forecasting of what is known about the relative stability of a certain inertia, if I may put it so, in economic growth. For example, a medium-term forecast of production cost dynamics can be based on the correlation models of the base period. It involves the following main stages:

(i) analysis and qualitative characterisation of factors affecting production cost in the base period;
(ii) study and estimation of the possible dynamics of all factors in a longer term perspective;
(iii) prognostication of new factors and estimation of their effect on the subject under investigation; and
(iv) substantiation of the prospective level of production cost with due account of the whole complex of factors affecting overall normative spending in the prospective period.

In applying analytical and computational methods the final result of investigation is either the production cost indicator or some other parameter of the economic system. Its characteristics are a kind of function of the series of variables taken as initial data for such analysis.

The normative and estimative methods presuppose a different approach. In economic forecasting a number of prospective parameters and interrelationships in the national economy can be predicted (estimated beforehand) on the basis of what is known about the operative qualitative and quantitative forms of economic laws. Correspondingly, these norms can be formulated in a general way: for instance, 'full employment of the able-bodied population', or 'the growth of labour productivity must somewhat exceed increases in average wages'.

The results obtained through the use of analytical, computational and normative methods make it possible to outline hypothetically not only the probable parameters of individual economic categories, but also possible interrelationships between them. In short, they help to produce several variant descriptions of specific sections (blocks) of the national economy or the operational mechanism of individual laws.

The third group of economic forecasting methods (consolidated, comprehensive) is used to sum up the information from different sources, and construct the final forecast of economic growth which makes it possible to foresee the development of the national economy as a whole in a complex totality of functionally interrelated complicated processes and phenomena.

Formal mathematical methods cannot solve this problem. As pointed out earlier, in forecasting individual elements of the national economy each parameter is of a probable and considerably vacillating nature. Any mechanical arrangement of all these elements will make the whole system almost untrustworthy, while the vast spread between the maximum and minimum parameters will call in question the scientific and practical value of such a model. A more realistic consolidated economic model for a long-term period needs to be mission-oriented in keeping with economic laws, its parameters being adjusted on the basis of additional political and ideological data about the prospective growth of the whole social system, of which economics is just a major subsystem. In other words, forecasting is enriched with social and economic policies.

Large-scale work is under way in the Soviet Union to forecast the country's economic and social progress up to 1990 and a longer term period. It is estimated that in 1976–90 the Soviet Union's material and financial resources will almost double as compared to the previous fifteen years.

V WHAT IS BEING DONE TO IMPROVE PLANNING IN THE SOVIET UNION

A qualitative reconstruction of national economic planning to adapt it to the specific functioning of the economy of advanced socialism is under way in the Soviet Union. Its major directions are as follows:

(i) deeper scientific substantiation of the national economic plan, aimed at making all the plan indicators more realistic and more stable;
(ii) transition to comprehensive planning of the mounting efficiency of social production;
(iii) better methods of planning scientific and technological progress; and
(iv) closer cohesion of national planning with the planning of economic co-operation and integration with CMEA member-nations.

Let us have a closer look at these guidelines.

(1) *Realism and stability*

A major condition of a *realistic* plan is its all-round scientific substantiation. The solution of this problem is made easier due to the recent reorientation of social sciences to the study of applied socio-economic issues. Simultaneously, a stronger emphasis is laid on the analytical aspect of planning itself. Increasingly wider use is made of the programme and mission-oriented method which makes it possible to single out the 'key link', as one out of two or several interlinked problems in economics is always pivotal in the chain. The aim of the programme and mission-oriented method is to tackle the totality of such central problems, reveal as fully and as thoroughly as possible their inner structure and map out their extent and possible ways, sources, and deadlines for their solution. Several layers of cause-effect dependencies are analysed. Investigation of direct and inverse relationships between various economic phenomena and processes makes it possible to take a more sober stock of both the real potentialities, and the difficulties and contradictions that may be involved in solving a problem. This, in turn, is an important condition for making the national economic plan as a whole more realistic. At the same time the programme and mission-oriented method enables various ministries and departments to pool their efforts and resources for fulfilling national economic targets without violating the required sectoral and territorial proportions. For example, almost ninety research organisations and enterprises belonging to twenty ministries are involved in the Soviet Union under a single programme in developing equipment for drilling deep and super-deep oil and gas wells.

Experience indicates that planning of pattern changes through mission-oriented programmes, no matter how important, should not be absolutist. It is always necessary to balance all such programmes against the limited resources of a specific prospective period, and to link them with the other objectives of the national economic plan.

Practically, it is possible to balance mission-oriented programmes with national economic resources only within the framework of long- and medium-term planning. Thus, the rising role of five-year plans is now an important prerequisite for a more harmonised functioning of the entire economic machinery. What is implied is a gradual departure from the practice of annually reviewing and approving current plans, and a switchover to stable five-year plans with specified annual assignments propped up with material incentives of a long-term nature. Fulfilment of a five-year plan will be taken account of accumulatively, starting with its first year.

In practice the switching over to this system of planning has caused quite a few difficulties. The point is that the pattern and number of indicators, as well as the extent of their substantiation, cannot be the same in five-year and in annual plans. But then how can they be adjusted without a return to an annual review of five-year assignments? The current plan specifies in detail the respective parameters of the five-year plan for the given year; with due account of latent reserves and additional difficulties; unexpected 'zigzags' in fashions and, correspondingly, in the population's demand; and also of changes in the international situation. But this is not the only difficulty. The essence of the problem is that it is necessary to pass over from the aggregate indicators of the five-year plan to more specific, complicated and contradictory annual assignments, including the technical, industrial and financial plans of enterprises (associations).

The annual plan is directly linked with non-state financing, budgets, operative prices. All these specific forms of production relations have a direct bearing on the economic interests of society, collective bodies of workers and individual working men. Certain difficulties arise here in harmonising them in the indicators and norms of the annual plan, without violating the rates and proportions of the five-year plan. The problem was also complicated by the fact that until recently five-year plans directed and co-ordinated the flow of social product only in its *physical* volume and pattern (i.e. at constant prices), whereas annual plans cover in unity its physical, material and cost-value aspects. The switching over to planning cost-value indicators in current prices, i.e. the real commodity-money relations, raises the problem of self-sustaining efficiency or, on the contrary, the inefficiency of manufacturing specific products, including the new types; and thus the problem of material incentives to be drawn by working collective bodies from keeping certain proportions in the national economy.

All this indicates that if the five-year plan is to become the main form of planning it has to be reconstructed as follows: the role of its quality indicators should be raised; a consolidated financial plan and prices ought to be worked out for the prospective period; and additional reserves must be created. A major prerequisite for better substantiation of the five-year plan is to improve the system of aggregate norms in physical-material and cost-value forms. It is the norms that help co-ordinate the requirements and the resources. The quality of balances, and to a great extent the degree to which the plan as a whole is realistic, is contingent on how well the norms are justified technically and economically. These norms characterise in a concentrated and very clear-cut form how intensive and effective the use of each type of productive resources is. Besides, we have important reserves for growth in this field. All this leads to consideration of another form of improvement in present-day planning: transition to comprehensive planning of the mounting efficiency of social production.

(2) *Comprehensive planning*

This orientation of national economic planning stems from the understanding of a simple, but a very important interrelationship: that a high level of popular welfare can be based only on the highly effective functioning of the whole economic machinery. Therefore, it is particularly urgent to evolve a new methodology for a conscious and fuller use of the time-saving law in national economic planning.

In this connection the whole set of planning instruments is changed: much wider use is made of the final result of production for analysis, target-setting and appraising the activities of working collective bodies. It is also important that, unlike the previous years when the indicators of efficient use of productive resources were often based on expected results from planned technical and organisational improvements, the present-day planning assignments for increased efficiency of social production are becoming normative, i.e. they serve as the starting point for a certain complex of technical and organisational measures.

(3) *Planning scientific and technological progress*

From here follows the objective need for the third direction: better methods of planning scientific and technological progress. Planning faces extremely important tasks of directing research and development towards finding and substantiating radically new methods, instruments and forms of human interaction with nature conducive to an essential rise in the economic efficiency of production, better conditions and character of labour, and environmental protection. Already today the Soviet Union plays a leading part in constructing giant hydropower stations, high-voltage transmission lines, atomic powered ships, spaceships, electric welding equipment, etc. At the same time a considerable part of its products still fails to match the best world standards in their qualitative parameters. Therefore, it is necessary to improve the methodology of planning more effective relations between science and production, and to put the achievements of science into economic use more speedily.

Planning helps concentrate scientific efforts on the most prospective aspects of technological progress (atomic power engineering, laser and plasma technology, development of systems and complexes of machines capable of sharply increasing labour productivity and the quality of products, development of new types of transport vehicles, etc.). Comprehensive programmes also play an increasingly important role in our time. Their function in planning is not only to elaborate vital problems of scientific and technological progress, but also to achieve effective practical results. Some of them are included in the national economic plan. For instance, the current Soviet five-year plan includes assignments to draft over 200 scientific and technical programmes.

Through planning, the scientific and technical programmes to be put into effect are co-ordinated with the respective sections of the plan on production, capital construction, material supplies and personnel training. In the process efforts are made to improve contacts between research and production organisations as well as the system of non-state financing and incentives which ensures a fast and effective advance of scientific discoveries from research institutions via designing and testing laboratories to serial and mass production of new products.

(4) *Planning of Foreign Economic Relations*

The fourth direction, i.e. improved planning of foreign economic relations and economic co-operation with the CMEA member-nations, is also an important factor accelerating the growing efficiency of social production.

Socialist integration created new and complicated problems for economic planning. At the same time it made an important contribution to the improvement of the latter. Within the framework of this integration scientists, economists and planners fruitfully co-operate to develop the theory and methodology of planning. In recent years the theoretical and practical activities in this field have been directed to improvement of the following forms of co-operation: mutual consultations on pivotal problems of economic, scientific and technical policies, which to a large measure predetermine the main trends and nature of the member countries' joint planning activities; elaboration of general economic, sectoral, scientific and technical forecasts; co-ordination of five-year and longer term plans of the individual member nations' economic growth which raises the level of planning and economic efficiency of the entire community of socialist countries; joint planning of individual industries and lines of production, which is a more advanced form of jointly solving large-scale problems of key importance for higher production efficiency and more stable proportions in the member economies; and drafting of long-term, mission-oriented programmes and harmonised plans of multilateral measures to be effected through pooling the members' material, financial and labour resources. These programmes and plans gradually cover an increasingly larger range of important problems which cannot be tackled by each country alone.

It is also important to stress that the socialist countries' economic, scientific and technical co-operation has become an integral part of their national planning: their annual and longer term plans have a special chapter designed to provide for the implementation of agreed measures on international co-operation and socialist economic integration. This linkage between the international and national planning activities makes it possible to particularise assignments (in volume, pattern, deadlines and contractors) in capital construction and the manufacture and mutual deliveries of specific products within the framework of socialist economic integration.

VI ECONOMIC REGULATORS IN USE

While analysing the specific features of Soviet economic management one cannot help saying a few words about the methods and instruments of indirect regulation of individual aspects of economic growth. The process involves a whole system of economic levers such as credit, prices, profits, bonuses and other incentives.

Lenin insisted on the need to use a single national economic plan in combination with economic regulators. But he viewed this combination not as a mechanical sum of the plan elements and commodity-money relations, but as a complex in which they supplemented each other, with planning playing the leading and determining part. This can be exemplified by the new economic policy of the twenties. Sometimes the NEP is lopsidedly treated as a deal aimed only at activising market relations. This is not correct. Lenin's wisdom was more far-reaching. Firstly, he discerned in the commodity-money relations an important factor for the rehabilitation and development of the economy of numerous peasant holdings and, at the same time, the whole national economy. Secondly, he found an effective tool to limit the free market forces, namely, a single state plan designed to bring about the victory of socialist production relations.

This skilful combination of planning and commodity-money relations made it possible to overcome the economic chaos and hunger of the twenties, to reach the pre-war level of production in a comparatively short period of time and to start the technical reconstruction of production and its further growth at a rapid pace.

It is important to emphasise that an effective combination of planning and economic regulators is possible only if the commodity-money relations, including demand and supply, are well balanced and if inflation is barred.

Apart from directives and other binding assignments Soviet planning agencies are now making a wide use of economic regulators (prices, credits, bonuses, sanctions, etc.) in effecting national economic plans to raise the quality of products and enlarge their assortment, encourage saving and better organised production, render material aid to families with many children, and for other purposes.

Practice is the main criterion of whether national economic planning is well-substantiated and realistic. That the Soviet economy has succeeded in a com comparatively short historical time in climbing the steep ladders of its quinquennia from century-long backwardness to the heights of world progress is convincing proof of the vital advantages of planning. The crisis-free expansion of production, the full employment of the able-bodied population, the steadily rising living and cultural standards and stable prices – all these features distinguish the progress of the Soviet national economy and are evidence that the theory of scientific planning has become an important practical reality of today.

17 Reflections on the Nature of National Planning

Krzysztof Porwit
INSTITUTE OF PLANNING, WARSAW

I THE NATURE OF SYSTEM-WIDE PLANNING

The views offered in this paper pertain almost exclusively to the nature and role of national planning in the conditions of a socialist socio-economic system. More specifically they are related to experiences gathered in Poland. Any recommendations formulated in the paper should be considered in this context. The issues will be discussed from the viewpoint of economic theory, of its relevance for the solutions in the sphere of system-wide conscious control over socio-economic processes[1] or, in a wider sense – for the premeditative behaviour of the system.[2]

It is necessary to pose and discuss the problem from this angle because it is then possible to make a distinction between various interpretations of planning, as well as to assess them. The most frequent interpretation connects planning directly with managerial functions of decision-making. In this sense planning, as a managerial subfunction, is related to management (control) centres who make decisions concerning a given object. The delimitation of such an object, and consequently the scope of decisions, depends on the location of a given management centre in the institutional and organisational structure of the national economy. In this sense Gościński (*op. cit.*, p. 246) defines a process of planning as a set of activities preparing the decision on the future desired state of the system as well as on the manner of implementation of tasks and goals. A plan as a planistic act is considered as identical with

[1] This problem was raised and discussed by J. Pajestka in his paper 'Kształtowanie procesów sopłeczno-gospodarczych (Shaping the socio-economic processes)', *Ekonomista* (1977) no. 1.

[2] This term, based on R. Ackoff's typology of systems, is used and explained in more detail by J. Gościński in '*Zarys teorii sterowania ekonomicznego (An outline of economic control theory*' (PWN,Warsaw, 1977), pp. 40–3. In short – the premeditative system can set and change both the aims of its behaviour and the ways of their implementation. It is characterised by the will and possibility of a consciously set behaviour.

a decision. There are certainly many merits in such an approach as far as it leads to emphasis on important features of planning as a process, dealing with the processing of information and involving methods and techniques of decision-making.

These aspects should not be underrated, but they cover only part of the nature of planning. Using this approach one cannot understand why certain types of decision are (or should be) within the scope of the functions attributed to particular management centres; to what extent planning is (or should be) different, depending on the nature of these functions; in what sense these functions, and the corresponding processes of planning, are mutually interconnected and conditioned. One may say that in such a context planning is considered in terms of the scientific disciplines called by Lange[1] auxiliary to political economy, rather than of political economy itself. If one looks at national (system-wide) planning from this viewpoint then it is usually identified with planning performed at the central level of management (i.e. in central government institutions) and serving centralised decisions. The substance and scope of such decisions are seen then as mutually exclusive with those concerning decisions made at the lower echelons (e.g. by the managers of enterprises or by regional authorities). This leads in turn to an oversimplified view that the strength of national (systemwide) planning and its practical influence on the behaviour of the whole socio-economic system, depends on the degree of concentration of decisions at the central government level. If such terms of reasoning are adopted then it becomes difficult to understand and explain the true meaning of democratic centralism, which is rightly considered as the most important principle for the control of behaviour of the socialist socio-economic system.[2]

Such difficulty is especially evident, if – as in the case of Poland – a diagnosis is made that the basic economic units (i.e. the socialist enterprises) have not enough freedom of choice and decisions to be able to act efficiently, but it is seen to be necessary, as a remedy, to strengthen both the central planning and the scope for initiative and choice, the forces of innovative dynamism in the enterprises.[3] The remedial conclusions are correct but misunderstandings are likely to emerge if the framework for reasoning is not adequate, i.e. if it is not based on principal features specific for the behaviour (the manner of action) of the socialist social formation.

[1] O. Lange 'Ekonomia polityczn (Political economy)' in *Wielka Encyklopedia Powszechna* (*Great Universal Encyclopedia*) (PWN, Warsaw, 1964), vol. 3. Econometrics and planometrics, cybernetics and operations research were mentioned within this category of disciplines.

[2] Cf. W. Nowożyłow *Zagadnienia rozwoju gospodarki socjalistycznej* (*Development problems of the socialist economy*) (PWE, Warsaw, 1976), pp. 343 and 388–9.

[3] Statements to that effect were made at the VIth Congress of the Polish United Workers Party (in 1971) and confirmed at the VIIth Congress (in 1976).

From this viewpoint one should note that the most important characteristics which shape the nature of systemwide planning and control in a socialist formation are the creation and strengthening of socialist modes of production based on social (national and co-operative) ownership of the means of production. This is considered as fundamental because it constitutes the basis for those changes in attitudes and motivations, in institutional and organisational structures, in patterns of interactions among individuals, organisations and institutions which are driven by the will to strive for consciously chosen common aims. In this way the possibility of a harmonious development of the whole system is created, but the utilisation of this possibility is not automatically ensured, as it depends on the abilities of the society to understand the nature of economic laws and to act accordingly. There is a gradual process of mastering these abilities which involves difficulties and conflicts but the latter can be resolved as there are no fundamental sources for self-perpetuating controversies within the socio-economic system.

In Afasanjew's words:[1]

> Social laws manifest themselves always as the laws of behaviour and action of the masses in concrete specific behaviour of individuals. As a result of interactions among individuals there arises a general tendency, a common ultimate outcome of interactions which forms a law. In pre-socialist formations each individual was acting according to his own goals which were not consistent with general and ultimate outcomes, with an overall tendency and law. As a consequence there were some spontaneous forces mastering the people. There was no possibility for the society, as a whole, to set a common goal and to mobilise all its members around the task of its implementation.
>
> In principle there are no inherent conflicts between the individual goals in a socialist society and the general outcome. Consequently there is no dominance of any exogenous spontaneous forces but the ultimate outcome can be shaped according to goals previously chosen and planned.

This seems to be the main feature relevant for discussing the nature of national socio-economic planning under socialist conditions, i.e. to consider it as a major organising and co-ordinating force used by the society to integrate intrasystemic actions around the tasks of implementing social goals; the latter being perceived and articulated according to socialist criteria and norms of evaluation.

[1] W. G. Afanasjew, *Naukowe zarzadzanie społeczeństwem* (*Scientific social control*) (Warsaw, WP, 1976), p. 139; translated from Russian: *Naucznoje uprawlenije obschestvom* (Moscow, 1973).

What this implies also is the importance of striving for an understanding of economic laws, the objective manifestations of which have to be consciously utilised within the framework of systemwide planning instead of being spontaneous masters of the system's behaviour.[1] Three main categories of laws are to be considered, i.e. technological and balancing laws of production, laws of human behaviour and laws of interaction among human activities.[2] Especially relevant for national, systemwide planning are the latter two categories, and also their interconnections with the technological and balancing laws of production.

II THE EMPHASIS ON THE PLANNING OF PRODUCTION

Planning of the national economy has for many years been considered as an important subject of scientific research, and of theoretical formulations within the framework of political economy of socialism. However, the emphasis has been placed on the problems of internal consistency in shaping the structural development proportions (in their interbranch, interregional and also inter-temporal aspects); and on the problems of finding solutions corresponding to certain predetermined criteria of optimality. Writing on this subject in the early 'sixties Lange made the observation[3] that the political economy of socialism was concentrating attention first of all on the real terms and structural balancing aspects of the economy. Other aspects, related to the internal dialectics in the development of socialist modes of production, to inherent conflicts and driving forces of development, less frequently formed the subject matter of scientific analysis.

In other words, one may say that the approaches have been based mainly on the premises of technological and balancing laws of production, which must have involved certain assumptions making the impact of other premises[4] either neutral or exogenously estimated. This meant also that progress in the theory of planning was one-sided in the sense of being concentrated on 're-ified' categories (of the stocks and flows of products and resources) and their interrelations. Much less attention was devoted to such issues as the manner in which social and partial (subsystemic) objectives are articulated, the criteria of their evaluation and choice are formed, in which attitudes and motivations of people[5] are evolving (either contributing to consciously designed final outcomes or creating mutually controversial tendencies).

[1] Cf. O. Lange *Ekonomia polityczna* (*Political Economy*) (PWE, Warsaw, 1975), pp. 291–7.

[2] Cf. O. Lange, *op. cit.*, pp. 270–8.

[3] O. Lange, *op. cit.*, pp. 804–5.

[4] The premises related to the laws of human behaviour and their interactions.

[5] Those who form plans and implement them.

III NEW APPROACHES TO PLANNING

In the course of the last fifteen to twenty years we have witnessed several important new trends in scientific research and in theoretical formulations related to the issues considered in this paper. Let us draw attention to the following:

(1) The framework of national planning, especially in its short- and medium-term operational aspects, gradually became more explicitly connected with considerations of self-regulatory mechanisms characteristic for current planning and management; in particular micro-organisations and their horizontal ties. This involved the terms of economic and financial mechanisms utilising various parameters and normatives which regulate the behaviour of economic organisations (prices, wages, credit and related interest, taxes, rules for the distribution and utilisation of profits, etc.) parallel to selected sales targets and/or allocations of resources. The principal issue in this respect which still demands a more explicit analysis and theoretical treatment is related to the intertemporal relations between the teleological and systemwide premises of evaluation[1] on the one hand, and internal driving forces at the micro and subsystemic level on the other.

(2) Much insight has been gained in the field of dual relationships between real and value terms of analysis and design for structural proportions. This line of research may open promising prospects for better understanding of the issue mentioned above, i.e. related to a 'missing link' between systemwide future-oriented planning and current regulatory mechanisms based on commodity-money categories. However, there are many difficulties in this field, especially related to a different time-perspective and an informational role of accounting and current prices, as well as their consecutive changes.

(3) There are several attempts to enrich an economic analytical framework for development and its structural proportions. Firstly, there is the approach related to recognition of the fact that in order to link consumption patterns with the notions of human needs and their satisfaction it is insufficient to rely on autonomous consumers' preferences. Such preferences are, of course, of great importance, but they are always conditioned by various social and environmental factors. Important issues then pertain to the interrelations among such phenomena as (i) social perception of human needs; (ii) factors contributing to such conditions which would allow the needs to be perceived and satisfied in line with social criteria of desirability; (iii) factors causing differentiation in perception and satisfaction of needs among individuals, i.e.

1 Those which must exert an influence on the future place and role of a given organisation within the whole system.

reflecting a real diversity of needs and not the differences in conditions imposed by exogenous and social factors.[1]

These aspects are considered essential for an enriched analysis of income distribution, including centralised redistribution and supply of 'benefits in kind'. Simultaneously attempts have been made to identify the links between patterns of satisfaction of human needs and those of the factors promoting efficiency. In this sense the level and pattern of needs satisfaction are considered not only as defining the aims, but also as essential factors promoting development.[2] However, this is still a field where more concrete and quantifiable analytical approaches are very difficult.

Secondly, there is a line of thought related to observations that various input-output relations used in an economic analytical framework, especially the conditions and possibilities for their change, depend not only on the technological characteristics of corresponding processes (which primarily reflect the respective physical and/or chemical properties), but are also influenced by a range of factors depending on the manner in which such characteristics are utilised by people, especially in wider sets of interactions. Attention is also drawn to the manner in which new possibilities, formed by science and R & D activities, are made available for practical application and are assimilated in practice.

Thirdly, more attention is devoted to relationships between socio-economic activities and the state, and changes in the natural environment, especially from the viewpoint of ecological conditions for human life and of depletion of non-renewable resources and conservation of renewable resources. The point is to consider these relationships in a manner promoting a conscious and active environmental attitude in shaping socio-economic development patterns.

(4) There is a growing tendency to consider national planning in a wider context as socio-economic, instead of the formerly used notion of national economic planning. There are two aspects of this shift in emphasis. On the one hand, it reflects the determination to get a deeper insight and stronger justifications for the tasks of articulating social goals within the framework

[1] These aspects are discussed, *inter alia*, by J. Danecki 'Egalitaryzm społeczny a modele konsumpcji w perspektywie do 1990 roku' (Social equity and consumption models in the perspective of 1990) in *Społeczny rozwój Polski w pracach prognostycznych* (Social development of Poland in prognostic studies), ed. J. Danecki (Warsaw, 1974) and also by Z. Ferge, 'Social Policy and the Types of Centralized Redistribution', *Acta Oeconomica*, vol. 15/1, Budapest.

[2] Cf. J. Pajestka, *Determinanty postepu* (*The Determinants of Progress*) (Warsaw, 1975); K. Secomski, 'Czynnik ludzki a baza materialna rozwiniętego społeczenstwa socjalistycznego' (Human factor and the material base of a developed socialist society), *Nowe Drogi* (1976), no. 10, Warsaw.

of planning procedures. On the other hand, it involves the problems of getting wider popular participation in assessing and evaluating alternative patterns of goals and of policies leading to such goals.

Both of these aspects are meant to enrich the rationality principles employed in the optimising framework of comprehensive national accounts, in the sense of getting a stronger base for evaluations related to the choice of desired final outcomes.[1] This raises various problems:

(i) the level of living of the population and its particular groups, including such issues as identification and perception of manifold kinds of needs, the extent of their satisfaction, and basic conditions formed by the society in order to satisfy their needs;[2]

(ii) specific areas of concern such as social care for children and youth, education, social care for elderly people and for disabled and war victims, development of health protection, housing, satisfaction of cultural and intellectual needs, development of physical culture, tourism and recreational facilities;[3]

(iii) the problems of employment, characteristics of the people employed from the viewpoint of their professions, skills, qualifications, types of occupation, the length of working time, conditions of work, etc.

One should also note a significant line of research, characteristic for contemporary scientific thought in the socialist countries, which concentrates on a comprehensive approach to important changes being effected in many aspects of the socio-economic system's development in a stage when a *mature* socialist society is formed. Comprehensiveness means that not only the above aspects are included but also that much emphasis is given to the patterns of social and individual 'way of life' at that stage.[4]

An important matter in dealing with all these problems is the manner in which the options for choice are formed and evaluated and in which the criteria for making the choices are gathered and transformed into policies. One should note three interrelated channels serving for implementation of

[1] One may consider this as a way in which a code concerning the objective function (in a formalised 'shorthand' notation) is deciphered.

[2] Cf. e.g. F. Hronsky 'Metodologicheskie problemy analyza zhiznennogo urovnia v sotsialisticheskom obshchestve' (Methodological Problems of Level of Living Analysis in a Socialist Society) in *Sotsializm i narodnoe blogosostoyanie* (*Socialism and National Welfare*) ed. K. Mikulsky (Moscow, 1976).

[3] Cf. e.g. Z. Czyżowska *Społeczny rozwój Polski* (*Social Development of Poland*) (KiW, Warsaw, 1975).

[4] As examples of publications in this field one may mention the collection of papers in a volume edited by K. Mikulskij (*op. cit.*) as well as a number of contributions published in a Polish monthly *Nowe Drogi*.

such processes, each of them having different properties, and consequently using different kinds of procedures and indicators. The first is based on specialised scientific research; it involves relatively specific and 'technical' sets of categories, analytical tools and corresponding indicators for particular areas of needs. Its basic tasks are to form a background for the identification of issues and the corresponding conditions for possible options.[1]

The second pertains to public planning agencies (central and regional), where attention is focused on comprehensive feasibility and relative effectiveness studies. Here there is the difficult problem of an adequate language for presenting the conclusions and options for consideration by Parliament, by the organisational units of the Polish United Workers Party and other political organisations, by the trade unions, regional councils and collectives of workers in enterprises. Popular discussions on the issues involved, opinions expressed and suggestions made, form the third channel of the process of choice, which should exert a feedback influence on the ultimate formulation of the elements of the plan.

The problems just described are a typical example of an area where there is a continuous interaction of premises, deduced from scientific research, reflecting organisational and informational efficiency as well as socio-political processes. The networks of such interactions are changing, they are in motion and have to be considered along a time-axis. From this viewpoint one can hardly envisage the possibility of having a positive and normative theory, which would provide ready-made prescriptions for practical applications or a true mapping of reality in any kind of a theoretical model.[2] Generalising statements represent the prevailing tendency, and they reflect elements of normative thinking concerning the desired paths of evolution for the processes under consideration. This seems to be a legitimate approach, because the concrete patterns of social economic laws depend on manifold conditions, which influence the manner of the system's behaviour and – at the same time – can be subject to consciously devised influence. In this sense the behaviour

[1] Cf. e.g. 'Standard of living indicators', paper by the Economic Research Institute of the USSR State Planning Commission in United Nations, *Approaches and Methods Used in Long-Term Social Planning and Policy Making* (New York, 1973).

[2] One may indicate in this context that human and socio-economic systems are of the relatively highest level of complexity, whereas the most subtle, analytical and theoretical instruments available reflect the properties appropriate to much lower levels in a typology of systems. It is useful to develop and use such inadequate schemes and instruments because a higher level system incorporates all features of those below it. However, there is a caveat not to accept '. . . as final a level of theoretical analysis which is below the level of the empirical world we are investigating'. See K. E. Boulding, 'General Systems Theory – The Skeleton of Science' in *Management Systems*, ed. P. P. Schoderbek (New York, 1971).

of the system in a given time period is influenced by the conditions formed earlier, whereas present activities directed towards changes in such conditions will contribute to a different shape of the system's behaviour in the future.

(5) The observations just made are in the background of this line of research and socio-economic thinking, according to which intertemporal relations must be taken into consideration both in traditional economic planning, concerned with stocks and flows (of resources, products, services); and also in relation to the manifold conditions which influence the shape of economic processes.[1] One has in mind here institutional, informational and organisational conditions relevant for shaping the interactions among enterprises, households, public (non-profit) institutions and governmental bodies; as well as various forms of language used for communication in such interactions (the language of economic parameters and normatives, and of financial instruments here playing a distinct role). In other words, the manner of the system's behaviour, the rules which govern the functioning of enterprises and interlevel ties, and the manner of systemwide planning are not treated as exogenously given, but are considered as subject to consciously devised actions. Moreover, it is recognised that the desired pattern for shaping such processes cannot be discussed in an 'ahistorical' way, as a programme to strive towards an ideal model. In this sense the notions of meta-control and meta-planning are introduced to represent systemic functions which design, prepare and organise the implementation of changes in the conditions of the system's behaviour.[2]

It is interesting to note that a similar recognition of the need for a wider, systemic approach to planning can be found in 'The Bellagio Declaration on Planning' agreed upon by the participants of the OECD Working Symposium on Long-range Forecasting and Planning in 1968[3] where the following statements were included:

> . . . the pursuance of orthodox planning is quite insufficient, in that it seldom does more than touch a system through changes of the variables. Planning must be concerned with the structural design of the system itself and involved in the formation of policy. Mere modifications of policies already proved inadequate will not result in what is right. Science

[1] This was emphasised by J. Pajestka in the sources referred to in the notes to pp. 289 and 294.

[2] Cf. Y. Z. Maiminas: 'Razvitie sistemnogo podkhoda va narodnokhozyaistvennom planirovanii' (Systems approach in national economic planning), *Ekonomika i Matematicheskie Metody* (1974) no. 5.

[3] E. Jantsch (ed.), *Perspectives of Planning* (OECD, Paris, 1969). One should also add that the socio-political context of changes in the structural design of the system differs depending on the nature of a social formation, i.e. mainly the nature of the modes of production.

in planning is too often used to make situations, which are inherently bad, more efficiently bad.

The need is to plan systems as a whole, to understand the totality of factors involved and to intervene in the structural design to achieve more integrated operation. All large, complex systems are capable of some degree of self-adaptation. But in the face of immense technological, political, social and economic stresses, they will have to develop new structures. This can easily lead to grave social disturbances if the adaptation is not deliberately planned, but merely allowed to happen.

Returning to the previous arguments, let us note also that the need for meta-planning should not be interpreted in a too literal and simplified way. This type of 'future-creative' activities cannot be based on strictly predetermined programmes, the consistency and timing of which would be centrally co-ordinated and directed. Certainly there is a need for comprehensive co-ordination and control, but this has to be considered along the time-axis in the sense that the teleological, systemwide influence should be combined with adaptive, 'self-learning' processes having their source in the elements and subsystems. What is important here concerns innovative attitudes and motivations within organisational and institutional structures themselves.

IV THE FEASIBILITY OF SYSTEMWIDE PREMISES AND CRITERIA

This brings us to the last line of thinking to be discussed in this paper. As its background there is an inevitable question concerning the reasons for an assumption that teleological, systemwide premises and criteria for shaping the future will be correct. The point here is not whether they are desirable, nor whether one should try to use them, but rather – to what extent, in what sense, under what conditions they are feasible as a correct basis for action.

One may start in this context with an observation that the quality of a cognitive process, in which a situation is assessed, a problem identified and a choice made, depends on: (i) the validity of the information available; (ii) the characteristics of the evaluating criteria; and (iii) the motivations which may influence the manner of interpreting information and of applying evaluation criteria. The problem of feasibility is linked primarily to the availability of information and the manner in which it is interpreted and used. In this context we have witnessed a growing appreciation of the fact that the quality and validity of systemwide planning depends very much on the extent, scope and quality of various auxiliary analytical, diagnostic studies as well as future-oriented prognostic, simulation and programming studies. There is also a growing emphasis on the so-called strategic role and function of central planning, in contradistinction to operational and tactical functions in management and planning.[1] Observations are made that the capacities of units involved in systemwide planning (viewed upon from the viewpoints of personal, information-processing and organisational capacities) preclude simultaneous emphasis on strategic and operational problems. It is argued then that priority must be given to strategic problems because they cannot be dealt with in a different manner (i.e. without full involvement of these capacities), whereas there are such possibilities with respect to operational problems.

However, this is not only a problem of limited capacities but also of a significant difference in approaches applicable to strategic and operational planning respectively. If there is a multilevel procedure of operational planning (involving decisions at a higher level) then the emphasis is necessarily shifted to technological and organisational feasibility, issues essential for the choices of the manner in which to implement given objectives. Consequently a higher level planning unit concentrates attention on separate internal characteristics of particular subsystem organisations, and it relies for this purpose on data flows gathered from these organisations. This may often involve two kinds of dangers. Planning data sent upwards may be biased, and at the same time the subunits of a higher level institution who are responsible for particular subsystems are likely to identify themselves with a subsystemic viewpoint or – in some cases – to enforce difficult ('progressive') input-output relations in order to induce subsystem organisations to economise on certain resources, raw materials, etc.

There are, of course, various balancing accounts serving the tasks of consistency checking, but these tasks are performed under twofold pressures, i.e. to find the ways to reach social objectives desired for a given time period; and parallel with this to reconcile such ways with subsystemic viewpoints concerning the expected effects of their activities and the inputs necessary for that purpose. In short – the characteristic features of operational planning, its close links with decisions concerned with the activities of particular sectoral organisations, create certain specific attitudes on the part of the people involved in planning which weaken their ability to assess and judge the problems from the viewpoint of comprehensive, systemwide criteria. It then becomes difficult to develop strategic planning on the basis of data flows, informational procedures and organisational structures which were shaped according to the features of operational planning.

The following are the main conditions essential for the validity of teleo-

[1] The borderlines between these types of function are not quite clear and uniformly defined. The attribute of strategy is usually defined as: (i) dealing with a problem crucial for the existence of the whole system; (ii) concerned primarily with the choice of objectives (which involves, however, alternative ways and also the feasibility of their implementation); and (iii) reaching relatively further into the future.

logical, systemwide premises of analysis and strategic planning:

(i) there is a need for the most objective assessment of data reflecting various factors influencing past, present and probable future behaviour and performance of the system, i.e. the data should be unbiased by sectoral and operational interests;
(ii) it is essential to recognise that the ability to gain information is different from having access to data: it involves the skill of drawing information from data through its processing, which in turn must be consciously designed according to the questions of interest for those who need the information;
(iii) in this context the processes of gaining information for strategic, systemwide planning must have a specific design which allows particular subsystems and sectoral problems to be looked at against the background their interactions within a comprchensive whole;
(iv) it has to be recognised that some of the problems dealt with are unstructured or highly stochastic;[1] consequently, *continuity* of the information-gaining processes, which may make it possible to verify hypotheses and develop learning processes, is of particular importance;
(v) the ability to gain information useful for estimating the desirable level and structure of reserves (in terms of their types and time distribution), including reserves with 'a decision potential', allowing for flexible adaptations is of particular importance for strategic planning.

In view of all these conditions one may draw the conclusion that strategic planning should have its own informational base, consisting of a consciously organised network of diagnostic and future-oriented exploratory procedures, with an emphasis on problems of systemwide relevance and significance. One may say that there is a need for a 'stock of knowledge' (continuously revised and supplemented) representing this, which one might call 'systemic wisdom'. This would form the basis for social evaluating norms and criteria and be a counterweight to operational and partial (subsystemic) criteria and pressures. There is some reason to believe that the tasks of operating 'information producing' procedures of this kind may be performed better if they are not located in organisational units directly charged with management and administrative functions.

One may also pose the question of whether the tasks of strategic planning, and those of producing information for that purpose, can be identified with long-term (perspective) planning. It is true that a number of strategic problems

[1] These issues were discussed *inter alia* by A. Kaufman, 'Concerning the notions of operation and optimation' in *Scientific Thought* (Mouton/UNESCO, Paris–The Hague, 1971); and J. W. Sutherland, 'Beyond System Engineering: The General System Theory Potential for Social Science System Analysis' in *General Systems*, XVIII (1973).

must be considered in a relatively long-term perspective. It is equally true, however, that the premises of strategic thinking (its criteria and approaches) should be continuously present and should exert an influence on shorter term operational and tactical control functions.

If one looks at all the issues discussed above in a comprehensive way, one comes to the conclusion that each of them, although different in its nature, is equally important for the theory and practice of national socio-economic planning. If the significance of some of them is underestimated, then difficulties are likely to arise in the field of others, both from a cognitive, theoretical viewpoint and from that of practical applications. One is inclined then to conclude that there is no reason to question the relevance of theory in the social sciences, especially of political economy and its auxiliary disciplines, for dealing with the issues involved in systemwide planning and control. There is only the important condition that the approach should be comprehensive enough in the sense that it should recognise specific features and their interrelations for such aspects as the principal socio-economic laws for the system's behaviour and development; the praxiological aspects of rationality; the specific features of commodity-money relations and their role in regulatory mechanisms; the manner in which human needs and social participation manifest themselves in the system's behaviour and its conscious control; the various aspects of data flow and information-producing activities; and the institutional and organisational conditions mutually connected with the above aspects.

Discussion of the Papers by Professors Belousov and Porwit
(Chairman: Professor Malinvaud)

Academician Mateev (Bulgaria) opened the discussion. He said that he would not try to summarise Professor Belousov's paper, which was itself a successful summary of a large subject, but he would draw the attention of the conference to some of the more important topics raised in the paper. He referred first to the great importance of the development of an effective system of national planning as indicated in the opening paragraph of the paper and expressed his agreement with this assessment.

Secondly, he noted that the paper showed the connection between centralised planning and the need for planning of the component parts of the system. The problem for the central planners was to arrange in a consistent system the decisions taken at various levels by numerous separate bodies. The third point to which he wished to refer was the distinction which was made (p. 275) between two approaches to the choice of criteria in appraising the efficiency of planning activities. One concerned the degree of *attainment* of the specified objectives, the other the extent to which the economic potential of the enterprise, industry or region had been realised. Professor Mateev thought this was a very productive distinction; but observed that distinction did not signify counterposition, and emphasised the connection between the two approaches and their transition into one another. The change in criteria which had been made, as correctly pointed out by Professor Belousov, was probably related to a larger extent to the transition of the socialist economy towards an exclusively intensive type of development, after filling the gap in developing the key economic sectors. Both the Soviet Union and the other socialist countries of Europe were no longer in possession of those additional resources of manpower for an extensive expansion of production which were supplied by the rural economy in the past. Besides that, the introduction of the familiar technology and equipment marked great successes. There remained only one road to further development: *new technologies* based on *new* or further improved means of production and directed towards *new* consumer objects.

The fourth point to be stressed was the need for long-term planning and the need to improve still further the connection of long-term to current planning. Complex and interesting problems were emerging in this field and required theoretical treatment and practical solutions. They had a bearing on both the stability and the flexibility of the five-year plans and also of the annual plans.

Finally, Professor Mateev pointed to a special feature of macroeconomic planning. The more distant the period covered by the forecasting, the greater was the uncertainty, though at the same time the longer was the period available for overcoming the inertness of the system; and *vice versa* for brief periods. This showed that the contradiction which had emerged must be attacked simultaneously from both sides: first, to reduce the uncertainty to the minimum; second, to improve the mechanism of planning – that of operative management in particular, including for this purpose the use of mathematical models and electronic equipment – in such a direction that the system should be in a position to react ever more flexibly. In other words, inertness should also be reduced to the minimum possible for a given stage of development and a given degree of complexity.

Turning to Professor Porwit's paper Academician Mateev said that its main topic was the interconnection between the central plan and the planned activities of subordinate bodies. Great attention was given to this and it was even introduced into the definition of planning. He shared most of the views expressed in the paper but considered that the problems raised by Professor Porwit could easily be dealt with if it were realised that planning had to do with complex multilevel systems involving individuals and groups. Planning was always and at every level a linking of aims and means within a determined time horizon.

Dr Desai (India) referred to the distinction made earlier in the conference (p. 59) between system rationality and component rationality. He thought it was possible to decide such issues as the allocation of public goods if it was certain that individual agents would give correct information. However, if they reacted in a perverse way the system rationality might be undermined because of behaviour which was rational from the point of view of the components but not of the system. He asked whether this problem did arise in the planned economies, particularly in relation to the gathering of information and the formulation of plan targets.

Professor Mujzel (Poland) discussed a number of topics arising from Professor Porwit's paper. He referred firstly to the distinction between two aspects of central planning: the real aspect, i.e. the making of decisions on the allocation of resources, and the social aspect, i.e. the institutional framework and scope of planning and the interrelationships between agents within the plan. He thought that the state of planning theory was reasonably satisfactory with respect to the first aspect and that the USSR and Eastern Europe had achieved a great deal in the practical work of planning; but that the second aspect was much weaker. Some very general formulae had been produced, but these could not be applied and lacked both deep theoretical insight and empirical evidence. The development of this socio-political aspect was an urgent task for economists and others.

His second point was the problem of the relationship between the principles of (a) strong central planning and control and (b) autonomy of firms. The traditional view in the socialist countries had been that there was some contradiction between these two principles – that one could only be strengthened at the expense of the other. However, there was now a much deeper understanding of this crucial issue. It was appreciated, on the one hand, that only strong central planning could produce the basic conditions in which the autonomy of the firm could be developed; and, on the other hand, that the autonomy of firms, with its associated rationality at the micro level, was a basic condition for rationalising and strengthening central planning. The first proposition followed from the realisation that firms could not be given autonomy unless there was strong and efficient central planning. Only in this situation would firms find a state of equilibrium (balance) in the economy; and only an efficient central planning agency could generate the appropriate tools (prices, incentives, financial systems, etc.) to influence the firms and so enable them to act autonomously and rationally within the given context. The second proposition followed because there were strict limits to the number of decisions the central planners could handle – if they tried to do too much they became inefficient and it was, therefore, necessary for them to enlarge the scope of the decisions made by the firms.

Professor Mujzel said the real way to strengthen central planning was thus (a) to deepen the social orientation of the central planners and improve the procedures for social approval of the plan; (b) to harmonise the units in acting according to the plan targets; (c) to increase the efficiency of the techniques and the information used in making plans; and (d) to improve the implements used to influence the behaviour of the subordinate units.

Dr Owosekun (Nigeria) said that planning in Nigeria was being reappraised in the light of recent experience. He was of the view that the type of planning which took place in the socialist countries would not be effective in a mixed economy for a number of reasons. First, there was the lack of basic data and, where such data were available, their inaccuracy represented a major constraint. Second, in a mixed economy where consumer sovereignty dictated not only what was to be produced, but also the quantity that should be produced, planning was destined to be ineffective. Third, in a political system which allowed for pressure groups and changes in social rationality very frequently, plan discipline could not be ensured.

Professor Green (UK) said that Professor Porwit's paper illustrated what he meant by intermediate theory (see p. 264 above). It was not a general model of national economic management independent of political economic systems and contexts, but it was much more than a description and analysis of options and problems unique to Poland in the late 1970s. It raised issues which he, as a practising strategic planning adviser in two quite different states, Tanzania and Namibia (as envisaged by the Liberation movement), often found both relevant and difficult, and threw light on options, constraints and sequences which were relevant to those two societies.

There were four questions on certain implications or possible lines of development of the paper which he wished to ask.

Professor Porwit had stressed (p. 297) the importance of meta-planning and the influence of the past on present behaviour and of present decisions and actions on future behaviour (pp. 296–7). With this Professor Green fully agreed.

The planning agency in its operational micro and macro roles was seen as responsible for testing alternatives for relative efficiency (p. 296). Did this not raise problems for meta-planning? Meta-efficiency in the future was likely to have current micro and macro efficiency costs. How then could one choose (or pose trade-offs) between these two potentially divergent efficiencies? Even if there were parallel strategic (meta) and operational (micro and macro) planning structures (pp. 297–301) how could one safeguard meta planning against component rationality which was likely to oppose systemic and structural transformation?

Second, was the approach proposed one of moving (balanced) equilibrium or of planned moving (imbalanced) disequilibrium? At least in respect of meta planning Professor Porwit's paper (p. 297) would seem to suggest that deliberate, selective imbalance (disequilibrium) was the appropriate approach.

Third, the interaction of strategic (meta) and operational planning poses complex institutional and power problems. As pointed out in the paper merging the two roles might be inefficient in both strategic and operational terms.

However, if the two were separated how could the following dangers (tendencies) be averted?

(i) operational planning having more visible and immediate power and therefore better access to data;
(ii) operational planning appearing to be more relevant and to have a faster pay-off inducing a decision-taker bias in its favour;
(iii) operational planning decisions in sum either blocking or altering the course of strategic planning because of inadequate communication and interpenetration;
(iv) strategic planning becoming isolated in one unit and not being seen as a function of concern to individual institutions and productive units?

Fourth, the importance of making provision for reserves in planning (p. 300) is matched by the difficulty of seeing how to make strategic planning allocation *ex ante* of reserves operationally meaningful. The known tendency of planning to estimate resources optimistically, allocate them 100 per cent (or more) and trust that no unforeseen calls on (or shortfalls of) resources will arise is clear and needs built-in safeguards in the planning process process, i.e. planned reserves. But how can these be specified operationally? Generalised financial or investible surplus or (perhaps) foreign exchange reserves can be planned but specific physical resource or knowledge or manpower reserves appear to pose more severe problems. Still more is it hard (even if critical) to see how to define 'flexibility capacity', to allocate some of it and to have planned reserves available to meet specific institutional emergency requirements.

Professor Pajestka (Poland) said that Professor Green had raised a number of much discussed issues with his reference to intermediate theory. Many of the problems encountered in planning were of this character, and sophisticated logical theories needed substantial amendment so as to take account of practical questions including socio-political forces and the behaviour of institutions. Generalisations at this apparently 'primitive' level were more important than very sophisticated mathematical or logical models.

With regard to the distinction between macro and micro planning Professor Pajestka thought that initially the socialist countries, under the influence of Marx, had put the main emphasis on the macro level. Today it was believed that both levels were equally important. Macro planning was principally strategic in character, and could take account of long-term changes in a way which was extremely difficult for the component units to do.

In reply to Dr Owosekun, Professor Pajestka said that planning was not a technocratic calculation – it had to be seen as a socio-institutional process with full allowance for the real nature of the society for which the plans were being made. He accepted that plans could only be applied to the private sector if it was possible to guide and influence the market mechanism, but in practice this could generally be done as, for example, in the case of Japan.

Professor Porwit (Poland) said in reply to Professor Mateev that he thought the more technological definition of planning omitted certain important aspects. He also thought the issues raised by Dr Desai were very relevant. In reply to Professor Green's question about the strategic function of planning he thought this could be treated in two ways. On the one hand, there were certain strategic decisions which had to be made – that was already a decision-making process. On the other hand there was a question of systemwide premises and information for evaluating and appraising possibilities. In this case it was not done from the point of view of decisions already made but as a means of assessing possibilities for the future. What was needed was thus a set of organised pre-plan studies of options and possibilities. This could create a counterpart to all the biases and deviations created by the existing interests. With regard to some of the other problems raised by Professor Green he would not say that these could be avoided, only that the planners must strive to do so.

Academician Khachaturov (USSR) said that he regarded the theory of socialist planning as being based in part on the fundamental laws of political economy and in part on planning practice. He discussed the nature of long-term planning and said that in the Soviet Union they were no longer satisfied with a period of five years. Many processes (e.g. demographic changes or scientific advances) took place over a longer time-span, and it was necessary to plan accordingly. He also referred to Dr Owosekun's comments and said that he thought the problem of collecting suitable information had been exaggerated. There were in the USSR many local agencies which collected the data needed for planning.

Professor Malinvaud (France) said he thought it might be appropriate to turn briefly to economic theories that had been developed in the West and concerned planning in market economies. Before doing so one must recognise that, during the last decade, the role of medium-term national planning had somewhat decreased in Western Europe, this being particularly true of French indicative planning. Simultaneously, however, organised forecasting had made progress and short-term economic policies had been studied in a longer term perspective, since stagflation had shown the importance of the medium-term consequences of monetary and fiscal policies.

The 'theory of decentralised planning' had been the object of a good deal of attention among mathematical economists. Was it relevant? We must recognise that, although it started from problems faced in actual planning (see the paper by Kornai-Liptak, or his own written in 1963), it did not react on it and the practice of planning had not been directly influenced by this theoretical research.

If it was relevant, it was at the more fundamental level of the theory of resource allocation: it helped us to understand the possibilities, limitations and conditions of concerted decision-taking in a society in which agents were endowed with different and complementary information. This concerted decision-taking might concern the planning of the whole of production or the building of basic equipment or the provision of public goods. Studying it had brought significant results, freeing us from oversimple stereotypes. For instance we had understood that many alternatives to the famous Walras tatonnement process were relevant, and often better as procedures of resource allocation. Or we had seen that various procedures were unequally robust with respect to the temptation that agents might have of distorting the information concerning them; the 'free rider problem' appeared less formidable than was once thought for public goods, but also the market mechanism turned out to be less reliable for private goods than was formerly claimed.

Mention should also be made of the recent work on the optimal control of economic policy. Direct applications of this methodology had not been more than illustrative examples. But some of our previous intuitions had been revised, as for instance the one according to which a 'stop-go' policy would necessarily be bad because it would be destabilising.

Index

Entries in the index in bold type under the names of participants in the Conference indicate their papers or Discussions of their papers. Entries in italic type indicate contributions by participants to the Discussions.